T0374185

God's Direction

Our Journey

Earl Goatcher

WESTBOW
P R E S S®
A DIVISION OF THOMAS NELSON
& ZONDERVAN

Copyright © 2017 Earl Goatcher.

All rights reserved. No part of this book may be used or reproduced by any means, graphic, electronic, or mechanical, including photocopying, recording, taping or by any information storage retrieval system without the written permission of the author except in the case of brief quotations embodied in critical articles and reviews.

Unless otherwise noted, all Scripture references are from the (NASB) New American Standard Bible. C 1977, The Lockman Foundation, Holman Bible Publishers

Scripture quotations marked NASB are taken from the New American Standard Bible®, Copyright © 1960, 1962, 1963, 1968, 1971, 1972, 1973, 1975, 1977, 1995 by The Lockman Foundation. Used by permission.

This book is a work of non-fiction. Unless otherwise noted, the author and the publisher make no explicit guarantees as to the accuracy of the information contained in this book and in some cases, names of people and places have been altered to protect their privacy.

WestBow Press books may be ordered through booksellers or by contacting:

WestBow Press
A Division of Thomas Nelson & Zondervan
1663 Liberty Drive
Bloomington, IN 47403
www.westbowpress.com
1 (866) 928-1240

Because of the dynamic nature of the Internet, any web addresses or links contained in this book may have changed since publication and may no longer be valid. The views expressed in this work are solely those of the author and do not necessarily reflect the views of the publisher, and the publisher hereby disclaims any responsibility for them.

Any people depicted in stock imagery provided by Getty Images are models, and such images are being used for illustrative purposes only. Certain stock imagery © Getty Images.

ISBN: 978-1-9736-2205-5 (sc)
ISBN: 978-1-9736-2228-4 (hc)
ISBN: 978-1-9736-2204-8 (e)

Library of Congress Control Number: 2018902788

Print information available on the last page.

WestBow Press rev. date: 5/2/2018

ACKNOWLEDGMENT

Those who have written a biography or family history can understand the unique difficulty of giving credit where credit is due. That is especially true in this chronicle which covers an extended period of time with stories and quotes from many people who have passed on. Many of our missionary co-workers all over the world have also passed on, making verification of some events difficult. My brother, Truett Goatcher, now deceased, and my sister, Lavelle Rollins, have helped tremendously as we attempted in our later years to reconstruct what little we had heard and learned in our earlier years. Our children, Lisa Schuttger and James Goatcher, have been helpful in adding to or correcting our memories of some of our family escapades and, in some cases, providing editorial assistance. Their memories of family life and events were often better than mine. As I have discovered in my later years, memories can be malleable things. They can play tricks, tending to recall an event in a preferred version rather than the factual version. My intention has been to be factual.

I have tried to verify stories, dates and historical events but I was not always successful. Songs emphasizing faithfulness, especially by our ancestors, have hovered quietly in the background of our lives and ministry. Our parents and grandparents have been an inspiration to us. We pray that all of our descendants will continue that heritage of faithfulness. Psalm 78:5-7 (NIV) speaks to the hope, prayer and desire that Joann and I have for those who follow us. "For He established a testimony which He commanded our fathers, that they should teach them to their children, that the generations to come might know, even the children yet to be born...that they should put their confidence in God."

Finally, and most of all, I am thankful to and for my wife Joann. No words can fully express my gratitude for the part she has had in shaping and sharing this journey. Without her there would be no book. Traveling and working in such a variety of ministries over such a long period of time and extending over much of the world, has provided a fertile field of material, much of which remains untold. It is impossible to thank everyone who has contributed. Although I journaled most of my work for the last 40 years, many gaps remain. For those who provided correspondence we are most grateful. May God be glorified in all of it.

It is the wonderful nature of God's plan that we will soon complete our earthly journey and join our heavenly family. May the Lord find all of us faithful until we meet again.

FOREWORD

Our decision to chronicle our journey has been nudged and sometimes shoved along by our children and grandchildren. Partly because of that I have included many details of our early years, perhaps even to excess. But as others have said, no one can be fully understood aside from their historical context. Our children have been persistent...and I do thank them.

In addition, several issues have stimulated my willingness to follow their urging. One of those issues has been the absence of written records or stories by our ancestors. Dad married late and we three children came along even later. I never knew any of my grandparents and never had any conversations with Mom and Dad about our family history. Joann did know some of her grandparents, but with her also there is a sad absence of letters, conversations and information concerning her ancestors. Many questions remain unanswered. That huge gap in knowledge of our own family history has prompted us to try to recover and record as much as possible before it is irretrievably lost. It will be obvious that much of what I relate in this chronicle is both autobiographical and historical, with equal priority. We want our descendants to know something of our roots, and something of what life was like for those of us who went before them and what experiences helped shape our lives. We also want them, and all who read this, to know how our story fits into the larger story; the historical context. Our God is not only a God of history, He knows us and leads us personally.

For Joann and me, our years and ministry together confirm Jeremiah's affirmation that God had a plan for us, a plan that was good and that provided a hope and a future for us. There is a divine plan for everyone, in which each event of life has its place. The longer we have lived the more obvious it has become that God was leading us. We were only following; and we are the blessed. All who follow Him will be blessed.

Another issue has been the continuing erosion of the Biblical standards of right and wrong within our nation and culture. Joann and I have lived during the greatest changes in the briefest time period in our nation's history. In the physical and material world there has been unbelievable progress. Unfortunately, in the world of morals, ethics and spiritual values, there has been a frightening decline, especially since WWII. Our hope and prayer is that in relating our wonderful and gratifying journey that all who read our story will know our God as one who blesses those who follow Him.

A final prompting, and the greatest issue, has been our desire to share with everyone the faithful, loving and continuous hand of the Lord in our lives. Sometimes with a light-bulb moment, more often with a little nudge, a quiet whisper or a light touch of an invisible hand, God has led us through an incredible journey. As we reflect on our more than 60 years of life and ministry together we see clearly the providential, sovereign hand of God directing us. This is not so much our story as it is His story. But we were not robots; we were very willing participants in the journey. We have been only bit players in a drama far greater than the two of us could ever have fashioned. His directing has been gracious. Thousands of decisions, events and circumstances have been brought together to form a beautiful, meaningful mosaic that goes infinitely beyond coincidence or luck.

It has been said many times that it takes only one generation for a people to forget God. Joann and I pray continually that our children, grandchildren, descendants and all who read this will not forget God but will see our journey as one guided by a loving God who lives and calls all of us to follow Him as He leads each one into a full and abundant life. In our twilight years we see more and more clearly the benefit and blessing that comes from living lives in accord with the will of God.

CHAPTER 1

Beginnings

The quietness and isolation of our births never portended the scope of events and ministry opportunities that would emerge for us in the subsequent six decades of spiritual work together.

Although born seven hundred miles apart geographically, there were many similarities in family circumstances, as well as contrasts. Faith in God, loyalty to church, continual financial struggles through the Great Depression, and commitment to biblical moral principles were common to both families. There was contrast in work situations; my family were farmers, and Joann's were mechanics and laborers. My early education in the hills of Arkansas was deficient, especially in math and the sciences, but a focus on the need for an education came after military service. Joann's early school years were in a one-room schoolhouse in the small village of Carlsbad, Texas, where she had excellent teachers who challenged her and fostered a desire and determination to learn that never diminished. That can-do attitude has never wavered.

My world was in the foothills of the Ozark Mountains of Arkansas, an area of rocky ridges and narrow valleys about two miles from the little town of Formosa. It was part of an isolated, insular world with a culture of its own and much language that reflected my ancestors' earlier lives in Virginia and Kentucky. My great-grandfather, Maston Goatcher,[1] was born in Illinois on February 18, 1824, moved to Arkansas (date unknown), and died in 1860. My dad and mom had 168 acres of unproductive, rocky land on a hillside.

Joann's early years began with her birth on a ranch in the arid, open range of West Texas, miles away from any doctor or medical care.

We have wondered what prompted our ancestors to cast off their moorings and break ties with their homes, other family members, their churches, their schools, and their villages and move to new and unsettled areas. What part, if any, did God have in their daily lives and decisions to move? Did they, like Abraham, feel led by God to leave their "place" and go to a "new place" to which God would lead them? We have no answers. We would like to have some indication of their character and the recounting of events that shaped their lives. What about their struggles, goals, victories, and defeats? What was life like in covered wagons on their westward journey? What was life like in their new land? We have no answers to those questions, but those places became our homes. And because home is a place in the mind as well as a place on a map, both had a part in shaping our identities and characters. Place does matter.

What Joann and I desire to accomplish in telling our story is well expressed by the psalmist when he says, "O God, do not forsake me until I declare thy strength to this generation and thy power to all who are to come" (Psalm 71:18). We want to tell our story so our

---

[1] The first appearance of the Goatcher name was in Scotland in 1343 with the marriage of Willelmus dectus Godechere, recorded in the records of Scotland during the reign of King David II of Scotland, 1329–71. The Goatcher name also goes back to Sussex, England, beginning in 1544, with an indication they emigrated from France in the late thirteenth century. Both records have a variety of spellings and suggest that the name comes from *gode*, meaning "good," and *chere*, meaning "aspect" or "appearance."
Goatcher surname may be found at www.surnamedb.com.

children, grandchildren, our descendants, and others may know the compelling force in our lives, what God has done and how He has directed us, and what He can do in their lives also, if they are willing to follow Him. Whatever legacy we leave, our greatest desire is that it will magnify our Lord. As we reflect on our lives together, we become more certain with each passing day that the Lord has led us on a wonderful, adventurous journey from the very beginning.

Telling our story often involves going back in the stream of our lives to remember narratives and events that relate to the larger story—what God has done and how He did it. Stories can be mundane or sacred. The mundane stories may be funny, unusual, or just unique to the time, place, or family, but they don't have a hidden spiritual point. They may, however, convey an event or a special time of bonding that is memorable. Sacred stories are those that reflect the behind-the-scenes presence and sovereignty of God in causing the events to occur. Or the narrative may contain a redemptive analogy that enhances our understanding of God's part in the story. It will be obvious that we use both in telling our story.

The mix of geography, family, church, culture, and other elements of our early lives helped forge our characters and worldviews. As Joann and I have compared and considered the similar circumstances of our early years, although widely separated geographically, we have realized what a rich and similar heritage we have. However, I feel some of that heritage of identity of place and of home has been lost in recent generations, and that is one reason we want to share our story. Each new generation needs to forge and record its own identity and character, not out of an historical vacuum, but out of an awareness of what part God had in leading that process.

Moving, Moving: The First of Many Moves

The need to make a living led to many moves by both families. In my case, we moved in 1931 to a smaller farm closer to Formosa, closer to church, and closer to school. With Truett, my older brother, already in school and me starting in a couple of years, it was a much better living location. However, it was not large enough for our needs. Dad continued to farm some of the fields on our "creek" place. It was there, just as I was turning five, that personal memories of what life was like started to become implanted in my memory. Somewhat strangely, I have clearer memories of those earlier years near Formosa than I have of the later years (1935–1942) in Missouri.

In Joann's place, her dad, a skilled mechanic, was able to advance in work situations, culminating in additional training that led to responsible positions during World War II, but those opportunities required frequent moves.

It was accepted in both families that children were to help with the work of the farm and home. It was not abuse or unfair to the kids; it was a learning situation that developed a sense of responsibility, character, maturity, and self-discipline. Joann's early home life was very similar to mine, and both of us have realized how blessed and fortunate we were to be raised in such an atmosphere.

In my place, the changing seasons brought changes in the type of daily work done. The morning chores remained similar. For the kids, it usually involved feeding the stock (mules and horses, cows, hogs, and chickens) and milking the cow(s). Mother would cook breakfast (biscuits, eggs, milk gravy, and sometimes meat) from scratch. Dad would either help with the chores or start getting things together for whatever farm work was to be done that day. Since I was the youngest and not yet able to do the heavy work, I would do the lighter chores such as churning butter, gathering eggs, or bringing in firewood.

Joann also gathered eggs for their family, but their hens laid many of their eggs under the house. She had to crawl to their nests, which was not her favorite place. Spiders, snakes, lizards, and a few other creepy-crawlies liked the coolness under the house. She still shudders at the memory of crawling there in the semidarkness early in the morning or late in the evening.

In addition to food preparation, both of our mothers had other occasional necessary tasks, including making clothes, quilts, and lye soap. Lye soap, made properly, could be an excellent, fragrant, foamy cleanser, but lye is very caustic and can cause burns, so it was handled carefully. They used wood ashes as lye. Either a cold process or a cooking process could be used to make soap. Recipes varied, but all contained the same three basic ingredients: lye, lard, and water. Lard substitutes were sometimes tried, but good, pure, pork lard was the best. Some women used additives at times, including coloring, fragrant oils, honey, and other ingredients to make it more appealing.

Making quilts was an on-again, off-again activity that most housewives took seriously and pursued with pride. They were needed in the home, could be worked on at any time, and served as a special occasion for friends and neighbors to gather for socializing. The frame was made of straight sticks or pieces of sawed lumber (or whatever was available), and it would be suspended from the ceiling of the living room so it could be raised or lowered as needed. Out of that crude setting came many beautiful works of art, often kept as valuable examples of a skill almost lost in a high-tech age.

We made our own toys too.

Walking sticks (stick walkers or tom walkers) were eight-foot-long saplings about two inches in diameter with a four-inch-long side limb (for a footrest) cut off about eighteen inches above the ground.

A paddle and wheel were made with an iron ring and a one-to-two-inch diameter stick or straight limb about four feet long, with a compressed Prince Albert or Velvet tobacco can formed into a U and nailed to one end of the stick. The wheel was an iron ring about ten inches in diameter and an inch wide that had been removed from an old, worn-out wagon wheel axle. We used the paddle to push the wheel around the yard or road. (To my surprise, I saw similar toys made by Indian children when we worked in India many years later.)

A bean flip was a half-inch (diameter) by six-inch-long Y-shaped fork cut from a tree. To that, we attached two elastic strips (usually old, worn-out car tire inner tubes about half an inch wide and two feet long) with a two-inch piece of leather pouch attached at the end. Using small rocks as ammunition, we often became accurate enough to kill birds and squirrels. It was a good feeling for us as kids to help put meat on the table, but Mother frowned on our practicing on the chickens.

We also made slingshots (David used this little weapon against Goliath a long time ago). We used two four-foot-long heavy cords (if we could find them) or twine strings with a two-to-three-inch-long leather strip attached in the middle. With a small rock in the leather pouch, we would whirl it rapidly a time or two and let it fly. It took much time and practice, but sometimes we would get lucky and hit something.

Kites are still familiar today, but we made ours from scratch. We used a flour-and-water mix to make glue with which we glued paper to the wood stick frame.

We also played with marbles. Obviously we did not make them, but every boy tried to have a pocketful.

Tops were too expensive for us to have most of the time. When we did have them, we became experts at spiking them, so they did not last long.

In some school districts, a short school term would be held after the crops were laid by and before the harvest was started. School could easily be interrupted by some need on the farm. The farm work took priority.

But during the drought in 1934 and '35 I began to realize the real difficulties Dad and Mother were facing. The spring grass faded from green to brown, and dust devils hopscotched across the dry fields. The creeks dried up, some of the wells went dry, the ground cracked, and the stock grew gaunt. The corn was so stunted we picked only a couple of partial loads of nubbins and finally just turned the stock into the field and let them graze it. For those two years, we picked only two small bales of cotton off of eighteen acres. (But every year was a good year for growing rocks. It was a fail-proof crop. We could have picked up fifty bushels of rocks per acre every year ... without planting a single one.) Dad made only a few hundred dollars to take care of the entire family for a year. The Christmas gift for Truett and me for those two years was one nickel each. During those same years, Joann, living in West Texas, received the same doll for Christmas, with a new dress for the doll made with cloth from a feed or flour sack.

For the kids, it was understood that we went barefooted in the summer. Shoes were not worn (except on Sunday) until after the first frost. Going barefooted was not deprivation; we preferred it that way.

We later learned it was the time of the Great Depression, but there was no change in our situation; it was just life as usual. Both our families were in similar circumstances. To live was to struggle, and keeping the home supplied with food, fuel, and other necessities was an unending task. There was little time for other considerations. What we did not have we learned to do without.

It was because of our move to be closer to Formosa that Formosa Baptist Church, and the people who were in the church, began to make an impression on me. It made an impression on others too, as I learned in 1999 when I wrote a brief history of the church for its seventy-fifth anniversary. According to the old church records, the church was organized in 1924 with twenty-one charter members. Of those twenty-one, six were Goatchers, two were Goatchers with other last (married) names, and three were cousins of the Goatchers.

Dad was listed as one of the charter members, but Mother was not. I wondered why. Truett told me later. When Dad and Mother married, she was a member of a General Baptist church. The Formosa church was organized as a Missionary Baptist church (later becoming a Southern Baptist church). They would not accept her as a member without rebaptizing her. (They had a doctrinal difference of opinion concerning baptism that still exists in some churches today.) Mother refused, saying she was satisfied with her baptism and did not need it again, so she was not listed as a charter member. The church relented later and accepted her as a member.

She became a much-loved Sunday school teacher. My uncle, Rev. Calvin Goatcher, a pastor in another area, preached the first revival.

Early church records were interesting and revealing. There were not many secrets in the church. Each person present was named, with how much each gave … or did not give. Ages were given also. Birthdays for members were observed by their contribution of one penny for each year of age. That could be significant. On February 13, 1927, Dad and Mother (with birthdays in the same week, his forty-fifth, her twenty-eighth) gave seventy-three cents as a birthday offering, more than twice the total church offering of thirty cents.

Sly comments revealing a sense of humor popped up frequently. In that same year, in the Sunday school record book referring to teachers, which was divided between male and female, a comment under male was "Handsome!"

Reticence to express opinions was not usually practiced, even toward the preacher. My first cousin, Maggie Evans, was the song leader for several years. And she led—she didn't follow. If the preacher started rambling without aim or gave no indication of bringing the sermon to a close as the clock began inching toward noon, Maggie started sending signals to the preacher. Obvious signals. Song book open. Sitting forward on the pew. Clearing her throat. Time to wind it down and turn it off. No preacher ignored those signals very long. She felt if he could not say what needed to be said in thirty or forty minutes, he couldn't say it in an hour either.

Preachers and pastors were either sometime, part-time, quarter-time, or half-time; they were rarely full-time. Not enough money to pay them. Pay would often be in kind: vegetables, meat, or fruit from the members. The church had many pastors during its first twenty years. Much later, Uncle Calvin served as pastor for two years after he retired from an administrative position at the Oklahoma Baptist Children's Home. I served four years as pastor (1993–1997) after I retired from the Foreign Mission Board.

Beginnings: The Missouri Sharecropping Years

The combination of summer heat (so hot we often slept in the yard instead of the house), thin soil, rainless clouds, and sparse harvests finally left Dad and Mother with no choice but to move. In the late winter of 1935, when I was seven, we moved to the bootheel of southeast Missouri, along with other relatives and friends. It was not a group move; it was individual families coming close to a breaking point and then making the difficult decision to move somewhere else to try to make a living. I have no memory of the move. In fact, I have only a few memories of our time in Missouri from 1935 to 1942. I have depended on Truett's memory for much of the story of those years.

How we moved, what we took with us in the way of stock, equipment and furniture, and what we left behind, I don't know. We went first to the little community of Pascola, where we lived from 1935 to '37, then moved a few miles west to Bragg City where we lived from 1937 to '40. That was where my sister, Lavelle, was born (November 23, 1940) and where we began to live a little above a subsistence level. Our next move was to Gray Ridge in 1941 for one year, then to Circle City in 1942. From there, we moved back to Arkansas when I was fourteen. The frequent moves, always in the middle of the school year, left me feeling a little shy and reluctant to take part in school activities.

Our move to Missouri brought Dad's first experience with sharecropping. As with all farming, sharecropping could be risky. If conditions were good—the contract with the owner was fair, the soil was good, the rains were timely, and the crop prices were good—it could be a profitable year, but the contract needed a close reading of the small print because other conditions could be imposed. The landowner (often a company) frequently established a cotton gin and a company store and required the farmer to use those facilities as part of the contract. The catch was that the company ginning fee and store charges were higher than what privately owned gins and stores charged.

The sharecropping ratio of farming income was usually between 20 percent and 30 percent for the landowner and 70 percent to 80 percent to the farmer. (A 20 percent return on investment wasn't bad ... for the landowner.) The farmer provided the capital—farm animals, machinery and equipment, seed, labor, harvest expense, and transportation to the collection point—and took all the risks. After production expenses were paid and the owner's share was paid, the farmer's share could be rather small. When the higher ginning fees and store prices were included, the farmer's portion would be even smaller. If the farming conditions were not good—due to drought, flooding, or low crop prices—the return for the farmer could drop drastically.

I learned later that Dad had something of an independent mind. When his income became so small he could barely feed the family, he would not take our cotton to the company gin or buy his supplies from the company store. Suddenly we would be without a contract and have to move somewhere else. That was why we moved so often. Even with those challenges, we did better than we had done on the rocky hillsides of Van Buren County. We did well in 1935 and '36, but then the massive Mississippi River flood of 1937 hit us. We awoke on the morning of July 3 to what looked like an ocean. Our farm had disappeared, replaced by small rippling waves of water that stretched for miles. Homes and barns appeared to be floating on the water. It was not all that deep, but the land was so level that the scene was frightening. We evacuated to higher ground in Diehlstadt, Missouri, to stay with our relatives, Alton and Dorothy Evans, until the water receded. Most of the crop was lost, and we had to start over. We were recovering and doing well again when Dad became ill in 1942, and we were wiped out financially.

In 1941, when I was thirteen, we were living near Gray Ridge and had our best crop ever. The corn crop was great—thirty-five to fifty bushels per acre. Cotton also was great; we were picking one bale of cotton per acre on the first picking. The short cotton stalks were loaded with bolls that opened simultaneously, leading to easy picking. I picked about two hundred pounds of cotton per day; Truett picked about four hundred pounds.

For some time, I had been asking Dad for a bicycle, but we could not really afford it. He finally told me he would get me a bicycle if I picked 350 pounds in a day. He offered it because he did not think I could do it. Truett asked what he could get if he picked five hundred pounds. Dad said he would give him one extra dollar because he thought he could do it. Dad had been paying us $1.25 per hundred pounds for what we picked. When we weighed our last sack at the end of the big day, I had picked 352 pounds, Truett had picked 502 pounds, and Dad had picked almost 400 pounds. Together, it was enough for a short bale, and we headed for the gin. I was one happy kid. Truett and I went to Dexter to get the bicycle, and I picked out the best one in the store. It was a Western Flyer with white sidewall tires, a battery-operated headlight, a horn, and a carrier basket. Fancy! Sadly, it cost a few dollars more than I was permitted to pay. Truett chipped in the difference for me, and I had the best bicycle in the whole countryside. Later, as I thought about it, and even now at times, I feel guilty that I did what I did.

I remember Sunday, December 7, 1941, "a date which will live in infamy." We were listening to the radio when we heard of the Japanese attack on Pearl Harbor. We had to look on the map to find the location. Truett and I did not realize the full implication of the event. I think Dad and Mom did. Dad had been inducted into the army just before at the end of World War I, but the armistice was signed before he was assigned to an active duty unit. He had vivid memories of stories of the fighting.

Early in 1942, we had to move again, this time to a farm (always forty acres) near Circle City. It was not a town, just a community. Truett had graduated from high school in Bragg City in 1941 and had gone to work at Sears, Roebuck and Co. in Memphis. World War II had begun, and Truett had received his notice of imminent call-up for military service. Dad and I put in the crop in 1942. I missed most of school that spring. We had bought a pickup truck a couple of years earlier for two hundred dollars, but Dad had never learned to drive. At age thirteen, I became the family driver. I learned to drive in wet, sticky gumbo mud, almost as slick as ice, but that learning experience came in handy many times in later years. The year had started well.

Back to Arkansas

In late spring, about the time the crops were laid by, Dad became ill. Truett was granted a six-month military deferment and came home from Memphis so he and I could gather the crops. Again, I have no memory of the work. Just as we were almost finished with the harvest, Dad was admitted to the hospital in Sikeston, Missouri, with a heart problem. His condition worsened, and he was transferred to Memphis. When we finished the harvest, Truett returned to Memphis to work. As Dad's condition became more serious, it was obvious that a major decision had to be made. He would not be able to work again. Truett's deferment would soon expire, and he would have to enter the army. I was too young to assume full responsibility for farming. The only option was to return to Arkansas, but that was not really a good option since we had no way to make a living.

Part of the move I remember clearly; part of it I cannot remember at all. I suppose we sold our stock and farming equipment; we certainly would not need it in Arkansas. In late November, Truett and I loaded everything we had on the back of the pickup truck: stoves, beds, tables, furniture, chairs, bedclothes, cooking utensils, clothing, and all the "stuff" every family had, but especially all the food Mother had canned and dried. The four of us piled into the small cab and took off.

It quickly became apparent that something was wrong. The load was so heavy and so high that the truck became uncontrollable above twenty-five or thirty miles per hour. When we hit a bump or rough place in the road, the front wheels came off the ground. We did not have the money to pay for a place to stop for the night, so we kept going.

Just before dawn on a cold frosty morning on a gravel road near the little town of Vilonia, Arkansas, the engine died. When we stopped and looked, the trouble was obvious; the fuel line was broken, and fuel was draining onto the ground. The truck was so heavily loaded that the pickup bed had dropped to the point of touching the fuel line. With the truck bouncing on the rough road, it finally ruptured. While Truett walked back to town to find someone who could help us, Mother, Lavelle, and I walked up to an unlighted farmhouse to see if we could stay with them until the truck was fixed. They very graciously opened their home to us, built up the fire, and fixed breakfast for us (and later for Truett). They fixed sandwiches and other food for us to take on our way. Angels of the Lord! It was years later before I began to understand (and I could never understand fully) the pain, agony, and anxiety Mother went through during that move. It was so traumatic she was never able or willing to talk about it.

Arrival in Formosa was bittersweet. It was good to see loving relatives and friends we had not seen in years, but circumstances, especially for Mother, were heartbreaking. In September, perhaps knowing he would not live long, Dad and Mother had bought a thirty-acre tract of land adjacent to the school grounds on the northwest side of town. The deed is dated September 14, 1942. It had a three-and-a-half-room vacant house on it and an enclosed well on the back porch. It sounded good, and it was fortuitous for us, but it needed a bunch of attention.

The floor joists (beams) were placed on rocks about fifteen inches above the ground, allowing the wind to blow freely under the house. With cracks in the floor, the winter wind was sucked up into the living room heating stove area, providing unwanted air-conditioning. The outside walls were clapboard, narrow, beveled boards that overlapped horizontally to cover the spaces in the outer walls. All the lumber had long since dried up, leaving air spaces all over the house. Truett and I had some major work to do; it was not ready to receive Dad or us.

After we partially completed the renovation, we moved in. Truett returned to work in Memphis to await his call into the army. The hospital in Memphis could do no more for Dad, and he was brought home to Formosa. Over Christmas, he became worse again and was admitted to the hospital in Morrilton just before the end of the year. He died on January 3, 1943, at the age of sixty-one. The diagnosis was heart failure, complicated by pneumonia. He died just before penicillin came on the market, an antibiotic that probably would have saved his life.

After the funeral, we all went back to the house. Mother finally broke down in grief. She had lost her husband and the father of her children. All our money was gone, the last of it used to pay medical and hospital bills. Truett's deferment had expired, and he was called to report for induction. Mother was left with two children, fourteen and two years old, with no money, no job, and no safety net of assistance. I can only marvel at her emotional strength, her faith in God, and her perseverance through those indescribable days and months. She was a saint of God.

As a side note, there was one small incident from those early days in Formosa that I have used occasionally as an analogy in teaching and preaching. Our neighbor across the road, Early Webb, was a blacksmith. As with many in his field, he was a real artisan. Shoeing horses and mules was his most frequent task, but he did a lot of custom iron and steel work. I was fascinated as I watched him heat and then shape a piece of bar steel into a horseshoe and then shoe the horses or mules. He was adept at sharpening or repairing damaged plow points, taking a piece of scrap steel and fashioning it into a wagon wheel, or fitting a smaller piece on a double tree. He could take an apparent piece of scrap and make it a perfect part for a farm implement. He knew exactly when the metal had been heated to the right temperature. He knew how long to keep it in water to cool it for the proper hardening. Even the leap of sparks as he shaped it with his hammer told him what he needed to know.

It was that leap of sparks, and the reaction that came from it, that triggered the analogy that I used as an illustration. Often the farmer's dog came with him when he came to get something fixed or made. Some of the projects could take a few hours, and the dog would lie down in the shade of the smithy's shop and enjoy a nap. When Early would take the red-hot steel out of the fire and begin to hammer it on the anvil to fashion it to its final form, sparks would fly in all directions. At first, the dog would wake up in fear and run off. After a bit, there would be no sparks and the dog would return and take another snooze. Then there would come another shower of sparks and the dog would flee. After some time, the dog seemed to think the sparks did not cause harm, and he ceased to flee from them. Then Early would strike a new piece of metal on the anvil, causing a shower of sparks that would ignite the hair on the dog.

I finally saw the analogy. Sometimes we can find ourselves close to a potentially dangerous situation, or a part of an activity that we know is wrong (sinful), and when we realize it, we immediately flee from it. Later, we realize we were not really injured. We really did not need to flee. The next time we are in a similar situation, we don't flee as quickly or as far. Eventually we see no harm and wind up being a part of the situation or activity that we abhor. We allow ourselves to become inured or addicted to something that gradually distorts our sense of danger, sin, and guilt. The sparks don't seem to harm, but one day, they will bring great pain, and we wonder how we could sink so low. Beware of that first step—that first involvement that ignites a seemingly harmless spark.

Now back to our early days in Formosa. Not long after Truett went on active duty, we received some unexpected good news. The military had instituted a policy of providing financial help to family dependents of active duty personnel with demonstrated needs. We qualified, and Mother began receiving a few dollars each month. What a godsend! When school was out that spring, Ed Bird, the owner of Bird's Store, the biggest store in town, gave me a job. It was about ten hours a day for six days a week, but he paid me forty dollars per month. It was a lifesaver for us.

I worked in the store as a clerk four or five days a week and drove a delivery truck the other days, delivering groceries, feed, fertilizer, and farm items to people living within eight or ten miles of Formosa. Because I was only fifteen years old, I could not obtain a regular driver's license. Ed met the required bond for me to obtain a permit that enabled me to drive. The money was great, and greatly needed, but what really pleased me was that I was able to drive a large truck all over the countryside. I was the envy of the other boys. Mother realized it was the Lord's doing and was grateful to Him for it, but it was only much later that I realized how significantly God was working in the whole situation and how His intervention took care of us. His loving provision has continued faithfully through the years.

When Ed was out of the store, usually one or two days a week, I was the only clerk. I granted or refused credit, pumped gas, candled eggs (to determine fertility status), decided the price to pay farmers for produce (a barter economy), and helped maintain the inventory.

But delivering store goods was my favorite work time. During the week, farm women would send in their orders via three-cent postcards. It was usually a wide variety, including orders for groceries and household supplies, stock feed and fertilizer, with a strong demand that the sacks be a specific design. Feed and fertilizer mills often packaged their products in cloth sacks with various designs: floral, checked, striped, or whatever. The women used them to make dresses, curtains, tablecloths, quilts, and other household items. They would sometimes get a sack with a design they really liked, but one sack would not provide enough cloth for their need. Their next order would insist that the new order be filled with the same design as the previous order. They usually omitted identifying the design; I was expected to remember and bring the right one. Woe unto me if I did not fill it correctly. Whoever thought of that idea as a marketing tool really hit a home run.

Those summers helped get me in the best physical shape ever. The feed sacks weighed one hundred pounds; the fertilizer sacks often weighed one hundred twenty pounds. Loading, stacking, unloading, and carrying those sacks to the barn or wherever was hard work though not unpleasant, but by the end of the day, I was not interested in going anywhere or doing anything else. The benefit of that work lasted for years. Army basic training was a cakewalk after that.

When summer was over and school started, we were blessed again when I was hired to be the school janitor. The Formosa school was actually established in the early 1880s or '90s. The school building I was taking care of was of native stone, built in 1928, the year I was born. All twelve grades met in the same building. It is still in use as part of a church camp. My pay was twelve dollars per month, but combined with what Mother received as a military dependent, it enabled us to get by.

My job description was slightly vague: "Keep the school clean and keep fires in school rooms as needed and keep the gym floor dry before scheduled basketball games." Writing the description was easy. Doing it was another story. Heat was provided by a potbellied wood stove in each of the three classrooms, plus the auditorium. The rooms and auditorium were fairly large, and so were the stoves. The school board could not afford to buy firewood, so each fall, the older high school boys would come to school two or three days before school started, come on to our land (adjacent to the school grounds), and cut the wood we needed. The wood would still be green when the cold weather hit.

Starting the fires was a somewhat challenging daily process. After breakfast and milking the cow, I would get to school before dawn, gather all the scrap paper I could find, place some in each stove, put in a little kindling, add a few small sticks of wood, and soak it all in kerosene (coal oil). I would repeat the process for each stove, then go back and throw a lighted match in each stove. (I know, I know, there was a safer way.) Most of the time, the system worked, but sometimes, the wood just refused to cooperate. The answer was to pour on more kerosene and throw on another match. In the course of a winter, that action resulted in a few stovetop lids being blown across the room. I'm sure the Lord sent extra helpers to protect the school and me.

The basketball gym was another story. It was a huge (to me) wood-framed structure with bleachers on one side and two dressing rooms on the opposite side (no running water). The walls at each end of the gym were only three feet from the end of the basketball court, making for close quarters during a game. It was covered with an old tin roof punctured by many nail holes. It leaked like a sieve. When it rained before a game, as it seemed to do regularly, the floor would be wet, with puddles here and there. My job was to have it dry before game time. My method for drying the floor was simple: pour kerosene on the wet places, set it afire, and let it burn until it was dry. I usually had it dry by game time, but the smoke could be as thick as a heavy fog. Wonder of wonders, I never burned the gym down.

The timing for this activity could get interesting. I needed to get the floor dry, but I also needed to get dressed to play ball. A few single electric light bulbs suspended from the high ceiling provided lighting. Primitive? Yes, but we could play inside. Some schools did not have a gym. As for our team, we made the most of it. We knew the slick and soft places and could avoid them while we hemmed the other guys into those same places where they slipped, slid, and lost the ball. All was fair in love and basketball. Formosa had a reputation for having a good team. For twelve straight years, we won the county and district tournaments and won the state tournament once. We had only old, worn-out playing suits, no warm ups, and no jackets.

For water, we had a perennial spring located on our land about a hundred yards from school. The previous owner had cleaned out the spring, built a native stone tank around it with an outflow pipe, and added a four-foot-wide flagstone curb around the entire area. It was a beautiful setting and provided enough water for the entire school. The boy's toilet—a three-holer—was down the hill in one direction from the school; the girl's toilet—a four-holer—(I think) was down another direction. No paper was provided and no water either. Ashes were used to enhance the atmosphere.

Smoking was the in thing, especially for the boys. Money was scarce, so we improvised. Occasionally one of the boys would bring a can of Prince Albert or Velvet tobacco to school, and we would roll our own cigarettes. At other times, we used what we could find, depending on the time of the year. We usually had about four choices—coffee, rabbit tobacco,[2] corn silks, and grapevine stems—but that does not cover the full range. Coffee was good. Rabbit tobacco was also good, but it was available only seasonally. The same was true with corn silks. Grapevines (dead) were okay, but they were really strong. Our coach did not want us smoking during basketball season, so we changed to chewing tobacco during that time.

School and church activities were our primary sources of social interaction, and for that, I will be eternally grateful.

One additional activity was "Music School," a two-week session each summer at which the basics of music were taught. That was where we learned to read music (shaped notes, of course), timing, key

---

[2] Many years later, I learned that rabbit tobacco was a well-known herbal medicine used first by the Indians and later by the early settlers. Those of us who smoked it just thought it was a good substitute for real tobacco. The plant grew to about three feet in height, with very aromatic white blossoms. It had long, narrow leaves that turned a silvery green color when it ripened in the fall. When ripe and fully dried, the crushed leaves made a good cigarette roll or a good corncob pipe mix. Medicinally, it was used for respiratory ailments, especially asthma, sinus problems, and fever. As a hot tea, it was used for sore throats, fever, and colds. It grew all over our place on Point Remove Creek.

signatures, directing, harmony, and whatever else the teacher might know. There might also be a piano lesson now and then.

All the churches inculcated biblical principles of morality and conduct in us, and that teaching helped set a moral compass for many of the students. Each summer, the Baptist church and the Church of Christ (the only two in town) would hold a revival. Well-known preachers and music leaders would be brought in, attracting people from the surrounding area to the services.

During the revival in our Baptist church in the summer of 1943, when I was fifteen, I was saved. I knew people had been praying for me, especially Mother. At one of the services, I was seated by an older friend. During the invitation, he leaned over and told me he had been praying for me and urged me to give my life to the Lord. I felt compelled to respond and made my first major conscious decision, which has led me on an incredible journey. It was not a dramatic, earth-shaking experience, but it was a time of confession, forgiveness, and salvation that was a defining point in my early years. Ed Bird, my employer, also made his profession of faith that week. We were baptized the following Sunday in the Chew Hole in Point Remove Creek at the foot of Wolverton Mountain, near where I was born. I was born and reborn near the same place. I have recalled that experience countless times through the years, and it has been an anchor for me in troubling times.

My high school years occurred under the shadow of World War II. News in the early months of the war was not good, and a sense of foreboding was very real. Some of my friends, eager for excitement, lied about their ages and enlisted before they were eighteen. Others of us, too young and dumb to know the horrors of war, were concerned that the war would end before we had a chance to get in.

Truett was in Europe but not in a combat unit. However, the troop ship on which he crossed the Atlantic was torpedoed and sunk on its next crossing. As word came of friends being wounded, and one being killed, a sobering reality came over the school.

Before the war began, I had become fascinated with airplanes and flying and had started building model airplanes. They were not fancy—just a few pieces of precut balsa wood, a sheet of ultrathin paper to cover the wings and fuselage, and a rubber band to turn the stiff paper (or balsa wood) propeller. They cost ten cents.

After the war started and many new military planes were developed, I did everything I could to get an extra nickel or dime to buy and build models of the new planes. In the early days, the models were made of wood. Plastic came later. With patriotism at a high level but school funds still short, I was often asked to suspend my aircraft models over school class or social functions as decoration. That love of aircraft and flying has never diminished.

Joann's Early Years

As noted earlier, Joann was born on a ranch a few miles outside the little town of Carlsbad, Texas, on July 13, 1931. She was not seen by a doctor until several days after her birth. Her mother was attended by one of her sisters, totally inexperienced for that role. It was a difficult delivery. She has little information about the family circumstances at the time, except that financially, it was similar to ours.

The places of our births were different in many ways, yet they were also similar in some ways. They had a garden, a cistern for water, and killed a hog in the fall and a calf in the spring. As with my mother's situation, her mother had a cast-iron washpot just outside the kitchen door, with the standard rub board nearby. Doing the family wash early every Monday morning in the middle of a scorching West Texas summer (or freezing winter wind) was not pleasant. There was a great improvement when her dad splurged and bought a used electric Maytag washer with an attached wringer. Wonderful ... until the day Joann was placing wet clothes through the wringer. When she bent over to get more clothes the ever-present Texas wind blew her hair into the wringer, wrenching out a handful of curly blond hair. Her screams brought her mother who unplugged the washer barely in time to prevent a horrible tragedy. It was close. And the missing hair never grew back.

Her family history has many gaps also. Even though her mother's dad, Walter Henson, lived with them in his later years, Joann remembers no conversations concerning her family history. It was a subject rarely discussed or perhaps rarely remembered. As their names suggest, the Hortons and the Hensons were from a Scotch-Irish-English background, but she has no family records to establish an ancestor line. Because the names are common names at their point of origin, it has been difficult to pinpoint a line of ancestors. They came from the same general area in the eastern part of the United States as did the Goatchers and the Allens, but they settled in totally different regions. Some of her ancestors came through Arkansas but continued on to East Texas, and a few settled near what is now Wills Point, Texas. Others continued on to West Texas and settled near San Angelo in an area that became the little town of Carlsbad.

With many of her family having a farming background, the question is obvious: Why did some stop and some continue on, especially into the semi-arid area near San Angelo, deep in the heart of Texas? It was typical plains country, slightly rolling, desolate, lonely, with a variety of cacti, mesquite, and creosote bushes typical of the region. In the distance, mesas could be seen. It was far different from their previous home. Water was scarce. Shallow wells could be drilled in the Concho River Valley to feed stock and help with a vegetable garden, but it was no place for row crop farming. Why stop?

A separate set of circumstances may provide part of the answer. A large tract of land known as the Hughes Ranch was located along the Concho River where Carlsbad is now located. It was purchased by a land company and divided into large parcels. A tract on one of the sites was selected as the location of a town and was named Carlsbad in 1907. At about the same time, medical research suggested that rest in a dry, sunny climate might be the best treatment for tuberculosis. Acting on that finding, the Texas legislature appropriated funds to build a TB sanitarium in Carlsbad. With parcels of land ranging in size from 80 to 320 acres selling very cheaply, and with employment available at the sanitarium, that could have been an inducement for Joann's ancestors to relocate. Later, she learned that her maternal grandmother and paternal grandfather had tuberculosis, ultimately resulting in their deaths. Those circumstances could well have influenced them to settle there.

Though widely separated in miles and geography, our families had some things in common. Both families would be considered poor by today's standards, but friends, relatives, and neighbors were in similar situations. To them, it was normal. Difficult, yes, but not unusual. Both families were deeply religious, living out and displaying a strong faith in the Lord and a loyalty to His church. Both families were active in their local Baptist churches. Both families had a similar belief in the disciplining of their children and in inculcating a strong sense of honesty, responsibility, and Christian character.

Work vocations were different, as described earlier. Mine was the typical small farming operation; Dad (and the kids, when older) worked the fields. Mother kept the home, did the cooking, did most of the gardening, and made much of the family clothing. Joann's Dad, J. W. Horton, though limited in formal education, was extremely skilled in welding and in understanding and repairing mechanical and electrical equipment. He worked at a local auto and motorcycle repair shop and did general repair work in the community. For Joann's Christmas present one year, he collected bicycle parts from wrecked bicycles, made her a bicycle, and painted it silver. A minor issue was that the frame was from a man's bicycle, which was just a bit awkward for her young years. In a dress, climbing over the high frame, shoving off and maintaining enough momentum to remain upright, and placing her feet on the pedals was a challenge, but it did provide the motivation to learn quickly.

Her dad finally obtained a job with the dairy for the sanitarium. Her mother, Toy Horton, supplemented the family income by working as a cook in the sanitarium and by preparing lunches for the schoolkids and teachers who wanted them. Similar difficult struggles and experiences by both families helped develop a very frugal mind-set that saw them through those trying days. That mind-set, present in both families, was passed on to Joann and me and proved to be a great blessing when we lived in primitive situations on the mission field and thought nothing of it. That frugal, conservative attitude was balanced with a strong sense of stewardship, always conscious that God had blessed us far beyond anything we had ever dreamed or merited and that we must therefore be good stewards of those blessings. Her dad taught her to tithe as a young girl. "For," he always said, "one can never out-give the Lord." For him, that translated to mean giving beyond the tithe—to the church or to anyone in need.

Our education opportunities were similar in our early school years, but they varied greatly in our middle and high school years. Joann's first school was in Carlsbad, a one-room school with a curriculum for six grades. Mrs. Louise Hansen was the firm but fair and excellent teacher. The older kids who did well were expected to help tutor the younger ones. With the schoolhouse being near her house, Joann went home for lunch. Very convenient—except for the day a buttin' billy goat broke through the barb-wire fence when she was about halfway home. They saw each other at about the same time. It took off after her, and she took off for home. It was a close race, but she won ... by one small step. She still does not care for goats or goat meat.

Classroom time was not enough to satisfy Joann; she was not content to leave it at school. When she came home, she set up school again, this time with herself as the teacher and James, her little brother (five years younger) as the student. It was only a short step to then set up for church, with her as the preacher and James as the congregation. She was also the music leader.

She spent her middle school years in the rapidly growing Pyote school district, a school greatly helped by the nearby Pyote Bomber Base. It was a good school. In contrast, my middle school years were spent moving from school to school, missing many classes to help on the farm. The curriculum was limited and varied from poor to average. Our high school experiences were totally different. Joann's family moved to Odessa in the fall of 1945, which had one of the best school systems in the entire state of Texas and one that very ably prepared her for college and medical school.

Formosa High School was barely adequate for the time and place, but it was totally inadequate by today's standards. Our school board did not have the money to pay for competent instructors. It was also remote and hardly attractive to well-educated teachers. One beginning algebra class and one beginning biology class was the total math and science offering by my high school. No chemistry was ever offered. We did have one excellent teacher, Mrs. Anna Bell Shipp, our English grammar and literature teacher. She was outstanding. College entrance a few years later revealed just how unprepared I was academically in math and science. I felt that inadequacy throughout my undergraduate and graduate studies. I was a little better prepared in English and literature.

This brief overview of our early years affirms ever so strongly just how important it is for families, especially the children, to be involved in church. Our early church years had similarities and differences. Both of us were in small churches, but my early churches (except in Formosa) had no classes or programs specifically for the young. In contrast, Joann's early churches did have classes and programs for the young. They also had circuit-riding preachers who came when they could and shared the good news that a loving God was calling everyone to come and follow Him. Joann heard that message from her earliest years and came to believe that God had a plan for her. Her young, sensitive heart was responsive to God's call, and she was saved at the age of seven. At age nine, she felt God calling her to be a missionary, influenced greatly by mission studies in Girls' Auxiliary and life stories of missionary women.

One story in particular had a life-changing impact on her. Blanche Groves, 1889–1986, was an indomitable, highly respected missionary to China for forty-eight years. In a testimony directed specifically to the younger generation, she spoke of the overwhelming need for someone to come help her in her ministry to the masses of children who were victims of famine and the ravages of war resulting from the Japanese invasion of China. Her ministry of loving care to the impoverished became well-known in her area of China and created needs far beyond her ability to meet alone. She pleaded for some of the youth in the churches to heed God's call and come to China. That touched Joann's heart, and she responded to that call. (Joann's immediate response to God's call, even as a nine-year-old, but which has continued throughout her life, has been a remarkable characteristic of her focused resolve to obey God immediately, whenever or wherever He leads. It has been a characteristic that has challenged and encouraged me countless times when I tended to hesitate.)

She immediately took her first steps on her focused journey toward her ultimate goal of being a missionary serving some of the neediest people of the world. When she was thirteen, she wrote the Foreign Mission Board, telling them of her decision and asking what kinds of missionaries were most needed. Their reply indicated that doctors were the highest priority. She said, "Okay, if that is what is needed, that is what I will be." Thus began the difficult but sure path on her eighteen-year journey to her appointment to serve the Lord as a foreign medical missionary. That response has brought her more joy and gratitude to God than any other decision of her working life.

Her story sharply accentuates the important role of parents in giving their children the opportunity to hear and sense God's calling on their lives while their hearts are young and responsive. Later, I'll relate how God took the seemingly haphazard wondering path I followed, leading to my ultimate fulfillment on the mission field.

There was one other element in our early school years that was important for both of us: the spiritual component. God was acknowledged. Biblical standards of right and wrong were taught and practiced. Moral or other misconduct brought appropriate consequences. The Bible was respected. The spiritual heritage and principles of our nation's forefathers were accepted as foundational to our nation's beginning and to our continued existence. Much of that spiritual component has been lost in today's secular, hedonistic culture. Family values—Christian values—are no longer reinforced by culture. Consequently, our society is suffering, and many of our present generation appear to have lost their pole star of reference.

In recounting the differences and similarities of our early years, then later the confluence of our lives as He brought us together, the rhyme and reason for it all began to come to me:

> My home was the green, green hills
> Encompassed by clear sparkling streams,
> Wonderful for scenes of beauty
> But wanting in the substance of dreams.

The Ozark Mountains are beautiful, yet without other influencing factors, those same mountains served as barriers to isolate and retard an awareness of the larger world into which God called us to go. The contrast in our green hills and the plains of West Texas was stark.

> The stars at night are big and bright,
> But the eyes must be lifted to behold;
> What is seen in the brightness of a spiritual light
> Is a plan only God could unfold.
> The desert around Carlsbad appears dreary;
> No mountains, no trees and no streams,
> The struggle to survive grows weary,
> But appearances can't stifle the dreams.

And Joann had dreams. As noted earlier, the little country churches, with occasional circuit-riding preachers, dedicated parents, and teachers planted, watered, and cultivated the early stirrings in Joann's heart to follow the Lord. Our different backgrounds had little, if anything, to do with our differing early responses to His nudging. She was just more responsive to the Lord and more spiritually mature than I was.

The Lord overcame our geographical separation in ways that probably made Him laugh. He led her from the desert to walk the halls of the University of Arkansas Medical School for her residency, just on the edge of my green, green hills, where she fell in love with their beauty.

Concurrently, He led me in a roundabout way back to those same hills near where I was born and to which I did not want to return. Born and raised in the harsh, arid, semidesert around Carlsbad and Odessa, Joann came to dislike the desert, and once away from it, she never wanted to return, especially after seeing the green hills and streams near my home. Paradoxically, when we lived in Van Horn some years later, I came to love the desert and the mountains. I loved to hike and camp out in the region, especially in the mountainous Van Horn area where it was even drier than it was in Carlsbad or Odessa. Now those wandering paths of ours were about to merge.

The onset of World War II brought incomprehensible changes. I use that word deliberately. The invisible walls of our little villages of Formosa and Carlsbad were knocked down almost overnight, never to be rebuilt. Our small, insular communities were exposed to a bigger, far different, more complex but not necessarily better, world. I alluded to the effect it had on me earlier. The effect it had on Joann and her family was just as dramatic. Her dad's mechanical and electrical skills enabled him to get a job at the newly opened Goodfellow Army Air Base in San Angelo in 1940. After about one year (during which he was critically injured in a motorcycle accident), he—accompanied by his family—was sent to Dallas for further study. After completion of his studies, he relocated to the Rattlesnake Bomber Base (later called the Pyote Bomber Base[3]), a B-17 and B-29 bomber-training field, about fifty miles west of Odessa. He was given a lead role in bomber aircraft maintenance. By the time the war ended, he was responsible for the final inspection and approval of the planes before they were assigned to or returned to combat service. During the same time, her mother had the responsible job of packing parachutes for use by the bomber aircrews. With both parents working, their financial situation improved.

One of Joann's clearest memories of her Pyote school years was the bus ride to and from school, which was provided by the army. It was one of the perks of living on base. The "buses" were two-and-a-half-ton army trucks (we called them "deuce and a half" in my military time). Rain (rare) or shine (almost always), hot or cold, pleasant or in a stinging sandstorm, the trucks were exciting to ride. Never mind the difficulty of modest young girls in dresses trying to climb into and out of the high truck.

When the base was deactivated at the end of the war, Joann's dad became an oil well pumper for Gulf Oil. In late 1945, they moved

---

[3] The US Army constructed the Pyote air base in the middle of the driest portion of desert West Texas. In the process of leveling the land for the runways, a huge number of rattlesnake dens was found, the nesting place for countless rattlesnakes. The name for the base came naturally—Rattlesnake Bomber Base. It was later changed to Pyote Bomber Base, named after a nearby village. The base was the final training center for B-17 and B-29 air crews before assignment overseas for combat duty. With three thousand military personnel and two thousand civilian workers, housing had to be built on base. Joann's family lived in one of the units. The isolation/desolation of the base made it ideal for training. There was very little other air traffic, and the weather was clear 95 percent of the time. It was a major air base, with three 8,400-foot runways. After the war, it became a storage depot for aircraft before they were sold, sent to museums, or torn up for salvage. Among the aircraft stored for a while was the *Enola Gay*, the B-29 that dropped the first atomic bomb on Japan. It was later moved into the Smithsonian Air Museum in Washington, DC.

to Odessa from which he maintained a multitude of oil well pumps in the Permian Basin. In addition to the excellent school system, many opportunities for spiritual development came along. Her dad used those opportunities to encourage her, especially in the field of music. He was an excellent singer and music director, and he often took Joann along to help with the music. In fact, her earliest position as church pianist was at the age of nine when she knew but three hymns, sung weekly for months—or until others could be learned. He was frequently involved in starting new churches with members who had very little musical ability, providing Joann a wonderful learning atmosphere. She became an excellent pianist. As a fast learner, it did not take her long to realize that God was working in her circumstances to accomplish His purpose in her life. Those were wonderful, formative years for her. Her dad, her band director, Mr. Robert Maddox, her piano teacher, Mrs. Pierce, and her Latin teacher, Miss White, particularly challenged and encouraged her. It all combined to give her a can-do attitude that has remained strong through the years.

Meandering on My Journey

Graduation from high school forced me to start making my own decisions, a step I was not really prepared to take. Perhaps the reason—or excuse—was my family history. Our small farm family made most decisions based on external circumstances, in our case, the seasons. Springtime called for planting, so we planted. Fall and ripe crops called for harvesting, so we harvested. Same principle was true whether it referred to crops, gardens, hay, or cutting firewood for winter.

Decisions were mostly made for us by needs that had to be met. I can't fault my parents for what they did or how they did it, but by growing up in those circumstances, I can better understand their mind-set. For Dad and Mom, providing just a subsistence level of living on those rocky, unproductive hillside farms was a never-ending challenge. Their energy was focused on providing for the basic family needs. They had hopes and dreams, especially for Truett, Lavelle, and me, but to obtain a college education or to become financially stable was so far beyond their immediate conception that it seemed almost unattainable. Very few discussions were held concerning career choices, higher education, or what plan God might have for our lives.

The significance of decisions was lost on me for most of my early years. It was much later that I realized that decisions are the foundations of life, for good or ill. I had heard the parable of Jesus countless times before I connected it to everyday decision-making. Jesus cautioned us about building on sand; when the floods come, the building will be destroyed. If we build on a rock (meaning the Lord), we can withstand the storms. All of life is built on decisions. Lacking decisions means lacking directions. Lacking directions means drifting.

Drifting means an unproductive, pointless, fruitless waste of a life that God has blessed with talent, potential, skills, and gifts. It is a wasted stewardship of what we are called to do and be for the Lord. I have often wondered if the unused, wasted potential of His followers might be one of the Lord's greatest disappointments.

I cannot claim those circumstances of my early days as an excuse, especially in light of what some of my own family did. Dad had three brothers who did very well. Uncle Winfred Goatcher was a very successful businessman. Uncle Calvin went to college and seminary and was a well-known pastor and children's home administrator in Oklahoma. Uncle "Doc," A. L. Goatcher, MD, became a highly respected and honored physician. He was one of the founding trustees of the Arkansas Baptist Hospital System. All of them were outstanding Christian men and church leaders. They came out of situations similar to mine and did great things, so I have no excuse. At some point, they sensed and responded to God's call. God was probably trying to influence my decisions all along the line also, but I was still living in a mind-set of responding to external circumstances and did not seek His guidance.

I had no plans. I did not have enough money to go to college and had no idea what to study if I could have gone. As valedictorian, I had received a few scholarship offers, but they were too small to be of lasting help. For some long-forgotten reason (I later realized it was God working in the background) I decided to go to Coyne Radio and Electrical School, a vocational technical school in Chicago.

Truett was out of the army, home and considering his next step. He decided to go to Chicago with me. After one week, he realized that was not the place or work for him, and he returned to Formosa. Not long afterward, he and Lillian Williams (a grade behind me in the Formosa school) were married, and he enrolled in Ouachita Baptist College (now a university). Later, he received his master's degree in math from Peabody College, part of Vanderbilt University. He was on course for a long and distinguished career in education in Arkansas, capped by having the Arkansas Business Administrator of the Year Award being named in his honor.

In retrospect, I realize that God was beginning to step in and guide me in a more obvious way during my year in Chicago. The training I received in electricity, electronics, and refrigeration was needed for my later work at our hospital in Thailand.

Chicago was a wide-eyed, skyscraper-staring experience for me. I was a bib overall, hillbilly boy from the hills of Arkansas. Chicago was another world. I think it was providential that I had to scramble continually to make enough money to stay in school. Packing Christmas cards, sorting mail at the post office, and working as a grease monkey in the huge mechanical equipment room at Presbyterian Hospital were just a few of the many part time jobs I had. I did not have time to explore the red-light district along nearby Madison Street. In school, it was classes in the morning and practical training in the afternoon. Once in a while, I studied. Studies included building newly designed superheterodyne radios from scratch, learning to repair them, wiring houses, and learning to repair and rewind all kinds and sizes of electric motors. TV was just coming into the market (black and white only) so we learned some electronics and how to use the oscilloscope in repairing them. I also took a quick survey course in refrigeration.

Two events in my Chicago year are still vivid in my mind. One is related to church. With churchgoing being a regular part of my Formosa life, I went to church on my first Sunday in Chicago. Again, I felt I was in a different world. People were dressed way beyond anything I had ever seen. It was obvious that I was a country boy, out of my element. I felt uncomfortable, out of place. I was totally ignored and felt ashamed. I never went back.

The other event was a shocker to this naive Arkansas boy. An older student and an instructor invited me to their apartment for dinner (supper). I was excited about the invitation, but I was called back to work to help with some emergency and was unable to go. The next day, the subject was mentioned in a conversation with other students. They looked at me strangely, then turned quiet. I did not understand. Later, one of the students told me that the men were homosexuals. A little later, I began to realize that God must have had a hand in thwarting our getting together. It was an early reminder that perhaps God was looking out for me. It was just one of countless times that God intervened and prevented a disaster from occurring in my life.

After graduating from Coyne in early summer of 1947, I returned to Formosa. I was broke and needed to find some kind of a job. While waiting to decide what to do, word came that the tomato harvest was starting in Indiana and workers were needed. Four of us took off, including a high school classmate. We headed for the little town of Swayzee, about fifteen miles east of Kokomo, which was said to be a major growing and canning area. As we drew near, we saw a huge canning factory that was preparing for the incoming harvest. We had come at the right time. They hired the three other guys as pickers, but when they learned I had been to electrical school, I was hired as the factory electrician for the canning season. It paid better than the picking job and was good experience for later needs in the mission field.

After a brief but intense canning season, it was time to go home. Woody and I decided to save money by hitchhiking back to Arkansas. It went well until we got into Illinois and were picked up by a couple of men who had been drinking. It did not take long to realize we were in danger. We faked an urgent need for a bathroom stop and bailed out. Our next ride took us to Cairo, Illinois, the town where the Ohio River meets the Mississippi. While walking down to the river to get a ferry across to Missouri, my cardboard suitcase broke apart—and everything in it spilled out on the sidewalk. What a mess! The appeal of the open road was fading fast. I had a cousin and her husband, Bess and Orville Shipley, living not far across the Mississippi River in Missouri. We headed there for our first home-cooked meal in months. We had enough hitchhiking to last a while and took little intercity buses on home.

I had saved some money and opened my little radio and appliance repair shop. It was not a smart move. Few houses in Formosa had a radio or more than one or two appliances. The surrounding community had even fewer. There was just not enough need to justify a radio and appliance repair shop. After a few weeks, I shut it down and started looking for a job. The timing was right for me to get a job in Little Rock with Western Electric Company, the equipment installation unit of the Bell Telephone Company. My first couple of weeks were devoted to an intensive training period. We had to learn the wiring procedures (all color-coded wires) for connecting and switching the many thousands of numbers that were constantly going through the telephone-exchange system.

The work involved a team of three to eight people going to the towns in central, eastern, and southern Arkansas to repair, renovate, or expand the telephone office equipment as required. That was in the late 1940s when small towns still had manual telephone systems. When you lifted the phone, the operator asked, "Number please?" When told, the operator would plug the cord from your number into the number being called and manually depress the ringing button. It was a step up from the earlier crank-turning, manual-ringing method, but it was far short of the newer dial system. With the rapid changes taking place in telephone equipment technology, we were kept busy, usually staying in a town for two or four weeks, then moving on to the next town. (Present-day communications technology was hardly into the science fiction realm at that time.)

After a little more than a year, a big job came up in Springfield, Missouri. Western Electric was building a totally new dial system for the city. A few of us were sent to do the preliminary survey, stay through the total installation, and do the final checkout. It would take at least a year. It turned out to be a significant year in my life. I came to like the town very much, found a church home that impacted my life, and became the leader of the youth group in the First Baptist Church. When the new dial system installation was complete, we were to be transferred to Kansas City for another major installation. I did not want to go. God was dealing with me, and I felt I should remain in Springfield and in the church.

While still employed by Western Electric, my church wanted to send me to the Missouri Baptist Student Union's annual meeting. I demurred since I was not a student. They insisted, and I finally consented. It was there, after a message by Dr. Frank Leavell, that I felt led to commit my life to vocational Christian service. I was very unclear what that meant. I did not feel called to be a preacher, but I did not know what other choices were available. Even though I felt closer to the Lord and was slowly maturing, I was still a child in the faith and was still meandering on my journey. Thanks to the Lord, my wanderings did not go totally off course, but I was still not seeking His guidance.

I resigned from Western Electric and enrolled in Southwest Missouri State College in Springfield, majoring in math and civil engineering. I immediately hit major bumps in math classes, quickly realizing how inadequate my high school preparation had been. I struggled to try to catch up.

Again, I did not have enough money for college, so it was back to a series of part-time jobs. Those jobs also happened to be in areas that helped prepare me for later responsibilities on the mission field—just a few more pieces of the puzzle God was using to form a picture that would not become clear to me until years later.

CHAPTER 2

Military Service Inspires Focus

Just as I was completing my first difficult year of college, the Korean War came along. Now came a major decision time for me. Do nothing, and I would be drafted. That was not very appealing. My love of flying was still very much alive, so I decided to enlist in the air force and go to cadet school. I applied, passed the usual mental and physical tests, and was ready to sign on the dotted line. At about that time, the air force changed the term of enlistment from three years to four years for those selected for pilot training. For pilots, there was no guarantee that discharge would come at the end of four years. After a struggle, I decided against entering the air force. I would take my chances as a draftee.

I did not have long to wait. My "greetings" notice came, and I reported to Camp Robinson in Little Rock in January 1951. There were about one hundred of us who were inducted and immediately sent to Fort Chaffee in Fort Smith for further processing. Processing included intensive testing in a variety of areas, which was similar to IQ testing. The next day, I was called in and told I had qualified for officer candidate school.

"Are you interested?"

"Yes," I replied.

"Yes, sir!" he snapped.

"Yes, sir," I replied.

"Very well, you will be notified of the next available opening. You are dismissed."

I left. I forgot to salute.

We were sent to Camp (now Fort) Carson, Colorado, for basic training. Our training cadre was a unit of the Wisconsin National Guard. The training was not difficult for me; I was still in good physical shape from my earlier work. The mental challenge was minor. After basic training, we were assigned to the 998th Engineer Construction Battalion. After a few weeks, we were given the assignment to build a road through the San Isabel National Forest in southern Colorado. That was a great time for me. We bivouacked by a little lake at about seven thousand feet, surrounded by mountains that were up to thirteen thousand feet tall. We could easily see Pike's Peak, which was almost one hundred miles away. It was breathtaking. I was in a signal corps unit, stringing wires and maintaining a telephone connection between company headquarters and the heavy-equipment operators a few miles ahead, bulldozing a right-of-way through the forest-covered mountains. In the process of laying telephone lines, I learned tree climbing, sometimes climbing thirty or forty feet to stretch lines across gullies or small canyons. When we completed the road, we returned to Fort Carson to wait for our next assignment.

Somewhat surprisingly, our training cadre was recalled to Wisconsin after our basic training was completed. After they left, a few of us were chosen to take leadership roles. We started getting rapid promotions. Every two months, we would move up a rank. Eight months after completing basic training, I was a sergeant first class. Part of my pleasure with the promotion was that it greatly increased the monthly dollar allotment to Mother and Lavelle as military dependents. It enabled them to live above a subsistence level.

It was only after I returned home after discharge that I learned that Mother had set aside a portion of her allotment for my later use. She had sacrificed for me again.

Shortly after arrival back in camp, I was called to the company commander's office and told that a slot was open for me to go on to officer candidate school. Did I still want it? The choice posed a couple of dilemmas for me. The first dilemma was that the length of OCS had been extended from three months to six months, after which I would be required to serve an additional two years. That meant I would be in the army for almost three years. I was not at all excited about that.

The second dilemma was that as a sergeant first class, Mother's allotment as my military dependent would be more than that of an OCS student and almost as much as that of a second lieutenant. All things considered, I declined the offer and decided to take my chances. That decision led me to an event where I witnessed one of the most amazing sights of my life.

Those two decisions, whether to pursue military flight training and whether to pursue commissioning as an army officer, were made consciously and have occupied my thoughts many times in the succeeding years. Why did I make those particular decisions? What influenced me in the process? Viewed from the perspective of later years, it is clear that God was working silently but persistently in the wings, guiding me in the process, but at the time, I wrestled with both decisions. I wanted to be a military pilot, and I wanted to be a military officer. With my limited math background, I might not have made it through flight school in the new jet age, but I think I could have made it through OCS. Why did I not choose to follow my desires? I think God had a different plan for me, and I think He was leading me quietly but firmly to follow His plan, not my own. Later events revealed distinctly the hand of the Lord putting the pieces of the puzzle in place: the onset of color-vision deficiency would have canceled any chance of being a military pilot, and going to OCS would have prevented my participation in an atomic weapons testing program and my involvement in a significant construction project in Korea.

Much of that struggle was because I had desired to go in another direction for many years. In my late teens and into my late twenties, much of my thought and my greatest personal desire was to be involved in aviation. I really wanted to be a commercial pilot. If not that, then I wanted to be involved in airport management. I just wanted a career in aviation. What I wanted, however, did not fit with what I felt I ought to do. That ambivalence just would not go away. I had not yet felt called into a specific Christian vocation. Although I had responded to a vague vocational call at twenty, I was not really comfortable with an aviation career. I sensed that I should obey God's desire for me, although it had not yet been revealed.

The tension was between what I wanted to do and what I ought to do. It has been brought home to me a thousand times in the succeeding years how blessed I have been that I did what I ought to do rather than what I personally wanted to do. The call of Jesus to come follow Him was/is not a hardship to be endured—it is a way of life that results in God's blessings. That was made obvious to me many times on the mission field when I would be in difficult, demanding, or dangerous circumstances. I was at complete peace because I knew I was in His will. I had made the right decision, and God was affirming it.

At this point, I want to emphasize something very clearly. When I chose to do what I knew I ought to do, God gave me a love for that work and a total peace and assurance that I had made the right decision. Joann felt the same way, even though her formative decisions were made in a very different context. There were times on the mission field when we were in dangerous and difficult situations, but we were there by choice. We always had the option of walking away from those circumstances, but we never chose to do so. Now, in our later years, there is a constant song of celebration in our hearts, knowing that we obeyed the Lord. There are absolutely no regrets, only an overwhelming sense of gratitude to the Lord.

How can one know His leading? His plan? His will? There is no easy answer. For me, working through the struggle and coming to the final decision, I had a sense of discomfort in proceeding toward a specific decision about which I had reservations. Flight school and commissioning, as much as I wanted them, just did not feel right. I realized later that it was God's unseen hand leading me to a higher calling. Not that the other choices were inferior work, but for me, they were not a calling from God. They were not a part of His will for me. I am convinced that I made the right decisions because the consequences of those decisions have brought me blessings beyond measure through all the succeeding years. It is not with pride, but with great gratitude, that I say I think my willingness to obey the unseen, but very real, hand of God led me to make many decisions that I later realized were pieces of the plan of God for my life. Someone has said it better: obedience is the real test of love and dedication.

Atomic Testing

Now to the amazing sight I was able to witness. I have been blessed by seeing many of the wonders of the natural world in my travels. I have stood in awe countless times as I have observed God's creation in indescribable beauty and majesty, but what I witnessed in the Nevada desert was a sight equally indescribable, but a sight wrought by man.

About a month after I declined the OCS offer, I was invited to go to Nevada to participate in an above-ground atomic weapons testing program. Two or three military personnel (senior NCOs up to general officers) from army, air force, navy, and marine bases around the world were brought in to participate. I think there were about two thousand of us present. I wondered why I had been invited. I certainly had no education, skill, or experience to evaluate any part of the test. The only remote thing I could think of was that I had been chosen as soldier of the month for Fort Carson the previous month, and they felt that my going would be a reward for that. Whatever the reason, I felt honored.

The test was conducted at the Frenchman's Flat Weapons Test Area, a desert region about sixty-five miles north/northwest of Las Vegas. From the train depot in Las Vegas, we were trucked and bused to the spectator area and directed to a loosely defined, slightly sloping sand, gravel, and stunted brush desert spot. We were all required to be seated on the ground and were told to "stay on the ground" when the blast occurred. Extremely dark glasses were passed out to shield us against the brilliant light of the blast. Radiation dosimeters were also passed out to measure radiation exposure. The spectator area faced ground zero about three or four miles away, at my estimation, at the intersection of two trails on a slight slope facing us. The plan was for the bomber to fly a prescribed course at a specific altitude (classified) directly perpendicular to us. The aircraft instruments would determine drop time so as to hit ground zero. We were told the bomb was set to explode one thousand feet above the ground. About ten miles before the drop point, the pilot switched the aircraft intercom directly to the PA system used by our announcers, enabling us to hear the final in-flight comments of the crew just prior to the drop. Excitement built as we were kept informed of the plane's position. When the comments of the flight crew began the countdown to the bomb drop, all eyes were focused on the anticipated point where we hoped to see the plane.

We barely saw the plane as it neared the drop point, but we could not see the bomb when the bombardier called "bomb away." At that point, our seated, orderly group became disorderly. As one man would rise to see a little better, so would the one behind him. Then the next one. Soon, almost everyone was standing, just before the bomb was due to erupt. The announcer was screaming for everyone to get down—and being totally ignored. He knew what was coming and what would happen to those standing, but we were too caught up in anticipation to pay him any attention. Then the bomb exploded.

The announcers had tried to convey the magnitude of what was about to happen, but it was, and is, beyond fully describing. It ripped the sky with a firestorm of heat, color, sound, sand, and shock waves. A white light, many times the intensity of the sun, enveloped the desert slopes. We felt the flush of heat almost immediately—with sound quickly following. We saw and felt the flash, then watched as the shock wave moved over the desert floor toward us faster than we could react. The announcer was still yelling, and perhaps a few did get down, but most of us were still standing when the shock wave hit. Everyone was knocked down by the brutal shock wave like stalks of grass. Added to the power of the shock wave moving toward us, almost at the speed of sound, was the amount of sand and debris it stirred up as it moved over the desert floor. Any desire to get back up for a better look was snuffed out by the swirling, stinging sand.

The initial white blast was followed by the entire fireball quickly swelling to over a mile in diameter, becoming a boiling cauldron of brilliant red, pink, blue, and many other colors. We were too close to see the iconic mushroom cloud rising above. All we could see clearly was a huge mass of dust, smoke, and flame still boiling, erupting, and filling the sky.

The whole image has remained etched in my mind, played over and over countless times through the years. It is still beyond describing. The immensity of the event was a testimony to the power of the mind of man, but was that all it was? I think it was perhaps at that time that I began to have thoughts beyond my usual, small, circumscribed realm of thought. The event was overwhelming. Why had I been permitted to witness it? I had no right to be there. Something greater was going on. I did not understand it, but my thoughts and concepts of God were being dragged to a greater awareness. That was a massive demonstration of the ability of the mind of man, but man had not created the elements that made the event possible. He had just harnessed what God had created. That demonstration provided only a hint of the ultimate source of real power; not just physical/material power, but a hint and a sign of the infinitely greater spiritual power inherent in the God of creation. When David beheld the splendor of the heavens and the majesty of creation, he immediately thought of God's spiritual concern for man—the only one created in His image. We are staggered at the power God has to speak the universe into existence, but it is not that great physical, creative power that is His greatest manifestation; it is His great life-giving resurrection power demonstrated in raising His Son from the dead. All I can do is join David in proclaiming that "the heavens are telling of the glory of God" and join Paul in affirming that man's highest goal is "to know Him and the power of His resurrection."

The entire event highlighted the inadequacy of words to describe something that really is indescribable. Everyone has significant, even life-changing times and events that they long to fully share with others but can't find adequate words to fully express their thoughts and feelings. That is infinitely truer of spiritual issues. I can only imagine the thoughts of Jesus as He tried to convey to finite human minds with finite human words the infinite immensity of His creation, His drama of redemption, and the ultimate joy of His children.

After about thirty minutes, we boarded vehicles and were driven to ground zero to start taking measurements. A wide variety of test subjects/objects was in total disarray. Animals in cages, houses in different stages of construction, and all types of military equipment were arranged in groups so that the four cardinal points of the compass would be exposed. We were to measure the amount of movement of the subjects, beginning at ground zero and moving outward to the last subject. When we completed the measurements, we turned in our film badges and returned to Las Vegas. We were now on our own and could return to our bases. I thought it was all over, except perhaps a report when I returned to base. Not quite. Thirty-one years later, in 1982, there came a surgical surprise, and then again, sixty-two years later, in 2013, I received a letter from the Department of Justice concerning the testing and my part in it. (That part of the story comes later.)

My return trip to Camp Carson was somewhat anticlimactic, yet it too was memorable. I went to the transit lounge at Nellis Air Force Base in Las Vegas to see if I could hitch a ride aboard a military aircraft headed back toward Colorado. Fortunately, a flight was available. A colonel, the commanding officer of an air force base (he didn't identify the base) was in a B-25 twin-engine bomber that he had renovated to carry passengers and was on his way to Kirkland Air Force Base in Albuquerque, New Mexico. He invited a couple of us to join him.

The flight path out of Las Vegas took us over Lake Mead and then the Grand Canyon. It was beautiful from five thousand feet above, but the temptation to get closer was too much. He descended to just below the south rim of the canyon and flew along for several miles. It was an unforgettable experience! Coming up out of the canyon, he flew at normal cruising altitude for a while, then descended again to fly low over the Painted Desert. That was enough sightseeing; it was time to go on to Albuquerque. I got a bus (or a train, I don't remember) and returned to Camp Carson.

Soon after returning, I was sent to an intelligence training school. During that time, I was investigated by some unnamed government agency to be cleared for a "secret" clearance that would enable me to review classified information. Apparently, an agent also visited Formosa; Mother said there was much curiosity in the community as to what I had done to cause a government official to come around asking questions about me.

I was beginning to get a little antsy. I had been in the army for eleven months, almost to the time beyond which I would not be deployed overseas before discharge. On almost the final day before the deadline, I received orders that relocated me to Korea.

Military Service: Korea

We sailed from Fort Lewis, Washington, in early January 1952. We docked in Yokohama for a week of military make-work, time-killing activity.

What a relief it was when we boarded another ship and headed for the Yellow Sea. Sailing up the Yellow Sea to Inchon, Korea, I had my only view of a "glassy sea." The wind was totally calm, and the air was extremely hazy, making it impossible to distinguish the dividing line between sea and sky. The ocean was absolutely mirror flat with not a single ripple in any direction except our ship's wake. Eerie.

Our ship pulled in to Inchon in late January 1952. We anchored offshore, then offloaded onto small lighters to be taken through the shallow water to the dock and then on to the replacement depot. My new assignment was to a combat engineer unit up near the Thirty-Eighth Parallel, an ill-defined line of demarcation between North and South Korea. It was actually a winding, sometimes changing line, tentatively established in anticipation of an armistice being signed (which has never happened). Sporadic fighting was still going on.

No war area is a pleasant place. It was an especially discouraging and dangerous time for the unfortunate infantry grunts, as told to me by one of my friends, an infantry combat company first sergeant who was a part of a unit in central Korea. They would be ordered to take an area—maybe a hill—and then withdraw. The enemy would reoccupy it. Then they were ordered to retake it. Countless lives were lost for no good reason. It was that chaotic interlude that led to "Heartbreak Hill" (sometimes "Heartbreak Ridge") becoming a byword.

Another weird situation was described to me by another friend, also the first sergeant of an infantry company bivouacked adjacent to the MLR (main line of resistance) in eastern Korea. The battalion executive officer (XO) had come for a routine inspection of the company headquarters. While the company commander and the

XO were talking, a small arms rifle round was fired into the area. The XO immediately ordered a patrol to be formed to take out the sniper. The CO asked him not to do it. The XO demanded, "Why not?" The CO explained that the same sniper had been in position for over a week and periodically shot into the area, but he had never hit anyone or anything. They had come to believe he deliberately missed, perhaps hoping thereby to be ignored. They thought that if they took him out, he might be replaced by someone who might not miss. It was unusual, and it did not last long, but strange things happen in war.

Our engineering unit had three major tasks: building bridges (sometimes using World War II, prefabricated Bailey bridges), clearing off small landing strips for use by reconnaissance aircraft, and bulldozing any needed roads for military units to get to the MLR. That was before the DMZ (demilitarized zone) was established. We were a combat unit, but we were never actually in direct combat. Air strikes and artillery fire were frequent companions, but we were never hit.

One unpleasant incident (to me … some liked it) is still vivid from my brief time near the MLR. We had bivouacked in a remote field over a mile from any source of water. We could not have used it anyway since none of the water in the area was potable. Human waste was used as fertilizer, and all surface water was contaminated. All fruit and vegetables were contaminated also. We had a water truck deliver potable water to us each day. On one occasion, the truck broke down. We had no water for two days. Our supply room did have beer—just beer. For two days, beer was the only liquid we had to drink. I detested the taste of the stuff. For me, it was cruel and unusual punishment. That episode totally turned me off to any desire for any kind of alcoholic drink. I have no hesitation in saying no to any form of it—even apart from my religious convictions against it.

After I had been with the unit a little under two months, we were pulled back to Seoul as a reserve unit. I was appointed battalion

S3 operations sergeant, one of the senior NCOs of the battalion. The position called for the rank of master sergeant, but rankings for NCOs had been frozen in our area for some months. I never did attain the rank. That was a short assignment because our reserve status soon ended.

I had one other brief but intense duty between assignments. Heavy rains caused the Han River to begin flooding an island with more than one thousand residents, about four miles upriver from Seoul. The island had no bridge access. As the water rose and became dangerous, our unit was ordered to help evacuate the residents. I was directed to lead a group of GIs in large pontoon boats and get them off the island. The inhabitants did not want to leave and hid in brushy areas. Finding them in the middle of the rainy night in rising waters and persuading them to leave was daunting. Finally, when they realized they were in imminent danger, they were willing to leave. They quickly appeared in bunches and overloaded the pontoons. With only one thirty-horsepower outboard motor for each of the pontoons and with trees, portions of houses, barrels, and other debris roiling in the dark, muddy water, we had a few exciting moments getting all of them safely to high ground.

Korea: The Bell Pavilion

Then came my new assignment—an exciting one with a history that actually began in the fifteenth century. Even back then, Seoul was a major city and the capital of Korea, the "Hermit Kingdom" (as it came to be called). It was surrounded by miles of thick, high walls, and eight huge gates opened to the north, east, south, and west. The size and type of construction of the walls and gates resembled the Great Wall of China. Only six of the gates and about ten miles of the wall remain today.

Erected near the center of the city was a temple/pavilion housing a gigantic bell (twenty to forty tons, I was told). It had been molded of bronze, brass, silver, and a little gold in the 1400s (some Koreans say earlier). The bell was rung at the close of each day to signal the closing of the gates for the night. At dawn, it was rung to signal the opening of the gates for the day. The bell did not have a clapper. It was rung by men pulling back a large, horizontally suspended wood beam, then ramming it into the side of the bell. It had/has great significance for the Koreans, similar to the Liberty Bell for the United States. The pavilion had been destroyed several times through the centuries, the last time when the Chinese and North Koreans invaded South Korea in 1950.

In 1952, President Syngman Rhee of (South) Korea and the commanding general of the American military forces in Korea, felt it would be a wonderful morale booster for the Korean people to see the pavilion restored and the bell rung again. It was a timely endeavor; something was desperately needed. Korea was in chaos. Bombings and fires had destroyed most buildings in Seoul and other cities. There were acute food shortages, and refugees roamed the cities and countryside. There was almost no national infrastructure in place.

The assignment to rebuild the pavilion was given to the Twenty-Fourth Engineer Construction Group (a regiment, in army terms). From there, it came down to our company. With all the construction materials being provided by the US Army Corps of Engineers, they felt a United States Army representative should be present during the construction. That was me. I became the American military representative on the challenging construction project in the heart of Seoul. With my living facility being a few miles from the construction site and more miles to the materials depot, I was provided a jeep and driver to cover my travel needs. As with the atomic weapons testing program, no one told me why I was chosen. I had no experience or skill in Korean construction procedures. (For some unexplainable reason, at the time I was promoted to sergeant first class, my MOS—military occupational specialty—had been changed to 1059, denoting a construction specialist. It was an arbitrary assignment. I had no training and little experience in the field.) Whatever the reason, I felt greatly honored by the selection.

My responsibility was vague in some ways. Three of us were considered project directors: a Korean architect, a Korean engineer, and me. My major role appeared to be to serve as the liaison between the United States military and Seoul authorities. I was to assist my Korean codirectors, and I was to ensure that construction materials were ready when needed. I quickly realized that I was an amateur among professionals. The Koreans were sharp, well-educated guys who were easy to work with. There was no way I could advise them on how to do their jobs.

We had about twenty-five skilled carpenters, fifty sculptors and masons—the pavilion grounds were to be surrounded by carved granite figures of animals and mythological characters—and about fifty woodcarvers. They were the most highly skilled artisans in the nation. In addition, there were about one hundred laborers.

Ensuring that all construction materials were available when needed was a totally new and fascinating role for me. It was an exciting time of learning about their culture, religion, language, and customs. For the Korean people, it quickly became a major morale booster. The construction site was a busy place. Koreans came by in droves to ask questions and just watch, and so did many military and civilian personnel from the joint UN forces fighting in Korea. Later, I realized the whole project was just another piece of the puzzle in the big picture the Lord was compiling to prepare me for further responsibilities many years later.

Surprises popped up early and frequently. The first one was determining how to move the bell. When the pavilion had been destroyed by the North Koreans in 1950, the bell fell and became half-buried in the ground about fifty yards from its new hanging location. We had to get it to the site. As the United States Army Engineer representative, I could requisition any equipment or supplies needed for construction. I told them I would get a heavy-lifting crane to help with the move.

"No! Not permitted!" I was told.

"Why?"

"We must build it without any modern equipment—just as our forefathers built it centuries ago."

I had my first challenge: moving the bell to the pavilion site. Solution? We had them excavate under the bell and wrapped a long, heavy, two-inch rope around it a couple of times. More than one hundred men pulled one end of the rope and rolled the bell toward the site. When they got it to the site from which it would be lifted to its final hanging position, we had another little problem: how to tilt it and then lift it to the correct position, approximately ten feet above the ground. After much discussion, they finally allowed us to use three hydraulic jacks to lift it. It was a reluctant concession to modern technology. Other concessions were made later. There were no trees left standing in Korea at that time that were large enough to serve as columns and support beams so they allowed cement with iron rebar to be used.

After tilting the bell into its approximate position, we placed the jacks 120 degrees apart under the bell and started jacking it up. The jacks had only a six-inch lifting range. We would lift it to the maximum, shore it up with six-by-six timbers, fill in some dirt, remove the jacks, and then keep repeating the process. It took several days to get it in its precise location. We jacked it up almost two feet higher than its final hanging position in order to have room to build the supporting concrete beam and framework. When that was completed, the bell was lowered into its final position. Only then did the actual pavilion construction begin.

As they began building the interior portion and the surrounding porches and railings, another little surprise popped up. They would not use nails or bolts. I deferred to their decision. They precisely carved and fitted the wood beams with overlaps, angles, and carefully trimmed dovetailed joints so well and so tightly that nails and bolts were not necessary. The whole pavilion was filled with some of the most beautiful carving I have ever seen. The workers were artisans.

The entire pavilion was a work of art. (It is also now beautifully lighted with well-designed displays.)

Pavilion nearing completion Oct. 1952 photographed by the author
Seoul, Korea, Bo Shin Memorial Bell

When I was back in Seoul in 1986, I visited the bell site. The bell was gone.

Korea: A Defining Encounter

A side event, unrelated to the project, occurred in the course of construction and became one of the signal events on my spiritual journey. It had its beginning when I started working on the project. When I arrived at work each morning (we worked seven days a week), there would always be a jostling group of hungry, shouting, ragged little refugee boys begging me to let them shine my boots. I rotated my choices to give each a turn. As I rotated through the group, one boy began to catch my attention. Each time I would choose him, he would invite another boy to help him, but he rarely chose the same boy. When I paid him, he would divide the money with the other boy. One day when I chose him, and he and his buddy had finished the shine, I tried to pay him as usual. This time, he did not accept any pay.

I asked, "Why do you not take pay?"

"Today I do it as a present."

"What is the present for?"

"Present is for you. Today is Sunday. It is Lord's Day. I no take pay on Sunday."

His answer froze me in my tracks as I thought of what he had said and all that it meant. He was a very young boy, emaciated and dressed in rags, barely eking out a living, but sharing it with others equally needy. He was obviously a Christian, living out the Christian life to the fullest in a horrible, war-torn world.

I asked, "How did you learn about the Lord?"

He told me about a Presbyterian missionary who had come to their village in North Korea and told them about Jesus. He, his family, and others had become Christians. In spite of his circumstances, he remembered it was the Lord's Day and would not profane it. I was not even aware it was a Sunday. I had been a Christian for years, yet my life fell far, far short of the faithful witness he bore. He had to beg, work, and scrounge continually in order to survive. I had no worries about food clothing and shelter. I had never been as humbled as I was at that moment. After much discussion, he allowed me to share with him so he could share with his friends.

Some days later, on our way back to camp after dark, I glimpsed a couple of boys in the headlights of our jeep squatting under a torn tarpaulin. The tarp was propped up in an alley between two destroyed buildings. I told my driver to stop. Sure enough, it was my little shoeshine boy with one of his friends. They were getting ready to bed down for the night. That alley, with almost nothing for a roof or walls, was their home. I asked him to tell me his story. It was like thousands of others. His home and village in North Korea had been destroyed. Some of his family had been killed, and others had fled, some from persecution, some from the fighting and destruction. They were now gone, separated, probably dead. As far as he knew, he was alone. When I expressed concern for him—how he was going to find food and clothes or survive the coming cold winter—his answer again humbled me. "I no worry. Jesus take care of me."

I talked with him a little more, gave him some money, and left, knowing he would divide it with some of his friends. The memory of that encounter has never left me. God used it to stir my desire to serve Him as a missionary.

Back to the bell. A major celebration occurred in the middle of the project. In the United States, we usually consider groundbreaking and dedication ceremonies as significant times. These were considered minor in Korean construction culture. The most significant ceremony in their building culture was the "beam-laying ceremony," celebrating the placement of the primary roof support beam at the top of the building. For the bell pavilion, it was the granddaddy of all occasions, like a big blowout. The city officials, military leaders, and lesser stars were provided seating; other thousands were standing all around the site. The high point of the ceremony occurred when the beam was to be lifted toward its final position. Several long pulley ropes were wrapped around the beam with a laborer at each end of each rope. At a signal, they were to begin the lift.

When the elaborate preparations were complete, the signal was given. The men bent to the task. With exaggerated grunts, noises, and positioning, they began to lift. Nothing happened. Then another signal. With much loud groaning, grunting, and posture posing, they tried again. Still nothing. After another try, they collapsed on the ground, totally defeated. In the meantime, the crowd was going wild, shouting encouragement, urging them to try harder, and fussing at them for not even budging the beam.

Finally, one of the city officials came forward and placed a big container of money on the beam. The crowd cheered. The men tried again, this time getting one end of the beam off the ground a few inches. In spite of their best efforts and sound effects, it would go no higher. Then another city leader came forward and made a big contribution. A little more progress. And so it went. The point of the process was to maintain their custom of paying the laborers by this method. They were paid a very low regular salary, barely enough to exist on. Those offerings brought to the beams were their payment for their labor. Until they thought they had been adequately paid, they would not lift the beam. The company commander and I, who had seats of honor near the beam, were worn out with laughing. I still laugh at the memory.

After the beam was lifted in place, the speeches began. The United States, the army engineers, and our unit were commended for the contributions and efforts given to accomplish the rebuilding. The CO and I were then called forward to receive plaques of commendation (See picture) and an inlaid jewelry box. Mine are still displayed prominently in our home. I felt deeply honored by that opportunity and recognition.

Receiving award from mayor of Seoul

Korea: Final Days and a Return to the United States

Shortly before the project was completed, and about two weeks before I was to return to the States, three ROK (Republic of Korea) soldiers and I were to do a preliminary survey about a mile from the village of Panmunjom. Preliminary talks were already being held between the UN, Korean officials, and Chinese officials. The POW site straddled the MLR in the Korean sector of the war zone, about fifty-five miles north of Seoul. The MLR at that point was a little wet-weather branch running between slightly sloping hills. We were to remain on the South Korean side of the MLR.

With our UN flag flying high, we pulled up to the site and stopped well short of the MLR, which we could see clearly out in front of us. It was a bizarre feeling. Fully armed Chinese soldiers were patrolling just across the little branch. On the Korean side, the Korean soldiers had dug deep, well-fortified bunkers, but no one was patrolling. The ROK soldiers told us very strongly to not ever have more than two people near each other while near the MLR. When that happened, they said, the Chinese soldiers would open fire. We made sure to abide by that advice.

Our survey instructions were to shoot only rough contour intervals and make elevation change markings within the designated area. I estimated it to be about fifteen acres. It was expanded later. We completed the survey in one day. During that day, I took pictures of air strikes and smoke from artillery fire exploding just over the hill in North Korea, but my little Argus C-3 camera film didn't show much of anything. I could see and hear the planes making their bombing runs and smoke rising immediately afterward, but they don't show on film. As soon as we finished the survey, we headed back to Seoul. We completed our report, and I got ready to head home. I took the train to Pusan, and I spent Christmas Eve in a pup tent with snow blowing all around. Christmas dinner on Dec 25, 1952, was beans and franks, eaten in a mess kit outside in a snowstorm. The next day, we boarded a ship for Sasebo, Japan, stayed a day in port, and then headed for San Francisco.

As we left Sasebo Harbor, I noticed the dock and the buildings along the pier appeared to be fuzzy. That was the beginning of my near vision problem. I realized then that if I had gone into air force flight training, that deficiency would have disqualified me. I would have been reassigned to a non-flying job. I had made the right decision.

The Golden Gate Bridge was a beautiful, welcoming sight as we sailed under it just at dawn. Almost home!

My two years in the military was a growing, maturing time. I knew I should complete my college work and move on. When I was discharged at Fort Chaffee early in January 1953, I went directly to the University of Arkansas where the semester had already begun. After my time in the Army Engineers, I knew I did not want to major in any of the engineering fields. By default, I chose business administration. It was not exciting, especially economics. Without a career goal and with little motivation, my final college years were almost a nonevent. I did the work and graduated, thanks to the financial help of the GI Bill and a bunch of part-time jobs, but I was just an average student until I had some courses in industrial development, which were more interesting.

College was makeup time for dating, making up for the four years lost in my nomad years with the army and with Western Electric. I had a couple of semi-serious girlfriends, but as with my two previous big decisions, I was just not comfortable with going on to marriage. I have thanked the Lord thousands of times that I waited until I met Joann.

CHAPTER 3

Merging Our Journeys

After graduation, I joined the Little Rock Chamber of Commerce in the field of industrial development.

The type of work I was doing and the location of my work was just right for me to pursue a long-desired dream: learning to fly. In my spare time, I was able to use the remainder of my GI Bill to take flying lessons. There were times when incoming company executives wanted to see the central Arkansas area from the air. With my pilot's license, I could take them for a look.

But in the midst of interesting work and the fun time flying, I began to get an uncomfortable feeling again. Something was not right. Little did I know that the Lord had several surprising, life-changing events coming just around the corner. And they would not affect me alone. Someone else was about to enter the picture.

For background understanding, when I first went to Little Rock in 1955, I joined Baring Cross Baptist Church in North Little Rock, then became a member of First Baptist Church in Little Rock. I became more active in church, Sunday school, training union, choir, and youth activities, but that persistent, uncomfortable feeling continued. That confusion culminated in life-changing events in the next several months. One was related to my growing dissatisfaction with my work situation. My work, which had been interesting and challenging, just lost its appeal. A sense of unrest was constantly with me, yet I could not define it. Then a young lady came along, and things became more complicated.

The young adult group was going on a weekend retreat. We were to meet at the church and go together on the church bus. When I got to the church parking lot, I saw a beautiful, blonde, well-constructed young lady dancing a jig on the church parking lot in her cowboy boots. My interest jumped to attention, followed by immediate investigation, followed by consternation. She was a doctor in her last year of residency, committed to, and preparing to go to, the foreign mission field.

The fact that she was a doctor was not a problem. In fact, it elicited great respect and admiration. It was going to the mission field that caused me to hesitate. That just did not fit what I had been considering. We met, talked, and became acquainted, but by unspoken agreement, we kept the relationship platonic. We were both in the choir and saw each other frequently, but we did not try to develop a closer relationship. Then the music director decided to enhance the spiritual fellowship of the choir by appointing prayer partners. Joann and I found ourselves prayer partners. That was okay with us, and we continued as before.

It was summertime, and summer church trips were scheduled. Joann was to take a group of young women (Young Women's Auxiliary or YWAs) to Ridge Crest Retreat Center in North Carolina for a missions emphasis week; I was to go to Glorieta Retreat Center in New Mexico for music week. When we returned, we were to share our experiences with each other. As we returned and began our prayer and sharing time together, a little tension appeared. It was not a bad tension—it was a good tension. Another element came into our relationship. Sparks began to ignite. We both felt it, but we also knew there were some unsettled issues in our situation. They needed to be dealt with.

For Joann, falling in love and marrying someone who was not committed to going to the mission field was just not acceptable. It would be contrary to everything the Lord had called and prepared her to do. For me, as much as I loved her and thought of her, to consider marrying someone and going to the mission field, was such an upheaval in my thinking that it was also beyond my comprehension. We had to have time to process the full implications for both of us. We put a fence around our emotions.

Life-Changing Experience

In the meantime, our work responsibilities continued. For me, my discontent with what I was doing became more pronounced. My downtown office was only six blocks from the church. I started skipping lunch and going to the church to pray and read the Bible at noon. The pastor had resigned to return to the faculty of Southern Baptist Seminary, and the music director had resigned to take a position at another church. There was no one from whom to seek counsel. I just read the Bible and prayed—and not just at noon. It was day and night. I did not know the Bible well enough to know specific passages that would help. I would just read haphazardly. That continued for weeks, with my emotional and spiritual turmoil becoming ever more intense.

Then came that great and wonderful Monday morning when the Lord gave His answer. I was literally at my wit's end. Totally exhausted and spiritually drained, I cried out to the Lord to please let His Word speak to me that day. With no forethought of where the Bible might open, I just opened it. I saw that it was the book of Isaiah. I started reading in chapter 6. When I read verses 8–11, I almost collapsed: "Then I heard the voice of the Lord, saying, 'Whom shall I send, and who will go for Us?' Then I said, 'Here am I. Send me!' And He said, 'Go, and tell this people …' Then I said, 'Lord, how long?' And He answered, 'Until cities are devastated, houses are empty and the land is desolate.'" In other words, "Until I call again."

I had my answer. I made my commitment. After a heartfelt prayer of thanks to the Lord, I returned to my office. I was walking down the same street I had walked only a couple of hours earlier, but it looked different. The world looked different. Everything looked different. I felt totally different. I was different. It was as though a cloud of God's grace and love completely engulfed me. My view of the world had changed. My initial salvation experience, my call to vocational Christian service, and my months of increasing unrest had coalesced into a clear call to come and follow Him. I was ready. What I felt—what I indistinctly realized and was unable to express—was best expressed by Jeremiah when he quoted the Lord in saying, "For I know the plans I have for you, declares the Lord, plans for welfare and not for calamity, plans to give you a future and a hope" (Jeremiah 29:11).

A fuzzy future now became clearer, an uncertain vocation became a certainty, and anxiety was replaced with peace. What an indescribable blessing! Through the succeeding years, that experience has been a fixed, immovable anchor in all the vicissitudes I have faced, taking me back to God's irrefutable call and His unbroken promise to be with me. What a blessed assurance!

As a side note, reflecting back in later years on the turmoil and unrest leading up to that special time, I have come to realize that God does not usually meet us in the comfortable times and smooth places but in the tangled times and rugged, stormy places of life. It was also later that I saw the similarity of my experience with Isaiah's. In his case, the death of his king was what prompted his sense of turmoil and anxiety. He came to the point of desperation: "Woe is me! I am ruined!" His attitude of contrition for his sin and his guilt brought cleansing and forgiveness. When that forgiveness occurred, his burden was lifted, and he made his commitment to go wherever the Lord sent him. I could identify with him.

For the first time in my life, there was an exciting future, provided by God, just waiting for me to claim. The indecision was gone. I had a purpose, a goal. I really began to understand that my life had meaning and had a purpose. God had a plan for me, and I was on a journey with Him to fulfill His plan and obey His will. Oh, yes, there were a thousand unknowns yet to be faced, but now I was assured that God was with me, would guide me, and would prepare the way for me. What a burden-lifting time! There is simply nothing that can compare to being in the living center of God's will—in spite of whatever the circumstances might be.

I must emphasize that I consider that life-changing encounter with the Lord to be unique to me at one particular time. I do not feel it should be considered normative for other believers. God chose my haphazard opening of the Bible to speak to me; I recognized it was God speaking, and I was willing to hear. He will choose His own unique ways to speak to others. Our God is a personal God, and He deals with each of His children personally. I can say with assurance that God will speak in some way if we are willing to hear and obey. Obedience to God's call, wherever it leads, is the tether that assures a sense of His continual presence.

Concurrently with my mountaintop experience, Joann was in the midst of a debilitating illness and had been admitted to the hospital. She had a major infection, was on IVs, and felt totally fatigued. For obvious reasons, I did not want to burden her with my struggles while she was struggling to recover. In addition, she was chief pediatric resident, responsible for interns and other residents and also for a huge pediatric ward full of very sick kids (from whom she probably contracted her illness). The other residents and interns continued to consult with her. It was almost work as usual; she didn't get much rest in the hospital.

I guess my struggles became more evident. On one of my visits, she asked what was wrong. I shared only a couple of comments and left. That was on a Sunday night. The next day, Monday, was my wonderful day of revelation. My visit with Joann that night was different, to say the least. She had responded to IVs and antibiotics and was feeling much better. When I shared what had happened at the church that day, that hospital room became a sanctuary of worship. I was not sure what the call involved, and Joann said, "Could it be to missions?"

I immediately said, "Yes." I knelt on the floor by her bed, and we embraced with rejoicing and tears as we both realized that we could and would be on a journey together wherever God led us.

Pastors and other Christian speakers often encourage their listeners to get out of their comfort zones and serve the Lord more faithfully. If that exhortation speaks to those who are emotionally and materially comfortable in a lukewarm Christian commitment, I can understand. In my status, however, it was just the opposite. I became extremely uncomfortable in my indecisive, uncommitted status. It was when I responded to and obeyed God's call on my life that I moved into a realm of comfort and assurance that is beyond compare.

Coming Together

Events started happening in a hurry. Her illness occurred in late September. We became engaged in October, and we were married on December 21, 1957. In January, I resigned from my job and left for the seminary in Fort Worth. Joann stayed in Little Rock to complete her residency. When I announced my decision to the church, someone in the church (we still did not have a pastor) suggested that the church should license me to preach. I was not completely comfortable with the idea. I was called of God, and I wanted to serve Him, but I was not gifted as a public speaker and did not have the passion to preach. To serve, yes. To preach when the occasion called for it, yes.

But I was not comfortable in refusing the offer either. At that time, I was not aware of the many other vocational choices that would open later to missionary candidates. I saw no option but to preach. With all that uncertainty, I was licensed to preach by the First Baptist Church of Little Rock on January 8, 1958. Shortly after I was licensed, the church had its annual Youth Week, with young adults serving in the various offices of the church for the week. To my surprise, and humbled by the honor, I was elected youth pastor.

In a visit home a week or so later, I shared with Mother the news of what had happened in my life. Her response surprised me. "Son, when you were born, I gave you to the Lord and have prayed continually that He would call you into His service. This is an answer to my prayers." I asked her why she had not shared that with me earlier. She said she did not want her desire for me to influence my decision. She wanted it to be completely between the Lord and me. I have wondered if it would have made any difference in my decision-making, but her approach was probably best. That visit and conversation became even more meaningful a few months later when I was in the seminary in Fort Worth and could not visit home often. Later in the spring, Mother developed cancer of the liver and died on September 18, 1958. That visit was our last good time together.

Joann Meanders ... Briefly

Joann's focused charge toward the mission field as a doctor did have a few bumps along the way. One of the bumps was self-inflicted, but others came from unexpected sources. They occurred at about the same time some of my struggling meandering occurred.

As I noted earlier, Joann's instrumental music skills developed greatly in her high school years, especially with the piano and the bassoon. Those skills led to a tempting offer: a full-tuition music scholarship to a state university. The catch was that she had to major in music. That presented a dilemma. She had felt strongly that she should do her premed studies at Baylor University, but the money just wasn't there. The financial help provided by that music major offer, especially considering the high tuition at Baylor, was sorely tempting. It would ease a heavy financial burden on her parents. The difference in the curriculum for the two fields of study were significant. The course credits required for premed studies were generally the most difficult courses: biochemistry, chemistry, physics, trigonometry, Latin, and others. Even with that curriculum, she was salutatorian, just narrowly missing the top spot, but colleges did not offer scholarships to second-place finishers.

But, feeling that it was not the Lord's will for her, and with the concurrence of her parents, she declined the music scholarship. As the deadline for the entrance fee to Baylor came ever closer, the money simply was not available. She still needed fifty-six dollars to enroll in the first semester. Then a little miracle occurred. (Is any miracle "little?") She had been playing the piano for a youth revival team during the summer. Normally, pay was not provided for the pianist. At the end of the final summer revival led by the team, and before leaving for enrollment at Baylor, a paper envelope filled with change and a few little bills was placed on the piano as she was playing the last song. When she arrived home, she and her dad counted the money. Both of them shed tears as they counted the unusually large offering. It was $56.84—more than what she needed to complete the required enrollment payment. It was a huge affirmation from the Lord of her decision to go to Baylor. It also affirmed that God would somehow provide tuition in the semesters ahead.

But premed studies were not easy. Here came the next little bump in the road. Well into her second semester of her first year, her studies were not going well. She came to feel that she could probably serve the Lord just as well as a nurse as she could as a doctor. She changed her major. Troubles followed. Her studies still did not go well. Spiritual and emotional unrest were persistent. Finally, after hours of prayer, she realized she had made the wrong decision and had deviated from the Lord's plan. She changed her major back to premed. Not surprisingly, her grades came back up, she was at peace mentally and spiritually, and she knew she was back on track with the Lord.

I'll jump ahead and mention another bump that came along several years later. It affected both of us. After completing seminary, I was going back to Little Rock to do my residency in hospital administration. Since it paid only a small stipend, Joann needed to work to help us through the residency period. To our surprise, the Foreign Mission Board said, "No." They felt that Joann should be a stay-at-home wife for a year since we had not yet had that experience. We were not happy with the decision, but we abided by it. The board later partially relented and allowed Joann to teach a couple of courses in anatomy and physiology at the Baptist Hospital School of Nursing. With the two small salaries, we made it, but we were on short rations. We were told later that it was a new policy and that it had been canceled.

Back to medical school. Admission to medical school was a challenge. She fell short of several criteria, some unwritten, used to determine admission to school.

She was a woman, and a few of the faculty doctors on the admissions committee were vocal in their objections to women doctors, thinking they would marry and never practice medicine.

She had no proof of adequate funds to stay in school the full four years.

She did not have a single recommendation from another physician that she be admitted. (She didn't even know one.)

She did not plan to practice medicine in Texas, or even in the United States.

The interview took place in a small, smoke-filled room with her seated on a lone chair with the committee facing her from behind a semicircular table. They asked if she knew any graduates of that medical school or had any doctors in her family. She had to answer, "No." They asked if she had funds in the bank to complete four years of school. Again, she answered, "No, but I will work." Then they asked if she planned to practice in Texas. "No, I am called to practice on the mission field in Southeast Asia." Finally, they asked if she planned to marry. She did not know how to answer since she had no prospects of marriage at the time. Finally, she answered, "Well, I'm not against it." That brought a little laugh—but no change in attitude. The tone of the meeting left her discouraged as she left the room. Her responses had not coincided with the committee's preferences. Three days later, amid tears of rejoicing and prayers of thanksgiving, she received her letter of acceptance to the University of Texas Southwestern Medical School.

The rigors of medical school are too well-known to need recounting. Joann dealt with them, but with the added burden of dealing with a couple of professors who let it be known to the six women in the class that they intended to flunk them out of medical school. For Joann, with her stubborn, can-do attitude, it just became another challenge to overcome. She did overcome it and became a doctor of medicine at the ripe old age of twenty-three.

Graduation from medical school was usually followed by a year of internship and then a two-year residency. With an eye on the anticipated medical problems she would face on the mission field, she chose Sacramento County Hospital in California for her internship. It was a huge hospital with a heavy patient load, containing a mix of races and cultures as well as medical problems and trauma. She chose well, although after a few thirty-six-hour shifts of dealing with one crisis after another, she wondered about it. She frequently faced total exhaustion from work that involved life-threatening, emotionally draining decisions, but she saw and did things that she would never have seen and done in other locations. It was good preparation for the challenges she faced later in our hospital in Bangkla and in the jungle refugee hospital where she was the medical director.

Now came the time for the residency and the decision as to where. Several factors led her to choose pediatrics. It was a field in which she had a special interest, and it also would fill a void in many mission hospitals around the world. The next step was to choose where to go for the training. She had become aware of a nationally recognized pediatric expert who had become the director of the Pediatric Residency Program at the University of Arkansas Medical School in Little Rock. Since she always went for the best, she applied and was accepted. She was now on her way. Little did she know what lay ahead during the next few years, especially about the convergence of our two paths, but as usual, she was excited about it.

Joann joined the First Baptist Church and became part of the young adult group, but her work schedule caused her to miss many activities. The choir was a priority for her. She loved music and wanted to maintain her unusual vocal and instrumental music skills.

One event she scheduled far in advance was the youth retreat I mentioned earlier. She doesn't remember dancing a jig on the church parking lot, but she does remember our early meetings and the potential dilemma we faced if we became serious. Again, it was just something of an unspoken, yet understood, factor in our relationship. We enjoyed being choir prayer partners. In retrospect, it was a valuable time for us to really come to know each other and treasure each other as friends and fellow Christians. Both of us have seen marriages fall apart because the early physical and emotional attachment led them into marriage before they really knew each other. Only later did they realize their mistake. Joann and I knew each other well—and we were close friends—*before* love and marriage ever entered our conversation. Sixty years later, we are still best friends. And our love for each other has grown deeper.

Traveling in Double Harness

In my early days, I heard marriage referred to in several terms, often as traveling in double harness. We didn't care what it was called—we were just ready for it to happen. I was coming up on thirty years of age, and Joann was coming up on twenty-seven; we were ready to get on with it. With Joann's family in Texas—some in the extreme northwest near New Mexico—and my family in Arkansas, Joann felt Dallas would be the best location for the wedding. She chose Highland Baptist Church, the church she attended while in medical school. The big day was December 21, 1957.

We had a brief honeymoon of two days, then both of us had to get back to work. Limited by both time and money, we still made the most of it, especially one great fun lunchtime we remember with laughter. Our hotel was near Neiman-Marcus, the classiest department store in Dallas. It was having a red runway fashion show at noon, adjacent to the restaurant. We couldn't pass it up; we had to go. We were seated near the runway: the perfect spot for every model to parade her finest before the prettiest lady in the audience. Joann managed to look interested in and longingly at every beautiful outfit. Part of our fun was that only we knew that we didn't have enough money to buy even the cheapest of the outfits—we had ordered the cheapest sandwiches available just to be in the restaurant—but the models did not know that and gave their best in trying to persuade both of us to buy. We did not have the heart to tell them we were headed for the tropics where those winter outfits could never be worn.

Early in January, Joann was invited to attend a pediatric medical meeting offered by the University of Kansas Medical School in Kansas City, Missouri. With a little financial help from her residency program, we decided it would be a good time for both of us to go and enjoy a short extension of our honeymoon.

Our return from Kansas City was going great until a heavy snowstorm blew in and quickly carpeted the countryside with several inches of snow. Somewhere in south Missouri, the police closed the roads just as we reached a little crossroads town with one run-down motel. We got the last available room, with parking some distance away. Joann was still dressed in her finest, including new shoes, and looked with great disfavor on wading through the snow to the room. My big chance! I picked her up and carried her to the room, across the threshold, and into a stunning honeymoon suite. Stunning, that is, in amenities—or the lack thereof. If the exterior looked downtrodden, the interior was still able to outdo it. Sparsely furnished, with only the bare essentials, it had a small, damaged, gas-fired heater fighting a losing battle to keep the room warm. The bed was dilapidated, sagging in an alarmingly disconcerting fashion. The walls had been painted in some distant past with an undetermined color. What little was left was blistered and peeling. The uneven wood floor was filthy, splintered, and stained by unknown liquids, but so what? We were newlyweds, and this was good preparation for roughing it on some distant mission field. We laughed at the whole predicament and thoroughly enjoyed it.

Continuing on to Little Rock the next day, we hit the steep, slippery, snow-covered hills of north Arkansas just before noon. With only intermittent spreading of salt and sand, the snow had played havoc with traffic. On the untreated hills, the object was to start up the hill with just enough speed to maintain forward motion but not so fast as to slide off around the curves. I made it okay for a few miles, then misjudged and started sliding toward a steep drop-off on one of those sharp curves. Heavy posts had been installed in the highway shoulder to prevent that very event, and I plowed into one. I knocked it over, but it stopped us just before we toppled over an abrupt cliff. When we stopped, we just sat there for a moment, regaining our breath. Joann turned to me and said, "Let's thank the Lord for the post." We did. About that time, a truck came by spreading sand. Without getting out of the car, I backed up onto the highway and drove on to Harrison. When I looked under the front end of the car, it was not even dented. They don't make cars like that today.

Then the first of a multitude of separations that occurred in our years together came within a few weeks after our marriage. Knowing I had a lot of academic preparation to complete before I could be appointed, I moved to Fort Worth as soon as possible to enroll in the seminary. I frequently traveled the highway between Fort Worth and Little Rock. That was before interstate highways were in place, and that drive was a hard day's journey. Travel decreased when the money decreased. I had not yet found a job, and Joann's magnificent salary of seventy-five dollars per month as a resident couldn't handle all the expenses. Our few reserves, built up while I was working in Little Rock, were about to disappear. We were a happy couple when she completed her residency, joined me in Fort Worth, and found a job.

The seminary apartment I had rented was not much better, or bigger, than the motel room we had stayed in on that snowy night in Missouri. When Joann moved in, she decorated it with some of the wedding gifts we had received. One of the items was a couple of very nice candleholders with candles included. When I came home from class at noon one day, the candles had melted and folded over on to the table. Hot! It was over a hundred degrees—and no air-conditioning was available. It stayed hot through the night too. We found a better apartment near her work and lived there until we bought our own home near the seminary. Lisa was born while we were living in that apartment.

Lisa's birth was a scary time. I took Joann to the hospital as soon as her labor started and began the usual wait. The usual turned somber before long. After several hours of waiting with no word at all from the labor room staff, I became more and more concerned. While I was waiting, another man brought his wife in. We waited together. In a short time, the doctor came out and told him his wife had died but the child was okay. Then another man brought his wife in and began his wait. Not long afterward, his doctor came out and told him his wife was fine but the baby was dead. It had now been over twelve hours since I had brought Joann in, and there had been no word about her. My concern became so acute that I went into the labor-and-delivery suite, a "no admittance" area to me. I found her labor room, went in, and found her able to talk—barely. The doctor finally came out and told me she was having a difficult delivery but that she should be all right. I stayed in her room for a couple of hours, and then I went back to the waiting room.

Finally, after twenty-eight hours of very difficult labor, including sixteen hours on a Pitocin drip, she delivered a beautiful little seven-pound girl on November 19, 1958. We named her Lisa. They were discharged a couple of days later and went home for a little recovery time and the beginning of a new life with a larger family. Joann then promptly developed pneumonia. It held on for over a month. I called my sister for help, and she came for two weeks. What a blessing! The worst was over, but I still had my hands full with studies and caring for Joann and Lisa for another month. Good experience!

Joann's first practice experience in Fort Worth was not pleasant. After a few months, she found a better situation in the pediatric clinic at Carswell Air Force Base Hospital in Fort Worth. It was a good place, and she enjoyed it for the remainder of our time in Fort Worth. Her salary, plus my much smaller salary as pastor, enabled us to purchase a house.

It seemed like a good idea at the time. It was a new house near the seminary. We planned to live in it until we left for the mission field. While we were in the field, we would rent it to furloughing missionaries who were doing advanced study at the seminary. The rent would cover the mortgage. When we came home on furlough, we would have our place in which to live. The plan worked well the first year, then a renter trashed the house, and we could not rent it to anyone. Mortgage payments were still due, and we had no option but to make the payments. Our salary as missionaries was low; adding mortgage payments put us living on short rations for a couple of years. We sold the house as soon as we came home on furlough. (In fairness, I must say the FMB took care of missionaries in those years, although missionary wives did not receive separate salaries and did not accrue Social Security benefits. Health-care and retirement benefits were decent, and we are grateful for their provisions, all of which were made possible by the support and cooperation of Southern Baptist churches in the United States.)

Seminary was a wake-up call for me. I had little Bible knowledge and zero theological comprehension. My college studies had been in business and were not really difficult, but seminary was graduate-level study with much higher academic demands. I had been an average student in college, but this was different. My first term paper in my first seminary class was to "discuss the pros and cons of the ontological argument for the existence of God." Pardon me? I had a new motivation and a new goal, and it turned out to be an exciting time. I have continued to be grateful for my seminary studies, especially the biblical languages. Surprisingly, Hebrew turned out to be an easy language to learn—at least to read. I was reading the Old Testament in Hebrew in my second semester of study. Greek was more difficult but a joy to learn; it is the most descriptive and expressive language I have studied. I still refer to my Greek New Testament frequently for study assistance.

I realized early on that I did not have the gift of preaching. I felt more comfortable with teaching. Knowing an advanced degree would offer more opportunities, I decided to go ahead and obtain a PhD with a view toward teaching in a seminary. The program required translation capability in four languages: two ancient and two modern. My seminary Greek and Hebrew met the ancient requirement. For the modern requirement, I picked up German and French at Texas Christian University in Fort Worth.

However, it did not take long for me to realize that a PhD in a theological field and an MD would not likely be needed in the same place on the mission field. Some other avenue would be needed. About that time, another door opened. The FMB started appointing hospital administrators. That was good news to me. I already had some training and experience that would help in that area, and a hospital administrator and a doctor could often work together in the field. Through God's grace, it all came together just right and my indecisive status came to an end.

But there was still one not-so-small requirement to meet. At that time, the FMB required all non-MD male appointees to have two years pastoral experience, along with the MDiv, to be eligible for appointment. (That was later changed.) Again, with some timely help from the Lord, I was called as pastor of Jermyn Baptist Church, a small church in a small village in north Texas. It was all coming together.

Being pastor was a wonderful learning experience, one I really needed. As pastor of a small rural church, I quickly learned that I was expected to fill in wherever there was a vacancy. Music leader absent? I led music. A teacher absent? I taught. Learning to "do the needful" paid off later in all kinds of situations. That church was also where I was ordained to the ministry. Lisa was born several months before I was called as pastor. She became the star of the church, sometimes to our chagrin. With Joann playing the piano and me speaking, someone else had to take care of Lisa (the church did not have a nursery). Several ladies enjoyed doing it and spoiled her rotten. We still have friends in that church, over fifty years later.

After graduating from the seminary and before beginning my hospital administration training, I obtained additional training in pastoral counseling at Parkland Hospital in Dallas (part of the medical school system Joann had attended). It was a postgraduate course in clinical pastoral education (CPE), involving extensive interviews with a full spectrum of patients. Those interviews (recorded) were followed by sessions with psychiatrists, psychologists, and chaplains who reviewed and evaluated our interviews with the student. We also had sessions in which we monitored (through one-way glass) interviews by our professors. The whole summer was a very helpful study time.

As I neared completion of my seminary studies, I was admitted to the Arkansas Baptist Hospital's administrative residency program in Little Rock. I entered the program in September 1961. The program called for residents to spend time in every department of the hospital, learning as much as possible about every function of the department. In my case, I requested an extended training period in some departments, knowing I would need a more complete understanding in order to help train many of our personnel in Bangkla, especially in hospital equipment maintenance and in business office procedures. We would be building in a rural area with no reservoir of potential employees with the skills we would need.

Since I would be doing most of the purchasing for the hospital, I also spent extra time in the pharmacy, operating room, central supply, laboratory and x-ray, learning about the medications, supplies, and equipment I would be purchasing.

A useful feature of most training programs was for the resident to spend a couple of weeks in a small-town hospital in order to gain a better overview of an entire hospital operation. Mr. John Gilbreath, the hospital CEO and my preceptor, suggested that I find the nearest mission hospital and arrange to spend my time there. I was thrilled at the opportunity. It turned out to be the Guadalajara Baptist Hospital in Guadalajara, Mexico. When I told the FMB of my good fortune, I was taken aback by their response. I was told that if I went to a mission hospital for such a time of observation that I would jeopardize any possibility of appointment. I was completely shocked at their position, but I did not go. A few years later, they reversed the policy. I never understood their reason for adopting it.

A timely opportunity came toward the end of my residency. A friend of mine, Norman Roberts, was personnel director of Baptist Hospital. Norman was selected to be the administrator of the new Baptist Memorial Hospital in North Little Rock. He asked me to assist him in opening the hospital and getting it going. What a gift! I would soon be helping to open our new hospital in Thailand, and I could have no better learning experience than what that opportunity offered.

On August 29, 1962, near the end of my residency, our son, James, made his grand entrance. It was also a long and difficult delivery but not as critical as Lisa's had been. Joann had had two miscarriages since Lisa was born, one far enough along to clearly identify as a boy, so we were especially thankful that James was okay and Lisa would have a little brother to play with. His coming completed our family, and the two of them have been a source of much joy and pride since their first appearance. His arrival time was on target: born in the States but old enough to travel well when we left for Thailand in January 1963.

Requirements for appointment were gradually being met as we completed our training in Little Rock. The one remaining hurdle was the psychiatric interview. It was well-known and well dreaded by some appointees. Ours took place in Fort Worth shortly before we moved to Little Rock. The psychiatrist interviewed us separately and then together. As the interview progressed, the atmosphere became cooler and cooler. It became downright chilly as he closed the interview with us together, summarizing his perception of us. It was not good. His summary was in three parts: mine, Joann's, and the two of us together.

Mine:
- I married a doctor so I would have more income.
- I married a doctor because I felt insecure.
- I married someone who would mother me.

Joann:
- She wanted to marry someone she could mother.
- She became a pediatrician because she was not comfortable around adults. (I wanted to say, "And you became a psychiatrist because you are not comfortable around normal people." But I didn't say it. I felt we had already flunked his evaluation.)
- She wanted to marry someone with less income potential so she could be in control.

Together:
- We were going to the mission field because we were afraid we could not make it in the States.
- We were excessively codependent.

We were dismissed. We left his office angry and depressed. Not surprisingly, the director of the personnel department at the FMB called in a few days with the big question: "What happened?" The doctor had recommended that we not be appointed. We summarized our interview. She said she would arrange an appointment with another psychiatrist, a doctor in Louisville. I had just completed my residency in Little Rock when we were scheduled to go to Louisville. That interview was a 180-degree turnaround from the earlier one: warm, cordial, encouraging, and affirming. We were told the rest of the story later. The first psychiatrist was not a Christian. Questioning suggested he was opposed to any missionary effort. That may not have been his first interview for the board, but it was his last. The doctor in Louisville, a Christian, strongly recommended us for appointment, and we were on our way.

The entire process had been a little strange to us because of our long relationship with the board. Joann had been in contact with the FMB for more than nineteen years with much correspondence and many personal interviews during the previous five years. I had been in contact for more than four years, having personal conversations with several FMB staff personnel. Both of us had submitted our life histories for evaluation. We had submitted multiple references, and the FMB obtained references on the references. The background check was more thorough than an FBI check (which I had experienced in military service). I guess policies must be complied with. We were grateful they had enough personal knowledge of us to decide to send us to another psychiatrist for the required interview.

Our big day came in early December 1962 when we were appointed as missionaries to Thailand: Joann as a physician and homemaker and me as a hospital administrator. That event was a huge leap on our journey and has led to blessings and adventures we could never imagine happening.

The subsequent weeks were hectic. We went through a brief but intense missionary orientation period in Pass Christian, Mississippi, returned to Little Rock to sell, move, or store our furniture and things we would not be taking, and packed for shipping. With different electrical voltage and cycle frequency in Thailand, we needed to wait until arrival there to purchase some of the electrical appliances. A final round of painful goodbye visits had to be made in Arkansas and then in Texas. Leaving Joann's parents was especially difficult. Her mother was extremely upset with Joann for taking her grandchildren and going overseas for many years, maybe even into dangerous places. She was so hurt that she rarely wrote letters during our first few years in Thailand. Before closing the door for us to leave, she said, "As far as I'm concerned, you're dead!"

CHAPTER 4

Leaving Home, Going Home to Thailand: Adapting, Learning, and Working

Boarding the USS *Cleveland* in San Francisco was exciting. We were more than sailing the ocean (first time for Joann, and almost, but not quite equivalent to a cruise); symbolically, we were severing much that was familiar to go and establish a new home in a new country in order to share the good news of the gospel.

The journey started with a pleasant side trip—a one-day stop in San Diego before going on to Honolulu. We made the most of it and spent a memorable day at Sea World.

In Honolulu, Joann had a high school friend whose husband was a naval officer, at that time away on a training mission. She was a wonderful hostess and tour guide for our time in Hawaii. Waikiki Beach, Diamond Head, Pearl Harbor, pineapple plantations, blowhole—the island was just a scenic wonderland.

The remainder of that twenty-one-day sea voyage was filled with fun times. Lisa swam in the pool every day (except when it was drained in rough weather). James, four months old, loved the rocking and rolling of the ship and slept most of the time. Joann won most of the onboard passenger competition: the piano-playing contest (Chopin's *Polonaise*), the doll-making contest, the crepe paper costume contest, and others. She won so many miniature metal ships that it overloaded our luggage.

We had heard about the absence of some of our favorite foods in Thailand, especially steaks, so Joann had steak at every meal, including breakfast. Several days out of Honolulu, we ran into a major storm. We encountered very high waves with the bow frequently going well underwater. Saltwater spray was all over the place. The swimming pool was drained for three days. No one was on deck. Lisa loved it, and James slept through it all. None of us ever became ill.

We docked in Yokohama for a day and then went on to Hong Kong for a week before flying to Bangkok. The FMB had asked me to stop in Hong Kong for consultation with the missionary medical and administrative personnel. They were transitioning from a clinic practice to a full-service hospital, opening later in 1963. (They were of more help to me than I was to them. The board probably thought that would happen.) Hong Kong Baptist Hospital is now a highly respected major medical institution with more than eight hundred beds.

It was time for the final leg: the flight to Bangkok. It was a rough flight for James. His time aboard ship had been a peaceful, rocking-cradle sleeping time. Our flight was a mostly miserable experience. The plane apparently had a pressurization problem, causing James to scream with excruciating ear pain for most of the flight. As we descended for our landing in Bangkok, the pain finally went away— and we landed with a happy baby.

Our arrival stunned us with sensory overload. We left the States in the cold of January. We stepped off the plane in Bangkok on to the tarmac (no jet ways) in hundred-degree temperatures. It was like walking into a steam bath. Lining the rail on top of the terminal building were at least thirty missionaries and MKs from the Thailand Baptist Mission, cheering and welcoming us. We were overwhelmed, numb with the physical and emotional feelings that filled us. We were trying to absorb the reality that we were now finally home—home to a place we had never been before—and in a totally different world. This was where we would spend the next thirty or thirty-five years of our lives. This was where our children would grow up.

That kind of move can be a defining moment in the life of a new missionary. The previous years of preparation would have been filled with excitement and anticipation of a dramatic new life as a "real, live missionary." Anticipation is over. Realization is now beginning to set in. It can be daunting, difficult, and disheartening at times. It is at this point that a clear and distinct call of the Lord is either confirmed or it isn't. If it is there, there will be a burning desire to get the language, learn the culture, establish relationships, and get on with the work. If it isn't there, then it was only an altruistic or sentimental motive that brought you to this place—and now there is no power to sustain you. I saw this clearly years later when I was the mission administrator and welcomed new missionaries who were already having second thoughts about their call to missions.

Too much happened too quickly during the ensuing year to go into great detail. We were in a new world with a new culture, language, and religion and strange worldviews, customs, and foods; they were all different. And we did need to adjust, adapt, and sometimes adopt. We could not isolate ourselves in our own little enclaves and accomplish what the Lord had called us to do. The mission support staff saved the day for us. Housing, import customs, various permits and licenses, unending bureaucratic red tape, language school, transportation, driving on the opposite side of the road, switching to the metric system—the list of new things went on and on. One of the very minor but pleasant discoveries was the delicious Thai food and fruit, especially the fruit. Tropical, plant-ripened fruit with year-round availability was a continuing delight. I regret not having a picture of Joann surrounded and almost covered by ripe pineapples grown near our house in Bangkla. There would have been twenty pineapples, each one large enough to fill a two-gallon bucket, costing five cents each, for a total of one dollar. And sweet!

Of all the early experiences we had, great and small, I will relate only one small event that still remains vivid to me. It contained an analogy that conveyed the message of the gospel simply but profoundly. It could have happened anywhere, but it happened while we were in language school, shortly after we arrived in Thailand. After the hot, dry season, the very welcome rainy season began. Lisa loved to play in the tropical rain. As a heavy shower came one day, I heard her talking as she was playing in the yard. When I looked out, she was squatting down and talking. I thought it was to herself or maybe to the ground. Then I realized she was talking to the ants around an anthill. The water was rising, causing the ants to scurry around, looking for higher ground. Lisa was trying to tell them how to flee the rising water. She would push up little dikes near them so they would have a safe trail by which to escape, but they ignored her. She put a twig from them to the dike and tried to guide them with her hands. They continued to ignore her. As the water continued to rise, some of the ants found the rows of dirt and escaped. Others kept wandering around and drowned.

The analogy was apparent almost immediately. We are all surrounded by dangers or threats at various times. We scurry about for many reasons—security or danger—or for no reason. We find no sure escape route. In Lisa's case, the only way she could have led them to safety was to talk to them in their language. The only way that could happen would be for her to become an ant, yet retain the knowledge and ability to communicate that she had as a person. That is exactly what Jesus did. He came as one of us—man, but God incarnate. He knows the dangers we face and provides the way to safety through faith in His Son Jesus. He communicates to us repeatedly in countless ways to tell us and show us the way. It may be by His Word, a friend, an event, or a circumstance, but He speaks. He is always near, always ready, and able to lead us to eternal safety and joy.

Thailand: Language Acquisition

Language study is a simple phrase, but the ramifications are enormous. No matter how it is expressed, acquiring fluency in the local language is a necessity. It is one of the most difficult yet important early challenges faced by missionaries. If a missionary does not become capable of communicating to those around him/her in the heart language at the highest level—emotions, feelings, concepts, spiritual truths, guilt, and despair, etc.—the gospel may remain unshared or misunderstood.

Western missionaries in Asia face a particular problem. Many Asian languages, including the Thai language, are tonal, meaning the tone is integral to the meaning of the word, just as a letter or syllable. Tones may be high, low, mid, rising or falling. Meaning is usually determined by the tone as well as by long or short vowels. Many words look alike but are differentiated by tone. A classic example in Thai is the word *mai*. It is one of the most commonly used words, but it can be used with any of five tones, with each tone giving it a totally different meaning. Changing the tone can change the word. Westerners who cannot hear or reproduce the correct tones are driven to total distraction. It helps if they can sing or carry a tune; that ability enables them to reproduce the tones correctly, but if they can't do that, they usually say the wrong word and don't know it. They will not be understood. And they can't correct themselves.

All language students are haunted by mispronunciations. They may be funny or disastrous. Soon after starting language school, Joann found a new fruit that she loved and asked her helper to get two kilos of it. Her helper came home with two kilos of birdseed. The word for both items was the same except for the tone; one used a high tone, one used a mid tone. Joann used the wrong one.

A more serious mispronunciation occurred when a missionary preacher preached his first sermon in Thai after about a year of language study. The message was about Jesus dying on the cross for our sin. He learned later he had preached the whole message about Jesus dying on his trousers. It was an easily understood mistake. In Thai, the word for *cross* and the word for *trousers* is the same three-syllable word except for a tone and for a "soft" k instead of a "hard" k (the equivalent letter used in Thai). Examples could continue for pages.

A continuing minor dilemma for us (our language school was a Christian organization) was that the language school teachers did not teach us dirty, inappropriate or profane words. It was common for Westerners to say a bad word and not know it. And because Thai culture inhibited the act of correcting others because of the possibility of causing a loss of face, our teachers rarely corrected us. We learned some of the no-no words the hard way. I'll refrain from giving examples, but all of us fouled up at some time.

An additional complication was added for those of us (really all of us) who would be preaching, teaching the Bible, leading worship services, and referring to royalty (earthly or heavenly). At those times the "high," or "royal" language needed to be used instead of the "common" language used in everyday conversation and newspapers. Nouns, verbs, adverbs, adjectives, and pronouns were often different words in the high language. It was almost like another language, retaining some variations of Sanskrit from which much of it had originated. Fluency came slowly; I was well into my second term before I was thinking and dreaming in Thai. And I was still far from fluent.

Doctors had one additional major challenge that loomed large until they were over it. They had to pass the Thai medical exam, partly in Thai, before they could obtain a license to practice medicine in

Thailand. In addition to the regular Thai language study (including the "high" language), they had to study the medical language, pathology, and tropical diseases unique to Thailand. Part of the exam was objective, part subjective. It was notoriously difficult. Many foreign doctors failed it more than once. There was great rejoicing when all our doctors passed it. Some, including Joann, passed the first time.

Thailand: Beginning the Medical Work

Most missionaries began leaving China in the late 1940s and early 1950s because of the Communist takeover. Several of them transferred to Thailand where they were soon joined by newly appointed missionaries by the FMB. The new missionaries were appointed for various assignments but there were no medical personnel. Discovering acute medical needs in the rural areas, they requested personnel to address these needs. A corollary to that was the historic evidence that compassionate, competent medical care of the ill and wounded prepared hearts to seek and respond to the good news of the gospel. We wanted to respond to both the physical and spiritual needs. The Thailand mission was greatly blessed by a common desire on the part of both the older missionaries and the younger incoming medical missionaries having a similar philosophy of medical missions. That philosophy was played out in the choice of a location and in the scope of the proposed hospital: small, rural, great need, and no other Christian witness in the immediate area. That agreement in philosophy was a major key to the success of Bangkla Baptist Hospital.

Much research, thought, and prayer by the mission led to the selection of southeast Thailand as the preferred location. Not wanting to act unilaterally, they sought input from the Thai Ministry of Health as to their preference. Providentially, they also thought that southeast Thailand would be a good location for the hospital. When all factors were considered, Bangkla was chosen. It was a county seat town with a population of about six thousand on a river about fifty or sixty miles east of Bangkok, toward the Cambodian border. During the rainy season, access was sometimes by boat only. The primary area to be served had a population of approximately three hundred thousand with minimal medical care available. It also had very minimal Christian witness. No other Christian organization was working in the area.

Construction had just begun on the hospital when Joann and I arrived. The doctors already present at the time (Dr. Fred Medcalf, Dr. Harlan Willis, and Dr. Orby Butcher) were all in language school or about to leave on furlough. They started taking turns going to mobile clinics in the area around the hospital. Patients poured in; the response was encouraging. Joann immediately became a part of the team.

Bangkla Baptist Hospital

The area was undeveloped at the time, but we wanted the hospital to be a modern, well-equipped hospital that could provide excellent medical care. The design and equipment reflected that desire, but the contractor needed a little help in following the architect's plans. The second floor, containing the chapel, library, and several offices, was built over the Outpatient and X-Ray Department and other examination areas. The roof was flat, with drain pipes at the four corners to allow a quick runoff after a heavy rain. Without asking or questioning anyone, the contractor thought the drains were for support, so after they were installed, he had them filled with concrete.

He also had a little problem with the plumbing design. I guess he had never seen a septic tank sewerage system and did not realize the toilets, water faucets, and sinks were to be connected to the underground septic tanks. He just ran all the drain pipes into the ground and dead-ended them. Not long after the hospital opened, I started getting complaints about stopped-up toilets. By itself, that was not surprising; problems often occur when a new building is opened. When the problem persisted, I had the maintenance people crawl under the hospital and check it out. Surprise! Surprise! There was no interconnection of the pipes to the septic tanks. The contractor needed a little encouragement to make the necessary modifications.

We wanted to have a cordial relationship with the local Thai doctors in our province just as we had had with the health authorities in Bangkok in deciding on the hospital location. We extended invitations and always welcomed them when they visited. We were gratified with their warm reception of foreign doctors and a foreign hospital. Many visited our hospital to see how we had added new equipment and technology in the diagnosis and treatment of medical problems.

The variety of medical problems dealt with in those years could fill a book—certainly too many to give details here. Rabies was not uncommon. Diseases and pathology rarely seen in the United States because of vaccinations, inoculations, and other preventive measures were common in Bangkla. Some of them were related to traditional medicine, sometimes called folk medicine, that was practiced by many of the people in that area. The germ theory of disease was not well-known or accepted by most of the rural people. Treatments varied, but they often involved a variety of plants or some part of an animal, either of which might be made into a poultice or taken orally. There might also be an offering of money to an image or temple, or a gift of some kind to a folk doctor (shaman) for incantations that might bring healing. Many times, those treatments were tried first. When they were not successful, the patient would be brought to the hospital as a last resort. That often resulted in a heavy patient load of critically ill patients. In anticipation of that, our doctors had decided early on to install oxygen and suction outlets at every bed in the hospital, both IPD and OPD, which was rare in Thailand at that time. It saved many lives. Our patient load was always heavy, resulting in only the most ill being admitted. That meant the entire hospital was similar to an intensive care unit. With our occupancy rate usually above 100 percent, our doctors and staff were always pushed to their limits.

Some of the medical problems were seasonal, especially cholera. The dry (and hot) season was usually accompanied by an epidemic of cholera. When the rains stopped, it did not take long for the *klongs* (canals), cisterns, wells, and other water sources to become contaminated. When a patient developed cholera, the resulting diarrhea and vomiting caused acute dehydration, which could bring death quickly. Many died because traditional treatments did not provide for needed hydration. The hospital was often filled to overflowing. Officially we were licensed for twenty-five beds; in reality, our patient load was often far above that, especially during cholera season. We sometimes had up to seventy patients in the hospital. They would be on and under beds, on open floor spaces in rooms, in halls, and in waiting areas. We learned quickly to stock up on IVs and IV poles. People soon learned that if they could get the patient to the hospital before they died, they would probably survive. For those arriving at the hospital in critical condition, IVs would be started in all extremities. Recovery usually occurred if they came in time.

Medical Work: Fruitful Ministry with Leprosy (Hansen's) Patients

Another unusual medical situation developed when the mission inherited/adopted a leprosy (more correctly called Hansen's disease) clinic before the hospital opened. Unplanned and unanticipated, it came about through a combination of events that gave great impetus to our fledgling medical work and to our gospel outreach. We found ourselves involved in a major leprosy program.

For thousands of years, there has been a fearful fascination about leprosy. Much of that fear and many of the myths surrounding leprosy still existed when we began our work with leprosy patients in the early 1960s. Medical researchers had determined that good sanitation and sterile techniques on the part of medical providers made it highly unlikely that the disease would be contracted. It had a very low level of contagion. Our medical people were not really worried about it, but many people were still afraid of it.

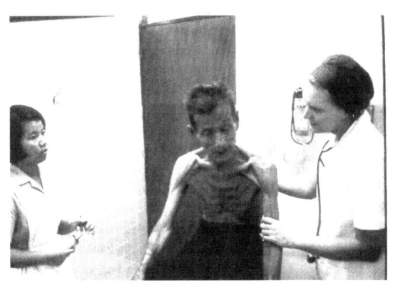

Joann with TB patient

The bacilli of leprosy and tuberculosis are related, but tuberculosis is more contagious than leprosy, and I learned it the hard way.

I started losing weight. It kept going down. Joann called for a checkup. I had turned positive for TB, plus amoebiasis. Joann and Harlan kept me on medication for a year. I have had no recurrence, but I still have a calcified node in one of my lungs as a reminder. It was hard to maintain sanitary procedures in the villages.

The McKean Leprosarium in north Thailand, part of the Presbyterian missionary work, was operating a major leprosy clinic in Cholburi, a city on the coast of the Gulf of Siam near our area of work. It was under the direction of missionary physician who was retiring in 1963 with no one to take his place. In the meantime, missionaries Ronald and Evelyn Hill had moved to Cholburi in 1959 to begin our work in southeast Thailand. When the clinic operators realized they could no longer continue the work, they asked our mission to assume responsibility. We accepted it, with Ron and Evelyn having immediate oversight, assisted by Thai national Christian with years of experience in taking care of leprosy patients. The transition occurred in 1962 and 1963, just as our doctors were arriving in Thailand but before the hospital opened in 1964. With almost two thousand registered patients already under active treatment by the clinic, our early medical teams, most of whom were still in language school, assumed a significant patient load. The retiring doctor provided a two-week practical workshop on the diagnosis and treatment of leprosy. It was not that new or unusual for our medical people, but it was a good opportunity for Jerry Hobbs and me to learn about the disease.

Part of our motivation for adopting the work was that the stigma and ravages of the disease had left many of them as outcasts of the world. They were the rejected, neglected, poorest of the poor—yet they were also created in the image of God. They also deserved to hear the gospel. They, of all people, needed to hear of a God who loved them, died for them, wanted to forgive them, and wanted them to have a truly abundant life. That was our opportunity to share that message. We took advantage of it.

Our leprosy work grew rapidly in the number of registered patients and in the geographical area from which they came. Jerry found many new patients in the area around Prachinburi, where he lived, eastward toward the Cambodian border. Others were found throughout southeast Thailand, many coming on their own as they learned of the treatment available. Within just a couple of years, we had about four thousand leprosy patients under active treatment.

Note: The following comments are made as a layman. They do reflect extensive conversations I had with many physicians, especially Joann. They also reflect research findings from several authors about leprosy, particularly by Dr. Paul Brand, a highly respected, international expert on leprosy[4]. In addition, as a nonmedical person, I have examined and distributed medicine to hundreds, if not thousands, of leprosy patients. This is my personal opinion, not a scientific treatise, although I think it is correct.

As we began our work with them, there was no cure available for all three types of leprosy. Dapsone was effective against two of the types, but it was only somewhat effective against lepromatous leprosy, the third and most contagious, deforming type. Otherwise, the best treatment we could provide, and it was important, was to take care of their skin lesions, treat other medical problems, provide symptomatic relief for complications, and give hot wax baths as a form of physical therapy.

In the late 1960s, another medication called B663 (Lamprene) became available. It promised a cure, but it had the unwanted side effect of turning the skin a darker color. That occurred when the ingested medicine settled into the infected tissues. With cooler skin areas like faces, hands, and feet being more attractive locations for the bacillus, those were the areas that became darker. In a culture where lighter skin was prized, that trait was a deterrent to many patients.

---

[4] *Pain: The Gift Nobody Wants*, Dr. Paul Brand and Philip Yancey, HarperCollins, 1983

In the early 1980s, another drug—Rifampin—became available. It was very effective against all types of leprosy and had few side effects. The disease became curable.

Thalidomide was also an important component in the total care of patients. It was not a treatment of leprosy but a treatment of the reaction to leprosy that many patients experienced. If left untreated, the reactions themselves could become serious. Thalidomide was very effective in controlling the reaction, but side effects of the drug raised red flags. It could cause congenital deformities in newborns whose mothers had taken the drug during pregnancy. It was later removed from the market. That was good news for young mothers whose babies were at risk, but it was bad news for great numbers of leprosy patients who were suffering from a reaction, some even life-threatening conditions, and had nothing else to equal the effectiveness of Thalidomide. Steroids helped, but they had some bad side effects also.

Clarification is needed concerning some misunderstandings about leprosy. The obvious evidences of leprosy—stumpy (or missing) fingers and toes, contracted/clawed hands, marred faces, blindness, and ulcers on the hands and feet—are not caused directly by the leprosy bacilli. The leprosy bacillus invades and affects the nerves, destroying the nerve endings and causing sensory loss (anesthesia, no feeling of pain). That loss of a sense of pain is what leads to most of the deformities because the patient makes no effort to treat injuries or lesions and develops infections. We have often seen leprosy patients pick up hot cooking utensils or red-hot coals with their bare hands and have no feeling of pain.

We have seen them cut their feet on glass or other sharp objects and not be aware of it. Those acts caused injuries that resulted in infections, sometimes severe, which caused a loss of skin and bone tissue. That was what caused the loss of fingers, toes, and other tissue.

The growth of our leprosy work called for more facilities and more services. We built a forty-bed leprosy unit on the hospital compound to house seriously affected patients until they could return home. We initially planned to use it for tuberculosis patients also, but it was not really feasible. For various reasons, we ended up using it for leprosy only. It was a multipurpose building: forty beds for patients (male and female) and a large open space under the same roof for a variety of meetings and occupational therapy treatment and training. The resident dorm director, Khun Manop (not his real name) and his wife, both of whom were leprosy patients, became skilled in several areas, especially making shoes and growing orchids. Both were fine Christians and were instrumental in leading many patients to the Lord.

Every three months, the hospital chaplain (John Patton, Bob Stewart, or Ron Hill at various times) would bring in twenty to forty leprosy patients for treatment, training in how to care for themselves and Bible study and worship services. Their response to this ministry made it apparent that they were very open to the gospel. Knowing their status in society, it was easy to understand. They had come out of an atmosphere of rejection to one of love and acceptance.

The common attitude by the public toward leprosy patients at that time in that area was similar to biblical times: shunning, separating, and excluding. Patients with visible symptoms could not ride public transportation, eat in restaurants, get jobs, become monks or priests, or gather in public meetings. Thai medical workers without proper training were reluctant to touch them. Even many families with a member with the disease would consign them to a little bamboo shack separate from the family house. Their own religion shunned them. The prevailing belief in fate and reincarnation had convinced them that if their previous life had been so bad that it resulted in their present condition, then they simply had no hope. When they started being lovingly touched by the people who treated them, people who showed compassion, who washed them and dressed their lesions, even on their feet, and who told them about a God who cared for them, they were ready to hear. They listened with hungry hearts as they heard about God, His Son, and the Holy Spirit. He was not a spirit to fear or placate, but a powerful Spirit that gave hope, joy, and loving forgiveness. Most of them were hearing the gospel for the first time, and it really was good news. Many of them joyfully accepted it. It so transformed their lives that they became some of the most effective witnesses in the region. That response by leprosy patients was the seed from which came many churches in southeast Thailand today. (Note: It should be obvious, but I will state it anyway: Response to or rejection of the gospel made no difference in the compassionate care provided to the patients. Neither did the lack of money or the severity of the disease.)

The increase in the patient load continued for both leprosy and non-leprosy patients in spite of travel difficulties for many of them. For patients living near Bangkla, it was not so difficult to get to the hospital, but most of the people lived in difficult-access areas. Hundreds of little villages were located throughout the region, scattered in the jungle, surrounded by a few small rice paddies, accessed only by a trail or by a klong. To go to the hospital in Bangkla and see a foreign doctor was a major undertaking, to be done only as a last resort, but it was during those visits that our doctors would find patients with leprosy or tuberculosis (and much other pathology). Both diseases required ongoing medication, but it required time and money to return to the hospital—and many patients would not return.

What to do? A small part of the solution involved two of us, Jerry Hobbs, living in Prachinburi, and me. Neither of us was a doctor, but we had received some basic training in the diagnosis and treatment of leprosy. We made regular visits to the villages to follow up on the patients who had been diagnosed by a doctor. Each of us would have the medications and records of patients with leprosy and TB in the villages we would be visiting. We would usually go to the house of the village Headman, squat down, and begin visiting. The entire village would soon join us, including the patients we were there to see. We would distribute medication, change a dressing, take vital signs, or whatever else was needed.

Earl at village clinic

An additional reason for going to see leprosy patients was to check family members to see if others were infected, which was often the case. If we saw something suspicious, we did a simple test. We blindfolded them and used a feather to see if the suspicious area had any feeling. If there were nodules or skin discoloration, or the feather test was not clear, we might use a sharp stick to see if the area still had feeling. If the signs indicated possible leprosy, we would take the patient back to the hospital for one of our doctors to confirm the diagnosis and start them on the appropriate medication. We did the same thing with TB patients. The procedure became more difficult in the rainy season when the roads became impassable. We would sometimes walk in and leave two or three months' of medications, but the rainy season left several patients either not found or not followed up.

But the provision of medical care, for leprosy or any other medical problem, as important as it was, was not our ultimate mission. Even with the best of care, physical death would, and will, ultimately prevail. Our goal was to share the gospel of Christ among a people, most of whom had never heard of Jesus, knowing that, as they came to know Jesus, they would attain eternal, abundant, spiritual life. One of the many ways we did that was through a regular schedule of preaching, teaching, and personal sharing within the hospital setting. We had staff worship and prayer time each morning before regular work was begun. Then we had a midmorning service in OPD during which we briefly halted patient registration. Beginning with the missionary staff, then gradually transferring to national Christian staff, we shared a brief message about who we were as Christians and what we believed. Then a brief summary of the gospel was shared. All Christian staff continued sharing that story as they provided compassionate medical care.

For those of us involved in the rural clinics, it was a wonderful opportunity to just sit, visit, and share the gospel with an entire village in a cordial, welcoming atmosphere. I began to realize I was talking and not always communicating. It was time to stop and think about it.

Learning: A Communication Challenge

While still in my first term, my Thai language skill was woefully inadequate. Often when I spoke, I read incomprehension on the faces of the listeners. It was disturbing. It was time to rethink how I was presenting the message. Most of us as new missionaries were facing the same issue. Communicating cross-culturally had been a frequent topic of study and discussion in the seminary and other venues, but doing it was a different story. We had been trained in our own language, our own culture, and usually in our own religion, but now our circumstances were very different. Limited language ability and minimal cultural understanding drove home the necessity of learning how to communicate more effectively. We faced three barriers: religion, language, and culture. (Race was not a barrier for us).

As to religion, Thailand was and is a Buddhist nation. Their religion was integral to their nation, but it was a cultural religion, not a spiritual religion. To be Thai was to be Buddhist. To leave Buddhism was to betray their nation. Christianity was a foreign religion, good for foreigners, but not appropriate for them to adopt.

As to language, Buddhism had its own language—just like our Christian faith—but many of the same religious words have widely different meanings, unique to each belief system. *Sin* in Buddhism is far different to *sin* in Christianity. In a similar way, the word *God* has different meanings in each system. The *god* of Buddhism is far different from the God of creation and redemption. The God we worship as Christians is different from the Allah as used by many Muslims.

When we witnessed to people about the Lord we worshipped, we loved to tell them about our Savior, but there was no equivalent word for Savior in the Thai language. It was translated as a phrase, but that phrase fell far short of conveying what "Savior" really means. The same is true of many other "religious" words. Our challenge was to address and attempt to penetrate all three barriers. We needed a new method of communicating/interpreting the gospel message without changing it. (Incidentally, that is becoming more of a challenge in American culture also.) "Church" words, beautiful and meaningful to us who understand them, are often not understood by the younger generations who have not grown up in church. It may be easy for us to think we are communicating the gospel when there is little real communication.

Actually, the method was already there. Jesus used it extensively. He told stories and parables, and He used analogies, metaphors, symbols, and hyperbole (speaking ministerially) to help His hearers understand. He was the greatest example of using the "storying" method for sharing His message. Our challenge was to transfer His method to Thailand. Belatedly, we began to pick up on it. I'll give just a couple of examples.

The first example relates to the use of a redemptive analogy with which the Thai people could easily identify. Israel and Thailand were both agrarian nations. Planting, sowing, reaping, and harvesting were commonly understood terms. Jesus used them, so did we, adding the water buffalo to the analogy.

Every Thai (and Cambodian and Vietnamese and Laotian) farmer had a water buffalo (kwai). It was often his most prized and valuable possession. His rice farming required it. The children rode it as a pet. The family took good care of it, but thieves often stole the buffalo because it was valuable. In rural areas, there was no law or police force to help him find it and recover it. He had no appeal to a higher authority. It was up to him to recover what was stolen. Contact with the thieves was not difficult. They were, in fact, often known. The farmer often had to gather all his resources, or even borrow from others, to pay the high price exacted by the thieves before he could buy back and lead his beloved buffalo home.

The transition from the biblical story of the redemption (buying back) provided by Jesus to the farmer buying back (redeeming) his buffalo was not hard to understand. The strength of the analogy lies first in the action of the owner and then in the nature of the buffalo. The owner seeks out and buys back what is his by right—at great cost to himself. God had no higher authority to which He could appeal, so out of His great love, He came and paid the high price Himself. Christ, God's Son, came into Satan's (the thief's) territory and paid the ultimate price to buy back (redeem) his stolen possession.

As for the nature of the buffalo, it is helpless. It is a victim of a heartless master, doomed to a life of servitude unless someone intervenes and sacrifices in order to restore him to his rightful owner. Man, like the buffalo, is unable to help (save) himself. He too, is under the power of Satan, the evil one, is doomed to a life of servitude and suffering. Christ has paid that ultimate sacrifice to restore the man to his rightful owner (God). He has been redeemed (saved) by the sacrifice of Christ, God's Son. As the loving Owner, God eases man's yoke of servitude and lifts his burden. God loves man and wants only what is good for him. It was not hard to continue telling the story, using other passages to describe who Jesus was, what He did for us, and what He was now offering to all who would believe in Him. Later, as I tell of our refugee work, I will use another analogy to describe the refugee situation as an analogy of salvation.

The second example (although neither an analogy or metaphor) concerns their belief in spirits. Many of the rural Thai people were preoccupied with and fearful of them. Their "spirits" were similar to but not the same as "ghosts" in the Western world. They existed, hovered, moved, and permeated everything. A noise in the house? Spirits did it. A wreck on the road? The spirits caused it. Some bad luck happened? The spirits were disturbed. To many Thais, spirits were threatening entities, sometimes angry, often feared, and needing to be placated.

We countered that perception with stories of a great, powerful, and benevolent God who was a mighty Holy Spirit able to overcome all lesser spirits. As we/anyone believed in that God and trusted in Him, He placed His Holy Spirit in them to enable them to overcome the evil spirits that troubled them. That presentation often led to a discussion of who God really is and the role of Jesus in giving a new kind of life to those who place their trust in Him.

One of many examples about their fear of evil spirits occurred in the hospital. Joann had gone in the night to deliver a baby and was appropriately suited up in delivery room dress. After delivery of the baby, she dropped by the main ward to check on a critical malaria patient. She seemed nervous but otherwise improved, so Joann went home. On the next morning's rounds, she stopped by the lady's bed to check her. The lady claimed a spirit came to her bed last night, and she was sure she would now die. Joann realized what had occurred, assured the lady it was she who visited her, and told her she knew of a mighty spirit so much greater than the evil spirits the Thai fear. She told her about the Holy Spirit and how He not only is greater than the evil spirits but is available to her to protect her and help her heal and have peace in her life. She wanted to know all about this Holy Spirit.

The method of storying the gospel was a much more effective method and has now spread throughout the world, especially among people groups in less-developed areas with little formal education.

Learning: Village Visits and Hansen's Patients

After a while, I became a little more comfortable with my care of leprosy patients. I was less comfortable with my attempts to care for TB patients, especially in my amateur effort at doing the history and physical of suspected new patients. I tried harder to get the suspicious cases to go to the hospital for an exam but many were reluctant to go.

It was the other patients with whom I was most uncomfortable. When I distributed medicine and took care of leprosy and TB patients, they assumed I was a doctor. No amount of denial would change their minds. All the sick people in the village wanted to be seen. Some were obviously ill, but my limited competency in knowing what was wrong and what to do left me uneasy in advising them. I usually tried to get them to go see a doctor, but they rarely did it. Sometimes, if the patient appeared to be critically ill, I would take them to the doctor myself. The whole activity left me with ambivalent feelings. I was not a doctor, but I was acting like one in some ways. I was able to help many people who otherwise would not have been helped. And I made sure I did not harm anyone.

Spending hours distributing medicine and visiting in a tropical village could easily lead to dehydration, but drinking the local water was not a good idea. We had the ideal answer right in the village. I would give one of the village boys a baht (five cents) to climb a palm tree and bring me a few green coconuts. The coconut water was delicious, safe, and had the right electrolytes to provide almost perfect rehydration.

Coconut water was a good solution for the thirsty individual, and it had a much wider use in the more remote areas. We were close enough to Bangkok to purchase the IV fluids we needed, but remote, up-country hospitals did not have that opportunity. When a major dehydration crisis arose, such as a cholera epidemic, they could not have an adequate stock of IV fluids to meet the need. In that situation, it was not unusual for the hospital to attach a special pediatric filter to a green coconut and allow the water to flow directly into the patient's veins. It was not a perfect IV solution, but it saved countless lives. Isn't it great how the Lord provides?

From the beginning of our leprosy work, we were all very conscious that we could treat only the disease and its symptoms. Not even the doctors could undo the ravages that had already occurred. (Harlan did very successful tendon transplants on some clawed fingers and deformed hands.) Treatment could heal open lesions, delay further destruction of tissue, and, later, even cure the disease, but damaged fingers, hands, feet, and eyes could not be replaced. Skin biopsies could prove they were healed, but their families and the public still saw the deformities as evidence of leprosy. Many patients, although cured, felt they still had the disease because they still had crippled areas on their bodies. They continued to suffer rejection, separation, and exclusion. They often had to depend on others. They needed the next step: help with developing some degree of independence. We did that with a limited occupational therapy program.

Many of the Thai people were skilled in handcrafts, woodcarving, and making jewelry, ornaments, dolls, and flip-flop sandals out of worn-out tires. We provided facilities and materials for them to improve their skills and help in marketing their products.

We added another occupational activity on a four thousand-square-foot space adjacent to the leprosy building: a place to grow orchids. Thailand was famous for beautiful orchids, and there was a ready world market. We set many posts in the ground, interconnected with wires from which hundreds of orchid plants were suspended. Transplanting and maintaining the plants was simple and easily learned. Handicapped patients could often handle the basic physical requirements since orchids are primarily air-breathing plants requiring few supplements. Overall, it was a small operation, but it did allow many patients to become self-sufficient for the first time. As noted earlier, Khun Manop, the leprosy building resident manager, became skilled at making shoes. That was a huge step in the healing process for infected, deformed feet. The loss of flesh and bone tissue in toes and feet left the feet malformed. Normal shoes (even if they could afford them) made the problem worse because they did not conform to the shape of the damaged foot. Factory-made shoes created new pressure points that became inflamed and infected. With a space-age development, Khun Manop was able to make shoes that did conform to each individual foot. Microcellular rubber, a new material, became available and provided a major part of the solution we needed. When the patient's foot was placed on the warmed microcellular material, it formed a mold identical to the foot. When cooled, the mold became semihard and retained its shape permanently. Khun Manop then encompassed the mold with leather, forming it into the rough shape of a shoe. It wouldn't have won a fashion award, but it prevented a lot of damaged feet and helped heal many others.

For a variety of reasons, Thailand began a rapid transition to a more modern country in the late sixties and seventies, a transition that affected our medical work. Much of it was the result of the American military presence in Southeast Asia and the cooperation between Thailand and the United States. The United States helped in the transition by providing economic assistance. One portion of that assistance was the selection by the United States Army Corps of Engineers to build a modern highway from Chacheungsao (the capital of our province) to nearby Prachinburi, toward the Cambodian border. That highway came within four miles of Bangkla. The Thai government added to the American assistance by building several feeder roads from the new highway into the more remote areas. That opened the door for us to initiate a major mobile clinic ministry. We bought an extra-long wheelbase Isuzu truck chassis and designed a clinic with an exam area, x-ray cubicle, basic lab area, and pharmacy space. We towed a ten thousand-watt generator behind it (see picture).

Mobile clinic

The doctors rotated in staffing the clinic on its rural visits. It relieved Jerry Hobbs and me of much of our clinic work for which we were grateful. (It's possible the quality of medical care was improved a bit also.) Even with the new road construction, the mobile clinic was limited in the rainy season.

Many wonderful stories came out of our work with leprosy patients. One of the most unusual stories concerns a patient brought in one morning in the middle of a typically full OPD. The whole hospital staff started scurrying when two large Mercedes-Benz cars pulled up to the OPD entrance. An obviously very ill man was helped out of one of the cars and taken immediately to an exam room. Harlan happened to be the doctor who saw him. His history was unclear; he could hardly speak, and his assistants did not know the full story. It was obvious that he was bleeding internally and that he also had some external bleeding lesions. Harlan recognized that he had lepromatous leprosy and had suffered major blood loss. He was at the point of death. Harlan and his team did their usual outstanding job and soon had him stabilized. His condition gradually improved, and Harlan was able to piece together his story.

Mr. Som (not his real name) was a very wealthy highway construction contractor who happened to have leprosy. Apparently, he had had a reaction to his leprosy (not unusual). A doctor in Bangkok had given him steroids to counter the effects of the reaction. The heavy doses of steroids had then precipitated an acute bleeding episode. He got to the hospital just in time. Harlan used the full range of treatment: blood transfusions, IVs, and medications (including Thalidomide), and his life was saved. As he recovered, he realized what he had been through and how close to death he had come. He wanted to show his appreciation. It so happened that his illness occurred during cholera season and the hospital was overflowing with patients with diarrhea. Cholera patients required clean water. Unfortunately, the Bangkla water system would sometimes run out of water during the cholera season—just when it was most needed. We had to have water. We explained our need to Mr. Som. "No problem," he said. "I will station a water truck and driver here to bring water as long as you need it." He did, and it was a literal lifesaver.

Later, after he had recovered from his acute episode, word came that Thalidomide was being removed from world markets and could no longer be used. Again, it was bad news for leprosy patients. It was the best medication available for the treatment of reactions. When Mr. Som learned of its removal from the market, he immediately dispatched a fleet of vehicles all over Thailand to visit pharmacies and buy up their total stock of the medicine. It might not have been the most ethical thing to do, but he did share some of it with others with the disease. He continued to be a friend and supporter of the hospital for many years.

I'll add one more note concerning the care of critically ill patients. Trauma patients from wrecks, shootings, stabbings, and animal maulings made up a major portion of our patient load. Abdominal and other masses were also common (including extrapulmonary TB masses). The reputation of our doctors, especially our surgeons (Harlan Willis, Orby Butcher, Fred Metcalf, and Al Hood) brought in a continual stream of patients. Harlan was board certified in surgery, Orby had advanced training in orthopedics, and Al and Fred also had some advanced training in surgery. In that situation, they were all general surgeons—and they all did what was needed. It was almost like an ongoing residency in many specialties. Joann had her boards in pediatrics, but in Bangkla, and in most mission medical settings, every doctor is a generalist. She concentrated more on the OPD clinic, but she also did anesthesia and some obstetrics. She later picked up more of the leprosy work.

Inevitably, there were head, chest, and other injuries beyond the surgical skill and equipment capabilities of our little rural hospital. In the early years, they tried to transfer the most severe cases to Bangkok. I was often the one to take them in. At first, I would take them to the emergency room, make contact, explain the situation, and leave. Later, we would learn that when I left, the patient would usually be ignored (especially if he couldn't pay). I tried getting the patient admitted, talking with the surgeon, and even going to the surgery suite. Still nothing was done. At times, I had to take the patient back to Bangkla. Our doctors soon realized that if they did not do something, nothing would be done. I hurt for them many times when the final burden of a critical emergency fell on them and they had not been trained and did not have the equipment to cope with such severe cases (such as brain surgery).

Only a doctor who has faced a similar situation can fully understand the burden faced at a time like that. There was no referral capability. The patient's life was in his hands alone. Whatever complications developed after surgery began—and many unexpected problems were possible—were his to resolve. It was a heavy, emotionally draining responsibility. In cases of unusual, heroic, and even miraculous surgical interventions with the Bangkla staff, I have been struck by their responses, especially Harlan, but they often could not recall the cases. It was not the successes they remembered—it was the cases when the patients died. Those stayed with them. Inevitably, they sometimes questioned their handling of the cases. Memories of those episodes faded very slowly.

Two unusual cases illustrate the skills that led to our increasing reputation and patient load. In one case, a patient had been mauled by a bear. His face, shoulder, and upper chest had severe injuries. His right arm was deeply lacerated. He was Harlan's patient. A lengthy and complex suturing process began the restoration program, coupled with a major skin graft. Harlan cut a very large skin flap from the patient's abdominal area, bound the patient's mauled arm under the flap, closed it over, and sutured it until the graft had taken. The end result was an absolutely remarkable recovery.

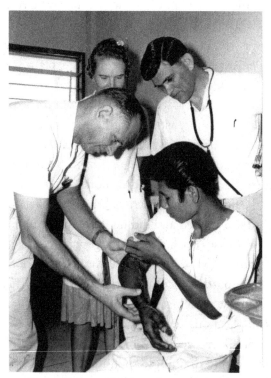

Harlan, Joann, and Orby seeing mauled patient

Another case involved a patient who had been shot and stabbed numerous times, including in the liver and other vital areas. When it occurred, he insisted on being brought to our hospital because of its reputation. A slight problem was that it would take about twenty-four hours to get there; he might not live that long. He came anyway, but he barely made it in time. He was Orby's patient. Much exploratory surgery in the GI tract and other areas was required to repair all the damage, but Orby did it, and he recovered.

In that particular case, Joann remembers the "rest of the story." His serious condition required a long stay in the hospital. That gave him the opportunity to hear and accept the gospel. As Joann was making patient rounds one day in Orby's absence, she found him reading the Bible. He was worried. He had read in the Bible that a Christian man was to have only one wife. He had eight. What was he to do? Joann was stumped. "Let's pray about it," she said. When he was discharged to go home, his family came to get him. Only one of his wives showed up. "That's my answer," he said. Problem solved, prayer answered. The hospital's reputation spread even further.

Working Women ... and Other Terms

It has been common for the doctor to receive most of the attention in a family because of the dramatic nature of their work, but the doctor's wives in Bangkla did their share and more. Jo Willis was a nurse and often helped in the OPD when she was not teaching mission kids (MKs). Olga Hood had several children of her own, so teaching required a major part of her time. That, plus the time and effort it took just to keep a household going, combined with her church work, fully filled her days. Betty Butcher's children were just a little older, so when they started at the International School in Bangkok in the ninth grade, Betty was freed up to do other things. And did she do them! Her big legacy was, and is, Thai Country Trim (TCT).

Thai Country Trim was born out of an acute need. The Thai custom of the men taking multiple wives, or mistresses, often left the women with children but with no support for them. The man would tend to take a newer wife and relegate the older one to a lower status—or discard her. Life became sad and difficult for many. Betty saw a great need and decided to do something about it. She began—in her home—teaching them how to do handiwork with cloth and other material and then helped market the items. The women were quick to learn what Betty taught, plus many other handcrafted products they developed themselves. The result was, first, a local, then a national, and now an international network of crafts and decorations that are marketed worldwide. Part of that worldwide distribution is through Worldcrafts, a legal entity operated by WMU (Woman's Missionary Union). All profit goes to assist women and children who need to get away from similar situations. Betty's accomplishments brought her the distinguished alumnus award by Oklahoma Baptist University. Missionary wives don't take back seats!

There was a noticeable drop in photographs toward the end of our first term. Our first years were filled with new, strange, and unusual scenes of beauty and wonder. My camera stayed busy, especially in the hospital. The doctors wanted pictures of unusual surgical events for use on their furlough presentations. All around us were unforgettable scenes we planned to show when we went on furlough, but the new wore off and everyday life in the hospital and elsewhere became commonplace. The camera was left behind. Much of what really made up a very rich subject of life in a wonderful new country was lost because it had become commonplace. I have regretted neglecting it ever since.

A Memorable Christmas ... and Other Events

Christmas came almost suddenly to Thailand ... as a commercial enterprise. Merchants hopped on business opportunities very quickly, especially Thai (Chinese) marketing people who had studied in the United States. Lights started going up, Christmas trees were decorated (some with faux snow), and Christmas music was heard in many stores. There was a wonderful, unplanned side benefit from the commercialism in the business community. It whetted the curiosity of many people who began asking about the meaning of Christmas. That curiosity was our huge opportunity. With less than half of one percent of the population of Thailand being Christians, we were always searching for ways to make the gospel story known. Now many ways were opened to us, and we responded eagerly. One of the pleasant surprises was that a few of the Thai schools and temples invited some of the Christian leaders to come tell the story and explain what it meant. Missionaries and national Christians combined resources to use every venue possible—radio, TV programs, news articles, and public announcements—to tell the story.

One of the best ways turned out to be caroling. Thai Christians had adopted the custom of caroling with enthusiasm. It provided a good opportunity to visit people's homes in a cordial atmosphere, enjoyed by both the carolers and the residents. The Christians in Bangkla joined wholeheartedly in the effort. In order to visit more homes, they gathered in separate small groups and walked the streets of Bangkla, caroling at the homes of city, county, and school officials as well as business leaders. Naturally, they also caroled at the homes of missionaries, maybe partly because they knew there would be a big spread of drinks and goodies waiting for them. It was a thrill for us to see the nationals taking advantage of the opportunity and going all out to share their newfound faith.

The leprosy patients in our leprosy building also learned about Christmas, but they learned it primarily from the teaching and preaching of the Bible story. (Even so, we had a constant struggle trying to teach them the difference between Santa Claus and Jesus.) The custom of caroling also caught their attention, but because walking was so difficult, if not impossible, that activity was denied them. Or so we thought.

In the late 1960s, one particular caroling time by the Christians in Bangkla became an especially memorable Christmas. Caroling was usually done on Christmas Eve. Joann had spread her usual bountiful preparations, and we were prepared to welcome the carolers. We received them under the house (our house was on stilts like all others). The upstairs lights were off; only a couple were on under the house (burglar protection). At about ten o'clock that night, the first of two or three groups started coming by, did their caroling, enjoyed their refreshments, and continued on their way. Then other groups came by. Sometime around midnight, one more group came by and did their caroling. We waited until about one o'clock on Christmas morning, but no one else came. It was time to close everything down. Just as we started to clean up, a large stake-bed truck pulled up to our gate. In the semidarkness, we could barely tell that the truck was full of people, probably about twenty. As the driver took down the rear sideboards, allowing us to see better, we were dumbfounded. They were patients—leprosy patients. Most of them were Joann's patients. Because they could hardly walk, we had not expected them to come to our house, which was more than half a mile from the hospital. We learned later that they had pooled every baht (nickel) they had to rent the truck for the occasion.

Someone placed a makeshift ladder on the back of the truck bed so they could begin the very difficult process of climbing down. I glanced at Joann and noticed the anguish on her face as they struggled. All the patients had serious problems, not only with leprosy, but many of them had additional medical problems. We were shocked that they had left the leprosy building. All had on some kind of bandage or cast. Many were on crutches. Many had hands and feet so completely covered with bandages that their clawed fingers and stumpy toes could not grasp or hold anything to help move. They could easily have fallen off the truck.

Joann cried as she watched their struggle to descend and limp up the driveway. It was inappropriate for us to go assist them. Only she knew the damage being done to their tissues, even through the bandages. They were harming themselves even though they were feeling no pain. We knew bandages and dressings would have to be replaced the next day, and healing would be delayed.

When they had all reached the ground, they assembled to light their candles and do their caroling. Lighting and holding their candles brought more anguish to Joann. Because many patients had both hands wrapped, they had to use both hands to hold a candle. With no feeling and with all the jostling, the candles were held in all positions. Hot wax and open flames often touched bare skin. It did not hurt them, but it hurt us to watch.

They began by singing two Thai Christmas songs (translated from English). Then came the grand finale. They had memorized the phonetic English words of "Joy to the World" and proceeded to sing it, wildly off key. It was a glorious, wonderful, joyful noise. Most of them were Christians who had experienced the joy about which they were now singing. That joy was expressed in their faces and in their voices as they enthusiastically sang about the incarnate God who had come into their hearts. Joann and I could barely see and hardly join them because of the tears in our eyes. We just choked up. After sharing drinks and other goodies with them, they returned to the hospital. Our anguish resumed as we watched them struggle to climb back on the truck.

They left happy. They had joined with other Christians in celebrating their Savior's birth. They had shared their Christmas carols with their foreign friends who were also their brothers and sisters in the Lord. They never knew how much they had blessed us. That time of worship has continued to bless us through the years. The image of that experience remains vivid and makes it one of the most memorable Christmases we have ever had.

There was one other patient—out of hundreds—whose story needs to be related. It began on a day like a thousand others. Khun Supachai and I were dealing with some routine hospital problems in my office. My office was just inside the main building, adjacent to the entrance to the OPD. Since we had no air-conditioning, my window louvers were always open. The full visual and audio effects of the OPD were in full force. Babies crying, patients groaning, patients being brought in by every conceivable conveyance—it was chaotic but controlled. Just a routine day.

That morning, a major commotion developed right outside my window. Four men were carrying a patient who had been wounded in his chest and was obviously in critical condition. As they carried him by my window, I barely heard him saying (in Thai), "Please, God, help! Please, God, help!" The OPD staff immediately rushed him to an exam room and began emergency procedures. One of our doctors (I can't remember which one, and they don't even remember the case) came out, took a glance, and helped get him to the OR for immediate surgery. It was successful, and he was brought back from the very brink of death and began his recuperation.

Some days later, much improved and able to talk, I went to visit him. "Do you remember being brought in?" I asked.

"Faintly," he replied.

"Do you remember what you were saying?"

"Barely," he replied.

"What was it?" I asked.

"Please, God, help! Please, God, help!"

His answer struck me. Buddhism teaches that there is no God. Buddha emphasized to his followers that he was not God. Many people revere him as a god and refer to him as Lord Buddha, but this man did not call on the Lord Buddha. He used the name for God.

"Who was the God from whom you were asking help?"

"I don't know, but there must be a God who can help when there is nothing else."

"There is," I replied. "Let me tell you about Him." And I did.

When he said, "There must be a God who could help," a biblical phrase came to me. It answered the man's question and reinforced Paul's affirmation that all mankind is without excuse: "He (God) has set eternity in their heart" (Ecclesiastes 3:11). That statement brought home to me a new understanding that there is a universal seeking after God in the soul of every person. Because we are made in the image of God, there is a spiritual hunger that can be met only by God. That man had been led to believe there was no Creator God, only myriad spirits that must be placated, but in his crisis time, there was no help. In that vacuum, he called for help because eternity had been set in his heart. His soul hungered, and his spirit thirsted. And so it is with everyone, but what if they never hear? What if no one ever goes and tells them about that loving, forgiving, redeemer God?

The medical staff followed through with a continuing witness and with a kind of loving, compassionate care he had never before known. When he was nearing full recovery and had come to an understanding of the gospel story, he trusted his life to the only God who was really able to help.

Joann's Home, Hospital, and Other Ministries

Joann could easily have had a double full-time ministry. The pressure was there to do so. In that setting, her medical skills were always needed. She could have given all her time to that very worthwhile ministry, but she was also a wife, mother, teacher, and example of what a Christian homemaker should be. It was in that role that she was led to establish the family class. It turned out to be one of her greatest legacies from her work in Thailand. (Although it would be difficult to top her later accomplishments in the refugee work.)

It will help to make a brief comment concerning the context within which the class came about. The Christian message and Christian churches brought new teachings and new concepts to the Thai people. To them, it was a new religion, but they already had their own—a much older one. For many centuries, they had been steeped in the teachings, culture, and beliefs of Buddhism. To many of them, Christianity was a foreign, even frightening, new thing, good for the foreigners but not for them. To adopt it was almost a betrayal. To be Thai was to be Buddhist. To adopt a different belief system was to deny their country, their family, and their heritage. They were reluctant to attend Christian worship services. Those beliefs were difficult to overcome. They still are. It was, and is, a long, slow process.

A hint of a breakthrough in penetrating that wall of misunderstanding and rejection came as they noticed the differences in our Christian homes in contrast to the usual Thai home. Joann became aware of it first in the market in Bangkla. When she was shopping, getting her hair done, or just visiting, the women expressed curiosity about the faithfulness of missionary husbands and wives to each other and to their families and the closeness of the Christian family. They longed to have something like that. In Thai life, it was common for the man to take a second or third wife—and maybe also have a mistress or two. The result was a sad and often tragic home life for many, especially the women and children. Joann had begun to be aware of that sadness as she saw many of the women and their family members as patients, but a hospital exam room was not the place to fully discuss it. Her clinical experience, supplemented by the curiosity of her hairdresser and other market ladies, prompted Joann to begin a family class.

Her basic intent was to teach and describe the biblical/Christian view of the home and family. That included relationships between husband and wife, parents and children and others, appropriate discipline of children, trust, being responsible, and the basic doctrines of the Christian faith. She used it all to lead into a discussion about the place God should have in those relationships. (Little did she know at the time, but that was early preparation for a wider ministry she had later in the eighties and nineties as she spoke on similar subjects to missionary women and other groups all over Southeast

Asia.) That class grew to become one of the major conduits for channeling entire Thai families to the Lord and into the church.

In the early stages of our work, many Thai people were reluctant to enter a church building. That was one reason that led Joann to begin inviting women, and later the men, to our home every Friday night. They were curious. The class had an inauspicious beginning, but when they came and experienced the warmth and fellowship of our home, it appealed to them. As Joann spoke, taught, and invited them to share their thoughts, questions, and problems, they were encouraged and interested. They told others and invited others. Attendance grew. Other family members and friends began coming. At times, at the encouragement of Joann, a class member would invite the group to meet at their house. It drew even more to attend and check out what was going on. Our house was a full, busy place on Friday nights.

Joann began by teaching basic principles of family life that were generally accepted by most cultures and religions. She would then move to the Christian principles of home and family. Using Bible passages and simple language, she would deal with many of the basic doctrines of our faith, including God, humanity, the Bible, and sin. She would spend extra time dealing with sin because of the great difference in the concept of sin between Christianity and Buddhism. That presence of sin revealed the need for forgiveness and redemption. From there, she moved to the coming of Jesus into the world, why He came, what He did, and what He and the Bible writers taught about the need for all people to accept Him as Lord and Savior.

That is a terribly oversimplified summary of what she was attempting to achieve. It was not easy, and it was not quick, but it was wonderfully effective. Many of the women and children and a few of the men accepted the Lord and became a part of the church.

One of the most gratifying blessings to come out of those efforts was that the group continued—in Bangkla and surrounding villages—after she was no longer present to lead it. Dr. Somporn, one of our Thai national Christian physicians, and other Christian women started other classes in other areas.

Family Life in Thailand: Events, Places, and Activities

Foreign missionaries and missionary kids live in two different worlds. Sometimes they blend in, and sometimes they separate. How to appropriately balance the two worlds is a challenge for every family. Some choose to totally immerse the entire family in the local language and culture. Others choose to maintain almost total separation. Joann and I have seen both examples and have seen the benefits and the problems that can occur with either choice. The living situation can be so different in different areas of the world that it is not for us to question the choices others make.

Joann and I chose to assist and encourage our children to live in a harmonious balance with both worlds. Joann and I were on the mission field because the Lord had called us to it, but Lisa and James had no say about being there. We anticipated their growing-up years to be primarily in a different country—with a different language and a different ethnic group—but they were American citizens, and we expected them to choose to live in the States as adults. We did not want them to lose an appreciation and awareness of their American history and heritage.

But they were also a part of Thailand. We were living in Bangkla in a relatively remote, rural area, so it was natural that they would have both Thai and other MKs as playmates. Lisa soon picked up basic playground Thai. As with other MKs in Bangkla, Lisa and James were homeschooled. Lisa was able to do the required Calvert Home School curriculum in a very short time, leaving her free to do other things. We all concluded it would be well for her to learn to read, write, and speak Thai. In spite of a few curious encounters as a lone, blonde, curly-haired, fair-skinned foreign girl, she did well and continued in Thai school into our second term.

When James reached school age, we did the same with him. It didn't work; we had a problem. His situation was different. His hair was white, his skin very fair (like his mother's), and he still had only playground Thai. His classmates (five and six years old) had not come across another kid like him, and curiosity took over. His hair was pulled, his skin was pinched and rubbed, and classroom discipline disappeared. (I can't say it went out the window since there were no windows.) By mutual consent of all concerned, he was unenrolled.

I'll jump ahead with a postscript. When James was at Baylor University, he became friends with a Thai man. Dr. Nirand was a graduate student who was soon to receive his PhD. He and his family owned and operated a college in north Thailand. He asked James to come to his school after he graduated to help establish a department of computer science (his major). He returned and stayed for more than a year, helping to get the department off the ground and running. Much of his early Thai came back to him, plus more that he acquired, and it was a major asset in the whole program.

Joann and I discussed and prayed extensively about what degree of immersion in Thai culture was appropriate in our situation. We wanted to prepare them for living in both worlds. Learning the local language was a good first step. Going to a Thai school would help. Joann and I spoke only Thai in our work and in all our church activities, but when we were together as a family, we spoke English. As we looked around at our mission families in Thailand and Southeast Asia, we realized it was not unusual for MKs to have varying degrees of difficulty in transitioning to life back in the United States. If they were totally immersed in the language and culture of their foreign home, the change to the American way of life could be daunting. However, total separation also led to problems. For some MKs, spending most of their growing-up years in another country and culture, then moving to the United States for permanent residence led them to questioning their national identity. Loyalty could be divided. The transition back to the United States could be difficult.

Most of them handled it well. We have been grateful that Lisa and James have both expressed appreciation for the privilege they had of living in Thailand for those years and for their exposure to another culture and another language. They both had minimal difficulty in adjusting to life in the United States.

In order to help maintain their identity balance, we provided interesting and educational English-language material for their study and entertainment. When I went to Bangkok to purchase hospital and medical supplies, I often picked up documentaries, films, and books for their review. I would stop by the American, European, and other embassies to pick up what was interesting or needed at any given time. In those days, stores and medical supply houses stayed open as long as they had customers. I would often pick up educational or interesting material in the morning and shop for hospital needs until late at night.

Many missionary mothers homeschooled their children. That was our situation in Bangkla, with a little adaptation. Jo Willis, Betty Butcher, and Olga Hood taught the MKs in the mornings. (Later, we had a few teachers come out from the States to teach two-year terms.) Joann worked mornings in the OPD clinic at the hospital until it was finished, and then she taught the MKs science (and sometimes math) and piano in the afternoon. At times, the MKs from Chacheungsao and Nakorn Nayok came for piano lessons.

Learning to play the piano was a big deal. All the girls were expected to learn at least the basics. The boys were strongly encouraged to take lessons, but no arms were twisted. Each year, Joann and the class presented the annual piano recital. It was the social event of the year. The parents were to dress up, and those in the recital were to wear formal attire. Most of the Southeast Station missionaries came for the occasion. Every girl (and Joann) had a beautiful orchid corsage. As a challenge to the students and to maintain her own proficiency, Joann always played a difficult classical piece. (That was where Kay Willis learned to play the piano.

She later became national president of the Women's Missionary Union of the Southern Baptist Convention.)

Another task Joann took on in the music field was an arrangement of Thai Christian music for use in meetings and worship services. There was no history or tradition of Thai Christian music. For Western Christians, steeped in centuries of sacred music, that lack left a painful void in worship services. Attempting to merge the two genres was daunting. Thai music has five basic tones; Western music has eight tones. Some Thai and Western music instruments could not be played simultaneously without special arranging.

We also arranged other fun activities. For Lisa, horses and equestrian training were important. We had found a highly skilled German lady in Bangkok who had competed in the Olympics. She had a training facility in Bangkok as well as a horse camp in west Thailand near the bridge over the River Kwai (Buffalo River). Lisa learned English riding, a little jumping, and a little dressage. She lived horses; dolls were a nonissue. We bought her a horse—or two—or three. Since she had to dress properly, cowboy boots, hats, jeans, and six-guns came with the horses. A place to ride was no problem in the dry season since the rice paddies had no fences. The monsoon season was a different story. Luscious green rice made for ideal grazing for the horses so the rice paddies were off-limits during that time.

To accommodate her insatiable desire to ride, I built her a full-scale wooden horse. To complete the riding paraphernalia, we brought a saddle, bridle, and other tack back from furlough. She spent many happy hours riding that wooden horse, roping whatever came near, especially James. She and I both have much regret that we have no pictures of that horse. How could that happen?

The horse camp was in the edge of the jungle in an absolutely beautiful setting. The Kwai River and the famous bridge were nearby. Although Lisa only went to the camp a few times, she has wonderful, vivid memories of those outings. It was at the end of the last camp she attended that she developed typhoid fever from drinking the water at the camp.

I'll jump ahead several years to relate one of her best and last horse-riding experiences. We were back in the States, on the staff of the FMB, living in Glen Allen, near Richmond, Virginia. Through a nurse friend of Joann's, we arranged for Lisa to join a riding group for a traditional foxhunt and a ride to the hounds. It is a sport loaded with its own language, customs, culture, and protocols—far too many to note here. Well, maybe a couple of comments. The hound is never called a dog—it is always a hound. The emphasis is on the chase and the hounds—not on the fox. No killing takes place now.

Lisa went out to the plantation the day prior to the hunt to get briefed on some of the procedures, to get acquainted with her horse, and to get a preview of the hunting area. She was able to ride freely over the beautiful, hilly Virginia countryside, which turned out to be the pinnacle of her whole experience. The actual hunt/chase did not go well. Everything started fine—ceremonies, announcements, bugles, the works—and then it went downhill. Lisa's horse became ill, and she was unable to complete the hunt. As she relived it and recalled the two days, she realized that the first day and her free-ranging ride through the hills was really the most enjoyable and memorable portion of her experience. Her love affair with horses began to wane after that Virginia adventure.

Family Life

Eating out in Thailand could be an adventure. There was one restaurant in Bangkla that was a favorite of all of us. We called it the Howard Johnson. For the kids, it was about as good as going to McDonald's. It was in the heart of the market, equipped with a few rickety tables downstairs and about the same number up a barely climbable stairway to the upstairs, but the food (Chinese and Thai) was absolutely wonderful. United States health department bureaucrats would have a hissy fit if they saw it. Cooking was exposed for all the world to watch. Heat was by charcoal. Smoke filled the place. Cleaning the cooking and eating utensils was hit or miss. But, oh, how it tasted! And we never got sick. There was one Chinese dish that we always ordered: Goie-See-Me. Lisa and James still talk about it. Another thing health officials would not have approved was dogs hanging around under the tables to take care of the scraps dropped by customers.

Speaking of eating, we had a few social occasions with Thai officials when the food served was best left unnamed. We were once served a delicacy that our hosts insisted we try. It looked nice and harmless, like cranberry sauce, and we tried it. It was coagulated chicken blood.

One of the fun trips we took several times was to an unusual accumulation of house-sized granite boulders piled on top of each other (Khao Hin Sawn). About twenty miles from Bangkla, on the way toward Cambodia, it was a curious phenomenon to be at that location. It was just outside the rice paddy plain, but with no large hills nearby and no other rocks in the area. It was a fun place to go for a picnic. The piled-up boulders left many tunnels, crawl spaces, caves, and rock-climbing opportunities.

Another place we all loved, especially the children, was Wang Tha Krai. It was farther northeast, at the edge of the mountains. A small river came off the plateau as a hundred-foot waterfall, then became a fast-flowing, rock-filled stream that was perfect for tubing. At a turn in the stream, about a mile from the waterfall, an idyllic, picture-postcard swimming hole had been formed. On one side, growing through the rocks, a large tree leaned out over the hole with a rope tied around it about twenty feet above the water. It was perfect for backing way up high, turning loose, swinging out, and dropping or flipping over and diving down. Another place we enjoyed and visited as a family was a national park called Khao Keow (Green Mountain). Near the center of Thailand, it was particularly inviting when it was extra hot. Rising abruptly from the central plain to an elevation of over five thousand feet, the elevation change was enough to cause rainfall even during the hot season. Covered with a thick rain forest and laced with many streams and waterfalls, it was a refreshing place of beauty. At that time, it was mostly untouched jungle with elephants, tigers, and several varieties of deer and also monkeys played in the trees throughout the day.

One especially beautiful place was along a trail leading to a swinging bridge about twenty feet over a very swift, tumbling little river. Lisa, James, and I loved it; Joann hated it. I have a picture of Joann, Lisa, and James on the bridge as I am jumping up and down on it, rocking it dangerously. If our cabin had come with a couch, I would have spent the night on it. One of the attractions of the park was a diamond-in-the-rough golf course. It was a beautiful course in a beautiful setting. There was one feature about it, however, that was not mentioned in the brochure. A golfer needed an attendant to protect the balls from the monkeys that would rush out on to the fairways from the jungle and try to get them.

Our mission owned a camp on the beach at Pataya, on the shore of the Gulf of Siam. It was on a beautiful, curving beach about four miles long. In the 1960s, it was uncluttered and undeveloped. It was our getaway place for meetings, vacations, and family outings. Tourism and rapid commercial development started in the seventies, and by the eighties, it had become an international tourist destination. Much of the beauty and attractiveness was lost, but during our first years, it was the ideal tropical, coral-clustered, coconut palm tree-lined, memory-making place of our dreams. Wide, soft, sandy beaches sloping to the water that remained shallow for almost a hundred yards provided the ideal place for families and children to play. One slight problem at times was the presence of many jellyfish. Their stings could cause painful, slow-healing skin damage.

Of special attraction to our family was a group of coral islands located about nine miles off the coast from our camp. We went at every opportunity. In our early days, we could rent a converted fishing boat for five or ten dollars a day. We would prepare a picnic lunch, head out to the islands, and spend the day snorkeling in and around the islands. I don't have the words to describe the beauty of the coral. Every shade of every color, in every shape imaginable, in the clearest water we had ever seen—the coral just went on and on. And always, tropical fish in a variety of shapes and colors would be swimming and darting in all directions. With our glass-bottomed viewing boxes, we spent many hours just floating and absorbing the wonder of that water world. Isolated coves with perfectly secluded beaches were always available for lunch. It is no wonder that the four of us still recall those island trips with such happiness.

A little dash of danger popped up on one of the trips. It was a reminder that the unexpected can interrupt our tranquility at any time. We were concentrating on the beauty of that underwater world, unaware of a rain squall that developed nearby. We were away from our boat and separated from each other when some rather large waves enveloped us. James was the first to notice that his mother appeared to be having a problem, and he let out a yell. Lisa then noticed her, and both of them headed for Mom. James was closer and reached her first and started pulling her toward the boat. The water was so rough he was having a problem (he was only seven or eight years old) when Lisa reached them. With all three of them working together, they made it to the boat okay. I was the most distant from Joann, but I saw it all happen. I was amazed, both then and many times since, at the intensity with which both children went to help their mother. It was an immediate, spontaneous response, totally oblivious to any danger to themselves. It was just a glimpse of the sacrifice they were willing to make.

On another trip, our return to the mainland turned out to be extra exciting. This time, the squall formed immediately around us. As usual, the water became rather rough, causing the boat to act like a bucking horse. The rougher it became, the more Lisa and James yelled and screamed with delight. Lisa wrapped her arms and legs around the mast, and James wedged himself in the bow of the boat. As the boat pitched and rolled, Lisa would be whipped back and forth. James would disappear when the bow went completely underwater. Both were just delirious with happiness and excitement.

In those and other similar situations where there was the potential for harm, Joann and I stayed in close eye contact with each other. Obviously, we were concerned about their safety. If we saw real danger, we did not hesitate to step in, but we did not want to be overly protective. We wanted them to have the opportunity and freedom to exercise their judgment and independence ... and also accept whatever consequences they brought on themselves. In later years, they have thanked us for allowing them that freedom.

There was one final place we loved: the Cameron Highlands in Malaysia. The Malaysia mission had a cabin in the mountains that we were able to use. It was located at an elevation of over six thousand feet, and it was cool enough for us to use a fireplace (although Eskimos might not think it was needed). After sweating through much of the hot season in Thailand, the coolness of the mountains was a wonderful relief. Portions of the mountains had been cleared and developed as tea plantations, but much of the area was still covered with thick jungle. Monkeys and other jungle game kept up a lively discussion day and night. When it was time to go home, we would go back through the city of Penang for a little duty-free shopping. It sounds like we did more playing than work, but in reality, those fun times were few and far between, not bunched up like in the telling them here.

For a brief time in the late 1960s, I served as an auxiliary United States military chaplain. There was nothing formal about it; I was just asked to be available when needed. There had been a major buildup of military personnel in Southeast Asia due to the war in Vietnam. There were times when there were not enough chaplains to cover all the units scattered throughout Thailand. I spoke to both United States Army and United States Air Force groups. The army units were within driving distance, primarily in east Thailand. The air force bases were more scattered. I spoke at Takli, Udorn, Ubon, and others. I enjoyed going to the bases for the chance to see and visit with them, but what I really enjoyed was the flying time with the air force. I would drive to the air base in Bangkok to meet my plane. They would send a DC-3 (the historic World War II gooney bird) to pick me up and take me to wherever I was speaking and then return me to Bangkok. What a rough life!

Family Life: God Intervenes

There was one more significant event that occurred that we rarely discuss, but one that the family and others want me to relate. It could have been a tragic event, but it did have a happy ending. As noted elsewhere, I went to Bangkok each week to purchase medicine, hospital supplies, and equipment and family needs. Once each month, I would bring back the hospital employee payroll. We had no bank in Bangkla, and few, if any, employees had checking accounts. The payroll was always in cash. In addition, much of my purchasing was done on a cash basis. The combined activities meant there were times when I had substantial sums of money with me. With robberies being common in our area, I was particularly alert and cautious at those times. In spite of attempts to conceal my activity, there were few secrets from the nationals.

When I had a lot of money, I would try to get home to Bangkla before dark. I would stop at the hospital, put the money in the safe, and then go home. One Wednesday night in 1966, I was a little late as I went through my usual routine when I had a bunch of cash. After I put it in the safe, I went by the Willises to pick up Lisa and James. Joann was still at a prayer meeting at another missionary's home.

When we arrived at our house, Lisa and James helped me carry the house purchases upstairs. As we were putting them away, a robber gang of five men ran up the stairs, into the house, and surrounded us. Three of them had guns; two had machetes. The leader of the robbers came up to me, pointed his gun in my face, and demanded money. One of the other men pulled Lisa and James together and stood behind them. The three remaining robbers began rampaging through the house, shouting as they dumped dresser and cabinet drawers, overturned beds and furniture, and started gathering up everything they thought was valuable. In that tense and threatening situation, James and Lisa began to cry. (James was four; Lisa was eight.) The gang leader told me to keep the children quiet or he would kill them. I told them they needed to stay quiet—and we would be all right. Both of them immediately became quiet and still.

The tone of his comments and demands indicated he thought I had a lot of hospital money with me. When I told him I had no money, he became more threatening. After searching the house and me and finding no money (except fifty or sixty baht, about three dollars) he became very angry and agitated. The atmosphere suddenly became very tense. They finally, unexpectedly, decided to leave. Three of them left with all they could carry, two remained, forcing me to the floor, with one holding a gun to my head and the other holding a machete on my neck. The three who left took James with them, telling me that if I made any effort to escape or to notify the police, they would kill him.

When the three left, it became very quiet. Lisa was still standing quietly, but obviously worried. My thoughts and emotions were in a jumble. I was grateful that Lisa and I were still alive—but in turmoil about what was happening to James. After several minutes, I was allowed to get up and go to Lisa. After several more minutes, the remaining two robbers also left. I don't remember what I did next, but I think I had someone go for the police and also notify Joann and others. I took off in the direction they had taken James, praying they had not harmed him and left him on the trail. It was almost half a mile to the jungle where they had fled. Just before reaching the jungle, I saw him coming toward me. To say we had a joyous reunion would be a slight understatement. They had turned him loose shortly after entering the woods. There was just enough visibility for him to see a light at our house, and he headed for it.

There was great rejoicing at our return. Joann was beside herself. The police, national Christians, and missionaries were naturally thrilled that we were all safe. The police were also dumbfounded, amazed that we were still alive. The usual practice was for robbers to kill any witnesses to their robberies. They wanted no one left to testify. The fact that we were all allowed to live convinced several Thai people that our God must be a powerful God to bring about a miracle like that. We thought the same way. The event became well-known and was instrumental in bringing many people to the Lord.

In thinking about it later, I realized that God's gracious providence took control of me during the episode. Otherwise, we would have been killed. My initial reaction—natural tendency—was to resist. It would have been fatal. Lisa remembers taking her cue from me: "If Daddy was calm, then it must be all right." I can't take credit for that calmness. The credit goes to God.

We know God doesn't always intervene like that, but I do believe there are times, especially in areas where the name of God and Jesus are not known, that He intervenes in miraculous ways to affirm His existence and presence. I think that was such a time. Although I had known Him and trusted Him for several years, I felt His presence in that event with such overwhelming power that I am completely sure of His intervention.

CHAPTER 5

Hospital Administration in Thailand

The Foreign Mission Board appointed me as a hospital administrator, but whether as administrator, physician, nurse, preacher, professor, agriculturist, engineer, housewife, or any other profession, we were all appointed primarily as missionaries. We all had a story to tell—good news to share—and that was top priority.

Once in the field, however, work could become the priority, especially for medical missionaries. Life-threatening health problems were constant, day and night. If care was not given, people would die. However, that very care prompted the questions that could lead to spiritual discussions. That discussion, in that setting, required much time, resulting in other patients being neglected. The doctors and nurses were frequently in tension between the two needs. The immediate physical need often became the focus rather than the spiritual discussion. It is beyond the purview of this personal history to explore the ramifications of that dilemma, but it posed a continuing challenge that was never fully resolved. As a mission and as health-care people, we all tried to balance our response, but the combined medical and spiritual needs far exceeded our ability to fully address.

Much of my work as a hospital administrator in Thailand had similarities to American hospitals. Personnel, equipment, and financial issues were common, whatever the location, but to a much greater degree than the medical people, I had more discretionary time. That was made possible by Khun Supachai, the hospital business manager, my assistant and, eventually, my successor as administrator. There are not enough superlatives to describe him. Whether in his personal, professional, or spiritual life, he became my role model and a great example of a Christian. He is still one of my best friends. Orby hired him before the hospital opened and just before I completed language school and moved to Bangkla. He was a young man, a Christian, and a recent graduate of a business school. He quickly acquired the ability to handle routine administrative duties. As a Thai national, with both Thai and Chinese heritage, he was much better at dealing with Thai personnel and cultural issues than I was. I delegated more and more of my duties to him in full confidence that he would do a good job.

Khun Supachai's abilities freed me up to do other things, especially visits to the villages. As I saw the dilemma faced by the doctors in trying to share the gospel in the midst of a full OPD, I was grateful for the opportunities that Supachai made possible for me.

There were some responsibilities I needed to retain, which were mandated by the FMB and the mission. I continued to do those. My governing board was the institution committee of the mission, and I met regularly with them. And there were the ubiquitous mission committees formed to cope with the 1,001 nonissues brought forth for immediate urgent action. There was constant maneuvering among all of us to stay clear of committees.

As would be expected, we had events, personnel issues, and problems that were unique to Bangkla. I noted a couple of those that occurred while the hospital was undergoing construction. Others developed later.

Potable water, or the lack thereof, was a perennial problem. The city water was unreliable, often failing in the dry season, our time of greatest need. Bangkla was located on a good-sized river (it would be considered a huge river in Texas) about twenty-five miles inland from the Gulf of Siam (as the crow flies). The city used the river as its source of water. Most of the time, the filtering system worked. However, in the dry season, the water level in the river dropped and the ocean tidal water, salty and contaminated, backed up to Bangkla. The city filtering system couldn't cope. Storage reservoirs dried up. Water faucets stopped flowing. As a hospital, we had to have water. We tried test wells at varying depths, but they all produced only non-potable salt water. We finally decided we had to build an underground water-storage system to help us through the dry times.

Harlan was interim administrator while I was on my first furlough, and he arranged for the excavation and installation of the system. Into an excavation of more than four hundred cubic meters, multiple interconnected concrete tanks were placed. We installed drainage pipes to capture the hospital roof runoff during the monsoon season to replenish the underground tanks. Adjacent to the underground tanks, we installed a water tower system with eight elevated tanks. Pumps kept the elevated tanks full; gravity kept the faucets supplied. It was a lifesaving solution, especially when Mr. Som's water truck driver kept the underground tanks filled during the dry season.

Intermittent electric service was also a problem. When doctors were operating in the middle of the night and the electricity went off, I heard about it. We had a twenty thousand-watt generator installed with an automatic start system (my past electrical training came in handy). We also installed our own telephone system (my past telephone experience came in handy). Our houses were deliberately not built on the hospital campus since we wanted them closer to other Thai houses, but that did cause a slight delay when a critically ill or wounded patient came in. The phone system was a huge help to the doctors, especially when medical problems could be handled over the phone.

Our maintenance director, Mr. Som Song (not his real name), was special. He had many talents, some of which even related to maintenance. One of his many fascinating non-maintenance talents was in landscaping, specifically in developing topiaries. He created plant sculptures over much of the hospital campus. Hedge sculptures of all kinds of animals lined the driveways and operating suite courtyard area. They were beautiful, but sometimes, a burned-out light bulb or stopped up sink might be unattended for a while.

Every couple of months, a few of us would try to get a day off together. Harlan, John Patten, and I would try to go to Bangsaen to play golf. The course was laid out over the hills near the coast, providing a gorgeous, panoramic view of the Gulf of Siam. Mango trees lined some of the fairways, producing luscious fruit in season. Local girls were the caddies. Tough life.

Orby provided a perfect "Kodak moment" at some unnamed occasion when several of us were down by the riverside in Bangkla. A little Thai dugout canoe was pulled up on the bank, and Orby decided to try it. He got in, pushed off, and began an astonishingly brief demonstration of how not to travel by dugout. The push-off, aided by a few tentative strokes, got him out into the river a few feet, and then he tried to return. Physics intervened. The equilibrium between Orby's weight and the displacement of the dugout became unequal. With only about one inch of freeboard, water started making the dugout more like a shallow bathtub. Somewhere I have a picture of Orby, grinning widely, arms and paddle raised triumphantly, slowly sinking into the river.

Furlough: 1967–68

In the early spring of 1967, excitement began to build around the Goatcher household. We had been in Thailand for more than four years. It was past time for our furlough. The usual pattern was to stay in the field for four years and then spend one year on furlough. Our time had been extended by six months to avoid two doctors being absent from the hospital simultaneously. Our delayed furlough enabled the medical staff to provide complete, continual hospital coverage.

Furlough was not vacation time. We were to do "world mission conferences," deputation speaking in churches, required meetings by the FMB, and perhaps additional training. It was a highly anticipated time for all of us. James, of course, could not remember the United States, grandparents, or other relatives. He had just heard about hamburgers. Lisa did remember a little, and she was excited.

Bangkok is on the opposite side of the world from Little Rock, which was to be our furlough home. We had a choice of going home either across the Pacific or the Atlantic Ocean. With the kids still too young to enjoy Europe, we chose the Pacific. The first stop was Hong Kong and the first pleasant surprise for the kids. The hotel room had air-conditioning, carpet on the floor, windows in the walls, and a bathroom they couldn't believe (all pink).

The next day, Sunday, brought a serendipitous blessing to Joann and me. We attended Tsim Sha Tsui Baptist Church, a large Baptist church in the heart of Hong Kong. (I had been in the church earlier in the year for a meeting.) The sanctuary was packed out—standing-room only. The building (as I remember it) was eight or ten floors, with the open lower floors, minus walls, being the sanctuary, with multiple balconies rising on three sides. The service opened with the choir processing in singing in harmony, in Chinese, a familiar beautiful Christian hymn. We were surrounded by hundreds of Chinese with tears streaming down their faces. We could not understand the words of the service, but there was an overwhelming sense of the presence of the Holy Spirit. After the service, I asked the pastor about it. He explained that hundreds of the people present were mainland Chinese who had just fled China, and that was their first opportunity to be in a public worship service in almost twenty years. They were shedding tears of joy. What a service and what a blessing!

We had an early flight on Japan Air Lines into Honolulu. We were happy to learn they had a no-smoking section. The happiness was brief. The dividing line for smoking extended from the front to the rear of the plane exactly between the middle seats. Smokers and nonsmokers were seated immediately adjacent to each other for the full length of the plane—and the trip. After a few hours, Joann was having respiratory problems. She was in distress by the time we landed. Thankfully, Honolulu provided for some recovery time, and that was all we did.

Arrival in Los Angeles brought joy and a surprise. Joann's parents met us ... with a brace around her mother's neck. She had neglected to tell us that her neck had been broken in a car accident. We were grateful there was no paralysis.

We were back in the United States, in Los Angeles, and driving on the "wrong" side of the road. I was not about to offer to drive. One of the first stops on the way out of town was a Tex-Mex restaurant. What a feast!

The Grand Canyon was all we had hoped it would be with an unexpected adrenaline rush. While Joann and I were gazing in awe at the canyon, we did not notice that Lisa and James had climbed through the barrier and gone out to the drop-off. All of a sudden, they were standing right on the edge looking straight down a two thousand-foot cliff. They were not concerned, just excited. Joann didn't die, but she almost fainted. I calmly told them to come back to the fence. They did. My calmness was faked. I was about to have a fit myself. The kids still laugh about it. We did not think it a laughing matter. I thought then, as I have thought hundreds of times since then, as I have viewed amazing sights of nature (Grand Canyon, the Himalayas, Mount Everest, and Niagara Falls), events (atomic bomb detonation and the Easter presentation in a refugee camp) and experiences (my call to missions and God's presence and deliverance in the robbery), How can I put this in words? How can I capture what I am seeing and experiencing with my limited, finite vocabulary? I want others to see and understand what I have seen, especially my experiences with the Lord. Ultimately, words are inadequate, but I try.

It was time to go home. From the Grand Canyon, we drove to Carlsbad, New Mexico, then Pecos, Texas, and then to Joann's home in Odessa. The drive from Carlsbad to Pecos has to be about the most forgettable drive in the United States It is similar in some ways to Death Valley, California, only larger. Maybe not quite as hot, but almost. A look at a map of West Texas gives an idea of the size and isolation. The eastern (unmarked) edge of the region begins roughly at a north/south line through the town of Kermit, then extends westward well over 150 miles. The southern delineation, also with no clear line, might be Interstates 10 and 20, with Pecos being in the southeast corner. The northern line might be the New Mexico border. The western edge, also without a line, would extend almost to El Paso, with Van Horn being in the southwestern area. United States Highway 385, which we used, bisects the eastern region, roughly paralleling the Pecos River from Carlsbad, New Mexico, to Pecos, Texas.

Texas State Highway 54 bisects the western portion, extending north from Van Horn to the Guadalupe Mountains. The Apache Mountains, Delaware Mountains, Baylor Mountains, and others are inside that bleak area. Trails from the surrounding areas start off into that isolated barrenness and disappear. The whole region is a rough, sun-dried semidesert. It is not a sand desert—just rocks and gravel and low mountains. The mountains are just high enough to draw a little moisture in the "wet" season, so there are mesquite and creosote bushes along the draws, a little cedar, tumbleweeds, and a variety of cacti in the canyons, arroyos, and draws, but it is very desolate, unproductive land. If someone had told Joann and me on that drive that we would be living in Van Horn in about five years, we would have said they were crazy. I was sure no one would ever choose to live in that area, but the Lord works in mysterious ways.

I think He smiles sometimes when he knows how He is going to turn us upside down.

On our way to Little Rock, Norman Roberts caught up with me by phone and invited me to be his administrative assistant at Memorial Hospital in North Little Rock while we were on furlough. It was a helpful, much-appreciated interlude, both for that time as well as for a later time. There are always changes occurring in hospital operations and health-care developments. Being back in Memorial allowed me to get brought up to date with them, along with a few other new technical developments.

Norman did me a huge favor without knowing it. Committee meetings are the bane of administrative people, especially in hospitals. To get out of another committee obligation, Norman asked me to take his place on the Central Arkansas Hospital Council. One of the other members of that council was the commanding officer of the Little Rock Air Force Base hospital. We became acquainted, never realizing how our paths would cross again in a few months on the other side of the world.

Furloughs are busy times, often with irregular schedules. Joann had two special events that were just for her. One was her trip to New York City to take her examination to become a board-certified pediatrician. That sentence is a long way short of conveying what was involved. Lengthy, intense studying was required to review old material and cover new developments in the field of pediatrics while she was overseas. New York City was a little larger than Bangkla. She was an attractive lone woman taking taxis around New York to unfamiliar locations. She did not know if the drivers were going correctly or not. There was some unrest in the city with a couple of disturbances occurring. It was a threatening time of concern for both of us. There was much thanksgiving to the Lord when she returned safely to Little Rock. Later word that she had passed her boards also brought thanksgiving.

The other special event was her attendance at a one-week leprosy (Hansen's) medical seminar at Carville Leprosy Institute in

Carville, Louisiana. It was conducted by Dr. Paul Brand, director of the institute and a world-renowned specialist in Hansen's disease. Dr. Brand had been a medical missionary in India, born to missionary parents who lived in India for many years. He did much of the pioneering research related to the disease, including surgical correction of deformities caused by the disease. His wife, Dr. Margaret Brand, was an ophthalmologist. She was extremely helpful in reviewing treatment options for leprosy patients with eye problems. It was a good educational experience overall for her leprosy work.

Homeschooled children in foreign countries often had no routine medical checkups. It was true with Lisa and James, even though their mother was a doctor and we were related to a hospital. We were surprised when a routine exam of Lisa while on furlough revealed that she was very nearsighted. It was correctable with glasses, but Joann was put out with herself for not discovering it earlier.

Back to Thailand

The one-year furlough was over quickly. We soon found ourselves back home in Bangkla, doing our usual routines. Khun Supachai had done a wonderful job covering for me while I was gone. I resumed my visits to the villages to follow up on leprosy and TB patients. The hospital inpatient load began to level off (at full occupancy), but the surgery load continued to increase. Joann had a little more flexibility with her time than the other doctors and assumed more of the outpatient leprosy patient work. She went to the Cholburi clinic on a regular basis, leading to a temporary increase in the patient load.

The introduction of B663 (Lamprene) began to make an impact. The early resistance to it started to wane when the patients saw that the darkening of the skin disappeared when the drug was discontinued. That occurred when the disease was cured. The number of patients began to decrease in the late sixties and early seventies. The decrease became more rapid with the introduction of Rifampin in the early eighties. It provided a cure for all types of leprosy with no side effects.

A few months after we returned to Thailand, Joann developed a severe case of peritonitis. She became semicomatose—with high fever and increasing respiratory difficulty. It was a virulent infection, resistant to all the antibiotics we had available. It was susceptible to the new drug Ampicillin, but Ampicillin was not yet available in Thailand. I went to the U-Tapao United States Air Force Base at Sattaheep on the coast to see if their hospital had any. In one of those "it just happened" episodes—arranged by the Lord, I believe—it turned out that the commanding officer of the hospital had been the commanding officer of the Little Rock Air Force Base Hospital when he and I were both on the Central Arkansas Hospital Council in Little Rock. It "just happened" that he had one treatment course of Ampicillin from which only one dose had been drawn. The CO gave me the remainder of the Ampicillin, and I headed home flying low. Joann was comatose when I arrived. Harlan started her on the Ampicillin, and within a few hours, she began improving. She had been on the verge of death. There were too many "it just happened" features for it to have been coincidental. We were convinced God's intervention had made it happen.

When she first became conscious, she thought she had gone to heaven because there were little white wings all around the perimeter of the hospital bed. After a bit, she realized it was not angel wings but nursing personnel with white nurses' caps on their heads gathered around her bed and praying for her. They soon realized their prayers had been answered. Praise God!

Family: A Major Little Addition

Shortly after beginning our second term, we had an addition to the family. We obtained a little dachshund puppy that brought joy and outstanding protection. Scooter was small, but he had a deep bark that intimidated any unwanted intruder. He was loving and affectionate to us and our friends, but all others had better beware. We first became aware of his ability to defend us when we watched him in action one day. A huge cobra was climbing over the fence into our yard when Scooter got wind of him. He got after him in full voice and with a full-frontal attack. The fight didn't last long. The snake started searching desperately for a way to get back over the fence. Scooter got an extra bone that night, plus a bunch of loving.

An equally significant act of protection occurred late one night. We had a twenty-foot trimaran boat, powered by a forty-horsepower motor, parked under our house. We accepted it to see how useful it would be in conducting medical clinics along the river upstream from Bangkla. We also used it sometimes for recreation at the beach.

Late one night, a big truck pulled up just outside our fence and parked. The light under our house was out, and it was dark. Joann could not identify anything about the truck. (As was often the case, I was out of town.) Scooter began to growl and bark, rather quietly at first. After a while, subdued noises could be heard from the back of the truck. Scooter's barking became more threatening. When the voices could be heard along the fence, Scooter went to full voice. Joann began to suspect an attempt to steal the boat, but she still could not see any people. Finally, the noises diminished, the truck was started and began to pull away. As it left and passed near a streetlight, she could barely see the emblem of the Thai navy on the side of the truck. She knew they had intended to steal the boat. In the darkness, they could not see Scooter—but they heard his booming, roaring bark and decided not to tackle him. I don't think the Thai navy was behind the attempt; it was probably a few navy personnel who tried to pull it off. Whatever was behind it, we were convinced that Scooter had prevented a theft. We have been attached to dachshunds ever since.

Family: Audience with the King of Thailand

In May 1966, there was excitement all over the Bangkla area. The king and queen of Thailand were coming for a visit to open and dedicate a new school. We were interested but not too excited. Then word came that he wanted to meet some of the foreigners working at the Bangkla Christian Hospital. We became excited. Joann and I were chosen to represent the hospital. It was an honor. Non-Thai people can hardly understand the respect and reverence with which the king and queen are held. They have earned it. They have been a unifying, stabilizing force since their reign began more than sixty years ago. Both are model leaders. For us to be granted the privilege of having an audience with the king and queen was a very high honor.

Audience with king and queen of Thailand

We were to meet them under a little grass pavilion erected near the new school they were visiting. Several of us from the hospital were waiting as a group for them to come by and greet us. I had not been briefed, but I had done a little research to be sure I did not completely mess up the protocol. As he came to us, I introduced the staff and then we began conversing (my High Thai language training came in handy). As with royalty in many countries, the term "Your Majesty" is used in speaking directly to the king. To use the wrong term is to be uncultured. I tried not to goof up. He soon changed to English. He was born in the United States and liked to use English when speaking with foreigners. His English was surprisingly good, as was the queen's (see picture). After a brief conversation with the two of us, he moved on, then the queen came by and spoke briefly to both of us. Joann curtsied and presented her a bouquet of flowers.

Afterward, I was very thoroughly debriefed. His assistants wanted a word-for-word recap of everything the king had said to me and my word-for-word replies to him. They wanted a complete record so they could follow up on any questions he had or promises he had made. I have recalled that occasion frequently, wondering how I will conduct myself when I have an audience with the King of Kings and the Lord of Lords.

Changing Circumstances

Within a year or so after our return to Thailand, there was a gradual shift in my work and responsibilities. Part of it was because Khun Supachai had picked up more of the administrative load. Part of it was the result of a changing emphasis in my village visits. My earlier visits were primarily to villages where leprosy and TB patient medications needed to be replenished. As their numbers decreased due to the efficacy of new medications, my visits to those villages decreased. I continued occasional visits to a few villages for patient follow-up, but our hospital chaplains very ably met that need. They were aided by local pastors. I still did the primary purchasing, payroll, necessary board meetings, and other required responsibilities, but they were diminishing also.

We now had a national Christian administrative staff taking major steps toward a larger role. That was not yet true, however, concerning a national Christian medical staff. We were still lacking in that area. It was not because we were not trying. We had established a scholarship program for Thai Christian medical students who were willing to come to Bangkla after their training was completed, but it took time for the program to become successful. We spent much time in prayer and in contacting prospective Christian doctors.

The motivation for our attempt to find national leaders reflected a basic principle of many missionary organizations: the principle that missionaries should work themselves out of a job when it was possible and practical. There simply was/is no way a limited number of foreign missionaries can evangelize the world. National leadership must emerge and assume most of that responsibility, but in pioneer areas, the national Christian churches/organization rarely had the resources, either personnel or financial, to reach out to new areas. That role then (and now) often falls to missionaries. We were very conscious of that principle in Bangkla.

Just as we were well into our second term, we received an encouraging boost in our national physician staffing. I had been in contact with a young lady physician, Dr. Somporn, a very strong Christian who was active in one of our Baptist churches in Bangkok. She had completed her training and was considering her practice location. I urged her to come join our staff in Bangkla, noting that it would provide her a wonderful opportunity to become a medical missionary to her own people. After she prayed about it, she concurred that the Lord was indeed calling her to serve at Bangkla. We were now fully staffed. She became a very valued member of our medical staff and served faithfully and effectively until she retired. She was an excellent physician, had a loving compassion for the Thai people, and led many to the Lord.

A Growing Sense of Discontent

Everything was going great. We had settled into a familiar routine in our adopted home. We were becoming more comfortable in the Thai language. (We were now thinking and dreaming in Thai.) Khun Supachai was gradually picking up more administrative responsibilities. Better medications were helping to reduce our leprosy patient load. Dr. Somporn was able to cover the OPD, do some of the surgery, and cover OB (we had five bassinets and a continual stream of newborns), providing some much-needed relief for Joann. Although response to the gospel was still slow, a few new churches were being established—and we felt a breakthrough would occur in the not-too-distant future. We were living the missionary dream. So why were we not feeling on top of the world?

The same little sense of unease and discontent that preceded my call to missions several years previously began to rear its ugly head again. It was totally unexpected. I had never experienced acute or chronic depression, so I felt that was not the problem. Although it was unusual and disquieting, I did not mention it to Joann. I thought her response would be total shock. From early childhood, she had been called by God and had been prepared to be just where she was. Now leave it? Incomprehensible! For me, it was so contrary to all my previous thinking about being on the mission field that I simply could not accept it. As career missionaries, we understood—and embraced—the thinking that career missionaries went to the field and stayed unless emergency family matters arose. Our family had no problems. The whole issue was so illogical and contrary to what I thought was the will of God that I was left very disturbed. It couldn't be the will of God, could it? Was Satan trying to deceive me? Who was disturbing me? Joann began to act a little suspicious. "You okay? You feel all right? Maybe we should get some lab work done." I finally had to start talking.

To my surprise, she was not shocked. In fact, she was beginning to have a few questions herself. They were not yet as serious as mine, but they were there nonetheless. She had stayed quiet about it just as I had. The more we discussed it, the more we came to believe it might be the Lord trying to get our attention. The ultimate consequence of our line of thinking, praying, and discussion could lead to only one conclusion: we would leave the field. That was almost unthinkable. Could that really be God's will for us? After much more thinking, praying, and discussion, we concluded that we would not be leaving missions—we just needed to leave Thailand at that time. One reason for leaving temporarily was to allow the Thai professional staff to fully assume their specific leadership roles. The culture of that Asian situation would have made it difficult for the nationals to assume full authority while Joann and I were still on the scene. We were still committed to going wherever the Lord led us, including back to Thailand, but for that immediate time, our thinking meant leaving Thailand, going back to the States, and waiting to see where the Lord would lead next.

Conveying to the mission and to the FMB our decision to leave the field was extremely painful. Our emotions were in turmoil. It was difficult for others to understand our decision. It was still difficult for us also. Later circumstances revealed how the Lord was working through all the pain and questioning, but we could not see it during the storm. We even had a few questions about it while in Van Horn. Years later, after returning to Thailand to the refugee work, we could see God's hand at work much more clearly. During the storm, however, our faith was strongly tested.

Closing out our responsibilities, preparing to leave, and then actually leaving was one of the most painful experiences we ever faced. We felt almost like deserters. It hurt.

CHAPTER 6

New Home, New Ministry

We returned home through Europe. Lisa and James were old enough to appreciate the experience, and we doubted that we would ever have another chance. We left in July 1971, when it was hot. After a brief stopover in Karachi, Pakistan, we began our abrupt reentry to the Western world in Rome. I rented a little Fiat station wagon. The four of us, with all of our moving luggage, utilized every cubic inch of space in that little toy car. And, of course, the steering wheel was on the "wrong" side. In fact, traffic was on the "wrong" side, but we were now in Rome! So, I did what Romans did—I drove like a madman on the "wrong" side of the road. With roundabouts for intersections and every driver primed to play chicken, I felt right at home. I had been inoculated by Bangkok traffic. The kids loved it, but it was white-knuckle time for Joann. For me it was almost as much fun as a demolition derby. What? Me worry? We were in Rome!

We saw the usual sights: the Mamertine Prison, where many believe the apostle Paul was imprisoned, the Colosseum, Saint Peter's, the Sistine Chapel, and others. The contrast between that world and

Thailand was so dramatic that we could not fully absorb it at the time. Later, however, as we read biblical references to those places, the memory of actually seeing them enhanced our comprehension. We saw Rome (and much of Europe) without having a wreck, much to Joann's surprise and relief (mine too).

On to the leaning Tower of Pisa, which was a bunch of fun. Joann decided it was better to let the rest of us have all the fun climbing to the top. Then on to Milan, Florence, the Lake District, and cathedrals too numerous to mention. Wonderful, beautiful houses of worship, but only a few worshipers. Sad.

We were just into the Alps when we came to the Swiss border. The police stopped us with good news and bad news. It was snowing hard on top of the mountain; he strongly urged us to take the tunnel instead of driving over the top. Unfortunately, the kids heard what the policeman said. "Over the top! Over the top!" It was bad news for me. I had to drive up a winding mountain and then drive down the other side in a heavy snowstorm. The scene on top was the greatest the kids could ever hope for. They had rarely seen snow (just a minor snowfall on furlough) and just had to play in it. Small problem. We had been in tropical Thailand for nearly four years and did not have one single piece of winter clothing. No problem. Play in it anyway. And they did. The cold snow finally got to them, and we went on to Zermatt to shop for winter clothing and spend the night. The next morning, we drove to the foot of the Matterhorn and took a cable car up to its final stop. Over a foot of new snow had fallen overnight, and the sky was cloudless. The picture of us near the base, with the iconic peak of the mountain clearly showing in the background, is one our most treasured family pictures. We traveled over much of Switzerland, by car and by train, just gazing in awe at the mountains and waterfalls. After spending years in hot, flat, rice-paddy country, the rugged, snowcapped Alps discharging their summer snowmelt into a thousand waterfalls was a continuous indescribable scene of beauty. We were reluctant to leave it.

The Sound of Music had just made its very popular debut and had already become one of our favorite movies. Salzburg, Austria, where much of it was filmed, was not far out of our way to Germany and the rest of Europe. We just had to see it. It was all we hoped it would be—perhaps even more.

We were on a limited budget and had already exceeded it. Hotels and restaurants were expensive, so we started using pensións and picnics. The markets had wonderful choices of fruits, cheeses, meats, and breads. We actually enjoyed the picnics more than the restaurants. Picnic spots were easily available along the mountain highways. The pensións were similar to American bed-and-breakfast houses, but they were much more interesting to us. We traveled across Europe very economically and probably enjoyed it more than the more expensive way. We were having a great time until we reached Amsterdam. We enjoyed the canals, museums, and art, but the stop was a bummer. The city was full of American college kids "doing their thing." Many of them were drug-induced zombies, sleeping (or passed out) on sidewalks and steps of many buildings. It was a very depressing, discouraging sight. We were getting a little tired of travel by that time and decided to cancel the England portion of the trip and go on home.

New York! Almost home! Well ... not quite. First, we had to get out of New York City. We landed at JFK airport just before five o'clock at night—the worst possible time. No midsize car was available to rent, so I ended up with what seemed like a forty-foot-long Dodge. Herding that monster vehicle, again on the "wrong" side of the street, through heavy New York traffic, looking for the tunnel to get to Manhattan, then searching for our hotel, was white-knuckle time. Checking into the hotel brought a surprise. They would not take cash. Our travelers' checks had been used, and we had no credit cards—they were not used in Thailand. After a little intense bargaining, they took cash (cash apparently had a short life span at the check-in counter). The remainder of our stay in that hotel turned out to be very pleasant. We took in the sights of New York that were free!

Washington, DC was a must-see, and we did the usual tours. We were finally finished with sightseeing and were on our way home. Well … almost. We took the wrong exit on the interstate when leaving the city and ended up in Maryland. After some unintended sightseeing, we finally reached home.

Our families were obviously happy to have us home. Our feelings were still mixed, but whatever our feelings, life was going on. I had to find work. The Hortons had a mobile home on LBJ Lake not far from Austin, Texas, and we moved there until we could get settled permanently. We placed Lisa and James in the Burnet schools, and we all began our adjustment to life in the USA. And it was an adjustment.

My search for a job brought a response from the Presbyterian Hospital System in Albuquerque. They were seeking an administrator for the hospital in Taos, which was a part of their system. I went for an interview and was offered the position. It put me in a dilemma. It was an excellent opportunity. PHS was a very reputable, statewide system, and the hospital was a regional medical center. I wanted the job—I needed the job—but I was just not comfortable with it. I declined.

Not long afterward, there was a meeting in San Antonio of several agencies of the Texas Baptist Convention, including representatives of the Rio Grande River Ministry. Raymond Sanders, director of missions for the Big Bend Baptist Association in West Texas, invited us to attend. With much of the River Ministry's work located in the Big Bend area, he was also directly involved in the River Ministry work and wanted to brief us on it.

We had heard the name, but we were unfamiliar with the work. As we learned of the scope of their existing work and plans for expansion along the river and more deeply into Mexico, especially in the field of rural health care, we became very interested. At the time, volunteer groups from churches north of the border were making a growing number of trips to the river, often with teams of medical people. Those initial, probing visits revealed the great needs along the border and deeper into Mexico. As Raymond described the work, Joann and I were struck by the similarity of that ministry with our work in Thailand. The region was remote, undeveloped, and had few roads, very distant medical facilities, and few schools. Another plus factor in considering expanding the work was the willingness of the Mexican health officials for our people to respond to the needs in the rural areas, but the work was becoming too big to remain haphazard. Someone was needed to coordinate and give direction to the rapidly expanding medical ministry.

The discussion led inevitably to Joann and whether she might be available and interested in providing that needed coordination. Whatever her/our interest, there were a couple of problems. First, the River Ministry did not have the resources to pay Joann a salary (and I didn't have a job), and second, we would need to live in West Texas, either in Alpine or Van Horn. The work was exciting and appealing, and we were interested, but there were obstacles. We told Raymond we would have to pray about it and give much thought to it before we could give him an answer. He accepted that, and we parted.

Back home in our little trailer by the lake, our thoughts were all jumbled up. No work prospects were in sight, and we would soon exhaust our resources, but the possibility of becoming a part of the River Ministry and returning to direct mission involvement was appealing. Finally, late in the year, we received a letter from one of the hospitals I had applied to in the Texas Panhandle, saying they had hired the administrator from Van Horn, Texas, and that I was no longer being considered. We looked at each other and said, "Then Van Horn must need one, right?" With no information about Van Horn or the hospital, I just addressed my letter of inquiry to the Van Horn Hospital in Van Horn, Texas. I soon received a call inviting me to come for an interview. Again, I was offered the job. This time, I accepted it. Joann and I could only thank the Lord and shake our heads at the way He had worked His sovereign will in all the circumstances. Joann considered it miraculous. God was doing His part. Now it was up to us to do our part.

Home to a New Culture

In December 1971, we moved to Van Horn, into a small, well-used, two-bedroom trailer, the only place available at the time. Van Horn was in the middle of nowhere. Literally. The next nearest towns (with medical facilities) were Pecos, ninety miles east, Alpine, one hundred miles south, Carlsbad, New Mexico, 120 miles north, and El Paso, 120 miles west. It was a strip town on Interstate 10 with motels, restaurants, and filling stations. Talc and sulfur mines fueled the economy. It had been a cow town for over a hundred years, but it was primarily desert and a 640-acre section of land could support only four or five head of cattle in the best of times. (We laughed as we recalled our drive through the area five years previously and our amazement that any sane person would choose to live in such a place. I think the Lord might have laughed too.) Ranches under one hundred sections had a hard time making it on cattle alone. Horses were common on the town streets. Many of Joann's patients were cowboys who still had on their spurs. They were just part of everyday wear. Ranching was the prevailing culture, with roundups and branding still done on a regular basis.

Language Study: Spanish

One activity we needed to resume was a repeat of one we had done in Thailand: language study. Many of Joann's patients and many of my employees were Mexicans who only spoke Spanish. It turned out to be confusing. The Latinos and the Thai people had some similarities in appearances, and it was extremely difficult to refrain from speaking Thai to them at times. When we got a blank look, we knew we had goofed up again. We needed the language for our work and to be able to share the gospel. That tendency to mix the languages stayed with us for a long time.

The hospital was a relatively new facility. It was a twenty-five-bed, well-equipped, full-service hospital with a surgery suite, and a labor-and-delivery suite. One wing was equipped to function as an intermediate care facility if needed.

It is a well-known fact in the health-care field that a twenty-five-bed, rural, full-service hospital is about the most un-optimum size hospital one can have. Staffing is required for the full range of services, but the surgery and OB utilization is so small because of the low area population that wasted staff time is frequent. We cross-trained to the fullest extent possible, but that was not a total solution.

Overstaffing was expensive and inefficient, but understaffing could be dangerous to patients. In a remote desert town, it was difficult to find and keep professionally trained people. I was continually looking for RNs, lab techs, and x-ray techs. We quickly cross-trained lab and x-ray people. Good wages and good benefits drew a few people, but there was not much in Van Horn to keep them.

However much my becoming the administrator might have helped or not helped the hospital, Joann's joining the medical staff gave the hospital a big boost. Dr. Bill Lipsey had been the lone physician until we arrived. The medical staff was doubled with Joann's arrival. The hospital patient load soon reflected the addition of Joann to the staff. The hospital became almost self-supporting in less than two years.

Private Practice: A New Experience

Dr. Lipsey invited Joann to join him in his clinic when we moved to Van Horn. It was not long, however, before the combined patient load of the two was beyond the capacity of his clinic. Joann needed to get out on her own. We bought a vacant dental office, had it renovated, and she moved in. It was a great improvement. Her practice continued to grow. In less than two years, the new office became too small also. It was time to move again. We bought a much larger, vacant Western Auto store (adjacent to the dental office, which we retained and rented out to an insurance agency) and remodeled it. It was a major renovation. We built a nice waiting area, an office for Joann, a work area for the receptionist, three-patient exam rooms, one dental room, and a small area for basic lab work. It was just what she needed. Her patient load jumped again. She was extremely busy, drawing patients from a huge area, including many women who had longed for a female physician.

It was not only her growing office practice that kept her busy. As a family physician in a small town, she was always on call. If she was not in her office, patients would call or come to the house. In addition, she rotated being on emergency room call with Dr. Lipsey. With heavy traffic on Interstate 10, plus being the only medical facility in such a large area, the ER could be a busy place. At times, there would even be a line waiting for her after church because, as they frequently said, "I didn't want to bother you at the office." It could get heavy.

One of the unexpected, slightly disturbing surprises that came with her being in her first solo private practice was that many patients felt that because Joann was their friend, they should not be expected to pay for their service. She really disliked dealing with the financial side of the practice. She loved taking care of patients, and she gladly took care of those who could not pay, but the business part of the practice was a burden.

In our early years in Van Horn, since there was no veterinarian in town, she and Bill were also called on to provide animal care at times. Horses, cattle, and pets were the most common, but Joann also saw lion cubs and other circus animals when they became ill while traveling through Van Horn. When those calls came during the night, I usually went with her for obvious reasons.

One call, although a very minor case, became a particularly heartwarming event. At midnight, she received a call from the Holiday Inn that an elderly couple and their dog were in distress. When she entered their room, both of them were overcome with grief. They had discovered that their huge, aging, greyhound, their "only child," had gone blind. It was running into the furniture every time it walked around the room. They wanted Joann to euthanize it and bury it. As Joann observed the dog, it appeared to be walking normally. Some perceptive questioning led her to believe the dog had had only a minor seizure and was now recovering from it. The longer the dog walked around, the more normal it became. It was not blind. Medication would take care of the problem. She gave them enough medicine to last them until they could get home to California. Their grief gave way to rejoicing; their "child" had been brought back from the dead. Joann was an angel, coming at exactly the right time. Just one of many interesting calls. At least it wasn't boring.

One of the "in addition to" tasks that had been assigned to the hospital when it opened was that of operating the ambulance service for the county and the area, under the direction of the administrator. Because of the great distances involved, ambulance attendants frequently needed to do more than just transport patients. That was especially true when the interstate was completed through Van Horn. When drivers could see twenty miles or more straight ahead on a wide-open highway, speeding was common, often accompanied with sleeping. It was not a good combination. The resulting wreck could wreak havoc on the occupants. Knowledge of basic life-support procedures was required. I arranged for an emergency medical technician training course to be taught. Since I was responsible for the program, I needed to understand it also. I became an EMT. Many of the patients brought to our hospital were too seriously injured to be adequately treated with our limited capability, so after stabilization, another 120-mile ambulance ride was required to transport them to El Paso.

Helipad Installation

That time lost in travel began to be a problem. With immediate, excellent medical care becoming a common expectation of the general public, we needed a way to get patients to appropriate facilities more quickly. It just so happened that a United States Army Helicopter Evacuation Unit had been transferred to Fort Bliss, in El Paso, a few months earlier. I went to talk to the commanding officer about the possibility of helicopter transfers. The timing was right. They were implementing a policy of providing emergency patient transport of civilians when it would not be in competition with the private sector. Van Horn, 120 miles to the east of El Paso, was an ideal location.

With a little help from the county road crews and volunteers, we built a first-class helipad adjacent to the hospital. It was paved, with a lighted landing pad, a wind sock, and a paved passageway directly into the hospital. The hospital was near the airport, which had a nondirectional beacon, so the helicopter had a radio navigation aid to guide it to the hospital if the weather was poor.

Initiating the helicopter pad and patient evacuation program did have its lighter moments. Before we installed the pad, the helicopter crew chose an area adjacent to the hospital for temporary use. It was an uncleared area, still covered with a few mesquite and creosote bushes (sometimes called greasewood or chaparral), ocotillo, tumbleweeds, and other scattered desert cacti. Not thick, just spotted around. I had been briefed earlier by the crew on how to guide the chopper in to that particular area. We had a few evacuations that went well, then the pad was finished and no outside help was needed for the landing—or so I thought.

Unknown to me, one of the boys (academically challenged high school students) working at the hospital during the summer on a federal make-work program had been watching me guide the chopper in for a landing. One day, after the pad was complete, as the chopper was coming to pick up a patient, the boy was watching and waiting for me to guide it in as usual. When I did not appear, he thought he should do it. He just got the procedure a little backward.

Before we had the pad, the landing procedure had been well developed. When the chopper was coming in for a landing and was still at a little distance away, I would stand at the landing point. As it neared, I would back off and guide it away from any bushes or plants that would interfere, then guide it down, into the wind, for touchdown. When the boy saw the chopper coming in with no one there to guide it, he took over. He stood on the extreme edge of the pad until the chopper drew near. Then he went toward the center of the pad, rather than away, and motioned the chopper in. The closer the chopper got to touchdown, the closer the boy got to the center of the pad. He did not respond to animated signals to get off the pad. The pilot would lift off a little, and the boy would back away, then the pilot would start down again and the boy would head for the center spot. They were really doing a nice little dance. After a couple of do-si-dos, I called a halt to the show. The chopper crew couldn't stop laughing the entire time they were on the ground. The landing crew at Culberson County Hospital's helipad became the most well-known in West Texas.

That helicopter was a lifesaving instrument on several occasions. One occasion was especially dramatic. A young lady, living on a ranch several miles from Van Horn, had a ruptured ectopic pregnancy. Her husband happened to be home and rushed her in to the hospital with severe bleeding. Joann was her doctor, and she just happened to be in the hospital. While she started IV fluids and blood, I called for the helicopter. It came immediately. Severe bleeding continued. Surgery was required quickly—or she wouldn't survive. Joann rode with her in the helicopter en route to Providence Hospital in El Paso, forcing fluids and blood into Debbie. Her breathing became more labored.

Joann began yelling, "Breathe, Debbie, breathe! Breathe!"

Her vital signs indicated serious deterioration.

Joann asked the pilot to notify the hospital of the situation and request a doctor to meet the helicopter when it landed. The doctor met them, and they rolled Debbie directly to the operating room. Without any surgical prepping, the doctor went to work. He made the incision, reached in, clamped the ruptured artery with his hand, and the bleeding stopped. He turned to Joann and said, "It's okay now. She'll make it."

And she did. The whole episode was a series of timely, lifesaving acts. For many years after that, Debbie sent flowers to Joann on her birthday to mark the occasion, "Because on that day, you gave my life back to me."

About 20 percent of our inpatient load, and many of our ER patients, came from travelers on Interstate 10. We were so far from anywhere that many vehicles stopped for the night or to buy fuel. In our little town, there were fourteen motels and many restaurants. A high percentage of the patients who came in, or were brought in, had some kind of cardiac problem. Some wondered if our altitude of a little over four thousand feet might be part of the cause. After a long drive, it was tempting to take a brisk walk or do a little jogging. That, at least, was a common comment by many who were admitted. Whatever the reason, Joann and Bill obtained a lot of experience with heart disease. We started upgrading by installing a cardiac monitor system between the nurse's station and a room we set up as a mini ICU. That helped, but Joann and Bill were not comfortable taking care of critical heart patients who were not able to handle a fairly high-altitude (over six thousand feet) helicopter evacuation to El Paso.

Then a new, very helpful, service became available. A cardiac specialty group established a practice in Lubbock that was equipped to receive real-time cardiac monitor signals from remote sites. It was continually staffed by cardiologists, enabling Joann, Bill, and other doctors to consult with specialists who were seeing the same ECG signals simultaneously. An added feature of our monitors was the delayed printout capability, meaning that if/when a cardiac event occurred with a patient, the monitor would immediately start printing an ECG signal as of thirty seconds prior to the occurrence.

It was state-of-the-art equipment for a little rural hospital and elicited favorable comments from urban patients who were surprised at the capability of a little desert hospital. Joann was properly modest about her skills, but she brought many patients back from the brink with the new capability. She received gifts from several patients from the East Coast, patients and families expressing gratitude to her for pulling them successfully through a life-threatening episode.

River Ministry: Fruitful Ministry

God had done His part in shaping the framework within which the River Ministry could accomplish its mission under the umbrella of the Baptist General Convention of Texas. The separate pieces needed to complete that framework were already in place or were falling into place. It had started simply. Elmin Howell had been the visionary leader who had seen the potential. He enlisted Dr. John Bagwell, an outstanding Christian physician in Dallas, to give initial direction to coordinating and defining the medical component of the work. It was a vision whose time had come. The entire Rio Grande Valley was open from Brownsville to El Paso, a distance of almost eight hundred miles. Great needs existed over much of the region, especially in the Big Bend region where we lived, not only a ministry to physical and material needs, but also to spiritual needs. Resources were available to meet those needs. Churches and individuals from a wide geographical area were ready to get involved.

The vision was taking on form, but the scope of that form expanded rapidly. Many upstate church members, including medical people, were ready to go, but coordinating and effectively utilizing such a diverse mixture of talent and skill presented a major challenge. Today's communication technology was not yet available. The geographical area to be served was huge, comparable in size to several smaller states combined. Elmin and Dr. Bagwell were both based in Dallas, almost five hundred miles away. Help was needed.

With the scope of the work expanding so quickly, Dr. Bagwell felt he should step aside. He had a large practice and had already reached retirement age. Coordinating many medical teams going into distant, remote mountain villages over a huge area in the midst of a busy Dallas medical practice was just not realistic. Someone else was needed who was closer to the region. That was where Joann came in. The Lord's timing for her to be at that place at that time was right on target. Why should we be amazed?

Because this is a chronicle of our personal journey and not a River Ministry history, I will omit most of the details concerning organizational issues. The River Ministry was well underway before we appeared on the scene, but the timing of our arrival in Van Horn was clearly no accident. The confluence of so many events and circumstances culminating in a very rewarding eight-year ministry could well be seen as luck or accident by nonbelievers. For us, however, it was crystal clear that God was orchestrating His plan and had indeed been orchestrating His plans for the River Ministry work for years, and we were blessed to be a part of it. Subsequent day-to-day decisions and actions on our part were now needed to accomplish God's full intentions for the ministry.

I note above the progression of Joann's practice over a period of time. Her responsibilities with the River Ministry had not been fully delineated when she began practicing with Dr. Bill Lipsey. She needed other options until her own practice had developed. One of those options was with the Texas Department of Health. They had been trying to establish clinics in some of the remote towns in West Texas, but they could not find physicians to staff them. They needed a doctor one day a week. When Joann became available, they were elated. We were glad also; it added a little needed income, but West Texas was a big place. Time lost in travel was a problem. It was 131 miles one way to Presidio on the Rio Grande River. Going and returning in one day left too little time for clinic work ... and the patient load was heavy. It was ninety miles north to Dell City, on the New Mexico border, which was still a long way. She also covered Fort Hancock, Sierra Blanca, Marfa, and Van Horn. (Travel to those distant clinics was one reason we later bought a plane.) With Department of Health clinics, her growing private practice, her gradual assumption of coordinating more medical clinics on the river, and her involvement in our church in Van Horn, she was a very busy lady. (And she was also a wonderful wife, mother, and homemaker in spite of all the outside work.) In a common phrase, she became a victim of her own success.

Purchasing the former Western Auto store to accommodate her growing practice brought a good side benefit. The larger building provided needed space to store River Ministry supplies and medicine. We used the dental room for that rather than installing a dental chair. Making appropriate medicine available to the growing number of clinics was a continuing issue. Many doctors took some of what they needed when they covered a clinic, but it was not possible to provide for all needs. We needed a place to receive, sort, and store medicine to supplement what the doctors took. Our place in Van Horn was ideal for that.

That turned out to be almost too much of a good thing. Some of the volunteers were pharmacists or pharmacy employees who started sending/bringing a variety of medicine. That was soon followed by hospitals and independent pharmacies sending larger amounts of medicine, almost always unsorted. Someone had to spend a lot of time going through it and discarding all unusable drugs. What was left had to be sorted according to dosage strength and expiration dates. It was amazing to see the amount of outdated medicine, as well as controlled drugs, that came in. All of a sudden, we had a potential legal problem that could be serious. We did not have a license or a permit. It was a little sad to realize that many of the useless donations were made to achieve tax benefits for the givers.

With so many groups coming, many accompanied by a medical team, it was inevitable that the doctor would sometimes cancel at the last moment. With the receiving village having been told of a doctor being with the group, the crowd would be even larger than usual. Someone had to fill in. Sometimes the group would be able to find their own replacement doctor, at other times, Joann would try to fill in.

In addition to the medical component, there were many other activities for both adults and children. Bible studies and worship services were always provided. For many, it was the first time they had heard the gospel. The initial response was rather slow, but return trips soon led to cordial relationships and a trust level being established that resulted in growing numbers being led to the Lord. It was not long before churches were being established, first in homes and then in small church buildings.

Another component of the ministry was agricultural development. It was provided in the form of animal husbandry, particularly goats, soil development, and water supply. That was a major enterprise, requiring much equipment and many people. Van Horn was selected as the staging area. A tract of land was acquired adjacent to the airport. A large storage and maintenance building was constructed. The ministry obtained a Caterpillar, a road grader/blader, two well-drilling rigs, a backhoe, front-end loader, multiple diesel engines and pumps, and much other donated farm equipment of all types. There was also a hangar for the two River Ministry aircraft. It was a major depot. There were usually about four volunteer families living in the area giving full-time to agriculture and health-care development.

West Texas and northern Mexico are in the Chihuahuan Desert. There was always a need for water. Upstream from the Presidio area, extending to El Paso, much of the water in the Rio Grande had already been drawn out for crop irrigation. What little remained was not safe to drink. What replacement water the river did receive was primarily from the small streams and rivers flowing into the Rio Grande from Mexico. The people needed a safe and easily available water supply. Most of the villages were located near small, river-bottom farming areas, but with the river flow being so depleted and with rainfall being so scarce, an ample source of good water was a perennial need. In many of those villages, the River Ministry came to the rescue with water wells.

The medical component of the work was so needed and so rewarding that the number of clinics continued to grow. More of the clinics were becoming repeat destinations. The thinking grew that a permanent clinic was needed in several of the locations. That prompted Joann and other volunteer physicians and builders to jointly come up with an appropriate design. Their final design was simple: a medical exam room, a dental room, a registration/waiting room, and a storage room. It would be a prefabricated unit, with all sections designed to fit on a long-bed trailer that could travel on the rugged roads.

Volunteer upstate churches would assume responsibility for fabricating and funding each unit. Every village requesting a building was required to provide a building site and then pour a four-inch-thick reinforced concrete slab exactly the size of the building. When completed, the village assumed the responsibility for maintaining the building and guarding the contents. Having a clinic building and a regular medical or dental clinic became a matter of pride for many villages. All of it led to a cordial, welcoming atmosphere.

As noted earlier, Mexican health officials were kept informed of the type and location of the clinics. Their initial consent grew to encouragement to expand the clinics as they saw the results of the work and the response of the people. Another "it just happened" feature of the medical work was the part played by one of the Mexican health officials. The doctor who was the director of health for the town of Ojinaga, across the river from Presidio, became the medical director for the state of Chihuahua. We had known him in Ojinaga. After a few years in Chihuahua, he was promoted to become the minister of health for the entire country. In that role, he invited Joann to come to his office in Mexico City, show the clinic design plans, and relate how beneficial it had been in remote, difficult-to-access areas along the river.

Joann invited Dr. Lee Baggett, an FMB missionary physician in our mission hospital in Guadalajara, Mexico, to join the meeting. The national minister of health invited other state ministers of health to the meeting. Out of that meeting came a directive from the national minister of health to the ministers of health in every state along the Rio Grande River to give every assistance to all River Ministry medical personnel working along the river. It was also extended to areas where Dr. Baggett worked or planned to work in central and southwest Mexico. It was a miraculous conjoining of elements no one could have arranged but God. It opened a multitude of doors to ministries that are still bearing fruit decades later. What a wonderful God!

Some years later, Lee had formed nine teams, each led by a Mexican national Christian physician, accompanied by medical assistants, pastors, and church leaders, in establishing clinics and preaching points across much of northern Mexico.

In response to that open door to Mexico, Joann was instrumental in getting twenty-two permanent clinics, with buildings, opened in villages along the river before we returned to Thailand. It was not a surprise to anyone but Joann when she was given special recognition by the Texas Baptist Convention and the Rio Grande River Ministry for her accomplishments. Several years later, Elmin Howell gave a significant contribution to Hardin-Simmons University in Abilene, including historical background records of the achievements of the River Ministry. The records, plus a few special items, were placed in a designated room, with an inscription that it was given in honor of Dr. Joann Goatcher for her outstanding contribution to the work and accomplishment of the River Ministry.

Family: Van Horn Years

Moving to Van Horn was a paradigm shift for us. The geographical change was a small part of that shift. We had lived in Arkansas with tall trees, beautiful green mountains, and clear-running streams. We had also lived for several years in Thailand with year-round tropical lushness, clean white-sand beaches, and gorgeous coral islands. Now we were living in an isolated little desert cow town in a very sparsely populated region with yet another language and culture. For Joann, it was not a pleasant change. In fact, it was a return to unpleasant desert conditions she had known in her early years. The dry air was hard on her fragile skin and thin, curly hair and allergies were a major bother, sometimes serious. The dust disturbed her breathing and covered everything in the house. She missed the high humidity of Arkansas and Thailand.

For me, it was a little different. At first, the arid, treeless isolation was so different that I had a problem adjusting. Then it began to change. Zipping through that region on Interstate 10 at eighty miles per hour, which was legal, conveys a very different impression than walking, camping, observing, and listening in the middle of it. The desert has a life of its own, and it has a lot to say to those who will stop and allow the experience to be absorbed. I came to like it.

Van Horn was not a geographically favorable place for Joann to live, but affection for the people came quickly. The western ambiance was very much alive and well and still reflected the high level of ethics and character seen in earlier rural America. The kids could walk the streets at night without fear. Our doors were often left unlocked. We returned home many times to find patients waiting to see Joann, some from across the river. There was never any indication anyone had gone into the house. There was an atmosphere of honesty, trust, and integrity. Handshake deals were common; contracts were for legal requirements. It was not perfect—far from it—but it was a good place. And we were warmly received with open arms.

We had moved into a little two-bedroom house trailer when we first arrived. After a few months, a nice house became available on the edge of town. We loved it. Built with white slump blocks, it was of Spanish design, spacious, with a small courtyard in front and with the backyard transitioning immediately into the desert. There was no fence for over a mile—just wide-open desert leading directly to the mountains. The windows in our bedroom, living room, dining room, and kitchen were filled with panoramic views of the desert and the Beach Mountains. Dominating the view was the six thousand-foot craggy peak of Little El Capitan, which resembled the real El Capitan a little farther north in the Guadalupe Mountains. With Van Horn being a little over four thousand feet, Little El Capitan, about four miles away, provided a picturesque backdrop for the town.

We had a minor hurdle to overcome before we could buy the house; we were broke. We were already paying on a used car. Beyond that, we were off FMB salary, and it would take all we could scrape up to make the minimum down payment. We did it, we went six months without furniture. But that was no problem. In fact, Lisa and James were disappointed when we did get furniture; they had come to love the open living room space where they could romp, jump, and play.

Lisa and James adjusted well to the public schools, especially considering the contrast between a Texas public school and homeschooling in remote Thailand. Their homeschooling in Thailand had provided good academic preparation for Stateside schools—thanks to Joann and the other teachers. The Van Horn schools were not the greatest in the state, but they were good. Both did well academically as well as in band and sports. Lisa graduated as salutatorian with a difficult regimen of science and math. James was in the top 3 percent. Both won various awards, honors, and scholarships to Baylor University. They made us proud.

The wide-open mountainous spaces of West Texas were just begging to be explored. After many months of uncertainty since leaving Thailand, we were ready to go see what we could discover. We had heard of a series of small spring-fed pools near the southern end of the Van Horn Mountains and thought that would be a good place to start. One Saturday in February, we went looking. The pools were easily found, but the immediate setting was not all that impressive. We did not find the primary spring. We came to the upper pool unexpectedly, just appearing in the creek bed. It flowed into each succeeding pool and then continued down the creek bed until it began to disappear into the desert soil. One pool of water, large enough to swim in, was too much to ignore—even in February. Against their parents' wishes, Lisa and James went swimming. It did not take long for reality to set in. They came out shivering and with no dry clothes to change to. We had warned them. For them, it was a long way home. It was not much fun then, but it makes for a good story now.

The much larger area around the spring— within a radius of about ten miles—was more impressive. The southern end of the Van Horn Mountains was just one of three small mountain ranges (Quitman, Eagle, and Van Horn Mountains) that were actually part of the southern terminus of the American portion of the Rocky Mountains. They all ended on an upward-sloping area that culminated in an abrupt vertical drop off of two or three hundred feet. At the base of the rimrock cliff, the land began its steep descent to the Rio Grande River. That is the region where the Rio Grande bisects part of the western mountains of North America, which extend from Canada to the southern border of the United States. It is a beautiful, rugged, barren, mostly uninhabited, and undeveloped region, but it is a good place to camp and experience the desert.

Exploring West Texas

Our initial enthusiasm for exploring was short-circuited by busy schedules: work for Joann and me, school, including band and sports for the kids, and church for all of us. I think both of us, consciously and/or subconsciously, were determined to have family times together and to be present at their school affairs if at all possible. I think we realized their school years would pass quickly, and we knew we would not have a second chance. Joann was particularly aware of that because she would often get emergency medical calls while at school functions. It upset her. She did not want her responsibility as a physician to supersede her role as a mother.

Our church experience in Van Horn was good. We participated in the usual activities: choir (Joann was the church pianist), Sunday School, and youth activities and mission projects (in addition to the River Ministry projects). Busy.

We traveled quite a bit when there was vacation time. If you lived in West Texas and did anything, you traveled. We went too many places to list in detail. I'll mention just a few and then say more about some special trips.

We loved the West and saw many of the national parks: Yellowstone, Grand Tetons, Grand Canyon, Rocky Mountain, Zion, Redwood, Yosemite, Sequoia, Bryce Canyon, King's Canyon, Petrified Forest, Great Sand Dunes, Canyon de Chelly National Monument, and many national forests. With Big Bend National Park nearby and the Guadalupe Mountains National Park in our county, we visited them more frequently.

One of the most dramatic places we visited was one of the least known. One Easter weekend in the seventies, on the Friday and Saturday before Easter Sunday, Lisa, James, and I (Joann had total hospital and community coverage and could not join us) climbed to the top of Mariscal Canyon. It is in the southwest portion of the Big Bend National Park and is difficult to access—it was four-wheel drive only when we went. Even though it is in the park, it receives very little publicity. The canyon is actually where the Big Bend of the Rio Grande River makes the big bend northward. Many of us think it is the most colorful, scenic, and dramatic of the three canyons of the Big Bend (Mariscal, Santa Elena, and Boquillas). Our destination was at the point where the canyon walls extend straight up out of the river to a height of more than 1,100 feet, deeper than the Royal Gorge in Colorado. The canyon is a little over ten miles long, much of it a continuous wall of rock.

We had to park some distance from the abrupt beginning of the canyon and climb from the backside of the mountain to reach the highest overlook. The view was absolutely stunning, especially with the changing colors at dusk and dawn. To the east, downriver, we could see the top of the winding canyon cut through the mountains. To the south, we could view the Sierra del Diablo range (a rugged, sparsely populated region in Mexico), and to the west, we could see the river run relatively straight for several miles—all in full view from our bird's-eye perch. Our climb to the top, with full backpacks, was strenuous. The top was flat with layered levels of bare rock. That would be our bed for the night. Although we did not sleep by the edge, the fact that we were near a 1,100-foot drop-off, with no barrier at the edge of the precipice, made it a little spooky.

Because it was Easter, there was a brilliant full moon. We stayed up late, just looking and listening and drinking in the beauty. There was not a cloud in the sky, the stars were bright, and the river could be seen almost as clearly as in the day. No houses or city lights could be seen, and no manmade noise could be heard, but the sound of silence was almost a physical presence. All our senses were alive to the world around and above us. We had our own little worship service. That experience, with just the three of us, has remained vivid, real, and special to me through the years. All three of us have regretted that Joann was not with us to share it.

One of the serendipities of Joann's Van Horn practice was the open gate it provided for our family to explore the region. Many of the ranchers became her patients and gave her the freedom to ride horses or drive over their ranches. As we took advantage of that offer, my attitude toward the desert began to change. From initial reservation to grudging acceptance to admiration and affinity, I came to love it and enjoyed trekking and camping in the wide variety of terrain. Van Horn was in the high desert. Mountains were on three sides of us. Immediately north of us (Beach), west (Eagle), and south (Van Horn) were mountains—some with peaks over seven thousand feet. Climbing challenges, canyon exploration, and old

Indian camp remains provided unending sources of pleasure. James and I, especially, came to love it. Joann … not so much (most of the times, she was working). Lisa enjoyed the wide-open range for horseback riding, but camping was not her favorite thing.

One of many camping trips James and I enjoyed was with James Thomas and his son Mal. Mal and James were in school and church together. Both also learned to fly at about the same time. The Thomas family became our close friends. The four of us (Mal, James T., James G., and I) camped out one night near the Rio Grande. Unlike the nearby barren desert, there was a thick growth of salt cedar bushes that thrived near the river. As we settled in for the night, all kinds of noises started sounding off. Strange bugs and insects, javelinas (feral pigs), and armadillos scurrying through the bushes looking for cactus or mesquite beans, coyotes yapping back and forth—it was just noisy. Sleep wouldn't come. Sometime after midnight, an obvious camp prowler came too close to be ignored. Peeping out from my sleeping bag, I saw a skunk foraging for food. He homed in on James G.'s sleeping bag, trying to join him in the bag, probably smelling some hidden food. As James became aware of the intrusion, the bag exploded. James saw the skunk, wanted no part of it, erupted out of his bag, and sounded off with a high-decibel yell. I knew what was coming and prepared for the worst. To my great surprise, nothing happened. The skunk scurried away with not a shot fired. By that time, all four of us were wide-awake. Then another surprise: the commotion caused the other noisemakers to shut up. We all went to sleep and were undisturbed the rest of the night.

Not all desert forays were out in the mountains or down by the river. I noted earlier that our house was on the edge of town with the backyard opening directly into the desert. When there was a bright full moon, the clear, high desert and low humidity made it so bright one could almost read a paper. Several times when it was like that, I walked away from the house a few hundred yards, sat down on the edge of an arroyo, and just experienced the night. The windless night made the silence so powerful it could almost be heard. It would be still and quiet, maybe with a slight odor of creosote bushes drifting by. Some of the town lights could barely be seen, and once in a while, a train whistle could be faintly heard in the distance. Inevitably, a coyote would be heard, either yapping or howling (if there was a bright full moon, it was more likely to howl … so the old timers said), but after some time to become attuned to the quietness, faint sounds of desert night life could be heard. There was something about that time and that atmosphere in the desert that was addictive and still lingers with me today.

James, Mal, Steve Woods, and other friends were fortunate in having Otis Hill as their Sunday school teacher and public school teacher. Otis also loved the desert and took the boys on many camping trips to the river as well as into the mountains. In his hikes throughout a wide area, Otis was always on the lookout for Indian arrowheads. He had a collection of hundreds, many of which had been beautifully arranged in artistic mounting frames. He also had a sizable collection of other Indian artifacts. The Van Horn area was crisscrossed with trails and campsites used by the Indians, primarily Apaches, in their travels back and forth into Mexico. Otis found evidence of many of them.

Sometime in the fall of Lisa's junior year in high school, she wanted the two of us to hike up, across, and down the Guadalupe Mountains, located in the northern part of our county. They are the highest, most rugged, and most beautiful mountains in Texas. Guadalupe Peak is the highest at 8,751 feet, but there are eight peaks in the park over 8,000 feet, including the iconic El Capitan peak at 8,058 feet. We planned to camp out one night on top, then complete the hike the next day. Our family had climbed to the top of the first range previously, a three thousand-foot climb up a well-defined switchback trail.

Lisa and I thought if we could do that, then the two of us could handle the entire hike, even though we knew it would be exhausting and challenging. Lisa had picked up maps of the national park trails on an earlier trip, so I let her plan the excursion. The plan for the first day was for us to climb out on top, hike a few more miles through big timber, and pitch camp for the night in the "bowl." The next day, we would hike the remaining miles across the range to McKittrick Canyon, climb down the canyon wall, and return by shuttle to our car at park headquarters. It was a good plan, except for one small detail: the lack of a terrain map. There were several small canyons that cut across our trail. Those climbs and descents had not been included in the total horizontal mileage. We found ourselves struggling.

We made the initial climb and hiked to a campsite with no problem. Inside our tent, we could hear the night sounds as we had heard in the desert, but with our altitude at well over seven thousand feet, the sounds were different. Except for coyotes. We always heard them. Nothing deters them. We heard an elk calling about sundown.

We got underway the next day on schedule and in a good mood, but about noon, we began to glance at each other, knowing we had not covered as many miles as we should have by that time. The trail was actually 24.4 miles long. We thought we had made six or seven miles the previous day. We had not because we had not considered the vertical distance. Knowing we had a long way to go to get to McKittrick Canyon, then make a very difficult two thousand-foot descent down the canyon wall, we had to really step on it. We had to be at the mouth of the canyon by six o'clock to get the last shuttle back to the park headquarters. We finally made it to the top of the canyon in what we thought was good time. Then we saw the canyon. It was scary. We were already tired, our backpacks were heavy, and we had been really pushing it. The canyon was still before us.

It took some searching to find a little eyebrow of a trail that existed only intermittently. There were extensive places with no discernible trail. The canyon wall was almost vertical at times; a slip could easily become a fatal fall. Those who have done mountain climbing know that a descent can be as difficult as a climb—sometimes even more so. With our knees and legs trembling with the continual exertion, we were in a precarious position. About halfway down, Lisa reached total exhaustion and began to cry involuntarily. We had to pause a moment and then resume our descent. As we descended the canyon, the slope became less vertical. We finally reached the bottom—and the creek—with only a few minutes to spare. We took off our boots and luxuriated in the cool creek water. We made the shuttle with one minute to spare. Lisa looks back on the adventure as one of her most treasured memories. It was a wonderful bonding time for both of us.

Van Horn: Another Country

Although our move to Van Horn was a drastic change, it was a good time for us. We had seen too much evidence of God's leading in our relocation to feel anything but affirmation for the move. We felt He had brought us there for a purpose, and we were comfortable in His will. In fact, as the possibility of the move became a reality, I looked forward to living, working, and traveling in West Texas. I had long enjoyed reading about life in the West. The mountains, plains, desert, culture, ranching, and cowboy life—all had been appealing. Now we would be living in the middle of it, and that was good.

We were pleased to find that much of the earlier Western culture still prevailed, even with all the encroachment of the modern world. I mentioned earlier that ranching was the only feasible use of the semiarid land, but that activity required only a few people. (Later, a few mining activities were developed, but they had minimal cultural or economic impact.) The Van Horn economy—and most of the employment—depended on the business generated by the heavy traffic on Interstate 10 and by a few mines in the county, but the minority ranching and cowboy population was still the prevailing culture. Joann and I were glad; we liked it and felt at home with it. It was an exhilarating atmosphere.

To a great extent, that atmosphere existed because many of the descendants of the original pioneers still lived in the area and operated the family ranches. They were chips off the old blocks; the hardworking, honest ranchers with integrity were the pillars of the community. They continued the heritage and legacy of their ancestors. Their names were known and respected far and wide. Two of the most prominent family names in Texas ranching history are Means and Evans, both of whom were among the earliest settlers who came into the Trans-Pecos/Van Horn/Fort Davis area in 1884. Several of their descendants were still active in the Baptist church in Van Horn when we arrived and became our good friends. Many stories could be told of life in those early days on the range. Some of them might even be true. I'll relate only one, a modern one, but it is a carryover from life on the frontier. I know it's true because I tried it.

Paul Evans was one of the descendants of the original Means and Evans family of pioneers. He and his wife, Ms. Wordy, were retired and living in Van Horn when we arrived. He was unwilling to forsake all of his ranch identity when he moved to town so he brought his old, well-used, but still very serviceable chuck wagon with him. It had covered a lot of rugged territory in its days on the range and served thousands of meals to cowboys working roundups or moving herds to other pastures. Paul had cooked many of those meals himself and did not want to stop. Every year he had an open house, pulled out the old chuck wagon, put the Dutch oven in one fire, and used another fire to cook the meat. He would serve anyone who came by. There was always a waiting line. It was ranch food at its best.

His featured dessert was peach cobbler. The recipe has to be seen to be appreciated, so I am including it in its entirety. It was included in the book of recipes published by the Auxiliary of Culberson County Hospital, "How We Cook West of the Pecos" and received much acclaim.

How to Make Peach Cobbler
Paul Evans

Get enough peaches to make as much pie as you will need. You can tell how much you need by the number of people you are going to feed.

Drain juice off the fruit with a pan the size you will need for the right amount of the pie. If you don't have peaches, plums will do. Sometimes I make it out of apricots. They are good too. If you don't have enough of one kind of fruit, mix them all together. That makes it better.

Put a hunk of butter, or more, in the juice.

Put enough flour in the pan to make the right amount of pie crust. You make the pie crust just like you were making biscuits, only you put in more grease.

Make the crust dough stiff enough to roll out real thin. Take a saucer and cut dough into pieces. Put your fruit on the dough and fold over like you are making fried pies. Drop them into juice and butter, warmed enough to melt butter.

Add enough sugar and nutmeg to make it taste good. Cook it until it is the right shade of brown.

Serve it with good thick cow cream. (If you follow directions carefully you will never have a failure.)

I've never tasted better cobbler than Paul's.

Moving to ranching country with horses and cowboys a common, everyday sight piqued Lisa's excitement. "Daddy, I've got to have a horse." That was okay with Joann and me; we just didn't have any money. Our first priority was to get some living room furniture—and then the horse. She had to wait several months. When we were finally able to get one, we had a good place to keep it. Our home was adjacent to ranch land owned by the McVay family, friends from church. About half a mile from our house was an abandoned corral and shed the McVays were not using. We were welcome to use it.

We had the run of much of their seventeen thousand-acre ranch. It had terrain varying from the rugged, mountainous northwest portion to the sloping grazing area that came up to our backyard. Several canyons split the mountains, sometimes with recessed areas that contained some of the best petroglyphs in the Southwest. Darice McVay later established the ranch as a nature preserve and began conducting guided tours over what is now called the Red Rock Ranch.

My time was coming to get a horse and get some firsthand experience. As administrator of the hospital, I met most of the area's residents when they came to visit family and friends who were patients in the hospital. That included many of the ranch owners in the region. Acquaintanceship often became friendship. Friendship often led to an invitation to visit them at their ranch. One of the ranchers, Banky Stocks, went a step further and insisted I come out and help him with a roundup. I jumped at the opportunity. He was one of the old-school cattlemen, a man of integrity and character that reflected the basic solid values that represented the best of what was admired in Western culture. A committed Christian and a deacon in his church, Banky had a compassionate heart that reached out to everyone he met. He was the type of man who lifted others just by his presence.

Banky's ranch had well over eighty sections. That meant it was at least eight miles by ten miles. A section is one square mile, 640 acres. It was not considered one of the larger ranches. It was located about forty miles east of Van Horn, near the little village of Kent. From Kent, it extended northwest into the Apache Mountains, then eastward for several miles toward Pecos, then south to Interstate 10. I-10 was roughly the southern border. That description is very rough; I worked only a couple of pastures in the southern portion of the ranch and never actually rode in the Apache Mountains area. The size of the ranch was overwhelming to me. Pastures ranged in size from a few thousand acres up to ten thousand, depending on the water supply. It was rugged terrain, crisscrossed with deep ravines and sandy draws that were lined with mesquite, tumbleweeds, creosote bushes, and cacti of several varieties.

Four of us volunteers eagerly showed up when Banky called. I was the greenhorn. Banky and his two sons were the anchors of the crew. They were first-class cowboys. We gathered before sunup for our assignments from Banky, and then he led us in prayer before we headed out.

Banky thought it would be a two- or three-day affair, depending on how long it took us to roust the stock out of their hiding places in the thickets, ravines, and cactus patches and get them to the branding pens. The terrain was so rugged, the grazing so sparse, and the pastures so big that the cattle rarely saw cowboys until roundup. That meant they were wild, so when roundup started and we began hazing them out of their hiding places, they spooked easily. That was where cutting horses earned their keep. It was hard work on them. The cattle did not want to be herded. The horses could work only a few hours before they needed a break. In those conditions, a cowboy could easily wear out two, three, or even four horses in the course of a day.

I had ridden enough by that time to have just a faint idea of what had to be done. Learning what to do and how to do it presented me with a steep learning curve. Two of us were assigned a specific pasture of over three thousand acres. The other man and I started from opposite sides at one end of the pasture, working toward each other (when we could see), clearing a swath, then repeating the process, working toward the other end of the pasture. That is a totally inadequate description of the task. We wanted only the unbranded stock, which usually meant calves, but when we started separating the calves from the mama cows, things got interesting in a hurry. Keeping them separated and keeping them headed for the branding pens, while rousting out others that might be found, was not child's play.

Brambles, cat claw, spiny cactus, and ocotillo were all over the place. They all had spurs that would go through jeans like they were paper and tear skin all to pieces. Thick leather chaps were an absolute necessity, but even chaps were no protection against lechuguilla, a half-moon-shaped cactus growing in isolated thick patches close to the ground. It had a hooked, inwardly growing spine that enjoyed digging deeply into anything that came near, especially men and horses. Since the hook pointed backward, it was impossible to pull out once it was lodged in flesh. Joann spent a lot of time cutting spines out of the legs of cowboys and cowgirls who had gone too close. It was probably my imagination, but it seemed to me the cows and calves knew it was safer to stop inside a patch of lechuguilla than outside. Horses learned quickly to avoid the plant, so when we found calves in a patch, it was bad news. Of all places, that was not the place to be unseated by a horse.

We all tried to be back at the main corral for lunch. Tradition called for the rancher to provide barbecued cabrito (goat) to the roundup hands for lunch. Banky did not disappoint. He had an all-you-could-eat banquet spread out that was the absolute best.

We had completed most of the roundup by noon the second day and were ready to start branding. (It took more than one roundup to cover the whole ranch.) Since I couldn't rope, vaccinate, or handle the branding iron, the flanking fell to me. It required the least skill, but for the inexperienced, it was the hardest work. By the end of the day, I was ready to collapse. Flanking was totally exhausting.

Flanking Calves for Branding

There were too many variations of the flanking process for me to mention them all. I'll tell only about what and how I did it when I helped with the branding.

Speed and timing were the secrets of flanking. Each one needed to do his part quickly and correctly to keep the action going and complete it as quickly as possible. Banky's two sons were expert ropers, and their skill was what made the process go so well. After a briefing and demonstration of how it should be done, they started bringing roped calves up to me on a regular, rotating, timely basis.

They were kind to me early on by bringing me the smaller calves until I caught on to the technique. The calf might be roped around the neck or by the hind feet. Or by a "headin' and heelin' team," which was one roping the head and the other the heels. Since I was flanking by myself, Jody and Russell usually brought it to me as a team. They would pull a calf to where I was positioned, and I would place one hand over the hindquarters, grasp the flank, or fleshy, portion between the rear leg and the belly of the calf. With my other hand, I took hold of the rope near the calf's head.

Now came the tricky part. If it was a big calf (some of them weighed over two hundred pounds before they were found and brought in), I had to be quick to use the position of the squirming calf to lift it with both hands, fold it on the ground, grab the front feet and hind feet, and pull them quickly and firmly toward me. (That was the time for the flanker to be quick with the piggin' string, but I never really mastered it). The calf had to be held in that fixed position while the other guys did their jobs. That was a critical part of the whole process. The guys doing the branding, vaccinating, and cutting needed a still calf to do their jobs quickly and correctly. If I lost my grip or the piggin' string came loose (it happened once), the situation became dangerous. A kicking hind leg could break an arm, crack a skull, or bust a jaw. With dust flying, the calf bawling, blood splattering, and the smell of burned hair and flesh filling the air, it was not a tea party. I was glad we didn't have a whole herd of two hundred-pounders. Completing the branding brought blessed relief. I was wiped out. It was a fun, exhausting, exciting time for me, but I didn't change careers.

A Tragic Interruption of a Good Life

On March 7, 1973, I received a late-night call from my sister. Her husband, Don Lewis, had been killed by a drunk hit-and-run driver. They had three children—Evan, Todd, and Laurie—ages seven, five, and three. He was an engineer and a leader of airport development in Mississippi for the Federal Aviation Administration. He was also an excellent singer and an outstanding Christian. His death was a great loss. I went to Jackson, Mississippi, to be with her.

My time in Jackson with Lavelle, helping her deal with the post-funeral issues, was a time of disillusionment and anger, primarily with lawyers and the legal system. The damaged car was soon found, along with the driver. The evidence was indisputable. The driver had no defense. He was a young man, the son of a wealthy insurance company executive. A lawyer friend of Don and Lavelle, a fellow member of their church, volunteered to handle the case for Lavelle. In the course of a conversation, I learned that he was going to take 30 percent of whatever fee was collected. With it being an open-and-shut case and the police doing all the background work needed, there would be no investigation costs and no time spent in trial preparation. Since the other family wanted to settle out of court, there would be no litigation costs. The lawyer would spend very little time with the case. Under the circumstances, I felt the 30 percent fee was excessive. A mother with three very young children was left with no husband, no father for the children, and no provider for the family. His fee meant he would be taking almost twice as much as each one of the remaining family members. That settlement was what the family had to live on for a long time. Only a small amount of time would bring the lawyer many thousands of dollars.

Lavelle was reluctant to talk to the lawyer since he had been a friend—so I talked to him. He was irritated that I would bring up the subject. He said it was unprofessional for him to discuss his fee amount with a client, and if I did not like it, I could talk with the Jackson Bar Association. I did. I was rebuked and rebuffed. They also said it was unprofessional and unethical of me to even bring up the issue. What was being charged was standard practice and was not negotiable. I went to see the lawyer once more. It was a very brief visit. I told him his fee, his conduct, and his attitude were unprofessional, unethical, and unchristian. It was a sad and discouraging time.

There is a follow-up note to what developed later. A few years after Don was killed, Lavelle was living in Little Rock with the children, attending Lakeshore Drive Baptist Church. There she met Bob Rollins, another member of the church and a fine Christian man. In the course of time, they married and had a child of their own, Bobby Joe.

Bob was a commercial pilot, with all instructor ratings, including instrument. He was often a great help to me in providing the required proficiency training I needed to maintain currency.

Bob, Lavelle, and Evan (Lavelle's oldest son) came to visit us in Thailand. Scuba diving (Evan only), riding elephants, and seeing the sights and culture of central Thailand was a happy, memorable time for all of us.

Taking Wing: A Surprising Return to Flying

Our move to Van Horn resulted in both of us needing to travel much more than we had ever anticipated. For me, hospital business took me to El Paso every month. A much greater time requirement came when my hospital meetings occurred in central Texas, from Dallas/Fort Worth, Austin, San Antonio, and Houston, requiring a full day's drive just to get to the meeting.

Joann's trips were usually not as far, but they were more frequent. In addition to her clinics in widely separated towns in West Texas, she had been appointed medical director for Hudspeth County, director of maternal and child health for Culberson and Hudspeth counties (an area larger than many smaller states), and medical director for the Rio Grande River Ministry. That latter position alone called for her to provide coordination for medical clinics along a seven hundred-mile section of the Rio Grande River. One last task was to speak to upstate churches that had—or were planning to have—volunteer teams on the river. She needed to be back in Van Horn every day to see patients or make rounds at the hospital. With the distances involved, driving a car resulted in hundreds, if not thousands, of hours being lost just getting from point A to point B. Something had to change. Flying was the answer.

The growth of our travel needs far outstripped the growth of our financial resources. Joann's practice income was growing, and we were grateful, but we had started with zero on our balance sheet—and airplanes didn't come cheap. Joann, bless her little blonde, curly-haired head and heart, was the one who finally said we needed to get a plane. Okay, but how? The president of the Van Horn State Bank came to the rescue and said he would be glad to finance it. Our tax guy said our type of flying would qualify us to claim 80 percent of the expenses as business use. Great! But it took time for us to be able to do it. We still had a lot of driving to do. Finally, in December 1977, we bought our plane. We found what we needed in Austin: a new Cessna 182 Skylane II, fully equipped for instrument flying.

Joann and Earl with the Cessna 182

The 182 was a powerful, high-wing workhorse of a plane that would carry just about anything we could put in the cabin. It was what we needed: rugged enough for short, rough, remote dirt landing strips, but fast enough to move us rapidly across longer distances.

While we waited to buy our own plane, I used planes belonging to friends that were also based at the airport in Van Horn. In the meantime, Joann was bitten by the flying bug. With frequent trips to many widely scattered clinics, she felt she needed to learn to fly. She took flying lessons from Lois Ziler (and so did James), a flight instructor living in Sierra Blanca who had been one of the women transport pilots during World War II. Joann's primary trainer was the Cessna 150 and 152, but she was also checked out in the Cessna 172 and then our 182. She was on her way! But it was not all just fun flying and watching the mountains go by. West Texas is known for its high wind can play havoc with a small airplane taking off or landing in a crosswind, which often happened in those small villages where the terrain might not coincide with the prevailing wind direction. She can tell some tall tales about a few of her takeoffs and landings that left her a little shaky.

James and his friends Mal Thomas and Steve Woods also decided to learn to fly. Mal became an agricultural spray plane operator. Steve went to TSTI in Waco to become an aircraft (airframe and power plant) mechanic. To the great sorrow and distress of both families, and especially to James, both Mal and Steve were later killed in plane accidents. Steve was working on a large plane when a jack failed. The plane fell on him and killed him. Mal and his wife were killed when they crashed in a thunderstorm. It was extra difficult for James because Joann and I were back in Thailand, and he had no one to help him through those dark days. It was difficult for us to not be there when we were needed.

Lisa had no interest in flying. When I would take her back to Baylor or pick her up to bring her home for the holidays, she would get in the back of the plane and sleep the trip away.

With all the flying activity we were involved in, it didn't escape me for a second what was going on behind the scenes. When the Lord called me to missions, I had gladly accepted the lack of further involvement in flying or in aviation, but God was just waiting to give me a surprise gift. Instead of my former unfocused drifting, with a vague hope to fly commercially someday, He had given me a mission, a calling, and a sense of fulfillment that far surpassed what any other vocation could ever provide. I had rejoiced in the decision to follow His leading. Now He had thrown the door wide open to owning my own plane and using it to greatly expand our area of ministry for His glory. I could almost hear the Lord chuckling.

Van Horn was blessed/cursed with sunshine almost all the time, which was great if you wanted to fly only around Van Horn under visual flight regulations (VFR). Much of my flying, however, was in central Texas where clouds had a habit of appearing just where I wanted to go. Without an instrument rating, flying in clouds was a big no-no. I ended up grounded in places I did not want to be. Our plane was ready and capable of IFR flying, but I was not. It was time for me to get my instrument rating.

My instrument rating multiplied the usefulness of the plane many times over. Being in the Air Traffic Control (ATC) system enabled me to complete most flights unhindered—whatever the weather. Van Horn was in a very low air traffic area so it was easy to file a flight plan, merge with other traffic, and then fly directly into Dallas, San Antonio, Houston, or wherever. What a relief—and what a time saver.

As I began writing this section on our flying, I pulled out our logbooks and reviewed many of the flights we made. I was surprised, and even shocked at times, as I was reminded of how malleable our memory can be. Times, events, and places that we remembered as being one way often turned out to be wrong. Or we made a major flight or trip and forgot it completely. Disconcerting! (It couldn't possibly be age causing it, could it?)

Of the multitude of flights we made in the few years we had the plane, I will relate only a few. My first story is not about one flight but a composite of several flights, all of them over the same general area in West Texas. It's the area I discussed in describing our trip from Carlsbad, New Mexico, to Pecos, Texas, on our way home for our first furlough. That area included the desolate area east of Van Horn to Pecos and then up into the panhandle of Texas where many churches were located that provided teams for River Ministry projects. We had many occasions to fly up to the panhandle for a speaking engagement and then fly back home at night. Many of those flights over that region, especially on moonless nights, were like flying over the ocean at night or in clouds. It was desolate and unpopulated. There simply were no lights for reference points. Conditions were VFR (no clouds), but it was more like an IFR flight. I had already started my instrument flight training and had some "blind" flying experience, so flying that route was the best possible training for my flight test. Under those conditions, I learned quickly to keep my attention focused on the flight instruments— not outside. I had already experienced a few times of disorientation during instrument training when I was wearing the hood and was prepared for it.

Those initial flights in blind conditions brought home the reality of an analogy I had already heard. Our bodies have built-in systems that provide us with a sense of spatial orientation (up, down, turning). That sense is closely related to visual perception. When we have a visual reference point, we can tell if we are upright or not. With no visual reference, we lose that sense. A constant turn, climb, or descent can feel like straight and level flight. If we cannot see outside while flying a plane, we can't tell—just by how we feel— if we are properly positioned. If we are not, a tragedy can occur quickly. Aircraft instruments provide a reliable reference to enable us to maintain spatial orientation and fly safely. The critical issue is whether we are willing to trust the instruments when their reading conveys a signal that is contrary to how we feel.

In blind flight, we absolutely must trust the instruments. Our feelings are untrustworthy. The analogy is clear. In life, our feelings can betray us, especially in difficult times or in temptations. Our only reliable point of reference is God. We can read His Word, we can talk to Him in prayer, and He will guide us. He is our pole star of reference, always right, always reliable.

Circumstances changed the dynamics of that flight from the panhandle to Van Horn. We have flown that route in winter when it was covered with snow and with a brilliant full moon shining from a cloudless sky. At those times, there were reference points everywhere. Every mountain, hill, and canyon could be seen in clear detail. The Guadalupe Mountains, well over one hundred miles distant, stood out in sharp contrast. A night flight like that, in cold, very still air, provides a totally smooth ride in a setting beyond describing. It can become addictive. When it was beautiful like that, I often turned on the autopilot—and Joann and I just gazed in wonder and adoration at God's creation. Flying Joann to many clinics along the river and into Mexico, sometimes landing on cow pasture landing strips, was always interesting. On one trip to Presidio, the Rio Grande was flooding. Several Mexican officials were in a meeting in Presidio with their American counterparts and were unable to return home. At their request, we ferried them back across the border to Ojinaga. There was mutual awareness of what we were doing, so there was no bureaucratic red tape about passports or visas. The shuttle required several trips.

One time on a warm, late-summer day, I took Lisa for a local flight in Van Horn and climbed to an altitude of over twelve thousand feet. From there, we could clearly see snowcapped Sierra Blanca Mountain in New Mexico (twelve thousand feet high), which was well over one hundred miles north of us. In the high, haze-free, dry air, even details of the mountain could be seen.

For Christmas one year, I offered to take the employees for a ride in our plane. I gave them two choices: a flight around Guadalupe Peak and then a flight along the two-thousand-foot rimrock cliff around El Capitan in the northern part of our county, near the New Mexico border or a flight to take a close look at Capote Falls, the highest waterfall in Texas at 175 feet. It was on fenced, private property and could be seen only from the air. Paradoxically, it was located in the driest part of Texas, near the base of Capote Peak, but the creek ran all year. It is in the southern part of Presidio County, just a few miles before the creek runs into the Rio Grande. It is well over one hundred miles from Van Horn. Several employees took me up on the offer, and it was well into January before I had accommodated all of them.

I was flying to Marfa one day when cumulus clouds about five or six miles in diameter began to form in front of me at my altitude. The formation had not yet coalesced, so I flew through a wide gap just to see what I could see. It was too early in development to have severe turbulence. I immediately entered a cloud city with gigantic corridors and towering columns in all directions, with shadings from dark to sparkling translucent. Side corridors of cumulus clouds opened in all directions, like high-walled streets, allowing/calling me to bank sharply to explore beyond the next column. From one wing over (wings vertical) with an almost ninety-degree bank to an immediate opposite turn, often seeing the plane's shadow on a column right at my wingtip, it was an indescribably beautiful, intense, but brief view of another world.

For the pilots who read this, I had talked to all unicom and tower frequencies, I had talked to the FBOs in Marfa and Van Horn, and I was in contact with Albuquerque Center. There was no other traffic in the area. My maneuvering was within VFR altitude parameters, and I did not enter a cloud. There was no turbulence.

On another trip I was planning to leave Waco to return to Van Horn, but a thin layer of thick cloud cover (about a thousand feet thick) was hovering over much of central Texas. Once on top, it was severe clear all the way to Van Horn. On impulse, I requested a special VFR clearance on top, then to proceed VFR on to Van Horn. To my delight, and a little surprise, the clearance was granted.

I took off and entered the cloud cover about a thousand feet above the ground and was in it for about two minutes. I broke out suddenly on top into a bright, sun-filled, clear, blue sky.

That little event quickly became another illustration I have often used. It resonates because "breaking out on top" seems to be an apt metaphor for much of life. All of us go through some dark times, some perhaps with little hope of relief, but for many, especially those with a deep and abiding trust in the Lord, there comes a time when God seems to break through the darkness and surround us with His grace and light. The sullen dark clouds give way to the brightness of His presence and reassurance comes that, with His help, we can come out on top. We can see clearly now that the clouds are behind us.

One of our early acquaintances had a classy jewelry store in Van Horn. They became good friends and were Joann's greatest boosters in encouraging her to move her place of practice and expand her clinic capability. When we were considering buying the Western Auto store, they were the ones who most strongly supported Joann in going for it. They said they would guarantee that Joann's practice would double in two months if she would move. We said, "If she doubles her practice in two months, we will fly you to El Paso and pay for a steak dinner. If she does not double it, you will buy it." They took us up. We flew them to El Paso, had a great dinner, and we paid for it.

In discussing River Ministry work earlier, I mentioned a trip Joann and I made to Mexico City at the invitation of the Mexican minister of health. The trip was very significant and productive for the River Ministry in many ways, but the flight was interesting also. We were not in our plane. We were in a Cessna 337, a twin-engine, push-pull (one engine in front, one in back), high-wing airplane operated by the River Ministry. It was based in Van Horn, and so was the pilot. I flew as copilot on the trip, and Joann was the flight commander from the back. Our best flight path would be from Van Horn to Brownsville, Texas, then to Tampico, Mexico, then to

Mexico City. We flew VFR to Brownsville, went through the usual customs and passport procedures, and filed IFR with Mexico ATC for the remainder of the trip. The flight was uneventful, although we were directed to climb to and maintain fourteen thousand feet as we approached Mexico City in order to maintain radar contact as we crossed the mountains around Mexico City.

The return flight was more interesting. The direction of our return flight via Tampico called for us to climb and maintain thirteen thousand feet to maintain radar contact as we crossed the mountains. Shortly after we reached thirteen thousand feet, we started accumulating ice on the wings and windshield. It wasn't long before we had trouble maintaining our assigned altitude. The pilot informed ATC of our difficulty and requested a lower altitude. Permission was denied.

After a few minutes, the pilot called again with the same request. Denied again. By that time, we were beginning to lose altitude because of the ice, but we were also getting glimpses of the mountains below through breaks in the clouds. The pilot started calling ATC while toggling the radio switch, informing them that we were unable to maintain altitude and were descending to eleven thousand feet. By the time we descended to eleven thousand feet, we were in the clear. The ice was melting, and we continued the flight without a problem.

On our last instrument flight, Joann and I were visiting her relatives in San Angelo just before returning to Thailand after our first furlough. We departed for the Grand Prairie airport (near our house in Arlington) at about ten o'clock at night. There was solid cloud cover, so I filed an IFR flight plan. We entered thick clouds soon after takeoff and remained in them until we descended for landing. The clouds were so thick that I had to turn off the strobe lights because of the psychedelic effect they were creating in the cockpit. It was so late that the Grand Prairie tower was closed, so Fort Worth Center handed me off to Dallas Approach Control for vectors to runway 36 (north) for landing at Grand Prairie. We broke out of the clouds at about one thousand feet above the ground to a spectacular sight. Beneath the cloud cover, the sky was extremely clear. The entire horizon was filled with the lights of the Dallas/Fort Worth Metroplex—from the extreme west side of Fort Worth to the extreme east side of Dallas—in the clearest detail. What a beautiful, spectacular, final instrument flight for us to see together. We sold the plane a couple of weeks later.

Family Travel: Going Places, Seeing Things

Even with the extensive travel related to our work, we enjoyed family trips in the summertime. Big Bend National Park and Guadalupe Mountains National Park were both nearby, and we visited them often. The Mountain Time Zone line was just west of the Van Horn city limits and was a constant reminder that the Rocky Mountains, with all their national parks, were not far away. We made the most of the opportunity. At some point in our time in Van Horn, we visited most of the national parks in the western United States, including some of the smaller parks, monuments, forests, and recreation areas—plus other national parks in Canada. We enjoyed traveling. I won't try to provide details of all of those excursions, but there is one vacation that merits further mention.

When Lisa and James graduated from high school, we promised we would let each one choose the family vacation place for that year. In 1976, when Lisa graduated, she chose a horseback camping/pack trip of almost a week into the central Canadian Rockies. Joann cringed, but she grinned and said, "Let's do it!" We would begin the excursion from Banff National Park with a guide, cook, wrangler, the four of us, and nine horses. What an entourage! But first, we had to get there.

We flew to Sacramento, California, rented a car, and headed north through redwood country. The Crater Lake area in Oregon was cloudy, so we just circled it, returned to I-5, and headed for

Seattle. From some of the higher elevations on the highway, we could see Mount Rainier in the distance. So, why not? We were drawn to that massive 14,410-foot landmark for all of western Washington. We parked at a trailhead at 5,600 feet and headed up the mountain. The twisting, climbing trail paralleled a rolling snowmelt stream coming down from the higher elevations. As usual, Lisa and James climbed faster than Joann and me. They were soon out of sight. I became a little concerned and then a little irritated. Both of them had a tendency to take excessive risks. Would the knuckleheads stop before they got in trouble?

We finally came up to them and almost fainted. They were on the top of the arched, curving roof of an ice cave (with a hole behind where they were standing, it could have been called a bridge), well over twenty feet above the floor of the cave. The rear of the cave faded into darkness in the background. The stream was coming out of the mouth of the cave, the runoff from a glacier higher up the mountain. What scared us was that they were standing on the very peak of the arch, which was less than two inches thick at that point. There was much continual dripping from the roof of the cave, indicating rapid melting. The entire roof was ready to collapse. We could almost see it happening.

My first impulse was to yell for them to get off now, but fearing what rapid movement might cause, I quietly told them to carefully climb down immediately. They must have sensed something in my voice because they obeyed without hesitation. Our return trip down the mountain was done together and quietly. It still scares me when I think about it.

That was enough excitement for one day—and for many days actually. We headed to Vancouver, Canada, for a couple of relaxing days, including a full day on the ferry and viewing the beautiful city of Victoria. The Victoria Gardens were spectacular.

But it was time to get to the main action. We took off on the spectacularly beautiful drive through the Canadian Rockies on the transcontinental Canada Highway 1 to Banff. Our tour leaders were ready for us, and after a day of orientation and preparation, we took off.

We covered a lot of territory—but not in great comfort. Brief horseback rides in Texas, and very few of those by Joann, did not really prepare us for several days riding in the mountains. And wouldn't you know it? Joann got the most cantankerous horse of the bunch. It did not want to get its feet wet. We crossed multitudes of snowmelt streams. Joann's horse would get to the edge of the stream and stop. She would urge it on. The horse would shuffle around the edge, but it would not get in the water. Finally, she would kick it. Then, instead of walking through the stream, the horse would try to jump the whole creek in one mighty jump. Everyone enjoyed the show but Joann. Don't ask me why one of us did not change horses with her.

Sleeping in little tents at the snow line was not all that great, but we had done it before—and we would do it again later, many times, in India (sans the snow). It was what was just outside the tents that gave concern. We were in a national park in the brief Canadian summer. Wildlife was active. Even though snow was still on the ground, the berries were ripening and the bears were making the most of the opportunity before they went into hibernation. The odors from our cooking tent and the leftover food were also great attractions for the bears. The sounds of their activity in our camping area tended to discourage nighttime visits to do the necessaries. The kids loved it, I tolerated it, and Joann suffered through it. By the way, it was misting cold rain the whole time we were there!

To paraphrase one of my favorite Bible phrases: "It came to pass ... it didn't come to stay." It was time to head back to Banff. I had reserved a cozy hotel room in Banff with a fireplace. As we relaxed in wonderful warm surroundings, Joann informed us that that was her idea of camping henceforth and forever more. We spent a little time in Calgary, drove down to Great Falls, Montana, turned in the car, and flew home.

CHAPTER 7

1979: A Return to Thailand and Refugee Chaos

To all outward appearances, our lives in late 1979 could not have been going any better. The hospital was stable (adequate professional staffing was always an issue), our church life was good, the River Ministry was growing and leading people to the Lord and establishing churches, Lisa was about to graduate from Baylor, and James was about to graduate from high school and be on his way to Baylor. Joann's practice was booming.

But a vague, hard-to-describe feeling of unrest, or sense of discontent, began to nibble just on the edge of awareness. I had had a similar feeling several years earlier while we were still in Thailand, but that experience did not really answer my present question. It was not a desire to look for another hospital or move to another location (I had already declined that opportunity). It was more a sense of not really being fulfilled, and that was a little surprising. Our work in Van Horn had been rewarding and productive. We felt we had provided a positive influence in the community. Then why the hazy feeling of restlessness?

That feeling was shoved aside quickly by a new development in late summer. To her total shock and surprise, Joann was notified that she was being sued for medical malpractice. Several months previously, a female patient had come to the ER with a simple fracture of the small bones in her lower leg. After a thorough cleanup and casting, she gave the usual instructions for such an injury, with the admonition to return the next day for a re-exam and possible replacement of the cast if needed. She never returned. That was the only time she saw the patient.

The official letter ordering her to reply to the summons was her first awareness of any problem. The next few months were traumatic for Joann as she prepared to go to trial in early 1980. Exposure to the court system and litigation proceedings were emotionally disturbing. Totally false and degrading allegations of careless, inappropriate, and unprofessional conduct were made against Joann by the plaintiff's attorney.

James Horton, Joann's attorney brother, was present and kept reassuring her that such conduct was normal in litigation and not to worry about it, but the accusations against Joann were so contrary to the loving and professional care and concern she gave to every patient that it devastated her. It hurt her deeply, partly because all the allegations were made in open court before the whole world and were totally false.

It helped some when her defense attorney presented evidence that refuted the allegations. All the medical records documented the high quality and appropriateness of care given and the total untruths of the allegations. Partial vindication came when the jury quickly returned a verdict of "not guilty on all counts." After the case was over, the plaintiff's attorney commended Joann and told her if he needed a physician, he would gladly use Joann, but that did not really help. It just seemed to accentuate the hypocrisy of the whole system. The whole episode was so agonizing to Joann that the memory of it still brings pain. Perhaps fortuitously, I was temporarily in Thailand, preparing for our return, and missed the trial. Maybe it was for the best. It would have been hard to sit quietly while false allegations were made about Joann. I might have said something that would have caused a mistrial.

Most of the above events occurred during the last half of 1979 and early 1980: the Canada trip, Lisa's moving to Dallas and going to work for Texas Utilities, James working for the Texas Highway Department and preparing to go to Baylor, preparations for the trial, and then the trial itself. During that time, the vague feelings of unrest began to return to my thoughts. I mentioned it to Joann, and we began to pray about it. We wondered if God was about to do something—or have us do something. Joann's booming practice began to loom as a surprising problem. If the trend continued, she would have such a disproportionate share of the total patient load that she might find herself the sole medical provider in Van Horn. That would be a totally untenable situation. We simply could not remain in Van Horn under those circumstances. This time, the Lord provided an answer to our questioning before it became a crisis.

The answer came in the form of a telephone call from Bill Wakefield, the area director for Southeast Asia, which included Thailand. In November 1979, Bill called and asked if we would be willing to return to Thailand. I would be the coordinator of our overall refugee relief effort in Southeast Asia, and Joann would be the medical consultant for that work. She would also be available to provide medical care if/when/where it might be needed. Joann and I sensed immediately that God was doing something, and we might be a part of that. I told Bill our answer was a probable yes, but we wanted to pray about it and talk to Lisa and James before giving our final yes.

With our previous years in Thailand and with Thailand being the epicenter of the refugee-relief effort, we had been acutely conscious of the refugee crisis. Our mission (Thailand Baptist Mission), for reasons noted later, had already assumed major responsibilities in response to a catastrophic event, but more participation was requested and more leadership was needed to provide that assistance. If Joann and I returned, we never considered it would be a temporary assignment. It was another major career change. We would be reappointed by the FMB and return to Thailand as career missionaries. The family would be separated; the children would be mostly on their own. We felt we needed to share that telephone call and the implications of that call with our children and let them be in on the decision. Thanksgiving weekend was the week following the call from Bill. Lisa would be coming to Odessa, and Joann, James, and I would join her as we all celebrated Thanksgiving with Joann's parents. Joann and I would talk to Lisa and James at that time.

After the usual scrumptious dinner prepared by Mrs. Horton, we took Lisa and James for a ride and shared the whole episode with them. We asked them to share their thoughts, questions, and responses. Both immediately yelled, "Go for it!" Joann and I both teared up at their affirmation of us and the opportunity God was giving us to serve Him in that way. Our children blessed us at that moment as much—or more—than they have at any other time. We all worshipped as we expressed a prayer of thanksgiving to God.

The decision to return to Thailand had been made. Preparations for going were not so simple. I resigned from the hospital, effective in January 1980. Joann began the lengthy process of turning over River Ministry responsibilities to others. Her announcement about closing the clinic and returning to Thailand brought consternation and anger from many of her patients. It was painful for her also. Her practice had been extremely rewarding. She had formed many deep and lasting friendships with many people. It would be hard to leave.

We sold the Western Auto clinic building but retained the original dental clinic building. We were unable to sell our house, so we rented it and left Joann's brother with the responsibility of it until he could sell it. Her brother provided immeasurable help to us in so many ways during those years. As an attorney, and executive vice president of a bank, he had all the necessary knowledge and wisdom to handle many of our stateside needs. We have continued to be grateful to him.

Return to Thailand to Refugee Chaos

We returned to a chaotic Thailand in the spring of 1980. The influx of hundreds of thousands of Indochinese refugees, first to the Thai border and then into camps within Thailand, was creating a major crisis. Thailand Baptist Mission had a major part in the response to the crisis, but it also had to deal with a leadership change. Another missionary had been the excellent coordinator for TBM, but he had developed a medical condition that necessitated his resignation as refugee coordinator. That was what had prompted Bill Wakefield's original request to me. In January 1980, I spent almost a month in Thailand, reviewing our role and learning how to structure our response. When we moved back to Thailand permanently in late spring, much of the administrative structure was already in place, including roles for the international organizations and for the voluntary agencies (Volags). It was far from complete, but it was functioning.

The magnitude and intensity of the crisis was too great to explain in detail here. I will just note a few of the issues we dealt with.

The influx began on a minor scale shortly after the exit of American military forces from Indochina in 1975. It grew in numbers through 1979 as Pol Pot's "killing fields" slaughter of his people led many to begin their flight from Cambodia and the "reeducation" camps in Vietnam led many of them to flee their country, but Thai soldiers met them at the border and refused permission for them to enter the country. Much of the border, however, was either the Mekong River or jungle, so many refugees were able to find their way into the country. Many, however, could not enter, and their numbers began to swell. The situation became critical; they had no housing, no health care, and very little food. The international community applied pressure on Thailand to allow them in. Thailand finally agreed, with the condition that the international community assume total responsibility for the refugees and that they would be moved on to another country in a short time. When it became known in

Vietnam, Cambodia, and Laos that the border was now open, the floodgates overflowed. Hundreds of thousands headed for the border.

Chaos ruled. The original response to the refugees had started rather quietly in the mid-1970s when the first refugees arrived in small numbers. The Thailand Baptist Mission and other Christian missionary organizations had been the first to respond, providing food, health care, and other necessities. After a brief time of individualized response, the groups came together and formed a committee to provide a more coordinated response. The move enabled the acute needs to be addressed more effectively and also enhanced the Christian witness that was provided to the larger refugee groups. However, when the explosive influx of arrivals came in 1979, the needs overwhelmed that small group of Christian organizations.

Organizational Responsibilities: TBM

The problems were too large and numerous and arose too fast for them to cope. In an attempt to maintain order, the Thai authorities issued an ultimatum to the foreign agencies: get it organized or else (without defining *else*). It was assumed to mean that Thailand would push the refugees back across the border. It fell to the UN and the UNHCR to establish a structure under which all organizations would find their places of service and their assigned roles. The structure basically involved the organizations noted below, and their functions. A glossary of names and abbreviations is also given.

International Organizations

- UNHCR: United Nations High Commissioner for Refugees. Overall coordinator of refugee affairs. Had administrative responsibilities and funding responsibilities.
- ICRC: International Committee of Red Cross. They were self-declared coordinators of refugee medical affairs,

but with no authority. Had very minor administrative responsibilities.

- WHO: World Health Organization. Advisory role: No administrative responsibilities, but did have some minor operational responsibilities.
- WFP: World Food Program. No administrative responsibility but did provide some supplemental funding for others to use.
- Voluntary Agencies (Volags). Sometimes called Nongovernmental Organizations (NGOs). TBM was in that group. The NGOs could be Christian, secular, nonprofit, or other. We had operational responsibilities but no official authority. We did the daily hands-on work in the camps.
- CCSDPT: Committee for Coordination of Services to Displaced Persons in Thailand. This was the primary operating committee, made up of all the Volag directors. It was the primary avenue of communication for all the organizations involved in refugee work in Thailand.

Thailand Baptist Mission was one of more than fifty Volags from all over the world actively involved in the refugee effort, most of whom flooded into Thailand following the media blitz given the dire refugee situation in 1979. Early on, there was much scrambling among some of the big agencies for high-profile, preferred camp locations. That was what led to some of the chaos.

Now back to the issues we dealt with and the process used as the crisis developed. With that organizational structure in place, the chaos diminished and the response became more effective. As the overall refugee coordinator, the UNHCR chose to work through the CCSDPT. It became the primary operating committee of the Volags. That committee was made up of the directors of all the Volags involved in refugee work in Thailand. The monthly meetings of that committee became the venue through which the IOs, the Thai government, and other governments announced their plans, policies, and requirements in their areas of responsibility.

It was also the venue in which issues specifically related to Volags were discussed and decided. Those open meetings were used by the media as the source of much of the worldwide reporting of the refugee situation. A subcommittee of the CCSDPT was the Medical Director's Committee, comprised of all the medical directors in the various camps. Joann was one of those.

A massive organizational operation dispersed more than seven hundred thousand refugees in twenty-two camps along the eastern border of Thailand over a relatively short period of time. Cambodian, Laotian, and Hmong refugees were located primarily in land camps; Vietnamese were primarily in seaside camps. The camps extended from the northeast part of Thailand to the southern tip, a distance of more than nine hundred miles.

The assignment of camp responsibilities gave TBM a major task and a major opportunity. We were asked to become the lead agency in the Kamput refugee camp, with additional duties in three other camps. A table will show it better.

Camp	Average Population	Responsibilities	Location
Kamput	21,500	Hospital, OPD, food, utensils, fuel, utilities, sanitation, vo-tech training, and maintenance	In jungle, on border between Thailand and Cambodia
Mairut	21,000	Food, utensils, and vo-tech training	SE tip of Thailand
Laem Sing	1,500	Food, utensils	South Thailand, on Gulf of Siam
Songkla	1,000	Some food, utensils	Southern tip of Thailand
TOTAL	45,000		

Our camps listed above were primarily for two different groups of refugees: Kamput and Mairut were for Cambodian refugees; Laem Sing and Songkla were for Vietnamese refugees. There were also Laotian and Hmong refugees who were placed in camps in the northeast area of Thailand, closer to the area from which they had come.

The graph above falls short in conveying all that was involved in discharging our responsibilities. Providing food enough to feed more than forty thousand people daily was a challenge, not to mention the fuel needed to prepare the food and the needed utensils. Southern Baptists had been generous in sending funds to the FMB for our use, but those funds fell short of the amount needed to do what we were asked to do (for food and for other needs). Additional funding was needed.

The IOs were the funding agencies. None of us had the resources to do all we were asked to do, but the IOs did. They were prepared to provide the funds we needed, but we would have to sign contracts in order to receive the funds. That was contrary to FMB policy, which prohibited missionaries (or missions) from signing such contracts. Ron Hill, our TBM administrator, called Dr. Keith Parks, president of the FMB, and explained the situation. Keith checked with appropriate SBC leaders and legal people and received permission for us to enter into specific, limited agreements under those unusual circumstances. Over the course of our three years of refugee work, I signed contracts for major amounts of dollars. I deliberately did not handle any of the funds. I made sub-agreements with Thai companies to purchase and deliver specific goods and services. When I verified their compliance with the agreements, I signed off on their invoices. They submitted them to the UNHCR for reimbursement.

Kamput was the most interesting and challenging of our four camps. The camp was in the jungle, on the border between Thailand and Cambodia, several miles off a decent road. The access road was cut through the jungle without any overlay of gravel or other material. In the hot, dry season, it was prolific in dust production; in the rainy season, it became the granddaddy of all mudholes. To our great relief, there were elephants working timber in the adjacent jungle, and we frequently used them to pull (or push) our vehicles out of the mud.

Elephant pushing fuel truck

Champion of all mudholes

But there is no picture of Joann and other hospital personnel helping push one of her vans out of the mud one day. They were all pushing when the van wheels caught unexpectedly and suddenly jumped forward. Joann and the rest of them fell flat in the mud. It made for interesting camouflage patterns on their white jackets. Fortunately, it was the end of the workday.

One of the most challenging responsibilities we (especially Joann) had in Kamput was t providing medical care. We also provided occupational training, maintenance, sanitation, and some utilities. In addition, we provided food and fuel in all four camps plus a few other responsibilities in three camps. The UNHCR had built a hundred-bed MASH-type hospital in Kamput with an adjoining surgical suite and a crude OPD shelter. Those facility words don't mean the same in a jungle setting as they do in a modern Western setting. Maintaining a professional staff was a continuing challenge.

Of necessity, it became a diverse staff from twelve countries. I was primarily responsible for recruiting the professionals, but it was a greater challenge and responsibility for Joann to monitor, teach, and direct such a diverse group in those circumstances. And that role fell to her as the medical director.

Medical Director: Joann

There was some background confusion in the States that led to her having that responsibility. That was not to be her role, but I was called by the personnel director of the FMB and told that the physician expected to assume that role would not be coming. I was somewhat perturbed because I knew what it meant: Joann would have to become the medical director. We had been back in the refugee work long enough to realize the magnitude of the demands that would be placed on her. Among other ramifications, that meant that each of us would have more than a full-time job, each with a separate base of operation that would require us to live separately. Her responsibilities were in one camp; mine were in four that were hundreds of miles apart. Not good.

"Medical director" was a long country mile short of defining her responsibilities. The hospital was bare bones. The beds were just frames with bamboo mats for the patients. There were only portable x-rays, which were limited primarily to chest films and extremities. The laboratory could do complete blood counts (CBCs), some blood work, and type and cross-match for transfusions and malaria smears. Doctors were forced to rely upon their clinical skills for most of their diagnoses and treatments.

When the refugee status garnered worldwide media attention, many SBC church people volunteered to come help, including many physicians. That occurred just prior to our arrival back in Thailand.

Unfortunately, when the initial crisis began to stabilize and media attention shifted elsewhere, the flow of volunteers diminished—but the numbers and needs of the refugees did not diminish. Joann was still responsible for a hundred-bed hospital full of patients and an OPD that was seeing three to four hundred patients daily. Recruiting physicians became an urgent task—*my* urgent task. Since we required our professional medical people to be Christians, the task was a challenge. We ended up having more than fifty medical people from twelve countries in the course of the work.

To perform basic nursing care, including vital signs and bathing, Joann supervised a continuous training program of Cambodian refugee employees., That proved to be good preparation for what she did later in India.

As difficult as the recruitment was for me, Joann's follow-up task was greater. Many of the doctors were from non-English-speaking backgrounds. Their training was much different than American-trained physicians. Their treatment protocols for various diseases were often different. Several of them had no experience in tropical medicine. Joann had to take who was available and mold them into a team that provided excellent medical care. It was a daunting task, but she did it.

Strange as it may seem, a few of the American volunteer doctors turned out to be the most peculiar and most demanding group.

- One doctor spent almost all his time chasing butterflies with his net. He rarely came to the hospital.
- A couple of doctors spent most of their time sightseeing.
- One doctor came, spent one day in the hospital, and left. "This is not my cup of tea," he said.
- Two or three doctors were unable or unwilling to rely on their clinical diagnostic skills. Since we did not have high-tech diagnostic and x-ray capability, they would not stay.

Joann and I especially appreciated one volunteer who was not a physician. James was able to work with us briefly on one of his summer trips to Thailand, assisting in food distribution in Kamput. The food and fuel arrived in large quantities and had to be separated into individual and family packages, which was no small task when you are feeding and supplying about forty-five thousand people.

Joann's responsibility for the volunteers did not cease at the hospital. She had to provide logistical support for them, including housing, laundry, housekeeping, food, and transportation. Since they did not speak Thai, she also served as translator.

TBM was the lead agency in camp. As the senior TBM official working daily in the camp, Joann was the one the Thai army commander (always in ultimate charge) looked to her when problems occurred with other agency personnel. He could not speak English; they could not speak Thai. "Get Dr. Goatcher!"

She often had to leave her work to go translate. Her workdays often exceeded sixteen hours. It is impossible to convey the enormity of the physical, emotional, and spiritual stamina required to maintain her schedule, but she did it for almost three years. We used a phrase—*compassion fatigue*—to describe the many workers who were unable to cope with long-term, intense stress. The only explanation was that Joann was exceptionally strong in the Lord and looked to Him constantly for strength and wisdom. As a physician dealing with life-and-death decisions on a constant basis, she was forced to establish an emotional wall that enabled her to cope with heavy medical decisions with a loving attitude while dealing with many simultaneous issues. That situation, plus many others, strongly reinforced the affirmation that the Lord answers prayers. She prayed often, but she was not praying alone; many others of us were also praying. God heard our prayers.

Foreigners were not permitted to stay in Kamput at night, allowing the Thai soldiers to harass the residents. The first problem Joann usually had to deal with on arrival at camp each morning was to help resolve a problem that had occurred the previous night. As heavy and unpleasant as that task was, Joann realized she was in a position to prevent many of those incidents from becoming very serious events. She was known and respected by the Thai military, and they did not want her making reports of misconduct to higher authorities.

Many refugees found their way into the camp at night. The following morning, they would be rounded up and placed in a barbwire enclosure. They had to be seen by a doctor, usually Joann, before being considered for processing. She had to examine them through the barbwire.

Joann seeing new arrivals through barbwire

Kamput camp was constructed, utilized to maximum capacity (about twenty-three thousand), and closed down in just under three years. In the course of that time, Joann and the other doctors saw thousands of patients, many with unusual medical problems and strange pathology. I'll relate only a few.

Perhaps the most memorable heartwarming case (among countless tragic cases) was that of a young boy who appeared at the hospital one morning. Small, of indeterminate age, and emaciated, with typical pipe-stem legs and arms and distended belly, he was alone. He had malaria, intestinal parasites, severe anemia, and malnutrition. An additional condition was his congenital bilateral club feet (both feet pointed backward). He made no move to register or talk with anyone. Finally, one of the nurses noticed him and began helping him along his thrilling road to recovery—physically and spiritually.

His story unfolded slowly, in bits and pieces, over the course of treatment. As with many other similar stories, they were difficult to verbalize. Most of his family had been killed by Pol Pot's soldiers.

Finally, he fled and attached himself to a small group of people fleeing toward the Thai border. Because of the danger of being seen, they traveled only at night. Sometimes during the day, when soldiers came near, they would hide under corpses to avoid detection. Many miles of walking at night, in all weather, in dense, dangerous jungle, with grossly deformed feet, with little to eat, and knowing nothing of what lay ahead, revealed a journey of unbelievable fortitude, courage, and stamina.

Over a period of a few months, a series of surgeries straightened both feet, enabling him to walk normally. His other medical problems were cured. The accompanying pictures first show him not long after his arrival, then in one of his casts, and then, finally, standing in his new red tennis shoes, smiling, looking like any other normal boy.

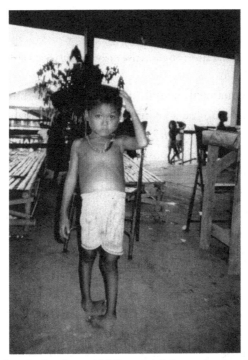

Newly arrived orphan with bilateral club feet and malnutrition

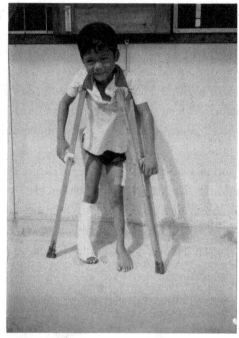

Same child after two corrective surgeries and good nutrition

But it was his emotional and spiritual healing that was most rewarding. Compassionate care and a loving fellowship, accompanied by stories of a loving Lord, made him curious and very receptive to knowing the God who made it all possible. He frequently told his story of what Jesus had done for him. It had all happened in the hospital, and that became his home. Hospital personnel became his family. His whole story was a thrilling, dramatic demonstration of how God's loving sovereignty is able to bring good out of the worst possible evil. Not long after he was restored to good health, a Cambodian family adopted him. They were granted asylum in another country. He was blessed, and so were those who had cared for him.

Malaria was an endemic, serious disease, especially cerebral malaria. It brought death to many people, both refugees and local Thais. Part of the problem for our medical people was disagreement about treatment protocols. There was not just one treatment that was universally effective for all malaria. Partial or inappropriate treatment could lead to medication resistance, resulting in an uncured condition—and then often to death. Joann had many years of experience in treating the malaria endemic to that area of Thailand. She knew what worked and what didn't work, and that was critical when dealing with cerebral malaria. Only Joann and a few other physicians in the camps had similar experience and knowledge.

There were physicians in other organizations without tropical medicine experience who insisted that other protocols were better and attempted to impose those protocols in all camps. That led to several heated discussions. They had scientific research that they thought proved their position was correct. Never mind that it was conducted by a French medical team that had not based any of their research on Southeast Asian malaria. The discussions were lively. No eruptions occurred, but there were some intense discussions. Joann stayed quiet, continued to use the "Southeast Asia–proven protocol," and saw the mortality and morbidity rates in Kamput become one of the best of all the camps.

Several of our volunteer physicians were from the academic world. The lack of first-class laboratory and x-ray diagnostic capability was disheartening for some of them. They were extremely reluctant to rely on their clinical skills, especially in dealing with pathology they had never seen before. Most refugees had not received vaccinations or inoculations, so diseases rarely seen in the United States and Europe were common in the OPD. Malaria, malnutrition, and parasites were most common, but there was much tetanus (especially neonatal), tuberculosis, leprosy, diphtheria, and whooping cough also. In addition, many babies were born with congenital abnormalities, thought by many to be the result of their mothers' exposure to Agent Orange. Our "high-tech" nursery bassinets were cardboard boxes with hot water bottles to provide warmth.

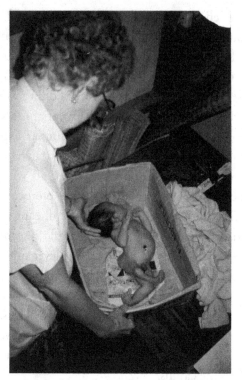

Joann with newborn baby in our incubator

Another intimidating factor for some of the volunteer medical staff was the frequent sounds of gunfire. The sound of artillery fire was so common that it often went unheard. Rather more intimidating was the sound of small-arms fire just outside the camp. No refugee worker was hit, but it was a reminder that the war was not taking place in some distant land. It was very near and very real. In fact, much of the trauma seen by the doctors occurred not far from the camp. Land mines had been placed indiscriminately along the border and then forgotten. Children or adults, males or females— the mines were not selective about their victims. There were many amputations but insufficient prostheses. The surgeons were kept busy. The whole hospital atmosphere was so different and frightening that some volunteers could not handle it. They just left.

That is only the tip of the iceberg concerning medical practice in camp, but it must suffice.

Camps: Spiritual Life

As with medical care in camp, so there were too many spiritual events and unusual worship experiences to describe them all. There were, however, enough extraordinary occurrences to make it obvious to everyone that God was manifesting His presence in camp in unusual ways that grabbed the refugee's attention. God was working, lives were being touched, and thousands responded.

The initial response to refugee needs was provided by a few Christian organizations, including a gospel witness. All assistance was provided unconditionally. Extreme care was exercised to ensure that all were shown loving concern equally. No enticements or preferential treatment was given to anyone, but it was not a surprise when that Christian witness began to face opposition. A little background will help.

As the refugee population exploded, the original small Christian group became unable to cope with the needs. A new committee evolved—the CCSDPT—which was comprised of all the Volags. Most of the new organizations were not Christian, but they were neutral in their attitudes toward the gospel being made available. One, however, was strongly anti-Christian. MSF (Medecins Sans Frontieres, now called Doctors Without Borders) was a French agency with some members who felt that the refugees already had their religion and to confuse them with the gospel story was wrong and unacceptable. They attempted to prevent any Christian effort being made in any camp.

We were able to counter their efforts in Kamput, partly because of the refugees' own experiences. They had gained a new hope in a living God that gave them boldness. Several thrilling events and activities totally neutralized MSF's attempts to banish a Christian witness.

One of those events occurred at Easter in 1981 and was brought about by the refugees themselves. Many of the Cambodians were superb natural actors. The believers conceived the idea of sharing the Easter gospel story of the death, burial, and resurrection of Jesus through a huge dramatization of the event for the entire camp. Surprisingly, the idea created an atmosphere of excitement that touched the camp even before the presentation.

A vacant, upwardly sloping area near the center of camp, slightly similar to an amphitheater, was chosen as the presentation site. Members of the cast cut nearby bamboo poles to build stage settings. Colorful cloth used to teach sewing in our vocational training center was used for costumes. Preparing the stage and practicing a few scenes publicly added to the excitement, enhancing the appeal to many non-Christians.

When the time came for the big event, an estimated ten thousand people filled the vacant space. As the drama began, clouds started to form (it was near the beginning of the monsoon season). As the drama unfolded on the stage, the overhead clouds increased. Sunlight became intermittent, and distant thunder could be heard. As the drama approached the time of the Crucifixion, the clouds grew darker, lightning came closer, and the thunder became louder. Many of the Christians began to pray, some of them fearfully, realizing that the unusual timing of the storm occurring just as the drama was portraying the death of Jesus meant that God was doing something. Many of the nonbelievers became concerned, knowing even less about the story but sensing a powerful manifestation of the Christians' God.

Some of the Christians later said they did not know how to pray. They were becoming frightened, but they did not want the drama halted. The thunder and lightning increased as the story neared the actual time of the Crucifixion. The clouds became darker as the Crucifixion took place, but the rain held off. Many of the women and children were weeping as the Crucifixion occurred. During the interval between the Crucifixion and the resurrection, the thunder diminished and the clouds began to lighten.

Just as the resurrection scene was being portrayed, the clouds parted—and the sun shone through directly on Jesus as he emerged from the tomb. A combination of sounds moved through the audience; some were sighing, some were awestruck, some were praying, some were singing and clapping, and some sat stunned and immobile. All knew they had witnessed a wonderfully unique expression of God's presence. The Christians had a better idea of what it meant and were vocal in their expressions of praise. They were quick to explain it to their neighbors and friends. That drama, with the accompanying weather phenomenon, was used greatly by the believers in camp as they witnessed to the other refugees. We have no print pictures of the event—only word pictures—but no picture could capture the atmosphere of the occasion. Many became believers as a result of the presentation.

Another event, a one-time-only, spectacular baptism, was also significant in the lives of camp believers. For many months, the response to the gospel in Kamput had been thrilling. Even with extensive teaching and testing of new believers before they could be baptized, the camp pastors were baptizing more than twenty-five new believers each week. The baptistery was simple but adequate. It was a one-and-a-half-meter sheet-metal cube with the top cut out. It was placed on a low platform, with steps leading from the platform up, over, and then down into the tank, then back up and down the opposite side of the tank to the platform. As the candidates came forward to be baptized, they would be halted as they started up the ladder to enter the tank. One of the pastors would then wash their feet before they entered the tank. After being baptized, they would climb the ladder out of the tank and descend to the platform. Only those with an understanding of the culture of Southeast Asia can understand the significance of the act of washing someone's feet, especially by a leader such as a pastor. Touching another person's feet is considered degrading to the one doing the touching. To do so intentionally is to put oneself beneath the recipient. The entire procedure demonstrated a meekness and humility on the part of the leaders that highlighted humility as an essential characteristic of all Christians. It was a moving, solemn, and joyful occasion for all believers.

But they still remembered their homes back in Cambodia. The older Christians had been baptized in creeks or rivers, and they told of those experiences with nostalgic longing. It led many of the new believers to want a similar experience. Unfortunately, there was no creek in camp, and the refugees were not permitted to leave camp. They were stymied. One day, I happened to be in camp when worship services were held. They asked if I could get permission for them to go outside the camp to be baptized. Knowing Joann had a good relationship with the camp commander, I asked her to take the lead in asking his permission.

We expected to be refused permission; there was a countrywide policy that refugees must remain in their camp until authorized to move. We doubted that the Kamput commander, regardless of his respect for us (and especially Joann), would ignore that policy. After much explanation and discussion, he granted our request, but with serious conditions to which we must agree: a record must be kept of everyone who went, with evidence of their return, and Joann and I must be aware that we would probably be deported should any refugee not return. We understood and agreed to his conditions.

On the designated day, 121 baptism candidates came prepared. An additional seventy or eighty relatives and friends also came. It was an impressive crowd of about two hundred people who walked joyously down the road almost two miles to the river for the ceremony. When we arrived, many of them were too excited to remain on the banks of the river. They jumped in the clear-running stream, splashing and rejoicing at that brief time of freedom out of camp.

Five national pastors rotated conducting the ceremony, sometimes baptizing simultaneously.

River baptism, Joann in upper left corner

It was gratifying, thrilling, and a blessing to Joann and me to watch them and listen to their expressions of praise and gratitude to God for all that He had done for them.

Too quickly, the time came to return to camp. When all were back and checked, not a single one was missing. The commander was astonished. That episode did not lead him to become a Christian, but it greatly affected his attitude toward believers and his trust of Christians. Joann and I still rejoice as we recall that experience.

The early days of the refugee crisis were so chaotic it was difficult to coordinate a Christian witness. There were a few national pastors and other church leaders in the original influx of refugees, but they were so caught up in the struggle to survive in the midst of life-threatening events that they could do little to maintain a Christian fellowship or arrange meetings. In any event, their numbers were too small to affect the general mass of refugees.

The Christian organizations that were members of CCSDPT tried to address the many-sided issue. I will speak to only one facet of that effort. It goes back to my story of our early days in Thailand and our attempt to discover redemptive analogies we could use to better explain the gospel to Thai people. In this case, the effort was made to provide redemptive analogies related to the refugee experience. The setting was obvious since the refugees had been living in fear for some time and become captive to that fear (also to sin). They finally abandoned everything and fled from imminent danger to save their lives and find a safe haven. It was a good analogy of salvation, analogous to the Israelites fleeing from Egypt. Several realities could be pointed out. I will briefly summarize a few of them.

- Life had no value to the enemy. Pol Pot and his soldiers killed indiscriminately, and Satan deceived and destroyed indiscriminately.
- Life has infinite value to God. The word *refugee* in Cambodian means "one who has escaped with just his life."
- One must abandon his or her former life in order to be saved. That also is required for salvation.
- There is no sure refuge or haven in any human institution, only in God.
- As refugees hear of the opportunity to go to another country, they must think, *What must I do to be saved?*
- There is a time limit for application. Those who wait too long must deal with the consequences.
- There are certain requirements and criteria for admission to their new homeland. They must follow the biblical path that leads to the new birth.

These analogies resonated with many of the refugees and prompted them to respond to the gospel. A side event—just a passing minor moment in the overall saga, and happening only to me—occurred in the midst of the major events. It occurred following one of the few times when I was able to attend worship services while in camp. There were about four hundred people at the service.

Church service in Kamput camp

As in Thailand, the Cambodian Christians had no heritage of Christian music. A few Western gospel songs had been translated into the Khmer (Cambodian) language, but the melodies were strangely mixed with local folk tunes … and they could not read music. At one particular service, as they were singing, often with each one singing his or her own tune, I began to hear a chord or a series of notes that seemed to remind me of a song I had heard somewhere in the distant past. As they came near the end of all the verses, it finally came to me. They were singing "This World is Not My Home." I laughed at the improbability of hearing and singing an old Stamps Baxter Melody Boys gospel song that I had not sung since I was a kid in the hills of Arkansas. Now I was hearing it sung in a jungle refugee camp in Southeast Asia. As they finished the song and some of the phrases began coming back to me, I stopped laughing. The words, the people, and the circumstances hit me almost as a physical blow.

These people had left everything. They had forfeited all their possessions. Their greatest loss was the loss of hope. Their religion had nothing to offer. Considered traitors by their home country, they could not go back. They had nothing in this world. They had no other home to which they could go, only a faint hope in some distant land, but they were singing with gusto: "O, Lord, you know, I have no home. I'm just a passing through, O Lord. I have no friend like you. If heaven's not my home, then Lord, what will I do?" They had all seen death, often of immediate family members. Many of them had barely escaped being killed themselves. Now what? Now God. He had come into their lives, and for the first time, they dared to hope again—not in houses, land, or treasures that were gone forever, but in a loving, living Savior that had given them a kind of life and hope they had never known before. They were not just singing some old song they had learned as kids; they were singing words that affirmed they now knew a gracious God who had prepared a home in heaven for them. I left that time of worship with far greater gratitude to God for His promise of eternity in His presence.

Later, as I reflected on my conversations with the refugees, I was struck by what they did not say. Not once did I hear them question why those horrible events had happened to them. In the face of the unspeakable atrocities they had experienced, including the killing of their own small, innocent children, they never asked why. Why did they not ask? Then I recalled one of the major tenets of Buddhism: suffering is inherent in life. To them, fate had worked its penalty. There was now no escape, except by impossibly difficult meritorious deeds. Hope was gone. There was no reason to ask why. The conversations were often heartbreaking. It was not the time for a theological discussion about an omnipotent loving God permitting such events to occur. Later, as they heard and believed the gospel and experienced the rebirth through the Holy Spirit, hope was renewed.

As I was driving back to Bangkok, thanking God for my own blessings and thinking I had reached the high point of the day— or maybe the week—another surprise blessing was poured out on me. I found myself singing out loud in the car. That just did not happen with me. Even I don't like my singing, but suddenly, I was strangely, surprisingly, wondrously happy. At first, I was shocked to be feeling that way. I had just come from hearing several refugees telling about their tragic, hellish experiences, many having watched their own family members being killed. How was it possible for me to be happy after hearing those stories? All of a sudden, an overwhelming sense of God's presence filled the car. There came to me the absolute assurance that I was exactly in the center of God's will, doing exactly what I was supposed to be doing, in the exact place I was supposed to be. On many other occasions, I had known that I was in the Lord's will, but that unique sense of God's assurance was beyond anything I had previously experienced. It was like what I imagined God's Shechinah glory to be like, totally enveloped in His indescribable splendor and grace, totally at one with Him. Paul's comment in Philippians 4:6–7 about "the peace of God that transcends all understanding" came to me as I drove on to Bangkok. What a day!

Joann and I were greatly impressed by the artistic skills exhibited by many of the refugees. The experiences that led to their being there could not be adequately expressed verbally, even if they had wanted to, but several of them were able to paint pictures that were more revealing than words. Joann and I bought several, but some were so disturbing that Joann gave them away. We have only a couple left. One is particularly stark.

It is an oil-on-canvas painting, all in dark tones. It is a night scene in the jungle that depicts a small group of refugees fleeing in terror from certain death by soldiers. They are glancing back in anguish at the sounds, imagined or otherwise, of soldiers pursuing them. Their faces reveal despair at their chance of success. A bundle of roots from a toppled tree extends outward and upward, entwined with outreaching limbs from other nearby trees, all appearing like a massive spiderweb, seemingly reaching out to trap them. It is frightening to look at it, yet it expresses better than words the fear, agony, and torment they are experiencing. The picture conveys the story better than words.

But there is also the "rest of the story" for many of the refugees who came to know the Lord in the camps. They were the nucleus of many Cambodian, Laotian, Vietnamese, and Hmong churches that were established by those new believers who became citizens of the United States and other countries. One of those was a particular blessing to Joann and me. When we came back to the States in 1987, for me to be on staff at the FMB, we joined Derbyshire Baptist Church in Richmond. We were unaware at the time that the church had a Cambodian mission with a Cambodian pastor. When we met him later, we learned that he had been led to the Lord by one of our missionaries and baptized by another while he was in one of our camps in Thailand. Now his mission/church in Richmond had an active WMU. That story was repeated many times, as I learned later when meeting other refugee pastors who had come through our camps in Thailand. We often had mutual acquaintances. Joann became active in the Cambodian WMU, and we were blessed again. It is a small world.

Similar stories could be told of events and response to the gospel in all our camps, especially in Laem Sing, a boat camp for Vietnamese refugees. Many of the Vietnamese Christians who came through that camp were instrumental in establishing Vietnamese churches in the United States, now a significant subgroup of the SBC.

Most of the Vietnamese boat people in our two camps at Laem Sing and Songkla were transferred to the Bataan Refugee Camp in the Philippines for further processing before moving on to their final country of refuge. One of our FMB missionaries was transferred from our Thai refugee work to the Philippines to provide assistance to the growing number of boat people who were arriving from Thailand and Malaysia.

Surveying that camp and seeing that area of the Philippines was a particularly moving time for me. The horrors of the Bataan Death March early in World War II had been big news in our area of Arkansas because one of the soldiers was from the area. The Bataan Peninsula extends west/southwest of Manila, beyond the island of Corregidor. The death march occurred along the road leading from

Manila Bay westward over a mountain range to the coast of the South China Sea. The account of the battles, defeats, and deaths that occurred in the Manila and southern Luzon area in those early days of the war has fascinated me since the days they occurred. Our refugee camp was located on the peninsula near the coast and was reached by a road that frequently traversed the original death march road. I would be traveling that road on the way to the camp.

There are many memorials along the road. The march was not just one isolated, struggling, desperate walk of survival or death. There were multiple battles and skirmishes extending throughout the peninsula before the ultimate defeat. Untold thousands of Filipinos lost their lives, plus thousands of American soldiers. The memorials provide an excellent history of the events, including references to General Douglas MacArthur's dramatic return to the Philippines.

My evaluation of the refugee camp was brief and encouraging. The missionary, with his experience in Thailand and his fluency in the Vietnamese language, had everything in order. He had established a very active church reaching out to other refugees who later became part of the fruitful Vietnamese church-planting effort when they were resettled in the States.

Camps: The Burmese (Karen) Refugees, Western Border

Refugee camp life and work on the eastern border of Thailand was our obvious focus, but our involvement went beyond that immediate area. The nature of my role necessarily led to other responsibilities, one of which related to Burmese refugees on the western border of Thailand. There was even more history behind that acute need than that of the Indochinese refugees in east Thailand. I'll not go into detail, but a brief background statement will help the reader understand how and why we had any part in that refugee relief effort.

Burma was one of the pioneer areas for Baptist missions in Asia, led by Adoniram Judson. (Another was William Carey in India, about whom I will write later.) His efforts were ultimately very successful among the Karen, Karenni, Shan, and other tribal groups. American Baptists gradually became leaders in evangelizing those ethnic groups. Thousands, then hundreds of thousands, became Christians. It is a thrilling story of a people movement to the Lord that is unknown to most people.

After World War II, however, when the British Raj pulled out of India, disorder and anarchy began to rule. The Burmese tribe became the dominant tribe in the area that came to be known as Burma. Over a period of years, they became the national rulers, contrary to the agreement that had been signed when the British left. There was serious suppression and persecution of other groups, especially Christians, and often with an iron hand. That remains the case today. It became so severe that many of the tribal groups near the eastern border with Thailand began to migrate to Thailand as refugees. From the 1960s onward, the basic needs of life for tens of thousands of people became more and more scarce, even as the number of people increased. Concurrently, diminishing resources of American Baptists, both in personnel and in other resources, led to a reduction in missionary presence and ministry outreach.

In 1981, I was asked by the American Baptist missionaries working in northwest Thailand if Southern Baptists could assist them in ministering to the thousands of Karen, Shan, Karenni, Lahu, and other tribal language and ethnic groups fleeing across the Salween River (the border between Burma and Thailand at that point) to escape persecution. The Thai government was not happy with the influx; the refugees were confined in a small area. No services were provided. There was no pathway to citizenship. It was becoming another humanitarian crisis.

I joined Paul Dodge, coordinator for American Baptists, in a survey trip up the Salween River to evaluate the needs and conditions in the many refugee camps that had been set up in the jungle along the border. It really was a crisis situation, and thousands of people desperately needed assistance. Thanks to the generosity of Southern

Baptists in their giving for hunger relief, we were able to provide lifesaving food.

On my first survey trip, I stumbled upon one of the most surprising and amazing worship times I have ever experienced. Paul had responded to their plea for help and had promised to meet them and learn about their needs. I had heard about their historical background and was glad he asked me to join him in the visit.

In talking about the camp situation, Paul somehow forgot to tell me what our travel to the camps would be like. The camps were just inside the extreme northwestern Thai border, adjacent to the Golden Triangle (juncture of Thailand, Laos, and Burma) in an isolated, rugged mountain range divided by the Salween River. The river was relatively benign most of the year, but the runoff during the rainy season coincided with the early summer snowmelt from the Himalayas, resulting in the river becoming a raging monster during the monsoon season. The river was confined to narrow channels between steep mountains, and it could move house-sized boulders at its peak flow. No one used the river at those times.

Up the Salween River to a Burmese refugee camp

It was a two- or three-day trip from Bangkok. We made our final segment of the trip up the river about thirty or forty miles in a long-tail boat after the peak-flow period. After leaving the river, we trekked through the mountains a few more miles to the first of several camps. Those camps had populations between one thousand and three thousand in contrast to the larger camps in eastern Thailand. They were usually established near water and near an area that could be cleared and cultivated so they could raise as much of their food as possible. Also in contrast to the Indochinese refugees, almost all the so-called Burmese (actually Karen and other tribal groups) refugees were educated and Christian (many were Baptists). A striking feature of the camps was that all the structures were built by the refugees themselves. After clearing an area in the jungle, they would build their first structure: a church building. The second structure would be a school. Individual family huts were built last. All buildings were constructed primarily with bamboo from the adjoining jungle. They also built a sparsely furnished hospital.

Many of the refugees were professionals, including physicians and engineers. They had been forced to flee when the Burmese army raided their home areas, burning homes, villages, towns, and crops that were ready to harvest. As with the Indochinese refugees, it was a tragic situation, but the world took little notice.

Now to the surprising event. As Paul and I neared the first village about midday, we began to hear intermittent singing. When we walked into the camp, we saw the source of it. A rather large group of people was seated on the open floor of the church. The group was made up of the choirs from four separate camps, coming together to rehearse for a choir competition to be held the following day in a joint-worship service. They were preparing to rehearse one of the major pieces that the combined choirs would present prior to the preaching time. Paul and I sat down to listen.

There were no music instruments; all singing was a cappella. The four sections were slightly separated. The sopranos began softly for a few moments, in the Karen language, then were joined by the altos, then the tenors, and finally the basses, all singing in beautiful symphonic harmony. Then all parts joined together, gradually increasing in volume to a semi-crescendo, then breaking into parts with sopranos and altos moving into antiphonal counterparts while the basses and tenors provided an organ-like foundation. They then all joined in harmony in a great crescendo that gradually faded to a soft pianissimo for the closing.

Paul and I remained seated, just stunned beyond words, both spiritually and musically. We had tears in our eyes. That choir, that presentation, would have received high critical praise in any concert hall or sanctuary in the world. For it to be presented with such finesse and spiritual fervor in a jungle setting by an unknown choir from a people group unheard of by most of the world was just unbelievable. It helped create a worship experience for Paul and me that extended far into the night. It was with great regret that we left the next day without hearing their full program. Later, I reflected on the enormity of what lay behind that presentation. The lyrics, the music, and the choir did not happen overnight. That event was the pinnacle of almost 170 years of Christian missionary influence in Burma, started by Adoniram Judson in 1812. His work was begun in a primitive setting among a people who did not know God, but God blessed those efforts—and we were seeing and hearing the fruit of that seed sowing and watering.

It was a particular joy for me to make several thousand dollars available to them for food purchases; it was all made possible by Hunger Relief funds given by Baptist Christians in the USA. They were in great need, and they were truly brothers and sisters in the Lord who would multiply that small amount of assistance many times over.

Election: Chairman, CCSDPT, and Issues

Not long after my survey trip to the Burma border, I was back in Bangkok for our regular monthly CCSDPT meeting. One of the agenda items was the election of a new chairman. I was elected. It was a surprise, especially considering that the secular Volag organizations had come to far outnumber the Christian organizations. We, as the Thailand mission, were well-known as a strongly evangelistic Christian organization. I was known for my efforts to maintain a Christian presence in every camp. Electing an individual from such an organization as chairman was unusual and unexpected. I did not want the position. We were on the verge of dealing with some major, divisive policy and position issues. There would be tense discussions, even confrontations, but the thought came that perhaps God had a hand in placing a Christian in a strategic position at a critical time. I remembered Ecclesiastes 3:7: "There is a time to keep silent and a time to speak." I felt someone should be in a position to speak on behalf of the refugees for their freedom to hear and accept the gospel, read His Word, and share their faith with others. I accepted the role.

A Christian witness in the camps was not a new issue. It had come up earlier, before I was present. Ron Hill, our TBM administrator, had dealt with it, but one agency would not leave it alone. Ron, the epitome of a wise, gracious Christian statesman, reminded all members of Section 18 of the UN Universal Declaration of Human Rights, which affirmed the very freedoms we were requesting for the refugees, including the right of refugees to read and hear ideas and views discussed in a free marketplace of ideas and choose their own religion. MSF refused to acknowledge any UN declaration. We were at an impasse.

Other Volag directors urged me to address it in an open meeting and bring it to a conclusion. I was reluctant to force it in an open forum. I knew no single Volag could force a personal opinion or a specific policy on all CCSDPT members, but there was a sharply divided opinion among some of the members. If it came to a floor discussion, it could become very explosive and divisive. Realizing ultimate decision-making lay with the Thai military, I went to a couple of senior military leaders and explained the situation. To our great relief, they concurred with our desire for complete freedom of witness and religion in the camps, and in a couple of camps, they even encouraged us. I conveyed that decision to the CCSDPT members. MSF was thwarted, and a Christian witness continued in all camps. (I cannot say that MSF was reflecting their official policy, but I think it was a reflection of the personal views of MSF personnel in Thailand.)

Camps: Harvest Time

How effective was our witness? In the three most active years of our refugee work, there were just over five thousand baptized in our four camps, the majority in Kamput and Laem Sing. An additional two or three thousand became believers, but since they were transferred out of camp before completing training and being baptized, they were not counted. Similar results were experienced in other camps by other Christian organizations. We had more new believers in our refugee work in three years than we had had in the more than forty years of our mission work in Thailand. It reinforced the historical record through the centuries that God draws more people to Himself through persecution and suffering than through a life of ease and affluence. Exactly why God allows, and uses, persecution and suffering is a holy mystery, but the fact that He does use those events is a certainty. By no means does that justify any type of persecution. Paul dealt with that misconception in the book of Romans, but those terrible, ugly, persecution events, and how God used them, could well be a lesson for the United States and other nations.

Another issue came up related to the status of Kamput and the makeup of the refugee population. Kamput had been considered a holding center since its inception. In April 1982, the UN reclassified it as a processing center. Receiving nations were provided spaces to interview refugees for relocation. A few were still coming in; many were leaving. The atmosphere in camp began to change. Previously, most of the refugees assumed they would be allowed to relocate to other countries. In reality, criteria had been established by each country that would determine eligibility for immigration. It turned out that many did not meet the criteria. It was seriously threatening the atmosphere and security in several of the camps. Unfortunately, much of it was being caused by changes in United States policies.

For many years, the Immigration and Naturalization Service (INS) has been under the Department of Justice. They determine the terms, criteria, and numbers for immigration under existing immigration laws. The Southeast Asian refugee crisis brought a variation in that status. The Indochina Migration and Refugee Act was enacted by Congress and signed on May 23, 1975. It allocated funds to the Department of State and the Department of Justice for the resettlement of Vietnamese and Cambodian refugees.[3] Now two (sometimes three) agencies were vetting refugees, but the criteria for granting immigration status were different. As an outsider, I did not know the specifics of the new procedure. They were very secretive about the process.

What I do know is what refugees who experienced the process told me. The United States State Department and the INS were both provided interview space in camp. The different criteria by the two agencies immediately caused problems; family members were being split by the different criteria. Some members fit one set of criteria by the INS, and others did not. It was the same with Department of State. Intra-agency tension developed. Portions of families would be divided to go to different countries; refugee consternation became volatile.

Then another element entered the picture that elevated the consternation to anger and possible conflict. What brought it about was a shift in the identity of several of the refugees. In the early stages of the crisis, all the Cambodian refugees were labeled "Khmer Seri" ("Free Khmer"). *Khmer* means *Cambodian*. They had suffered under the Pol Pot regime, but some of the "Khmer Rouge" (Communists, Pol Pot soldiers) started coming in to the camps as refugees.

The new category of refugees came about partly as a result of the murderous, killing-field philosophy of Pol Pot and his soldiers. World opinion was turning against them, and they were incurring military losses to the point of sensing defeat. Realizing what that could mean, several of the soldiers defected and headed for the camps at the border. Several of the early Khmer Seri refugees still in camp began to see Khmer Rouge soldiers coming in who had been among those marauding soldiers torturing and killing family members back in Cambodia. The atmosphere (in Kamput especially) became extremely volatile. When some of the Khmer Rouge soldiers began using false documents to obtain eligibility to immigrate, while the Khmer Seri were unable to do that, the situation was ripe for revolt. On that issue, I could document the allegations.

Someone needed to step in. We (CCSDPT) were generally accepted as the primary advocates for the refugees. The receiving governments were interested primarily in those who qualified to come to their country. A few of the other Volags and IOs had their own agendas that were alarming to the refugees, but when times of trouble came, we were looked to for support and assistance. That was one of those times. We were limited, however, by our status. We had no governmental authority and no leverage to make demands. Our authority and mandate came on the basis of our being a major refugee relief entity and the only moral voice being raised in the face of another potential disaster. Since we provided the forum and venue by which the world media was reporting the refugee developments, we decided to use that platform to alert the world to what was really happening. We felt we had to go public.

With the strong support of other CCSDPT directors, I began speaking privately with INS and United States embassy people about our concern. I emphasized that we were not for or against any refugee movement, but we were deeply concerned about the inconsistencies of the United States policies and the resulting rising tensions in the camps. The discussions were not successful. Their policies came from a higher level (meaning Washington, DC), and they had no control over them. I made it an agenda item for our monthly CCSDPT meetings. With world media present, American officials gave verbal commitments to address the issue, but over the next few months, there were no policy changes. The situation became more volatile. We had only one final recourse.

Declining Refugee Population and Confusing Immigration Criteria

Our annual CCSDPT meeting would be occurring shortly. Senior government officials from sponsoring nations, directors of the international organizations, senior Thai government officials, and world media would be present. Official spokespeople would be given a brief time to state their positions. As chairman of CCSDPT, I would be giving one of the keynote addresses. We decided to make the mishandling of the refugee interview process the focus of our message. In fairness, I informed our embassy and the INS of what I would be doing. I was strongly urged to refrain since they were already addressing the problem. Inside Kamput and a few other camps, however, nothing had changed, and it was becoming more explosive. We decided to continue as planned.

Embassy, State Department, and INS personnel were embarrassed and irritated. The United States had done far more than any other nation in providing resources and in accepting refugees for resettlement; now, they were being called on the carpet. I was extremely uncomfortable. As an American citizen, I was publicly questioning my own government. I knew how much our country had done compared to others, and I was proud to be known as an American, but I also knew an explosive situation was growing in some of the camps. It could easily lead to bloodshed and needed to be dealt with immediately. I made my presentation with deep concern.

There were no explosions. I was not vilified. For whatever reasons, and there were many factors involved in the final resolution of the refugee crisis, tensions began to diminish. Refugees were gradually resettled, camps began closing, and the crisis atmosphere began to abate. One of my best days was my last day as chairman of CCSDPT. The stress had been heavy, but time after time, I knew I was being sustained by the Lord's presence. And the spiritual harvest was abundant and inspiring.

Our heavy involvement with the refugee work started easing off in 1982 as the processing centers assigned more refugees to the receiving countries. The transit centers in the Bangkok area continued to process resettlement refugees, so Joann stayed busy with departure medical exams. We had a full-time Indian lady doctor, so Joann was not as loaded with work as previously.

But there was always another crisis popping up. During the rainy season of 1982, Bangkok (and many other areas in Thailand) experienced severe flooding, causing major problems in the low-lying slums. Joann directed multiple clinics in treating hosts of medical problems coming out of flooded areas that were inundated with contaminated water. FMB relief funds allowed us to provide some much-needed relief to many people. It also opened the door to several new ministry-outreach activities for the missionaries working in the Bangkok area.

As I write this in 2016, Bangkok is in the international news because it is sinking at an alarming rate. Thousands of wells have been drilled in the past forty years to supplement the unreliable city water system. The result is a major subsidence over much of the Bangkok area (over ten million population) causing increasingly dangerous flooding in the monsoon season.

Expansion: Other Areas and Nations

In the middle of some of the busiest refugee work, Bill Wakefield, my area director, did me a couple of great favors (unknown to both of us at the time). The first one was in 1980 when he asked me to go to the semiannual meeting of the board of directors of the Bangalore Baptist Hospital in Bangalore, India.

I was delighted with the invitation. India—and the medical work—were already well-known among Baptists. The pioneering missionary work of William Carey in the Calcutta (Bengal) and Serampore areas was of historical significance in the beginning of the modern missionary movement, and it all made me anxious to see India. That was the opening that led Joann and me to working intermittently in India for the next eleven years. That initial visit was soon followed by Bill's asking me to serve on the Bangalore Baptist Hospital board of directors. It was a most rewarding work.

His other favor occurred in September 1981, when he asked me to do a survey trip into Laos to consult with government officials concerning the possibility of reestablishing a presence in the country. There had been three FMB missionary families in the country when the upheaval of 1975 forced them to leave. Now, however, we were getting hints that our return to do development work might be welcome. That was what prompted the survey. I was delighted at the prospect.

Flying from Bangkok to Vientiane on an old Russian-built, unpressurized, single-engine, bi-wing Laotian Airlines plane gave me a hint of what was coming. Baggage was thrown loosely into the main cabin with passengers. No tie-downs, no assigned seating. Climb in, sit down, and hang on. As we neared Vientiane, the clouds became thicker. We could not see the ground. As we began to maneuver up and down and back and forth, I realized we were flying strictly VFR. There were no working radio navigation aids, and the pilots were looking for a hole in the clouds through which to descend and start looking for the airport. They finally found one, dropped through, oriented themselves, and landed uneventfully.

My trip had come about rather quickly, resulting in no scheduled appointments prior to my arrival. That was not the way it should have been done. To my surprise, I was cordially received and granted immediate access to everyone I needed to consult. The Laotian minister of health left a meeting with physicians from international organizations to spend more than an hour with me. I was told later that it was highly irregular for such visits to occur on short notice. To add to my pleasant surprise, everyone I needed to see was in the country at the same time: the minister of health, the minister of foreign affairs, the vice premier, the director of WHO, the director of UNICEF, the UNHCR chief of mission, the US embassy charge d'affairs (the US and Laos had no formal ties and no ambassador), and others. Absolutely remarkable! I was able to see much of the immediate Vientiane area as well as Pakse and other northern areas (but not the southern regions).

I felt the Lord had a definite hand in the episode. He was opening the door for the Laotian leaders to allow a Christian organization in who would share the gospel. The leaders I met were senior officials, especially the Laotians, but they were not members of their Politburo Committee so they could only make recommendations. They were sympathetic to our return, but they had little authority in decision-making. The real leaders blew it. They refused assistance—even in the face of desperate needs.

The needs, problems, and challenges in Laos were too great to describe in detail. I'll just give a few summary statements (some statistics were extracted from Business Journals and UNHCR reports, but I cannot name specific sources):

- All manufactured goods had to be imported.
- Medical care was minimal. (Strangely, antibiotics were plentiful.) Other medications, including IVs, medical and surgery equipment, and supplies, were absent.
- Ten percent of the total population left as refugees, but 60 percent of the elite left—the professional, educated, technical, and management people. The lack of skilled leadership raised concerns for us to utilize any available resources.
- There was minimal national infrastructure—few paved roads, primitive communications, few utilities, extremely high inflation—and the economy was a basket case. Ultimate

national decision-making was the big question. The national politburo was comprised of hard-core Communist believers. They were the deciders. Party philosophy determined decisions—not need, suffering, or what was just or right. Below politburo level (the people I talked with), there was a great desire for us to come in and help in every possible way, but they did not have the final say about the most important issues.

In discussions with Laotian officials, I mentioned mutual conditions needed if we provided resources for health care and other projects. I told them we would need ongoing visas and travel permissions that would enable us to evaluate and monitor the projects. They readily agreed, even to the point of assuring me there would be no import duties or taxes on equipment and supplies we brought in for development use.

Christianity was permitted—but only with government monitoring and with restrictive guidelines. I was told there was an active Christian witness in some southern provinces, with good response, but I was not able to visit or confirm. I attended services in the one Protestant church in Vientiane (a Baptist Christian, led to the Lord by an FMB missionary, was pastor), but it was restrained. A couple of pastors wanted to see me for a private visit, but they were fearful of being seen by authorities.

In spite of a very cordial response to my visit, I began to lose some enthusiasm. On the surface, the place was appealing. Both the city and the countryside were quiet, unhurried, and placid, a welcome change from the noise and chaos of Bangkok, but it was not an invigorating quietness. I began to feel a little down myself, which was uncharacteristic of me. Shortly after returning to Bangkok, it hit me. Yes, it was peaceful and quiet, but it was not a happy quiet or joyful peace. There was an atmosphere of apathy, anger, resignation, fear, and lethargy. It was a choking, suffocating presence, and it became contagious. I knew the antidote—hearing and believing the gospel—but I sensed a lack of openness to allowing us to accomplish our mission. There was a desperate need for God's grace to be made known, but walls of repression seemed to permeate the atmosphere. I left Vientiane slightly discouraged. They had overwhelming needs of every kind, and we were willing to share, but we could not force our entry. We left the door open, but they never responded.

I completed the survey and submitted my report to Bill, along with possible options for an initial, small response they would have permitted, but with no firm recommendation. I still had ambivalent feelings. I was too close to it to be totally objective. A few weeks later, when Bill was in Bangkok, we discussed the situation. In the meantime, I had attempted to obtain another Laotian visa with the intent to be ready should Bill decide to initiate an exploratory project. The visa was never granted. Without the ability to go in and evaluate any request they had made, and without the ability to monitor the use of the resources we provided, Bill felt we should hold off. I agreed.

One of many little side stories about snafus, problems, headaches, and foul-ups faced in attempting to help undeveloped areas of the world was provided by one of the largest landmarks in Vientiane. It was a little unusual—but not all that uncommon. Some of the background history is noted below.

The story started a few years earlier when the United States provided major resources for Laos to build facilities and infrastructure during the heavy United States military activity in Southeast Asia. American officials asked the Laotians what they felt was most essential to national development. They responded that a new runway for the national airport was greatly needed. They were right; they did not have an adequate runway for normal airline service. The resources were provided, work was begun, and vague progress reports were submitted. One small ingredient missing from the entire project, however, was the matter of American officials monitoring construction. When the project was nearing completion, a review was needed. I can only imagine the thoughts and consternation of the American officials as they viewed the finished product.

The finished product was not a new runway. It was a humongous, arched monument in the largest street intersection in Vientiane.

Vertical Runway Monument, Laos

Their explanation was that as they (the Laotian officials) considered the project, they felt a victory monument would be more fitting and of more benefit to the nation than a runway. I heard the story three or four times from lower officials who told it with a mixture of humor, chagrin, and embarrassment. They jokingly referred to it as the "vertical runway." After years of development work in third world countries, I could better understand how the foul-up could happen. We had similar issues (though on a much, much smaller scale) in a couple of our development programs, but we learned to mitigate the risk with closer monitoring. I'll tell about one of them when we get back to India.

Later in 1981, I took Joann on my fall trip to the semiannual Bangalore Baptist Hospital board meeting. With refugee work declining and with hints that Joann and I might be having increasing involvement in India, we felt it would be good for her to get initiated to the area. Little did we realize at the time what that benign beginning would develop into.

Interlude: Medical Surprise

In the spring of 1982, our refugee workload began to slow since Kamput was becoming a processing center rather than a holding center. Joann and I actually were able to get together in Bangkok once in a while. Our little apartment with two upstairs bedrooms was in the heart of the city. It was the middle of the hot season. We were thinking that we might be living there a little more in the future and considered putting an air conditioner in our bedroom. It was hot! Until that happened, I would go with minimum clothing, meaning only my underwear.

Then another overwhelming benefit came to me because of my physician wife and her sharp analytical eye. As we were talking one weekend, she noticed something not right about my right breast. The right nipple was inverted. I had not noticed it. She came over and began a very thorough chest exam. She found a nodule under the nipple. She became very quiet and stopped replying to my questions. She finally looked up with eyes filled with tears. When she was able to talk, she said she thought it was cancer. I was skeptical. A male with cancer of the breast? With no pain, no discomfort, no loss of movement? She insisted that I go to our hospital in Bangkla the following Monday morning and have Dr. Al Hood look at it.

Al's preliminary examination led him to think it was not cancer, but when he did a lumpectomy, he changed his mind. He sent the tissue to the pathologist in the Seventh Day Adventist Hospital in Bangkok where it was confirmed that it was indeed a malignancy. Al and the SDA surgeon agreed that, to be safe, a mastectomy should be done. I had a radical mastectomy done at the Bangkok SDA Hospital on April 3, 1982. The pathology report indicated it was encapsulated and all affected tissue had been removed, including lymph nodes, muscle, and other tissue.

Joann continued to keep her doctor's cap on. She called Dr. Gordon McGee, the pathologist at Hotel Dieu Hospital in El Paso, Texas. He had been our pathologist at Culberson Hospital in Van

Horn while I was administrator, and he and I had become friends. In that conversation with Dr. McGee, he told her he had just returned from the M. D. Anderson Cancer Hospital in Houston, where he had participated in the first medical seminar dealing with male cancer of the breast and possible treatment protocols. What a coincidence! He asked her to send him the slides done by the SDA pathologist. He would review them and then forward them to M. D. Anderson for their review. That was done, and the cancer was reconfirmed—with the designation of the cancer being changed from stage I to stage II.

All the doctors agreed that the surgery had removed all of the malignancy and no urgent, immediate follow up care was needed. However, the doctors at M. D. Anderson were intrigued and requested that I come to them for follow-up testing. Since we would be going on furlough in December, we made an appointment for a January 1983 visit to Houston. I thought that might involve a year or so of follow-up testing, and that would be the end of it. Not so. That episode was just one more step in the minor saga that had started in the Nevada desert several years previously. More steps were yet to be taken. Stay tuned.

That four days of tests dumped me into a very peculiar situation. Cancer of the breast was usually confined to females. I didn't fit the category, but they had no place or facilities specifically for males. I had to go with the females. That put some of the females in a peculiar situation. "What's a man doing in here?" I felt like an onion in a petunia patch or a thorn among the roses. Whatever it was, I was glad to get the testing completed and get out of there.

Back to the work in Thailand we realized the timing for surgery was not appropriate. As chairman, I was pressured from several angles. It was a crucial, hectic time. Thank the Lord (and I did, many times), I recovered quickly, but it was a stressful time.

Refugees: Winding Down and a Short Furlough

For many years, the FMB considered four years in the field, followed by one year on furlough, to be the norm. With the advent of speedy air travel and other factors, furlough options became available. Shorter terms became possible, with corresponding shorter furloughs. After almost three years of intense and—especially for Joann—very stressful work, we decided to cut our term short and take a break.

It just happened that a couple of years previously, China had begun to open the door to foreign tourists. Individuals were discouraged from going, but groups were invited, always accompanied by guides ("minders") and interpreters. Joann and I had longed to see China for many years, and this was our chance. In November 1982, we joined a group of twenty-five or thirty people, from many countries, at our designated hotel in Hong Kong. Our passports were collected, to be returned only when we were leaving the country. All of our names were stamped on a sheet of paper that served as our group visa. If anyone went missing, the entire group would be retained.

Our intended itinerary would take us from Hong Kong to Canton (Guangzhou), Guilin, Beijing, Xian, Shanghai, and back to Hong Kong, but travel schedules in China were subject to change.

Part of the fascination with China is their history, sometimes extending back three or four thousand years. It would be futile to try to review much of it here, but I will touch the high points. Canton was a good place to begin, with historical records going back at least 1,500 years and with religious structures existing for at least five hundred years. It was no wonder the Chinese and other Asians see the West as an upstart civilization. They pointed with pride to events and achievements that predated our history by many centuries. From Canton, we flew to Guilin. It is primarily in the twentieth century that Guilin has become known to the West, but it has been an ancient, almost sacred place to the Chinese for many centuries. Much of that attraction and reverence is because of the unique geography of the region. Spectacular karst rock formations, resulting from very irregular erosion over many thousands of years, have left towering geological formations of vertical upthrust limestone pinnacles and countless caves within mountains. It is a majestic landscape through which the Li River meanders, providing one breathtaking vista after another. It has been a magnet for Chinese artists since ancient times, and it is even more so today. Joann and I cruised on the river then-and again twenty years later. Absolutely astounding.

From the beautiful, subtropical, clear-flowing streams of the Guilin region, we flew to Beijing. What contrast! Again, I will limit my comments drastically. We saw the usual historical places, but one place made such a lasting, emotional impression that it has stayed with both of us. That was Tiananmen Square, infamous for the large number of people, mostly young people, killed there by Chinese soldiers. It happened primarily in Tiananmen Square, but also in the surrounding streets. When demonstrators asked for economic, political, and religious freedom, they were suppressed with deadly force. China will not comment on the incident. On the day we were there, a company of Chinese soldiers was marching back and forth in the square with loaded rifles, creating a very wide-open space among the many visitors in whatever direction the soldiers turned. The atmosphere was oppressive. Along with hundreds of others, we stood in line for a long time to view the preserved body of Mao Tse-Tung in his mausoleum whom the Chinese highly revered as the father of their present nation.

A side note just has to be made about the food we enjoyed (or otherwise) in China. It must have been cabbage harvest time somewhere in China: we had cabbage for breakfast, lunch, and dinner. We had cabbage stewed, grilled, boiled, fried, pickled, and fermented. We had cabbage as a side dish, in egg rolls, and as sauerkraut. However cabbage could be fixed, we had it. If we did not get enough at mealtime, there were piles of it along the roads that we could pick up. That was early tourism in recently reopened

China; it did not take them long to learn how to cater to tourists with top-notch food.

An amusing but semiserious episode occurred once when our guide asked if we were interested in experiencing a Mongolian hot pot meal. We all said we would. He did not explain that the meal was outside our prepaid package deal. When he asked for the money to pay after the meal, two ladies from England refused to pay. They claimed we had prepaid for *all* our meals. The guide then stated that, unless everyone paid for the requested meal, none of us would leave China. After a short but intense stalemate, several people volunteered to pay for their meals. That relieved the tense moment. Whew! (The two ladies, with one briefcase full of cash and another full of food, never did pay for the meal.)

The other place that must be mentioned was our visit to the Great Wall of China, only about fifty or sixty miles north of Beijing. It was the middle of November when we visited, and winter had arrived. A snowstorm was blowing, and it was cold. Countless pictures have been made of the wall, as well as many descriptions, but the magnitude and scope of the wall can't be fully grasped until it is seen from several perspectives, up close as well as from a distance (including from space). Aside from the obvious awe-inspiring wall itself, the analogies and symbolisms that can be drawn from it concerning our relationship to Christ and His care for us are almost endless—walls of false security, vulnerable defense, and unreliable protection—the list could go on.

In Xian, in west-central China, we saw the world-renowned, massive excavations of large-as-life terra-cotta figures of thousands of men and horses in full battle array. The exhibition is stunning and amazing. It was a mausoleum for a dead emperor. It stayed hidden for 2,200 years, possibly because the workers who carved and constructed the mausoleum were conscripted as slaves and were buried alive when the emperor was buried. No one was to be left alive who could identify his burial place. I am repeating what our guide told us; I could not confirm the story. We also saw many other ancient buildings, walls, temples, and artifacts.

We left Xian for Shanghai, but we were diverted because of "bad weather up ahead." Something happened, or changed, because our flight was shorter than scheduled, and we landed in Nanjing that night at nine o'clock. Nanjing is a city of about four million, but the airport was closed and the lights were out. Our tour guide was obviously stumped. We were taken into the dark, empty terminal building to wait. I'll skip the other details to report that we were finally housed in the "Comrade's Hotel," which housed only Communist officials. It turned out to be the best hotel and the best food we had on the trip. There was one quirk about it; there were no locks on the doors. Hotel staff came and went at will.

We went on to Shanghai the next day. With a population of about fifteen million at the time, it was the largest city in China. We saw and did the usual things and prepared to return to Hong Kong. We were doing our last event—touring the estuary of the Yangtze River—when Joann created a little excitement. The estuary of the river was huge and crowded with ships. It encompassed a major Chinese naval installation, one of their largest shipbuilding facilities and the largest commercial port in China. It was understandable that the Chinese were very conscious of security.

When our tour boat slowed for a moment to allow for a better view, a little one-man, one oar (scull) sampan pulled up to our boat to ask for money. It was a perfect Kodak moment, and Joann made the most of it. A few moments later, a Chinese patrol boat pulled alongside our boat and a Chinese naval officer came aboard and went directly to Joann. He demanded that she hand over her camera or be punished.

She was flabbergasted. "What have I done?"

"You took a picture of a Chinese war vessel; that is forbidden."

She denied it and refused to give him her camera. She told him she had taken a picture of the little sampan that was still alongside our boat. A few minutes of intense discussion followed. He finally relented and let her go. When we had the film developed in Bangkok, there was the sampan in full view—with a big Chinese destroyer clearly seen in the background. She was dumbfounded again. She had never noticed it. Neither had I. Oh, well. For a moment on the boat, the situation was not funny.

Time to go back to Hong Kong. Our flight left just at dark and would be totally over land, including some large towns. I had a window seat, and the sky was clear. I expected to see the usual beautiful night lights along our route of flight, but there were no lights. The countryside was in total darkness. As we came near the New Territory border (which extends from about five to about fifteen miles outside the Hong Kong city limits into mainland China), the pilot called our attention to the contrast below. He banked the plane to give us a better view. He didn't preach, moralize, complain, or condemn. He just noted that where the lights began was the border between China and Hong Kong. He didn't need to say any more. In a similar comparison to the Great Wall, the redemptive analogies were clearly seen. Official Chinese Communist doctrine states there is no God. There is a continual attempt to suppress the spread of the gospel. People are left in darkness, symbolized by the absence of light in the nation. As I write this, thirty-three years after that flight, there is encouraging news as countless pinpoints of light are appearing throughout China as Christians share the good news of the gospel in the face of much harassment and persecution.

Hong Kong had made its own statement when it installed a bright line of lights along the entire New Territory border. (All that was taking place before control of Hong Kong reverted to Chinese control in 1997.) Christian influence was evident in Hong Kong. A significant portion of the citizens were Christians. The gospel could be shared openly and freely. People were coming to the Lord. The land that was open to the gospel was a land of freedom, illuminated by countless pinpoints of light. Just across that fence was a land trying to suppress the Word of God, and it was a land of darkness. It seemed that many of the passengers on that plane saw and understood the symbolism. It was a quiet group as we landed and went our separate ways.

It was good to be back home in Bangkok, but our stay would be brief. We would be leaving for the States shortly. As we had done previously, we capitalized on being on the opposite side of the world from home and decided to make the most of it. We made our plans to go home through Australia and New Zealand. They were a little out of the way, but compared to the cost of a round-trip flight from the United States to Australia and back, going through there was not much more expensive.

We made a brief stop in beautiful Singapore, one of our favorite cities of the world. It is amazing what that little island city/nation has done to develop such a variety of tropical gardens, miniature parks, ethnic enclaves, multiple high-rise business and commercial centers, and attractive shopping choices.

From Singapore to Brisbane, Australia, then onward to Townsville was typical, routine flying. As we neared Townsville, however, it became atypical. Townsville was on the coast, opposite the approximate midpoint of the Great Barrier Reef, our immediate travel goal. Our final approach to the airport took us a short distance off the coast, still several miles from the Great Barrier Reef but close enough for us to get just a glimpse and hint of it. Even from that distance, we could see enough to tantalize us. Small islands and sand atolls extended in all directions as far as we could see. The Great Barrier Reef is more than 1,500 miles long, so we were seeing only a minute portion of it. The anticipation of beginning to explore it the next day was exciting.

With a strong wind discouraging boats from going to the reef the next day, I chartered one of the last small helicopters to fly just the two of us for a day of diving, snorkeling, and sightseeing. The flight out brought oohs and ahs. Our pilot told us the water averaged about two hundred feet in depth, but it was so clear that the ocean floor was plainly visible. Sand ripples on the bottom, large fish, small upthrusts—every feature could be seen in great detail.

We landed on a low-water atoll, just a small sand islet above water only at low tide. As the pilot shut down the engine, Joann and I both had the same question: "What happens if the engine will not start?"

"Get ready for a long swim!" the pilot answered.

Our pilot was familiar with the place. He suggested we go to the other end of the islet, swim out a short distance, look down, and then go down for a closer look. We did and found an old shipwreck about ten or twelve feet down. A small ship had apparently run into a coral outgrowth that gouged a hole in the boat and caused it to go down. It was fun and exciting to explore, but we did not try to go inside.

The indescribably beautiful coral and colorful tropical fish for which the reef is famous surrounded the islet, as well as the additional thousands of islands and islets making up the reef. After several hours of viewing just a small portion of God's amazing creation, it was time to head back. The engine did start okay, and we wound our way over the reef and ocean back to Townsville. We spent the next day exploring the tropical inland area around the town, then flew to Auckland, New Zealand.

The North Island of New Zealand was beautiful, but the South Island is justifiably considered one of the most beautiful places in the world. It is the setting for many movies. It had many places we wanted to see, starting with Milford Sound (fjord) on the southwest coast of South Island. Getting there, however, led us to one of those surprising, wondrous, serendipitous experiences that has been etched in our memory ever since.

The first part of the flight was from Christchurch to an airport at the base of Mount Cook, the highest mountain in the Southern Alps. We would transfer to a smaller plane that could handle the very short runway at Milford Sound. When we exited the plane at Mount Cook, we were approached by a man who wanted us to charter his plane for a special flight. He said Mount Cook (elevation 12,218 feet), which was enveloped in clouds over 90 percent of the time, was clear that day. In addition, there had been a significant snowfall the previous night. That day would be the ideal time to see it. We would have just enough time to see it before our flight to Milford Sound. Joann and I jumped at the chance. Interestingly, his plane was a ski plane, a Cessna 195, a type I had flown (minus the skis).

The second surprise came when we climbed to about ten thousand feet, and he turned directly toward the mountain. As we approached, he began to slow down, dropped partial flaps, and set up for an approach and landing. I was in the copilot's seat, on the edge, looking everywhere for a possible landing site. Every place on the mountain was covered with snow, and I could not see any possible landing site. As he dropped full flaps and throttled back, I noticed a straight, upward sloping bench on the side of the mountain in front of us that extended just far enough for us to land. He made a beautiful landing on the snow. After a brief slide on the skis, he kicked hard left rudder, revved the engine momentarily, and did a sharp 180-degree turn, leaving the plane facing downslope, but the plane didn't stop; it was slowly sliding down the hill. In all of the flight, he had never told us what he would be doing—so we had no idea what was coming next. He just looked over at me, grinned, and said, "I hope it stops!" It did, and we were ready to take off downhill when the time came.

We climbed out of that plane and just stood there. The cloudless sky was a brilliant blue, and there was no wind, both of which were rare. The flight, the landing, the setting, and the view left us speechless. Just a few days earlier, we had seen the beauty of the underwater world of coral. Now we were seeing God's creative beauty and handiwork from near the top of snow-covered mountains. To say it was overwhelming is an understatement.

After a few minutes of trying to absorb the experience, stamp the scene in our memory, and experiment with a snowball (big mistake!), we climbed back in, took off, and glided quietly the few miles back to the airport.

Our flight to Milford Sound was almost as spectacular. There were three of us plus the pilot in a larger, twin-engine plane. We wound our way between high-walled mountains to the head of Milford Sound. Our arrival had our full attention. We came in over a hanging valley about two hundred feet above the ground, passed over the precipitous edge, and descended in a tight spiral the two thousand feet straight down to the short landing strip. Thrilling? Absolutely, at least for Joann and me. Not so much for the other passenger. She was petrified. She covered her head with her coat and leaned down and forward so she could not see anything outside the plane.

We were not the only ones enjoying the geography. It was a favorite jumping-off place for hang gliders. On the day we arrived, since there was no wind, they could only jump off and glide to a landing. One of the glider pilots told me that on good days, with the wind from the right direction, they could sometimes catch a rising thermal or wind current and gain enough altitude to stay airborne for a long period of time. I was tempted to try a flight, but Joann untempted me. (Not really, she has never discouraged my adventurous impulses.)

A short cruise through the sound, out into the sea, and then back left us rubbernecking in all directions. Our boat driver nudged our boat up to the very wall of the sound, under the full flow of a five hundred-foot waterfall, and urged us to get out on deck to experience the sensation. Very few took him up on that. One of many amazing sights was seeing hundreds of seals sunning themselves on the rocks alongside the sound.

Time to leave. Our bus ride back to Queenstown was a continuation of spectacular scenery. Our canyon exit road was between granite walls almost two thousand feet high. It was the peak of the snowmelt time (their summer), and countless waterfalls were tumbling off from the higher mountains on both sides of the road.

The Southern Alps have some similarities with the Swiss Alps, and Queenstown is like a Swiss town in the middle of it. Ski lifts rise in all directions. Shopping was similar also, but with many items unique to New Zealand. We helped the economy just a bit.

Our last stop was back in Christchurch for a couple of memorable days. The first night, we watched a very professional local production of *The Nutcracker*, followed by a drum-and-bagpipe Scottish parade, complete with costumes. The next day, Sunday, was a surprising, welcome blessing of hearing portions of Handel's *Messiah* performed by a choir and recorder orchestra at a nearby Baptist church.

While walking back to our hotel from church, and for the remainder of our time in Christchurch, we were impressed by the conduct of the people. Drivers would stop in the street and ask us, complete strangers, if they could take us somewhere. I was buying something in the hotel when I realized my billfold was still in my room.

"Never mind," the attendant said. "Take this with you and bring the money when it is convenient."

We sensed a moral and ethical atmosphere and culture that was reminiscent of America many years ago. New Zealand would be the close second choice of our preferred place to live in the world. We headed home for Christmas.

CHAPTER 8

Home Again, Briefly

With great gratitude, we moved into a fully furnished missionary house in Arlington, Texas, for our furlough. It was provided, unexpectedly, by an individual family. We picked up our plane in Little Rock and flew it back to the nearby Grand Prairie airport for use until furlough was over and we could sell it. Absentee ownership of the plane had not worked as well as we hoped, but it was a great time-saver in our furlough travels.

I spent four full days of extensive lab and x-ray evaluation at M. D. Anderson Cancer Center in Houston in January. One new factor in my diagnosis turned up when a background interview revealed my participation in an above-ground atomic weapons test in Nevada in 1951. They felt there could be a possible connection between the testing exposure and my cancer, and with that possibility of recurrence, I should be followed with ongoing checkups. I was placed on a five-year regimen of soft-tissue (CEA) and hard-tissue (bone scans) tests. I did that, and the hospital has continued to follow up on my status, even to the present time. There has been no recurrence.

Furlough was a good time with family, speaking in churches, and other deputation engagements. Lisa had an excellent job with Texas Utilities, and James was doing well at Baylor.

One major event occurred on our furlough in early 1983 as we were driving around my old home place near Formosa. On the spur of the moment, we stopped at a Realtor's office to see what property might be available. I noticed a tract of land for sale that I had never thought would be sold. It had belonged to a pioneer family and their descendants for many years. It was the location of Ol' Piney, the swimming and baptizing spot that had been used by the entire area for almost a hundred years. It was at the confluence of Choctaw and Wolfe Creeks, both of which ran through the property. It was about two miles from where the creek ran into Greers Ferry Lake. When we saw it, there was no hesitation before we put down earnest money.

As soon as we left the Realtor's office, we went back to the place. Joann already had the house site picked out and the house halfway built in her mind. She was beside herself with excitement. On the east side of the creek, there was a bluff of sixty or seventy feet, beyond which was the remaining seventy-five hilly acres that were for sale. She picked a spot not far from the edge of the bluff and marked off the outline of the house. At the north end was the breakfast nook, then the kitchen, dining room, living room with fireplace, master bedroom, and master bath, all overlooking the bluff, the valley, and Culpepper Mountain. Ol Piney could be seen from all rooms except the master bath. Retirement was several years away, but location and house design were settled matters. We were thrilled with the purchase.

There was one final, major event that came up just before we returned to Thailand. Sometime over the 1982–1983 holidays Joann, Lisa, Lisa's "friend," and I were going to see someone at a camp somewhere west of Fort Worth. As we arrived at camp Lisa's "friend," Chris Schuttger, a coworker at Texas Utilities, asked me for permission to marry Lisa. It was a little surprising, but he was a fine Christian man, and it was obvious that Lisa was all for it.

I—and we—gave our blessing. One of the things that made it a little surprising was that Lisa had indicated considerable intent in high school in having a career in pharmacy or computers. She had always been a tomboy, never played with dolls, and had not shown great interest in dating. Situations, attitudes, and plans do change, however, and Lisa's did. She and Chris were married in May 1983, just before we returned to Thailand.

The extent and degree of those changes unfolded greatly in the next several years as Lisa and Chris had seven children, all of whom she homeschooled with great success. Now she is a grandmother several times over. (When your children have grandchildren, the reality of your mortality really begins knocking on the door. Ouch!)

Joann and I had wondered privately what we might be going back to when we returned to Thailand in 1983. We had had hints, but the more complete answer came in a letter from Bill Wakefield that we received on our arrival in Texas for furlough in December 1982. He asked us to assume two responsibilities. I was asked to become the consultant for hunger, disaster relief, and development programs for all of South and Southeast Asia. Joann would be the medical consultant for those programs in the same region. We would be traveling throughout the region, especially in India, investigating needs and opportunities for development programs. We had already begun those programs along the eastern border of Thailand, with several rural medical clinics already functioning, and those would continue. Our travels in India would also explore the possibility of our moving to India as a base of operation. The prospect was exciting—and very challenging.

Back to Thailand Again

Our arrival back in Thailand in June of 1983 was the beginning of our gypsy, tumbleweed years; we just did not know it at the time.

We resumed our work with the Thai people along the eastern border of Thailand. It was not a major activity, and that was the problem. Our small-scale provision of assistance in food and health care for the poverty-stricken Thai people, while providing everything for the refugees, had become a sore point with the Thai government. They asked us to do more for the Thai people. We started medical clinics immediately. We also started water- and agriculture-development projects with the help of very capable volunteers from Amarillo, Texas. The well-received and well-utilized assistance opened many villages to a gospel witness.

I had an ironic request from the American embassy. They requested that TBM assume major responsibility for multiple development projects throughout east Thailand, to be totally funded by the United States government. After our frank discussions some months earlier concerning the refugee resettlement problem, I was a little surprised at that request. One official told me that TBM had an excellent reputation for doing very effective agriculture- and water-development projects—as well as providing medical care in the neediest areas—with total integrity. With so much American aid being siphoned off into the black market, they wanted very much to work with a reliable organization like ours. They wanted to fund someone they could trust. That was entirely understandable. Unfortunately for the official, I had to say no. Our FMB policies would not allow us to accept or use government funding.

It was good to know that we had that reputation. It was really our agriculture missionary who was responsible for most of the agriculture and water development. It was a great success and prompted more requests to expand. Joann was responsible for the outstanding medical care reputation with the refugees and the rural Thais. She had become well-known and highly respected.

India: Getting a First Glimpse of Calcutta

It was time to take a closer look at India and implement some of the ideas Bill Wakefield had mentioned, but India was almost like a parallel universe, difficult to fully grasp or understand. We had a few ideas on how or where to get a toehold to begin our exploration, but they were necessarily tentative. Some of the story that follows is intended to convey the essence and variety of that work in the latter part of 1983 and is not necessarily in chronological order.

India was stunning. Lush beauty and exotic architecture often coexisted side-by-side with stark ugliness and poverty. Our senses were often overloaded with concentrations of colors, smells, tastes, sounds, and conduct. India could be a colorless land of black and white or a land of brilliant colors. It was rarely boring.

One of the many surprising things about India was that it had an estimated Christian population of several million with an estimated almost two million Baptists; the exact number was impossible to know. Many of them were in the extreme northeast area of India in Nagaland, Assam, and surrounding areas, but other areas also had a significant number of Baptist Christians.

In our early discussions, Bill had mentioned several areas with project possibilities, including Chandigarh, Calcutta, and Bangalore. Chandigarh was in the far northwest part of India, north of New Delhi, near Kashmir, adjacent to the Punjab, within sight of the Himalayas. The area had several Baptist churches with active outreach programs and the apparent ability to utilize assistance wisely.

Calcutta also offered a possibility. A wealthy Baptist leader among Mississippi Baptists in the United States had worked with and assisted Calcutta (Bengal) Baptists in some development projects and wanted the FMB to join in his efforts. It merited our consideration for involvement.

Bangalore, where our hospital was located and where several programs had been successful, also offered possibilities. We could look more closely at that area later when we went to Bangalore for one of the regularly scheduled board meetings.

Then another area became a very viable option. It came about through a request to the FMB from the Orissa Baptist Convention, a coastal state in east-central India, southwest of Calcutta. There were several churches in the Bhubaneshwar (capital) and Cuttack areas. Several Baptists were in civic leadership roles in those cities and were a respected Christian group. As a convention mission project, they wanted to reach out to a neglected tribal group in the Khond Hills in the western and southwestern area of the state. They had some personnel who could assist, but they did not have other resources. One ministry effort they mentioned had a medical component within our capability. They wanted the FMB to join them in their mission outreach effort. With dedicated church leaders and several churches with a heart to share the gospel, the potential for a successful partnership was high. That request opened the door for us.

As we discussed our options, we thought it would be good to begin our review area in Calcutta, visit with the church leaders in Orissa, then go to northwest India, and work back toward Calcutta. For whatever reason, Bombay was not high in consideration, although the door was not closed.

. I had been through Calcutta a few times on the way to or back from somewhere else; Joann had transited once, but we had not been really initiated to the city. We had heard and read about it, but that was totally inadequate preparation. We had transited through Calcutta earlier, but the real learning began in late 1982 when we landed at the Calcutta airport. As I went to collect our baggage, I was met by a short, emaciated, ragged little man, singing:

> God rest you, merry gentlemen,
> Let nothing you dismay,
> Remember, Christ our Savior,
> Was born on Christmas Day.

That was not shocking; in fact, it gave me a smile and an uplift, but the incongruity of it has remained vivid in my memory. It was stifling hot ... well over one hundred degrees. His few pieces of clothing barely covered him. He was one of only a few attendants who, we learned later, had been required to pay a heavy bribe for permission to be there. He made it back, of course—and more—in the tips he received.

When we exited the baggage area, we received our first shock. A narrow walkway was the only way out. Hundreds of people, male and female, from the very young to the elderly, leaned against the restraining chains with outstretched hands, begging for handouts. The shocking thing was that many of the women held out their babies who had been horribly burned or maimed as a means to elicit more gifts. Our emotions and thoughts were in a jumble. Our immediate desire to help had to be suppressed. If we had offered anything to anyone, a mob stampede would have ensued, resulting in injury and possible death to those who were the weakest. Memory of that scene still disturbs me.

Joann and I met with a group of pastors and church leaders on two occasions. I reviewed our FMB criteria for providing assistance with development projects. They listed projects currently underway or being considered. A few of them qualified for our participation. Without knowing any details, I asked if Joann and I could be shown one of their projects for which we had provided some funding, sponsored by one of the groups that had utilized a nurse. It sounded like a good model for us to consider. With a little reluctance, they agreed. We would be taken to it the next day. In the course of meeting with both groups, it became apparent that there were internal problems within the Calcutta association. We did not pursue the issue, but it did affect our development planning for the region.

We left early the next morning for an eye-opening series of experiences lasting until our very late-night return to Calcutta. We were told the project was on an island in the Ganges River Delta, several miles away in another district. It was one of many islands in the delta covered and surrounded by huge mangrove thickets. The thickets were home to a large number of Bengal tigers. We did not go sightseeing.

On our departure through the streets of Calcutta, we had our first close look at some of the (estimated) one hundred thousand "street people" of Calcutta who are born, raised, live, and die on the sidewalks. Dispossessed, disfranchised, and disregarded by the government and most people, they subsist primarily by begging and scrounging. It is a pathetic life lived without any privacy, without the necessities of life, and without hope.

Our road out of Calcutta took us by a garbage dump—a huge, long mound over thirty feet high with hundreds of people all over it scrounging for whatever might be edible or useful. After a few hours, we reached the river and boarded a small boat for another few hours to the destination island. The project was on the opposite side of the island, seven miles beyond where we docked. There were no roads or cars on the island—only trails and trishaws. We took our seats and headed out just as it started to rain.

The sole transportation mode on island with church

Our little procession of three trishaws provided the local residents with the best entertainment they had witnessed in ages, especially the blonde-haired foreign lady in the leading trishaw dressed in a bright sari holding a tree-leaf umbrella, sitting backward, with dangling legs, trying desperately to keep the mud and water from the trishaw wheels from splattering her.

Arrival at the project building brought a small dilemma for Joann; the area was one huge mud puddle. Not to worry. An Indian man promptly came up to her, leaned over, picked her up, carried her inside the building, and sat her down ... on the ground. She was too flabbergasted to do anything but remain still.

The building turned out to be a church. As usual, there was no floor. People sat on the ground—ladies on one side and men on the other. The ground was moist. After a moment, one of the men very thoughtfully invited Joann to come up front and sit on a box next to me. They had heard we were coming and were ready to have a worship service. (I don't know how it happened, but in all our travels, we could never make a surprise arrival at a village.) A couple of boxes were stacked up to serve as the pulpit. In a semicircle in front of the pulpit, there was a ring of smoking incense sticks ... frankincense? The air was full of it; it was similar to a Buddhist temple setup. The pastor stepped up, welcomed us, thanked us graciously for the building, and informed me that I was to lead in the dedication service of the building.

In conversations after the service and during the meal that followed, the story finally came out. The funds provided by the FMB (coupled with more funds through the Baptist layman from Mississippi) to conduct the agricultural project and the screening of children by the nurse had, instead, been used to build the church building. It was reminiscent of a previously described American project situation in Laos. After they had received the funds, the group decided it would be more meaningful to them to have a church building than to follow through with the project they had requested. It was a done deal; there was no way to undo what they had done. There was no point in chastising them now, but their action did prompt us to review our assistance protocols.

As I tried, diplomatically, to determine how and why they decided to use the funds contrary to their request, I could hear no sense of regret or of thinking the decision was unethical or inappropriate. Their thought appeared to be that the gift became theirs when it was given, and they could use it as they felt best for the group. The thought of using the gift according to the wishes or conditions expressed by the provider had not occurred to them. I began to realize that way of thinking might not be limited just to those island residents. It might also be true in other areas of India—and other areas of the world. (As it turned out, using the biblical principles of stewardship provided by the Lord concerning the use and purpose of spiritual and material gifts He has given to His followers, they came to understand our position, but they did not always agree with it.)

Given the problems within the Calcutta association and our inability to provide ongoing, on-site leadership and monitoring of the projects, we decided to assist only a few small-scale activities under the sponsorship and leadership of those with demonstrated integrity.

One of those small projects involved an oven design used by the rural women in the Calcutta area. Joann was reminded of an oven design used by many of the refugee women in the camps that appeared to work better. Both were made out of locally available materials. She had one built, demonstrated it, and let them try it. It did work better, and many adopted it. They made bread and pastries and sold them in the villages and along the trails.

The attitude and philosophy of one church represented a refreshing break from the usual Indian pattern of seeking foreign resources to fund ministries of the church. Joann and I were in Calcutta one Sunday and attended services at the Circular Road Baptist Church. A large, ministry-oriented church, it was founded in 1818 by one of the original groups who worked with William Carey, the father of modern missions. Dr. C. Devasahayam was the highly respected, warmhearted pastor. The service, the reports of what the church was doing, the profound biblical message he brought, and his philosophy of missions in the face of opposition from some of his own people made that service one of the high points of that trip into India. He strongly disagreed with the common Indian tendency to depend on outside resources to help take the gospel to his country. He, and his church, wanted no part in soliciting or using foreign resources. A visit with him after the service just added to the day's blessings. May his tribe increase!

As usually happened, we noticed a few uniquely Indian features in Calcutta. On the way to the Circular Road Church, we passed a compound of a generally run-down group of buildings that our Indian companion told us was Mother Teresa's place. The only water available to the occupants (we were told) was a faucet on the street outside the walls. The Writer's Building had been in existence 215 years. It had been established by the British Raj to provide a place where scribes, who gathered around the building each day, were able to transcribe letters and documents for illiterate people. When Britain pulled out after World War II, Indian nationals took over. It was still being used for that purpose when we were there in 1983.

Many companies hired multiple clerks just to get a telephone message through. The call frequently required hundreds of dialing attempts before a connection was made.

I was in a meeting with government officials when lunchtime came. Three of the Indian men left the meeting because I was considered beneath their caste, and eating with me would make them unclean.

Joann and I were on our way to the airport when a Communist peace march erupted into a mob fight and blocked the road.

Before we left Calcutta, we had one more interesting side trip to Serampore, about forty miles up the Hooghly River from Calcutta. William Carey College was founded almost two hundred years ago and was the first college in India to offer graduate degrees.

Founded by the father of modern missions, the college is still in existence, although its original purpose and mission has weakened in recent years. The museum on campus contains many of the original writings, furniture, and artifacts collected and cataloged by Carey. It was very historical and fascinating.

As we entered Serampore, we passed a juggernaut, kept on the side of the road between special worship celebrations. It was a massive, pyramidal, heavy wood framework structure about twenty feet high, capped by an image of Mother Durga, a Hindu female goddess of creation. It was located near a large Hindu temple, not far from William Carey College, kept there to be used for an annual Hindu worship ritual that brought it to fame or infamy. (Juggernauts in other areas were often different. Worship practices apparently varied in different areas of India. That variety is just one factor in the difficulty of defining Indian worship beliefs.)

The Serampore Mother Durga image would be carefully cleaned and attached to the top of the juggernaut, which was then rolled on logs along the street to a designated area adjacent to the riverside for a formal presentation. The image would be removed from the juggernaut and "baptized" in the river. In the process of rolling along the street, the emotion and frenzy of the moment would sometimes lead people to either throw themselves, or be thrown, into the path of the juggernaut to be crushed to death. That did not cause sorrow or anger since it was thought to propitiate whatever wrath the gods might have toward the people. It also might result in reincarnation at a higher level of wealth, looks, or status. For the female, it might be rebirth as a male. (The beliefs in reincarnation are far too complex to attempt an explanation here.)

We returned to Calcutta for the night, then flew to Bangalore for a regular hospital board meeting and a brief review of project possibilities. On our return flight to Calcutta, we stopped (unexpectedly) in Hyderabad for the night—and a special concert. When we went into the hotel dining room around ten o'clock, the local band felt they should accommodate and welcome their foreign visitors. They started belting out five or six straight-from-Texas country and western songs, such as "The Yellow Rose of Texas." They didn't know whether we were from the United States, Europe, or somewhere else, but American country and western songs were being played all over Asia. As a counterpoint to that performance, at four o'clock the next morning, we were blasted out of bed by an Islamic muezzin chanting grossly amplified calls to prayer through speakers perched on top of the prayer tower immediately adjacent to our hotel bedroom window. That kind of awakening makes you sit up and wonder where in the world you are.

We had planned an exploratory trip into the Khond Hills, but we learned in Calcutta that heavy rains had washed out the roads. We would not be able to go. So, we took a break. On the spur of the moment, we decided to visit Darjeeling, an Indian resort city in the Himalayas that was usually closed to foreign visitors. On impulse, we applied for a permit and immediately received it.

We flew to the base of the mountains and took a bus six thousand feet up a winding stair mountain to Darjeeling. The ride and the terrain were similar to that of our return to Katmandu.

Darjeeling must be situated in the most picturesque setting in the world. Across the valley northeastward, but relatively nearby, Kanchenjunga rises 28,156 feet, the third-highest mountain in the world. It is surrounded by fifteen peaks in excess of twenty thousand feet. To the northwest, less than seventy air miles away, is Mount Everest. The border of Sikkim, which is actually a part of India, is just outside the city of Darjeeling. The mountains of Bhutan are easily seen on the immediate east—Nepal on the west and Tibet to the north. Most of that panorama could be seen from our hotel window. Our most majestic view was of Kanchenjunga, covered with snow, glaciers, and huge ice fields. We were there at the end of the monsoon season so the air was washed clean, the clouds were gone, and—at our altitude—the visibility was almost unreal.

Joann and I made a four o'clock departure out of town to Tiger Hill (8,500 feet) to watch a sunrise in perfect weather conditions. I have long since run out of words to describe the scene as we watched the sun rise. As the dawn began to appear, the higher peaks could be seen emerging from the darkness. As the sun rose, the tips of the peaks turned pink, then orange, then as the full light of the sun hit, a brilliant white. From our viewing site, the top of Kanchenjunga could easily be seen before the pink of Mount Everest emerged. It was a time of worship for us as we watched the sunlight climb down the nearby mountains and then gradually move across the entire Himalayan rampart in a gradual unfolding of an indescribable scene of God's creation. That night, we watched another scene through our hotel window that was almost as beautiful. A full moon arose in the "severe clear" atmosphere that illuminated Kanchenjunga, almost as bright as day. Words fail me. It was time to get back to work.

We flew back into Calcutta and stayed at the new airport hotel. The Calcutta area was near the location of a major cantonment back in the British Raj era. The area was known as the Dum-Dum District, partially because it was where the "dum-dum" bullets had been developed. The Calcutta airport was built within that area and adopted the name. As we entered the hotel lobby, we noticed a sign that stated: "The Dum-Dum Rotary Club Meets Here Each Tuesday."

India: Orissa (Medical)

Our travels to review development/project possibilities continued as we flew to the province of Orissa, southwest of Calcutta. Calcutta was historic, influential, and significant. Bhubaneshwar, the capital of Orissa, was more rural, economically depressed, and mostly unknown. That is an oversimplification. No short statement is adequate to explain the complexities of the cities or rural areas of India. Come to think of it, neither can a long statement.

Orissa ranked as one of the most impoverished of all the Indian states. Part of that was because of the makeup of the population.

Much of the western and southwestern portion of the state (with ill-defined borders) was hilly, isolated, jungles that were peopled by tribal groups. In earlier days, they were sometimes known as the "untouchables." Today, they are euphemistically called "scheduled tribes." They are not a part of the caste system and have, therefore, been generally ignored by the government. One of the major tribal groups (not named for security reasons) was felt to have the greatest medical needs.

With the intermingling of several of the tribal groups, the precise population of each tribe is difficult to determine. Most accounts indicated that this tribe numbered approximately 150,000. When we worked there in the early 1980's, their language had not yet been put into written form. Many of them were beginning to use Oriya (Odia), the official language of Orissa, and one of the more than fifteen official languages of India.

By default, most of the isolated tribal groups have been cultural Hindus for centuries. This particular tribe had apparently first heard the gospel in the early 1900s when a British Baptist missionary family lived with them for a few years (the exact history is unclear.) In recent years, there has been a major response to the gospel. That response has prompted a backlash by militant Hindus. Persecution of Christians had started when we were there and increased in intensity through the years since then.

Arrangements had been made for Joann and me to meet with the Baptist church leaders in Bhubaneshwar and consider their request for FMB to join them in a major missionary effort. It had come about when they came to know a tribal Christian man who had overcome many obstacles to obtain a good education and become an outstanding pastor and leader. Through him, the Orissa Baptist Association had become more aware of the great needs of the tribal people and their response to the gospel. From that awareness came their thought that the Lord was calling them to reach out to them with the gospel. They had the desire and some personnel resources, but they were short of other resources.

Discussions led us to feel that some form of health-care training would provide our best opportunity. Living in very primitive conditions, with a very high mortality rate, with no health care available, with an illiteracy rate above 90 percent, and with little ability to travel, life expectancy was extremely short. Lengthy discussion finally led us to think the "barefoot doctor" concept of training a few local leaders would be the most beneficial project. In that situation, basic knowledge of what causes most health problems and the treatment of the most common diseases they faced would provide the greatest benefit. That was the basic idea. We worked out the details as we began to put the plan in action.

In preparation for the project, we provided the funding, and they prepared the supplies and equipment we would need, including an aluminum box, designed by Joann, similar to a fishing tackle box. It would have a place for basic medications, a blood pressure cuff, a stethoscope, a thermometer, soap, and a few dressings for each trainee. Each trainee would have one box. We knew adjustments would be made after we had conducted the first clinic in the hills, but it was time to move on to the next survey site.

From Orissa, we took a long jump to Chandigarh in northwest India, in the foothills near the Himalayas. It was unique in being a professionally planned city, the capital of three states. It was exciting to see the Himalayas as we flew from New Delhi into Chandigarh. Both of us had read *The Far Pavilions*[5] by M. M. Kaye, a historical novel that provided an excellent beginning comprehension of India. Kaye was an Englishwoman, married to an English army general, and lived much of her life in India. She was very knowledgeable and understanding of Indian culture. Her book contains many insights that were of great help to Joann and me in understanding the variety of cultures, religions, and geography of India. The book opens in the "Far Pavilions," as she called the Himalayas. That book, plus others,

---

[5] *The Far Pavilions*, M. M. Kaye, St. Martin's Press, New York, 1997

was of much assistance as we first glimpsed the Himalayas and later traveled most of the regions of India.

There was an active group of strong Baptist churches in the Chandigarh area, serving among Hindus, Muslims, and Sikhs, all intermingled and living in overlapping portions of the Punjab region. After much discussion, and for various reasons, we did not feel led to initiate any development projects in that part of India at that time. I did tell them I would return the following year for further discussions if they so desired.

We were near New Delhi, the capital and center of many centuries of Indian history, and near some architectural marvels of earlier Indian construction. It was time to take a break and take a look. We spent a couple of days touring New Delhi. On August 2, 1983, my birthday, we spent a memorable day in Agra at the Taj Mahal. No superlatives can describe it. Built of white, mother-of-pearl inlaid marble as a tomb for one of the wives of the emperor, it took seventeen thousand men twenty years to build. Extreme air pollution of recent years is beginning to have a noticeable effect on the entire structure. Indian authorities have just now begun to consider drastic preservation measures required to prevent further deterioration.

It would be just as beautiful and spectacular in the heart of Dallas or any other city in the world, but for it to be surrounded by the squalor and filth with which it is (or was) surrounded only accentuated its beauty in Agra.

But other structures were almost as impressive, especially the Red Fort in New Delhi, a high wall (one hundred feet in places) fortress, castle, palace, tomb, gladiatorial grounds, seat of government, elephant battle area, and I don't know what else. It was massive. Both the Taj Mahal and the Red Fort were built in the 1600s.

On to Bangladesh

The Bangladesh mission had asked us for a survey and consideration of possible projects. We went to Dacca, the capital, for a planned ten-day review. That brief statement leaves much untold. Traveling in South and Southeast Asia was rarely a matter of simply going from point A to point B. Our arrival in Dacca was a good case in point. We expected no problems on our nonstop flight from New Delhi to Dacca, but when we arrived in Dacca, we were told our baggage was lost.

"Sorry," the agent said. "Don't know where it is. We did not get it. Can't help."

If I had passed a few dollars under the table, he might have found our luggage, but I did not do bribes. All other counter attendants had left, and we were standing by ourselves. On a hunch, I wandered back into the cavernous freight and baggage area. It was totally disorganized. After several minutes of looking, digging, and shoving things around, I found our bags. As we left with our luggage, I exchanged glances with one of the attendants who had said our baggage was lost. He just shrugged as we left.

The mission administrator of Bangladesh had several places he wanted us to consider. In addition, one of the long-time missionaries working out in a remote area wanted to take us to one village in particular that was in dire need of medical help. The areas they had selected for our review extended from one side of the country to the other. As we got well into the surveys, I realized our scheduled ten days might not be adequate.

The southern portion of Bangladesh is mostly river delta, resulting from ages of river silting, primarily from the Brahmaputra and Ganges Rivers. They are massive rivers; the point where we crossed the Brahmaputra (more than once) was over three miles wide and moving fast. The actual coastline, on the Bay of Bengal, is ill defined. Many islands are continually forming and disappearing in the annual flooding and silting. The entire region is barely above sea level. When the monsoon season arrives, often with typhoons, a massive surge of water often moves up the Bay of Bengal, inundating thousands of square miles of land, causing great loss of life, buildings, and food production. It is a region just waiting for a disaster to strike. With such an inadequate foundation for large structures such as bridges, ferries have to carry the traffic. At that time, there were not enough ferries to carry all the people safely. The sinking of overloaded ferries was a common occurrence. Most of that situation is still true today. Some of the missionaries kept life preservers in their vehicles just in case.

Bangladesh is a little larger than Arkansas and a little smaller than Iowa. When we began our survey in 1983, the population was ninety-five million. In 2013, it was 156,600,000. It was wall-to-wall people. Economically, the country was a basket case. In 1983, at least 60 percent of the national budget was provided by foreign aid. As we crisscrossed the nation and got a glimpse of the massive needs, we were staggered by the challenge of how we could make a difference with our small effort. It was almost disheartening, but we could not turn away and do nothing.

Population records indicated the proportion of population was 90 percent Muslim, 9 percent Hindu, and 1 percent Christian. There were also tribal groups near the eastern and northeastern borders. Those were estimates; there was no way to get an accurate count. The missionaries worked with all groups. Response to the gospel, especially among the Muslims, was slow, but it was better with the Hindus and the tribal people.

Travel was difficult and unpleasant for Joann. Even though she wore appropriate Punjabi outfits and kept her head covered, it was obvious that she was a foreign woman. Everywhere we went, noses covered the van windows and windshields with men straining to get a look at her. She had to stay inside, and she could not go anywhere alone. Spooky.

I will omit most of the details of our survey except for three projects; one Joann did, one we started, and one we helped continue.

The one we started involved most of the mission. After one of the more disastrous floods, much of the duck population in the southern part of the country was wiped out. It was considered a national loss. I wondered aloud at one point how ducks could be wiped out by water. I never did get an answer. I suspected that most of them had been eaten because almost all food stocks had been wiped out and people were starving. I could understand. If my family were starving, I might eat anything available also.

Whatever happened, all the rural missionaries felt a resupply of ducks, channeled through their churches to those they deemed most needy, would meet a huge need and would be a marvelous mission outreach opportunity. So be it. When we returned to Bangkok, I chartered the largest jet freighter available, bought well over five hundred thousand ducklings (Thailand was also a big duck-raising country), and sent them on to Dacca. That brief statement hardly covers the behind-the-scenes work required to get it done. International shipments of live animals were not easy or quick. Much of that was done by our mission business manager in Thailand who was an expert in maneuvering through the bureaucratic maze for such a freight movement. The Bangladesh mission had arranged to receive and distribute them to the churches that capitalized on the act. The act was well received by Bangladeshi government officials as well. The entire project had been made possible by hunger relief funds given by Baptist Christians in the United States.

In an act revealing a new sense of stewardship, the Bangladesh churches distributed many of the ducks to non-Christian friends and neighbors to whom they wanted to demonstrate God's caring love.

The project Joann did was a clinic dealing with acute medical needs in a remote tribal village. It was a village the missionary had been visiting on a regular basis, and several adults had expressed a growing interest in the gospel. He wanted very much to demonstrate the compassionate concern Christians had for their fellow humans in distress. It was not as a superficial inducement to become a

Christian—but to show love and help with their obvious medical needs.

In one of those getting-there-is-half-the-fun episodes, I regret not having a picture of a star performance by Joann on our way to the village. As usual, the village was on the backside of nowhere, the last major segment having to be traveled on foot. It was the rainy season, and much of our walking was on narrow dikes separating rice paddies. Joann, dressed to the hilt in an off-white Punjabi outfit, slipped, teetered a moment, and slid down the dike. That was the shot I missed. What a shame! But she laughed and washed off most of the mud with water from the paddy, and we went on to the village.

The people in the village were in a pathetic condition. Joann needed only a glance and a listening ear to see two major problems immediately. One was the obvious visible symptoms of leprosy: clawed hands and lesion-covered bodies. The other problem, almost as obvious by the frequent heavy coughing, was tuberculosis. Many of the villagers were afflicted with both diseases. A more thorough follow-up exam revealed other medical problems, but they were not as severe. A one-time visit would not accomplish much, but Joann treated the ones she could, then spent much time with the missionary explaining how he could follow up with appropriate medication for the TB and leprosy patients.

There was one other project that had been initiated by the mission on its own that had been well received by government officials as well as the people. It was a water well project that was in distress after the massive flooding. Hundreds, if not thousands, of pumps had been destroyed. Bangladesh, like so many other places in the world, suffered many health problems as a result of contaminated water. In contrast to other places, help was easily available in Bangladesh. The water table was often only twenty feet deep in the low-lying delta region. With the soil being a mixture of sand, loam, and clay, drilling a well was an easy task, requiring only about four hours. The soil was so porous that a high-pressure hose, operated from a portable gasoline engine pump, could evacuate a two-inch hole through the ground down to the water table in a very short time. The hose could then be removed and a one-inch metal or PVC pipe, with a filter screwed on the bottom end, inserted as far as required. A very cheap, hand-operated water pump, partially subsidized by the UN, could then be screwed on to the pipe. The pump/pipe combination could then be attached to a crude but well-anchored wood pump stand. It was a wonderful addition to the village. Again, Hunger Relief funds were available and helped provide more than three thousand pumps to be installed in any given year. Over the course of a few years, several thousand pumps were placed in waterless villages over much of the delta. Unfortunately, massive flooding could also damage many of the pumps. It was just one disaster after another.

I'll summarize my comments about our first trip to Bangladesh with the old saying, "The half has not been told." We would be glad to get home to Bangkok.

Thailand, Briefly

We were back home again, but only briefly. We would soon be returning to India to begin the new type of medical ministry outreach in the Khond Hills. Joann needed time to prepare the materials she would need, organizing and writing much of the basic curriculum appropriate to new circumstances and trying to anticipate what and how much medication to take with us. A similar program of teaching/training nursing assistants in the Kamput refugee hospital was good background experience for her work in India.

As usual, I was gone much of the time. First, I went to the eastern Thailand border to check on our development projects and then back to northwest Thailand to the Golden Triangle of Laos, Burma, and Thailand to assist American Baptists in their attempts to encourage the tribal groups to discontinue their opium growing. The last major item was to obtain an Indian visa. It always required multiple trips, much paperwork, and much time. Permanent resident visas and work visas were almost impossible to obtain. We received visitor visas, meaning we could remain in the country only a few weeks before having to leave and repeat the visa application process. That was a continuing constraint for much of our work in India, but finally, preparations were complete. We left Thailand on November 14, 1983, for the first of many training sessions in the Khond Hills of India.

India: Another Era, Another Place, Another Work

Our first major stop was back in Bhubaneshwar to pick up our kits, supplies, and equipment we had ordered earlier. For customs' purposes, convenience, and economic reasons, we bought as much as possible in India. Each trainee would be equipped as noted above. Since Joann and the trainees would be seeing many patients, I bought much of the medicine in factory-packed bulk containers. The fun began as we left Bhubaneshwar by train on the first travel segment to Berhampore.

Our baggage and supplies weighed about six hundred pounds. It required eight porters, each carefully balancing about seventy-five pounds on their heads, maneuvering from one vacant spot to another through the crowded terminal. Our entourage, trailed by two foreigners, one a very white, blonde-haired woman, brought other traffic to a halt. Moving through the train station, boarding the train, then reversing the process at Berhampore was an amazing sight in agility. Indian travelers often arrived early for boarding, accompanied by family members and friends, so station floors would be covered with wall-to-wall people. Watching our porters step over, jump around, and wiggle through a throng was as exciting to us as we were to them.

We left Bhubaneshwar at 6:00 pm, arrived at Berhampore at 11:00 pm, off-loaded the baggage, and reversed the loading process to a convoy of pedal trishaws for a two-hour midnight ride to our sleeping place. The next morning, everything was loaded on a large Indian-made jeep for a five-hour drive to Raikia, our staging area on the edge of the Khond Hills.

We expected to go on the next morning to the designated village to begin the training and patient treatment. It didn't happen. The church and our hosts had other plans.

Raikia Baptist Church was a 250-member, very active church with many outreach ministries, including caring and providing for about thirty orphans in their own facility. They wanted Joann to do health screening for the group, since they had never seen a doctor. They also had other clinics scheduled for her. The clinics, mostly outside, had no privacy, but that was not an issue.

Typical outdoor clinic

They also had speaking engagements for me. Joann saw about four hundred patients in two days, and I spoke six times in three churches. We were off to a good start.

The following morning, we started for Pokari, the village where we would begin our Khond Hills project. Our transportation was an enlarged World War II jeep that was barely operable. Our baggage was loaded, plus food for twenty people for two weeks, plus eight of the trainees, plus Joann, an interpreter, and me. There was also a driver in there somewhere. I called that close communion. Perched on top of all of it was a commode seat. I'll say more about that later.

For the first ten or fifteen miles out of town, the road was passable, but the remaining thirty miles to the village became more interesting. It was a trail through jungle and rice patties, used primarily by people, goats, cows, and water buffalo. We had to stop frequently to remove downed trees or large rocks before continuing on. We went through a surprising number of villages, usually barreling through the major path in the village with baby chicks, chickens, pigs, cows, goats, and kids (two- and four-legged ones) scattering in all directions. I was clinging to the side of the jeep, Joann was clinging to me, and both of us were hoping and praying fervently that the erupting sea of fur, feathers, hair, and bristles would part before our barely guided missile arrived in their midst.

After about three hours, we started down a hill and came upon a sight that chilled us and is still etched in our memories. The entire trail area was blocked by about one hundred people dressed (some partially dressed) in all kinds of clothing. In front of the crowd were several costumed and armed men, each with a headdress arranged around the horns of a dangerous type of buffalo.

Welcome to Pokari

They were armed with machetes, tomahawks, spears, and bows and arrows. Somewhere in the background, someone was beating a drum. At a particular drumbeat, the crowd would sound off with a bloodcurdling, war-whooping yell similar to the sound of American Indians in the old western movies, but these were Indian Indians, and the action was not on a screen; it was right before our eyes and ears. We had to stop. Then we were told to get out. As they gathered around us—smiling, laughing, and dancing—we realized they were the welcoming party from the village of Pokari. We were escorted as honored guests in the midst of the dancing and yelling procession for the half-mile walk to the village.

It was so stunning it took a while to absorb the experience. We had seen similar scenes on National Geographic TV episodes and the "Wild Kingdom" program, but being up close, with all our senses on high alert, left us speechless. It was almost like stepping back hundreds of years to another world.

The trip was memorable—and so were the clinic days—but it was not all heavy drama and deep emotions. I gave it some thought.

> Upon our arrival in Pokari,
> At the end of a numbing safari,
> We eyed our abode,
> In search of a commode.
> But our host, with a nod, said, "So sorry!"

Actually, it wasn't quite like that. We were not looking for a commode, and our host could not speak English.

We made our way to the village late in the day and began our preparations. We were taken to our sleeping quarters—a private room. They had expelled the previous occupants (goats) to make room for us. Tigers would kill any small animals left out at night so the family took the goats, chickens, cows, and whatever else they had into their one room and let us have the goat house. The goats were not happy with the eviction, and they sounded off about it. There were no stores in the village, which had a population of about 1,500, but Joann and I had brought our own candles.

After we had settled in, the first order of business was dedicating the new bamboo, mud, and grass roof church building they had built to use as the clinic. I was directed to lead the service. The cooking fires were going strong, preparing to feed more than twenty of us at about ten o'clock at night, which was their usual eating time.

There was one more facility they wanted us to see ... a special one, the bathroom. When we saw it, we realized how much they wanted to please us and how much they appreciated our coming. Our curiosity about the commode seat was answered. We had not asked about it, but they wanted to tell us how it all came about. It had started thirty or forty years earlier when a British Baptist missionary had spent some time with them. They took notice of some strange foreign customs, especially one related to the bathroom. They never did fully understand all the foreigner's eccentricities, but they did want to duplicate his setup as closely as possible to show their thanks for our coming.

The first view was impressive. Four bamboo poles had been driven into the ground. A long slender vine was pulled off one of the nearby trees and wrapped around the four poles several times, leaving a small opening near one of the poles for going in and coming out. Intertwined with the vines were dozens of large elephant ear tree leaves and cut-off small limbs woven tightly in and out to serve as privacy walls. At the center of the bright green "function room" was a hole in the ground about ten inches in diameter and a couple of feet deep. Over the hole, they had placed a topless three-legged stool, firmly driven into the ground. On top of the stool was the commode seat.

Bathroom facility Pokari

We never learned what happened to the commode itself or to the water closet. We did, however, see the water closet floats again. They had been pried open, a few small rocks inserted, and then closed up again. They now served as the main percussion section when they sang at the worship services. They had spent a lot of time and effort to prepare that convenience for us, and we were very touched by it.

The "facility" served well … for the first day. By the second day, we had to start making adjustments. We were not the only ones who liked it. The goats and the cows had found a very tasty, convenient salad bar at just the right height, and they made the most of it. By the third day, most of the leaves and limbs were gone. The village children had front-row seating to the show that took place inside. We were strange aliens from another world. They took full advantage of it. It did not occur to the village elders to weave more leaves into the vines, and we did not want to ask. It was time to improvise. It was really very simple. I held Joann's sari around her while she bathed and did the needful, and then she held it around me for the same purpose. I'm sure it was an exciting peephole show to the village children, but we didn't mind. We enjoyed the whole episode. We were not paid much in salary, but we were highly and abundantly paid in adventures, memories, and a sense of affirmation by the Lord. Beautiful, rewarding times.

I happened to come up with another very useful idea while watching the "facility" one day. We were well into the clinic routine. I was taking a break, sitting down in the clinic area on a hot afternoon and just watching the proceedings and the surroundings when the activity around the outhouse caught my attention. Some goats and cows were still trying to find remnants of the former buffet layout. They would nibble on one side, move to another, and then move again. In my semi-siesta state of mind, it took a while to realize they were moving around in response to a change in the wind direction. It was toward the end of the hot season, and the swirling wind was shifting in all directions as it moved through the village. As it moved, it picked up sand and silt, irritating the eyes of the animals if they remained facing the wind. So, when the wind direction changed, they moved. After many drowsy moments, it finally hit me: the goats tell you the wind direction. Stake out goats at the airport! They could serve as a wind sock for an airport! When the pilot flew by to determine the wind direction for landing, he could just look at the goats. The direction the goats were facing would designate the downwind leg: fly down-goat. The final approach and landing direction was simple: land up-goat. It was a great solution, but it was not recommended for night landings.

After we had eaten and been given the full orientation tour, we called the trainees and the village leaders together for Joann to have a get-acquainted session with them. Again, the setting was right out of "Wild Kingdom" with a banged-up lantern suspended on a tree limb, supplementing the dying light from the cooking fires. A full moon was coming up over the hills and through the trees. The sounds from the nearby jungle were changing from the daytime howls of monkeys and squawks of birds to the nocturnal rampaging insects and the occasional scream of a tiger ... and always the buzzing mosquitoes. She did not prolong her comments; it was time to call it a day.

Joann had thought ten trainees would be the optimum size for teaching and monitoring. The association leaders wanted twenty. We compromised at fifteen. Most of them had a very limited health-care background awareness, rarely having left their tribal areas. Most of them were pastors and/or evangelists. All were literate, a prerequisite to being selected.

She wanted to learn as much about them as possible before the sessions began, including their thoughts about illness and accidents, what caused them, and how they treated them. For example, most thought illnesses and accidents were caused by evil spirits and not by germs. (The germ theory of disease was not known.) They thought bringing a chicken or goat to the local witch doctor as a sacrifice would scare away or placate the evil spirits so the person would get well. In that give-and-take time, she only briefly touched on biblical references to health, evil, good, and sin. Although all the trainees were Christians, they had received very little training or biblical teaching. They were babes in Christ, but, as we discovered over the next almost two years, they learned and matured very rapidly. All of them were so steeped in the myths and stories of the gods of Hinduism and their animistic spirit world that they still had some confusing thoughts about their newfound faith. Her questions elicited some revealing questions from them. It was an enlightening time for both of us. She would be more aware of their thinking while she was treating patients, and I would be more aware of their understanding when I had a teaching hour each morning before the clinic began.

I had a rude awakening the next morning. I had slept on a low bamboo bench that was the sleeping place of the goats. When I got up, I was covered with bedbug bites. Joann slept on a newly woven rope cot they had made for her, and the bedbugs had left her alone.

The day began with Joann reviewing the schedule with them. I would have the first hour, doing Bible study and dealing with the basics of our Christian faith, attempting to use the storying method of sharing the gospel. Joann would take one to two hours to teach the basics of health, hygiene, nutrition, disease, and medications needed for different diseases. In the first few days of clinics, it was necessary to teach them how to take vital signs. I could help with that but not with the history and physical. That teaching schedule was repeated every day throughout the project. The more they learned, the more curious they became. The afternoons were spent examining and treating patients who had come from surrounding villages. This was true in-service training.

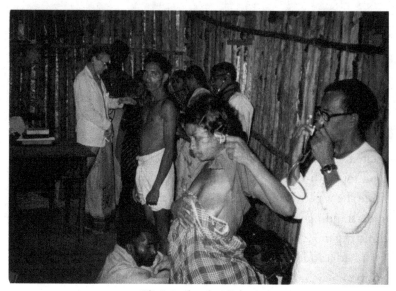

Clinic in church at Pokari

The trainees would take the medical history of the patients and then examine them. Through an interpreter, they would give Joann the history and physical results plus what they thought was wrong with the patient. She would then examine the patient and either agree or explain why she did not agree with the diagnosis. She would tell them what was to be used to treat the patient, and they would give the medicine to the patient with proper instructions. That would go on until dark. We had worship services at night, and everyone from the surrounding areas was invited. Our interpreter usually preached. Following all this would be the evening meal around ten o'clock.

That hour of teaching weighed heavily on me. Our time in each village was limited. To share the basics of our Christian faith in that brief time was daunting. It was tempting to consider only a few of the major biblical doctrines and not deal with other themes such as stewardship. The difference in the material wealth (or lack) of the villagers, living always on the very edge of abject poverty, and our relative affluence, often left me uncomfortable. Yet Jesus gave much attention to the issue, to a people who often were also destitute. He knew the rewards it would bring. Stewardship is a part of the gospel: our response to His great gift of life to us. We can't ignore it, and an offering was taken at each service.

Worship service in brush arbor

At one of the later evening worship services, this time with another missionary preaching, a haunting example of sacrificial giving was played out almost unnoticed by others in the service. Much of the following reflects his telling skill.

On the surface, there was nothing unusual or different about the service. The people made their way into the brush arbor, found a vacant spot, and sat down with the men on one side and the women on the other. The little children just wandered around. When the time came for the offering, one of the men and one of the women (with her two little girls) got up from their separate places and left together, obviously a family. In just a few moments, they all returned together, picking their way through the packed arbor, leading a little yearling heifer calf. Understanding came slowly. I can only

279

imagine them sitting in their little mud and bamboo hut, discussing their offering. I can only imagine their weighing their crying need for the very necessities of life against the call of Christ and their commitment to His call. I can only imagine the peace that entered their little home when the decision was made: "We will give our calf to Jesus."

They came in, leading their offering. The lead rope was a jungle vine wrapped in a piece of old ragged cloth. The man tied the end of the rope around one of the bamboo support poles near the offering table, ran his hand over the calf's head and ears, and slowly turned away. The woman reached out, touched it gently, and followed her husband. Then the two little girls put their arms around its neck and cried. They returned to their places unnoticed and sat down. So little said—but so much conveyed.

The little calf remained at the offering table, quiet as a lamb. It also remains in our hearts, standing alone, still tied to the bamboo pole in the leafy temple of their God who had given them new life and new hope. Years later, it remains a burning example of sacrificial giving, given by those who could not afford to give, but who could not bear to withhold the very best they had from the Savior who had given His best, His life, for them. That image is branded on our hearts every time we consider what we can give as an offering to our Lord.

We rarely sat through a worship service without seeing similar examples of sacrificial giving—maybe not as dramatic as the offering of the calf, but still so sacrificial that we remain humbled by them. Countless times, we have seen emaciated men and women bring a spoonful of rice, an egg, or lentils and place them in the offering basket. Their offering, like the widow's mite, was not out of their abundance, but out of their scarcity.

After the class teaching time, Joann and the trainees started seeing patients. That process took a while to be understood. They would have preferred for Joann to see the patients and just have the trainees observe, but the whole purpose was for them to learn to do it themselves. Joann would be there only temporarily; they would have to learn quickly and carry on by themselves. They had to be taught; the time was coming when it must be put it into practice.

Some of them had never seen blood pressure cuffs, stethoscopes, or thermometers, but to our pleasant surprise, they learned quickly. It was gratifying to see their excited comprehension as they heard heartbeats and measured blood pressure. The first week went by rather slowly as the process was learned, but it was heartening to see how quickly they learned and how rapidly their findings and recommendations turned out to be correct. After the first clinic experience in Pokari, the process picked up rapidly.

One of the things Joann and I both emphasized in our teaching times was that this new skill they were learning was to be used as an instrument to demonstrate the loving care and concern of Jesus—not for their own personal benefit. Our example was the Lord Himself. His healing ministry was prompted by his acts of compassion for those who were hurting. Jesus had added words to His works. We were to do likewise.

We had a visitor come at the close of our final clinic day in Pokari. He lived in a village several miles away, had heard what we were doing, and came to ask for help. A couple of days earlier, a tiger had come out of the nearby jungle and killed one of the boys who was watching and protecting the cows. He had mauled another boy who now needed medical help. Would we come and help their village? It saddened us to have to say no. Our time was up.

Our plan was to spend a week to two weeks in a village, see all the patients who came, move on to another area, and repeat the process. Our first visit to Pokari was longer, but the training and the rapid learning of the trainees went so well that we felt we had done enough to merit an evaluation and consider whether we were on the right track. With our visa about to expire, we headed home to Bangkok to catch up on our work in Thailand and start the visa-seeking process to return. Easily said—but not so easily done. It took four days to get from home in Bangkok to the villages, and it took the same time to get back.

India: Bus Travel

We were unable to find a Michelin Guide to bus travel in the Khond Hills. We learned by going on day buses or night buses. Our first trip into the hills had been by a jeep provided by the Baptist Association. The remainder of the trips were by bus, both into the hills as well as back to Bhubaneshwar. It required ten or twelve hours, depending on the usual vagaries of Indian travel. We tried it on the night bus, and we tried it on the day bus. They were equally uninspiring. One particularly demanding skill, especially for women, was coping with the lack of facilities. The bus would stop, but there were no rest stop amenities. Everyone was on their own. The men had no trouble. To them, any space was acceptable. The women were a little choosier, but Indian women had long since learned to cope with any circumstance, including lack of privacy. Just as Thai women could take a complete bath in a crowded klong and never reveal bare skin, Indian women could do whatever was needed without requiring privacy.

Joann had to adapt, improvise, innovate, or endure. The fact that she was a good-looking, blonde, curly-haired foreign woman added to the interest in the occasion. The thought occurred that maybe the night bus would be better—at least it would be a little cooler in the darkness—but India has all kinds of creepy-crawlies that come out at night, including sneaky snakes. Getting close to the ground in the darkness lost its appeal. So, it was the day bus.

There were some common elements in the buses to and from the Khond Hills, whether day or night: bench seats, glassless windows, untrained drivers, and overloaded buses. On both day and night buses, we often stood a few hours after boarding before getting a seat. Joann was usually the only woman on the bus so when the men were drinking, which was not unusual, and getting ideas about the foreign woman and how it felt to touch her, the situation could get interesting. I tended to object to the attention they gave to Joann by doing a series of unusual movements adjacent to the offending roaming hands, but it had to be done carefully.

The day bus exposed Joann to extreme heat, often up to 115 degrees. Her skin would burn, and dehydration was common—even inside the bus. Only one trip on the bus was needed to impress her with the need to prepare for the trip so she would not have to use the non-facilities en route. She did this by omitting liquids before the trip. We would take along a sack of oranges and eat on them sparingly while traveling. Bottled drinks and water at the stops were not safe.

These comments about the common, day-to-day physical aspect of life in the hills are not written to elicit pity or admiration. They actually became minor issues for us, never affecting our enjoyment of the work and never causing us to think of discontinuing the project. What experiences we were having! What a blessing! I'm sharing them to give a hint of what daily life was like for millions of Indians and other destitute millions around the world. We were no more committed or motivated than multitudes of other Christians; we just felt very blessed to be where we were. We were absolutely sure we were in the center of God's will, and He gave us complete peace at being there. Our laughing about our situation was not fake; we were just happy. We were being blessed more than we could have ever imagined. We were grateful beyond words that the Lord was allowing us to have a part in it.

Incidentally, Indian buses and bus travel were not the only places lacking in amenities. We were in many air and train terminals where the "function rooms" did not function and no paper or water could be found.

Nepal: Interlude in the Far Pavilions

In December, we arrived back home in Bangkok and heard the good news that James, Lisa, and Chris would be joining us for Christmas. I immediately made plans for an excursion into Nepal. We all wanted to see Nepal, but Lisa also wanted to show Chris where she had lived in Thailand. Her young life in Thailand had been pleasant, and she wanted to show her new husband some of the meaningful places where she had grown up.

The day after Christmas, we flew into Katmandu, Nepal. An energetic young guide attached himself to us and remained with us until we left town. Town was fascinating, unique, engrossing, and sad. Shrines, temples, images, monuments, relics—religious items dominated the place. I can imagine how the apostle Paul felt when he saw the city of Athens filled with idols. (In April 2015, a massive earthquake hit Katmandu and destroyed much of the city, including historic structures that were hundreds of years old. Many of them cannot be restored.)

On our first full day, we were driven to an eight thousand-foot hilltop overlook for a panoramic view of the Himalayan rampart, including a great view of Mount Everest, about eighty or ninety air miles distant. We chose to trek back several miles to our car and driver, descending over three thousand feet through valleys and villages with close-up views of village life. Walking through the countryside, hearing villagers call to each other, listening to bell cows and bell goats ringing out their (non-GPS) locations, listening to temple conch shells echoing through the valleys announcing some religious signal, and hearing the voices of children sounding like children everywhere provided such a sense of contentment that we slowed down and leisurely strolled through.

The next day, we joined a group for a chartered flight along the entire rampart of the high mountain range to Mount Everest and back. We were permitted to go into the cockpit for a better view. We did not get as close to the mountains as I wanted, but we were close enough to see details of the snowfields, ice fields, glaciers, and massive cliffs. What a view of God's creation!

Back at our hotel, I walked through an art display area where I found one of my favorite paintings of all I have seen in my travels. It is a scene in the Himalayan mountains of a deep, rugged canyon crossed by a swinging bridge. A tendril of cloud has drifted down from the upper reaches of the canyon, obscuring the bottom and opposite side of the canyon where the bridge was firmly attached. Two shepherds are trying to get their sheep and goats to cross to the other side, but the swaying bridge just disappears into the mist and makes them afraid to step out. The analogy just leaps out. We all come to frightening places in our life journeys. The future is often clouded with mists of uncertainty. We can't see the strong anchorage that holds the bridge safely for our crossing, but the shepherd knows it is there and his sheep follow him to safety. In like manner, we can trust the Lord to lead us in safety all the way—not just across this one bridge or one valley but to the end of the earthly journey. That painting always has a prominent place in our home, wherever we live.

The next morning, we left Katmandu to do an elephant safari in the Royal Chitwan National Park, on the border between Nepal and India. We traveled by Land Rover for several miles, then transferred to a raft for a wild ride down a roaring, whitewater river for three or four hours. The river, about the size of the Colorado, was running almost full and was a tad intimidating. I had made the float arrangements in Bangkok—with assurance that a trained crew would handle the raft. After we loaded our things into waterproof bags, we took our place in the raft and made ready to leave. Surprise! Surprise! James, Chris, and I were handed oars; we were the crew! Our guide had the steering oar. There was a novice trainee (his first trip) on the tiller who was not really helpful. It was a good thing James, Chris, and I had some experience in rafting. Lisa sat on the very front of the raft, and Joann sat in the middle. We were still adjusting to the new arrangement when we cast off. Within a hundred yards, we hit the first rapid, which was actually a cascade.

We dropped about five feet and found ourselves in very rough water. Lisa was often eyeball-to-eyeball with waves up to six feet, like riding a bucking horse, and loving every moment. It took only a few moments for all of us to be soaking wet with cold water. The three of us were working hard to maintain control and avoid the many huge boulders in the river so we were not cold, but Joann was sitting on a low seat, soaking wet and becoming more uncomfortable by the minute. For the next fifteen or eighteen miles, we had a ride we will not forget. We were ready to get out and move on to our jungle camp.

We arrived at our hotel after dark. They were mud huts with thatch roofs, no electricity, and no heat. We were still wet, but there were rugs on the floor. Supper was by lamplight and cooking fire. Actually, it was not that uncomfortable. We were having fun. After we ate, we enjoyed a program presented by a local tribal drama troupe of rice dancing, pole dancing, and sword fighting.

The big event came up the next morning: the elephant ride through the jungle to view wildlife. There was intermittent mist and fog as we made an early departure. The great variety of sounds of jungle animal and birdlife just awakening, heard from the back of an elephant, in that misty setting, created an eerie sensation. Our elephant mahouts had a good idea where the big animals would be and went directly there. We came close to a rhinoceros before it decided to move away. We also came close to a wild buffalo. We were glad to be on an elephant. Joann tried to take pictures, but only the mist can be seen. There were several Bengal tigers in the area, but we did not see any. Maybe just as well. The fog and mist grounded much of the birdlife, to our great delight. The great variety, in species and in color, made them too difficult to try to name.

As we were moving along on the elephants through the jungle with the undergrowth up above our feet, I dropped a small penlight out of my pocket. I thought it was gone. The mahout noticed the drop, turned the elephant around, and somehow directed it to probe with his trunk until he found it, picked it up, and dropped it in the handler's hand. Amazing!

Late in the day, we arrived at our next camp. It was a new camp; in fact, we were the first guests. It was New Year's Eve. We slept in two-man pup tents. In addition to the five of us, there were about fifteen Australians. A huge roasting pig provided a delicious supper. James stayed up with the Aussies to see in the New Year. The rest of us sacked out.

One final excursion remained: a walk through the jungle with the hope of seeing some kind of wildlife. It was a total fiasco; the guides got lost. We made enough noise to scare off any animals within miles. We finally made contact with camp employees who were looking for us. On our way back to camp in jeeps, we had to ford a river. It was wide but only about four feet deep. Our drivers thought speed was the best way to get through the river quickly. As we expected, all the jeeps stalled in the middle of the river. We sat there in the jeeps, bottoms in the water, for almost an hour until the jeeps would start again and get us back to camp. Let's go home!

Our bus trip back to Katmandu was the final segment, and it was a good finale. It was through a grand spectacle of mountains and snowcapped peaks. The views were indescribable, and so was the drive. The driver appeared determined to set a record, going all-out around hairpin turns and switchbacks at the very edge of precipitous thousand-foot drop-offs. He assumed the whole road was his; any oncoming vehicle was expected to move over whether there was room or not. It was a high-risk chicken raceway. After a wonderfully quiet night in Katmandu, we headed home to Bangkok.

A couple of days later, we took Lisa and Chris to the airport to go home and then drove James to Lampang, in north Thailand, to the Lampang Commercial College where he had been asked to set up a computer science department. The owner of the college was Dr. Nirand, who had received his PhD at Baylor University. He became friends with James at Baylor. It was his invitation to James that brought James back to Thailand for a little over a year to help set up the department. That activity helped establish an exchange student program with Baylor that is still going strong today—many years later. Dr. Nirand had become a Christian while he was in the States and was instrumental in initiating a Christian outreach in the Lampang area.

CHAPTER 9

Another Major Change: Khond Hills Revisited

The calendar said 1984, but it was just like 1983: busy, busy, travel, travel. After the kids were gone, we resumed where we had left off. Before we returned to India, Joann needed to fill in at the hospital in Bangkla while one of the other doctors was away. I was back to monitoring our project activity in eastern and northwestern Thailand. Both areas had realized benefits from the projects, and that prompted additional requests. That was gratifying, but successful projects are the direct result of having competent, dedicated people of integrity to provide leadership, and those were not easy to find and keep. The reservoir of volunteers who had been interested in the refugee work had dried up. Career missionaries had their own areas of work to which they were committed and were unable to assume other responsibilities. It became more of a challenge to sustain our development activities. The American Baptists were having even more difficulty; they were having to cut back. Our work responsibility throughout Southeast Asia was expanding, and we did not accept any new work in that area. Joann and I began looking at spending more time in India.

The inability to obtain permanent visas seriously impacted our work all over India, especially at the hospital in Bangalore. Key people were lost, both on the medical staff as well as the administrative staff. In my eleven years on the hospital board, I was asked to serve twice as interim administrator.

We would continue the Khond Hills project during our intermittent time in Bangalore. Coincidentally, Joann was needed at the hospital in Bangkla between my times in India. I was not excited about serving in India while she was serving in Thailand; we had already experienced far more separation than we liked.

Early in the year, we resumed our Khond Hills health-care training. For brevity, I will not describe each trip. There were too many areas of commonality to repeat them, but there were unusual, significant events in all of them, some of which need to be told.

Our first return after the New Year was to a different area. The driver managed to get lost, and we arrived well after midnight. Not to worry though. Fires were built, the food was cooked, and we enjoyed a delicious post-midnight snack.

It was in the middle of the hot, dry season, which was notable because of the effect it had on us. The village had built a brush arbor to serve as the clinic. One little problem was that it was built for their height, not ours. Most of the ceiling was a little over five feet high. Bending over all day—with the hot sun warming the crack-filled thatch roof right over our heads—was debilitating. We slept on the ground in the same area at night, continuing to keep warm with the always required mosquito net. We had the usual sightseeing crowd.

It was hot—not just a hand-fan, sticky-sweat, grumbling-about-the-weather kind of heat, but searing heat that burned Joann's skin. On our first full clinic day, we made the rude discovery that all the thermometers were ruined. It was so hot that the mercury expanded through the tops and ruined them all. We estimated the temperature to be about 115 degrees. From then on, we brought higher-quality equipment from Thailand.

The heat produced multiple dust devils that picked up an abundant supply of dust and debris. We quickly learned it was best not to chew our food—just swallow it and appreciate the roughage that came with it at no extra cost.

We felt sorry for the two ladies who were responsible for keeping us in water. The church was about one kilometer from the water source ... a spring used by other villagers as well as some animals. The ladies carried the water in pots on their heads.

Water carrier for the clinic

The water for the trainees, Joann, and me was boiled, but we still were not able to see the bottom of the cup. "Cool, Clear, Water," the beautiful song by the Sons of the Pioneers, a popular singing group of earlier years, came to occupy much of our thoughts, and finally our dreams. Again, I relate this not to elicit sympathy but to give a better understanding of the terribly difficult conditions under which those villagers, and many people of the world, live every day. As with countless other villagers I saw later in other parts of Asia, Africa, and Latin America, those Indian villagers who had never known an easy life wore the cloak of adversity with stoicism and perseverance. Joann and I could never complain about our brief sojourn.

We returned to the hills after our first training trip with some trepidation. A potentially dangerous skill had been placed in their hands; we wondered how they had used it. The first two or three days would let us know. To our great relief and gratification, the trainees eagerly began telling what they had found, what they had done, and how the people had responded. We were thrilled and praised the Lord. How meager it would appear in a modern, high-tech world, but how wonderfully significant the results were in that setting where almost no health care existed previously. We had the first indication of a coming drop in morbidity and mortality rates. It gave us a huge burst of encouragement. What was most gratifying was the response of the people as the trainees shared the gospel of Christ with those they treated and saw many of them come to know the Lord. Many new churches were being established.

Two days before the clinic ended, Joann had an attack of what many of the patients had; high fever, acute vomiting, severe diarrhea, and dehydration. The goats had gotten into the previously boiled water and contaminated it, unknown to us. We did for her what she had taught the trainees to do in similar situations: we boiled a liter of water, added a little salt and jungle honey, and I fed her sips of the water throughout the night. The next morning, she was able to get up. The people had seen many similarly affected patients die and were surprised when Joann got up and worked the next morning. It was the best example of the truth of what Joann had been teaching the trainees. When the foreign doctor received the same care she had advised the trainees to use, and she quickly recovered from her illness, it greatly strengthened their belief in the methods and treatments they had been taught. Fate and evil spirits were no longer dominant in life and illness.

Because of her illness, we left the village a day early, but it did not accomplish anything. We walked a few miles out to the road to catch the day bus, but the bus did not run that day. We waited another five or six hours for the night bus, but it did not come either. The next day, a bus finally came. The bus ride back to Bhubaneshwar was a marathon. We were on the bus for two hours before Joann was able to sit down. There was no glass in the windows in the bus, and the heat made the wind like a furnace, severely burning Joann's face.

Some of the trainees were also sick. Our interpreter was sick. Many of the medications and supplies we had ordered had not been obtained. So even though we saw much that pleased and blessed us, we headed back home with our flags at half-staff. It took a few days for us to get back to normal.

In relating this, I want the reader to understand clearly that I am not complaining. Though things had not gone according to plan, Joann and I found joy and fulfillment in the midst of discomfort. Throughout the whole episode, we felt the Lord's presence so keenly that we were still enjoying and laughing about all of it.

Belief that spirits, fate, a curse, or retribution by the gods was the cause of disease was so inculcated in the minds of the villagers that they were slow to accept any other explanation. Seeing or experiencing unusual healing was visible evidence that helped change their thoughts. Of the countless hundreds of patients Joann saw and helped heal, a few cases must be related. The cases are chosen for a variety of reasons but primarily to illustrate some principle related to a biblical truth and a loving, compassionate God:

- They refuted some of their long-held beliefs.
- They validated what they had been taught.
- They provided a redemptive teaching moment.

- They demonstrated the reality of a compassionate God who loved them.
- They were unusual.

A few days into one of our clinics, the morning routine was interrupted by a screaming toddler, brought in by his mother. It was not an angry scream—it was a scream of excruciating pain. Only a glance was needed for Joann to see the problem. The child had fallen into a cooking pot of boiling rice, critically burning large areas of its body. The mother had applied the usual treatment—a poultice of fresh cow manure—with the expected result. The indescribable surface pain added to a deep, terrible burn. The child was in obvious agony.

The trainees wanted to hold back and let Joann take over, but she had taught them how to take care of burns. They had, in fact, seen a few minor burns. They needed to take care of the child for the learning experience.

"What is the first thing you do?" Joann asked.

"Clean the wound area."

"Do it!" She directed them as they each had a small part in removing the poultice and cleaning the area completely, accompanied by the agonizing screams of the child.

"What next?"

"Apply some aloe vera gel from the plants we introduced earlier."

The use of a gel from a local plant had been a new thing for them. In one of our early clinics, Joann had noticed the frequency of burns and cuts. When she asked for a stem of an aloe vera plant, they did not have it. (It was well-known and used in Thailand.) On our next trip, she brought small plants, distributed them to the trainees to plant in their villages, and showed them how to take care of them. This particular village was one of those that had received a plant. Fortunately, it had plenty available. They brought her a stem, and she taught them again how to apply the liquid from the stem to the entire burn area. They taught the mother to cleanse the child with soap daily and reapply the aloe gel. They were to return in a week to see how the child fared. When the mother brought him back, he had a complete new layer of pink skin over most of his little body, and the family was very happy.

As the wound care was completed each time, the child would go to sleep. The villagers were amazed. They were even more amazed when the child healed rapidly with very little scarring.

Joann used the episode as a teaching moment, emphasizing that many of their illnesses and injuries could be cared for if they could learn and properly use what was immediately available to them. She was reiterating what she had taught the trainees—with the help of a very dramatic example. She repeatedly talked about how clean water, hygiene, and nutrition were the greatest benefits in being healthy. It was a slow process, and not all believed, but the trainees were more open and accepted many new ways of doing things. It was hard for them to believe in bacteria or germs when they could not see them.

That episode also brought another thought. That mother had applied that manure poultice thinking and hoping it would help heal her child. On the contrary, it caused much greater pain and harm. It provided no help whatever. In a similar way, people often apply a poultice of ritual or good works or good moral living to the cancer of sin, hoping—maybe even praying—that these actions will bring healing to an eternally fatal illness, but they offer no hope. There is hope only with Jesus.

There was also a good example related to nutrition. Joann noticed a lot of the children in one village had red hair. Because glossy black hair was desired by all, those children (and a few adults) who had red hair were embarrassed and sometimes ridiculed. On one of our trips, Joann brought a bag of soybeans and showed them how to plant them and mix a handful in their lentil soup along with some of the leaves from an ipil-ipil tree. She promised if they would do so daily, their children's hair would be black again. Within a year, their red hair had turned black. They were ecstatic. They were not aware of nutrition and protein, but when they saw the results, their eyes were opened.

Another example had an unhappy ending. A mother brought a very sick baby to be seen. A thorough examination revealed an infectious process for which we had medication that would help. The trainees carefully explained to the mother how sick the child was, administered the first dose of medication, and showed the mother how to give the remainder to the child before they returned home. The next morning, word came that the child had died. Joann, very saddened, went to the mother's little hut to see what happened. The mother, not realizing how seriously ill the child was, had not given the baby any more medicine. That baby's illness and death seemed to symbolize so vividly life's fragility as well as the vulnerability of those who are ignorant, weak, and defenseless.

On another occasion, in that same village, Joann was called to a home early in the night. A man was dying. Suffering from acute dehydration, diarrhea, and vomiting, he was at the point of death. Joann repeated to the man's mother what she had taught the trainees many times: mix some jungle honey and a little salt in a liter of boiled water and give it to him constantly throughout the night. She demonstrated how it should be done. She asked the trainees to explain again and then pray for the man. The next morning, he was able to sit up and talk, and he went on to recover. To the villagers, it was a miracle, but to the trainees, who had seen similar results from that treatment in other villages, it reinforced the validity of what Joann had been teaching and doing. They became strong believers in the new ways of treating illness and continued to use their training in succeeding years.

I note above some of our concern when we returned to the hills after our first series of visits. The trainees had the training and the opportunity to make money out of their newfound skill and ignore the spiritual dimension we had emphasized. When we returned on our second visit and asked them to review what had happened, our concern changed to celebration. They excitedly shared stories of both physical healing and spiritual new life. They were not using their knowledge to gain wealth or fame because they did not charge for their services. They only asked the patients' families to buy the medicine at the market to replenish their medicine kits.

One example stood out. One of the trainees could hardly wait to tell his story. He had been called to the house of the village headman to treat his sick cow. In the Indian Hindu culture, cows were considered sacred. In many cases, they were of greater monetary value than wives. That call to come treat the headman's cow carried severe implications. The trainee went hesitantly, explaining that he had been trained to treat only people, not animals.

"Never mind," the man said. "If your God is as great as you say He is, you can pray to your God—and He will heal my cow."

The trainee was praying desperately during the conversation, asking God to let him know what to do. Then he remembered that Dr. Goatcher had taught them to give ground-up, powdered charcoal from the cooking fire to patients who had eaten poisonous mushrooms or other poisonous plants. Considering that thought to have come from the Lord, he instructed the headman to get a generous container of charcoal from his fire, grind it up, and feed it to the cow.

The man did as he was told, and within a few minutes, the cow had a massive evacuation. Within a few more minutes, the cow got up and began grazing.

The headman was stunned. "It is a miracle," he said. "Tell me more about your God."

The trainee shared the gospel story with him. Over the course of the next few months, the headman and most of the village came to accept the Lord—and a church was formed. From that episode, I guess you could say one way to a man's heart is through his cow's stomach.

As other trainees told their stories of how the Lord had used their efforts to bring about much healing, giving God the glory for it, with many people coming to accept the Lord, we rejoiced that they were using this new skill in a way to honor God.

But other responsibilities were coming along, necessitating the phasing out of our Khond Hills clinics. I can't just stop the story, however, without some closing notes about those times and experiences.

During our Khond Hills era, there were far too many memory-making images and impressions to relate in detail. I'll mention a few in no particular order:

- Dismay at multitudes of forest fires set in the hills by the people seeking to obtain a small amount of fruit that falls among the leaves. The fires denude the hills, destroy a natural resource, reduce wildlife habitat, and—with the dust—make the air almost unbreathable.
- Sorrow at seeing the still-smoldering remains of a village where someone's cooking fire got out of control, igniting a wind-driven wave of destruction, laying waste homes and what few pitiful possessions the villagers had.
- Curiosity as to whether twenty pounds of fat would help cushion these old bones from the ground bed.
- Approaching consternation when diarrhea would not stop, the last roll of toilet paper was disappearing, the water was getting low, and we still had a few days to go.
- Anger at buying factory-packed medicine in large quantities, only to open them and find only about two-thirds of the stated number of pills. Corruption was systemic.
- Helplessness at the apathy, ignorance, suffering, and superstition that permeates the very core of society.
- Joy at seeing an idea gradually take root and grow in a mind, then translating it, effectively, into both the medical and spiritual worlds.
- Frustration at the unwillingness of so many people to do something for themselves that would dramatically improve their lives. Habits, superstitions, attitudes, and cultural mores are hard and slow to change.

- Relief at getting back to clean water, a bed, and clean clothes.
- Solace at getting off a windowless, spring-less, standing-room-only bus crammed with sweating, unwashed bodies after many hours. Somebody forgot to use deodorant.
- Fascination (and sadness) at the variety of means of eking out a living in a destitute society. A small sampling:
  o Ear cleaners, in most cities, using warm mustard oil to clean the ears of those able to pay for it.
  o Selling small packages (or jars) of sacred Ganges River mud.
  o Battalions of junk-men in an economy of scarcity where nothing is wasted and where recycling is not a slogan but a necessity.
- Chagrin at glancing back at these impressions and seeing how preoccupied I was with the minor physical amenities during our time in the hills.
- Gratitude for the privilege of seeing people grow in the Lord.
- Overflowing gratitude for a wife with true grit. She takes the rough with the smooth, bad with the good, and sickness with health. She would have been one of the first passengers on the *Mayflower* and one of the first in a covered wagon across the plains of America—just as she has gone with me into some of the most remote and difficult regions of Asia. And in the middle of it all, she has continued to be a Christian lady in the truest sense of that description.

Our wandering, tumbleweed mode of life during those months and years brought to life a verse in Psalms that still resonates today: "God has been our dwelling place in all generations" (Psalms 90:1). I read that passage one morning in our morning devotions while we were in the Khond Hills. A new insight came: God is our "dwelling place." As believers, we should be at home wherever we are. The person, not the place, is our dwelling. In a plane, mud hut, hotel, or jungle, we are at home. Home is the will of God. We felt at home in the hills because we felt we were completely in God's will, but we had also felt at home at the hospital in Bangkla, in the refugee work, back in Van Horn, Texas, and in other places. We went where we felt the Lord was leading; we felt we were in His will, and we felt at home.

Increased Involvement with BBH Board Chair

During our Khond Hills work, I had become more involved with the hospital in Bangalore. Visa constraints were hurting us in terms of maintaining adequate missionary staffing. The hospital was growing. Other hospitals were being built in Bangalore, equipped with many high-tech diagnostic tools and offering competition. That was not bad, but if BBH were to continue to exist and fulfill its mission, it would have to adapt to the new reality. The business, professional, and commercial enterprises in the area were adjusting to the more modern world and adopting more up-to-date business procedures. BBH needed to adopt and adapt, as appropriate, to remain equally up-to-date. Bangalore, with a population of around six million, had become the high-tech center of India. BBH was facing challenges.

In the spring of 1984, I was elected chairman of the board. Not long afterward, I was asked to fill in as the interim hospital administrator. As a temporary administrator, I was not comfortable initiating any major changes in those two brief interludes. There was no way I could really understand a totally new situation in that time frame, yet we could not afford to stagnate.

What was needed was a review of administrative procedures that would indicate a problem, or potential problem, in routine operations. That was not so difficult. Reports from every department were submitted each month. A review and comparison of those reports would reveal trends that were significant, either good or threatening.

That was where I started. Coincidental to my being in Bangalore, another issue arose that would eventually lead to a major shift in our medical mission efforts (and in all our mission work). Our area director was receiving signals that FMB resources that helped with operating budgets as well as capital needs for all mission institutions were not keeping pace with field requests. Reductions in financial support were on the immediate horizon. That was a frightening prospect for the Bangalore hospital. India was historically known as home for millions of poverty-stricken people who were unable to pay for health care even when it was available. That great need for health care was one factor that led to the decision to build the hospital on the north side of Bangalore, in a suburban area called Bellary. It was built and dedicated with the promise that all patients would be accepted regardless of their ability to pay. The threat of being unable to accept everyone who came, simply because of lack of funds, was distressing.

Several issues and needs were entering the picture simultaneously:

- The hospital outpatient load was growing. Additional exam rooms were needed.
- The hospital was known for its surgical capability; the surgery suite needed more space and patient beds.
- The charge for patient care was less than it cost; the more patients they had, the greater the deficit.
- The subsidy from the FMB would be decreasing; it would no longer cover the deficit.
- The cost center review I had done revealed that surgery patients had greater per-patient cost/loss than other department (medicine, OB, pediatrics, etc.)

Dr. Rebekah Naylor was the medical director and a surgeon (FACS, FICS). She had been instrumental in making the hospital so well-known and respected. The revelation by the cost center study that surgery was a major cause for much of the loss was distressing. That finding, combined with the impending decrease in FMB funding, disturbed her greatly. To her, any limitation of surgery would cause great harm to the hospital and loss of care to many patients.

Rebekah and I had been friends for years. (She had been a medical receptor in our hospital in Bangkla back in 1967.) We had many long conversations that were distressing, discouraging, frightening, and very painful at times. I identified with her feelings, but the inevitable was coming. We had to prepare for it. Fortunately, the FMB arranged for the reduction in funding to take place over a five-year period, with a 20 percent reduction each year. There was a little time to adapt.

Some options simply were not viable. We could not raise charges to equal the cost of service, we could not stop seeing charity patients, and we could not raise enough money locally to cover the deficit. So, what could we do?

I don't know who came up with the idea, and it was not original at BBH, but it was the right thing to do at the right time in Bangalore. The city was growing rapidly and developing a financial middle class. The decision was made to add the space, but make it an extra-nice and very high-tech place that was able to compete with the best that could be found in for-profit hospitals that were being built in Bangalore, and then charge accordingly. The additional funding realized from the new area would help supplement the necessary charity care needs. They did, and it worked. They have repeated that process in succeeding years—with continuing success. The hospital now has more than three hundred beds with accredited training programs for interns, residents, nurses, and ancillary health-care personnel. It is a highly respected Christian medical institution providing a wonderful, life-giving ministry in a key city in India.

Not all challenges faced by the hospital were resolved that successfully. An ongoing challenge was related to labor problems. It is too long and complicated to go into detail, but it began, and has continued, through the efforts of a small group of fanatical union agitators, most of whom had no connection to the hospital. They were angry that the hospital was not unionized, but Indian labor laws are such that that type of agitation can be exercised in what Americans would consider to be an unlawful manner. I was primarily an observer in the labor dispute, for obvious reasons, but I sat in on multiple meetings between the labor people and our hospital labor lawyers. What a hassle!

One of many incidents that occurred in relation to the labor problem that rankled then, and still raises my hackles, was what I saw one day when I returned to the hospital from a meeting. As I entered the hospital compound, I noticed an effigy hanging from the big column at the side of the gate. It was an effigy of Dr. Naylor, with written allegations of actions, conduct, and decisions that were blatant lies. A small group of people was standing around. It was not employees who had raised the effigy—it was the labor union agitators. I was strongly tempted to go out, tear it down, and tell them what I thought, but I did not do it. I knew it would probably cause a riot. Everything they had written was so contrary to her Christian character, her compassionate care for all people, and her efforts to help the poorest of the poor that my anger almost got the best of me.

Another issue, perhaps the largest in the history of the hospital, was what to do with the hospital as FMB missionaries were gradually being curtailed by visa restrictions imposed by the Indian government. With no missionary presence, the FMB had to decide what to do with the hospital. There were few options.

Selling it was an original FMB option, but that idea died when it was discovered that the funds could not leave the country.

Another option was to turn it over to a local Baptist entity in India, but the consensus, even among Indian Baptists, was that they did not yet have the administrative, technical, or financial resources required to assume such a huge responsibility.

Other options were considered and discarded after closer examinations indicated they were not feasible.

The option chosen was to enter into a contractual agreement with the Christian Medical College (CMC) in Vellore, India, for them to assume management responsibility, with an FMB representative continuing on the hospital board (I continued in that role until I retired.). That sentence covers years of studies, reviews, negotiations, and legal consultations—far too much to try to explain in detail. I'll mention only one thorny issue: trying to reconcile differing, sometimes conflicting, laws and regulations relating to legal and financial responsibilities under American and Indian legal systems. The huge conundrum was who would have ultimate responsibility under the management agreement—with assurances that it complied with Indian laws. Legal interpretations could change with changing government parties. Negotiations had begun in India years earlier. Dr. Rebekah Naylor was a major voice in those exploratory talks. She was the BBH medical director and was also on the CMC administrative committee. Dr. Pulimood, the medical director of CMC and BBH board member, also was a major voice.

In the United States, there was a meeting in our home in Richmond, Virginia, in September 1988. Dr. Keith Parks, president of the FMB, Dr. Pulimood (our house guest), Dr. Bill Wakefield, Dr. Van Williams, Jerry Rankin, and I considered the issue from the Stateside perspective. From that meeting, a framework was established for the Christian Medical College to assume the management of BBH. The CMC desired the name of the hospital to remain the Bangalore Baptist Hospital. A key component of the agreement was that the FMB would continue to fund and be responsible for the Chaplains Department. The final agreement was signed on January 1, 1989.

The growth, success, and spiritual impact made by the hospital in the subsequent twenty-six years makes it obvious that the management arrangement was a wise move. What appeared at first to be a disastrous situation for BBH has been turned by God into a bright and glorious lighthouse that continues to provide outstanding, compassionate health and medical care in India as a demonstration of the good news of Christ.

In the midst of my second stint as interim administrator of BBH, amid all the usual hospital crises, I received a surprising phone call from Ron Hill in Bangkok, telling me I had been elected mission administrator of the Thailand Baptist Mission. As noted below, that brought about many changes. I would need to discontinue my time as interim administrator at BBH as soon as feasible (although I would continue on the board), and Joann and I would need to discontinue the health-care training in the Khond Hills.

While I had been busy in the administrative affairs of the hospital, Joann had been equally busy in two major medical areas. One area was in the BBH Outpatient Department. The patient load had continued to grow rapidly, at that point exceeding eighty thousand patients annually. Her presence was of significant help when the national medical staff was occupied with surgeries and inpatients. Her other area was in conducting rural medical clinics in many of the villages around Bangalore, seeing patients, and giving many vaccinations.

The hospital and medical work in that area of India were becoming well-known. What was not as well-known, but of greater eternal significance, was the great number of churches established as a direct result of the medical work. Hundreds of churches have grown directly out of the BBH witness. Similar church growth has occurred in other areas of the world, led by people who were not primarily church-planter missionaries. The emphasis by the FMB (IMB) in recent years has been away from institutional ministries to individual church-planter ministries. There are valid reasons for some of the de-emphasis, primarily financial, but much has also been lost. The hospitals in India, Thailand, and several in Africa have been the most effective church-planting activities in our mission's history.

It is equally true of agricultural missionary activities, especially Harold Watson in the Philippines. His work has benefited tens of thousands of Filipinos, as seen by the special presidential recognition he was awarded by President Aquino of the Philippines in 1991. He also received the Magsaysay Award (Asia's Premier Prize, their equivalent to the Nobel Peace Prize) awarded to him by the Philippines in 1985. His agricultural innovations have been adopted by several other Asian nations with equal benefit. What is not noted in those awards—but what stands out in the eternal record—is the untold number of churches that have grown out of his work. My point is that institutional work can be one of the most effective church-planting efforts any organization can find.

CHAPTER 10

Another Call ...
Another Era

I was reluctant to become mission administrator. Ron Hill had been the administrator for several years, and we all wanted him to continue. He was the most humble, competent, capable, brightest, wisest, and most trustworthy leader I have ever known. He was also the most fluent Thai speaker of all the missionaries, a most important skill for the MA, but his first love was to be out in the field talking to the people about the Lord. Administration pulled him away from that. He wanted out.

We had between eighty and ninety missionaries under appointment to Thailand, scattered over much of the nation. We had six institutions: hospital, seminary, student center (with almost a thousand students enrolled), retreat camp on the coast, mass communications (radio, TV, and media/print material), and a bookstore. It was a major operation.

While I was occupied with MA responsibilities, Joann was called on to fill a sudden gap in the medical staff at the hospital in Bangkla. (I have long since lost count of the times Joann's skills as a physician have filled a critical need of some kind.) A family illness within the medical staff left the hospital short of a physician soon after our return to Thailand. Joann was available and obviously well qualified to fill in.

She was also able to pick up the medical responsibility of the refugee transit center in Bangkok. That position had been covered by a female Indian physician I had hired almost two years earlier. Now, however, she was being called to return home to marry. It was an arranged marriage. She had met her future husband only once or twice and barely knew him, but she was excited about the arrangement. Covering the transit center clinic was more convenient for us since it was in Bangkok. Going to Bangkla, however, was a little different. It was too far to commute, so she would be in Bangkla during the week and in Bangkok on weekends. Or I would go to Bangkla for the weekend. We were back to being separated again.

One of the serendipities of that time in Bangkok was that James had graduated from Baylor University (in computer science) and had come back to a college in Lampang, Thailand, to spend a year helping them establish a department of computer science. We were able to visit frequently and were also able to take a vacation together to Singapore. That was a choice time in a beautiful city.

Another benefit we had from James was that the mission was installing our first office computer system. James's presence and skills enabled us to get the system in operation at much lower cost and with much clearer instructions. He was our help desk for that year and a big help.

To be the mission administrator was not to be the boss. (It is hard to boss missionaries!) Some tasks were clear, but some were more nebulous:

- coordinate
- assist missionaries and institutions with budget preparations
- continually consider strategic planning for the mission
- liaison between the mission and national Baptists, both individuals and churches

- liaison with Thai officials and other organizations
- interpret compliance with FMB policies and procedures
- work closely with the area director (in my case, Bill Wakefield)

Working with national Baptists was a priority. The very limited missionary force could never evangelize a nation. At some point, the national Christians had to assume the primary responsibility for their homeland. As the national churches grew, matured, and became capable, we (the mission and FMB) would gradually hand over appropriate mission institutions to them. We needed to be careful not to prematurely burden them with excessive financial responsibilities. We began the process by adding nationals to the governing committees of the various institutions. As they grew in experience and wisdom, they assumed greater responsibilities. We were working ourselves out of a job—as we were supposed to be doing. We saw our role primarily as using resources made available to us by the FMB to continually extend, reach out to, and begin pioneer work in areas that a small new National Baptist Association would not be able to do.

I had been on the mission executive committee and was aware of some of those challenges as Joann and I returned from India. One appealing factor in the new assignment was that she and I would be living closer together again—at least we hoped so. I kinda liked that, even if it was in the middle of a city of around seven million people. We were in the Lord's will; we were home, and it was okay.

India: A Few Reflections

By the middle of 1984, we had lived, traveled, and worked in India almost a year. We had seen just a hint of the diversity, complexity, and drastic contrasts in the nation. It was a country, but it was not a community. Many writers have tried to describe the country, but

I'm not sure even an Indian knows all about India. There is simply too large a chasm between the ever-present extremes of affluence and poverty, the high caste and the outcast, the city and the village, and the highly privileged male and the servant wife/women.

Each ethnic, religious, and linguistic group, each tribal and caste group, each rich and poor individual lived part of their lives in their own cocooned world, always trying to attain to a higher position in this as well as the next life. It was often a violent land, and the extremes of the contrasts frequently led to violent confrontations (and still do today).

The caste system is a good example. By legislation and a new constitution, it had been outlawed, but it was still very much alive and well. The belief, design, scheme, practice, or whatever one wanted to call it was that one is born into a group or class (caste) that is fixed at birth. To a great extent, it is based on what the person supposedly did in a previous incarnation. There is no escaping in this life. If enough good deeds are done in this life, one can hope to be reborn in a higher class, or a higher level, but for the current life, there is no exit. As often happened in India, the interpretation of a cultural system varied in different areas of the country. For example, some Hindus eat meat.

I had been at the hospital for many months and had developed some close friendships before the caste issue would even be mentioned in my presence. And in the discussions, there was no explaining or defending the existence of the system; it was just assumed and accepted.

But that reluctance to consider it openly contributed to the tension-filled atmosphere that still lingered in some places in the country. The caste system was changing, along with other cultural phenomena. Attitudes of the younger generation were being affected by other worldviews. Marriages were gradually being based on individual choices instead of family arrangements, but many of the older generation were resistant to those changes. Change causes tension. With centuries of history and fixed cultural mores, change occurs slowly, but it is changing.

Part of the opposition to the Christian faith in India is the Christian belief that all people are equal in the sight of God. That idea neutralizes caste, race, economic status, gender, or any other criteria as a determination of worth or standing, but that idea runs counter to the religious and cultural ideas of many Indians, hence opposition, sometime violent, to any Christian encroachment on their value system.

So, what determines who has priority in business, social, professional, medical, and education interaction? High-caste status? Wealth? Some high-caste people are very poor. Some wealthy people are in a lower caste. Some of the high-caste people thought their caste status merited more favorable treatment. Some of the wealthy thought their wealth was a blessing bestowed by their god (similar to some Old Testament beliefs) and deserved preferential treatment. The criteria for determining priority varied greatly. It was too sensitive and complex for me, as a foreigner, to pursue at any length, and it was not my place to try to resolve it.

India was a conundrum for me. It attracted me greatly in many ways, but it repelled me in others. Joann accused me of changing personalities when I landed in India. I had to agree, and the fact that I had to agree irritated and disappointed me. One example was air travel in India. I would often be on a world-circling schedule, requiring me to take a particular flight, but many flights within India were *free seating*. In that situation, tickets were sold as long as people wanted to buy them. Many flights were oversold. People boarded until all the seats were filled. Those remaining were stranded. (I understand most of those policies are now changed.) To meet my schedule already set up in other countries, I needed to get on the plane, but boarding time was chaos. The strong, aggressive, rich, high-caste people were the first to board, and all others were left to fend for themselves. To make my schedule, I had to be strong and shove my way forward in order to get a seat. To act like that made me angry. Then I was upset that I was upset.

That negative attitude was countered by many extremely courteous Indians and by seeing a tremendous response to the gospel and observing lives and attitudes changing. I have seen the transformation of conduct when people came to know the Lord and adopted His servant attitude. Then I was shamed by my conduct. If I had grown up in a land where I was oppressed, considered to be inferior or unworthy just because I was poor, or was born in a lower class, I might act just like they did. Regardless, as a Christian, my conduct should be a part of my ministry. I often stumbled.

Surface travel in India gave me many more adrenaline rushes than I wanted. Indian roads and streets could vie with the best (or worst) in the world for hazardous travel. Often less than fifteen feet in width, with no shoulders, a great variety of vehicles would hurl themselves at each other at speeds ranging from crawling up to seventy miles an hour in a never-ending game of chicken. The bigger and mightier vehicles seized the right-of-way. There was usually a volatile mix of cars, trucks, jitterbugging motor bikes, bicycles, rickshaws, bullock carts, overloaded mini-buses (with passengers hanging on with one hand), rambling cows (never, ever to be hit), angry dogs, and surly camels interspersed with wild-eyed pedestrians playing suicidal dodgeball as they tried to stay alive while crossing the road. Then color the whole with blue-black diesel smoke from smarting exhaust pipes producing a cloud of fumes that burned the eyes, choked the lungs, and left clothing oily and dirty in only a moment. When the dry season ended, all paved surfaces were covered with a film of oil and grease. When the first rains came, the streets and highways became slick as ice; it was a demolition derby. Fun and games.

There was another peculiar Indian trait I never could decipher. Every language and culture has its own nonverbal communication quirks. In India, it is the head shake, nod, tilt, or rotation— sometimes all at the same time. It can mean yes, no, maybe, later, dumb, silly … or nothing. When I first saw them doing it, I knew they were communicating, but I could never decode the signals. I tried to do it a few times, but I got funny looks. I think I said the wrong thing. I quit trying. It was kind of like being at an auction and being afraid to raise an eyebrow or finger because you could send the wrong signal and get in expensive trouble. I was often in groups with heads going in all directions simultaneously. No one was confused but me.

We experienced much (much to us, but really only a small portion) of the diversity, complexity, contrasts, and extremes of Indian culture, economy, religions, and geography. There were so many times when Joann and I would observe an event, ritual, or scene and turn to each other and wonder how we could put it in words. It was impossible. In a much greater way, I have wondered how many times Jesus wanted to convey a message to His followers and was limited by finite human language in speaking to followers with limited capacity for understanding spiritual matters. Joann and I were in a different category, but we saw so many things and experienced so much that we have wanted to share with others but have not had the words to express it.

We were on our way back home to Bangkok, and Thailand did feel like home. Even though we were still babes in understanding all the complexities that existed in Thailand (Muang Thai, "Free Land") we considered it home. When we were in the Lord's will, we were home. Geography was irrelevant.

I was fortunate, in fact the entire Mission was fortunate, to have an excellent Thai office staff. Meeting the logistical needs (housing, travel, multiple types of permits, and financial) of that many foreigners living in another country was a time-consuming, never-ending task. They were of particular help to me as administrator because they knew and kept me informed of priority issues of which I needed to be aware.

As mission administrator, I was an ex officio member of all mission committees, but I spent more time with the institutions committee. From my time on the hospital board in Bangalore, I had already become aware of the decrease in funds that would be available as subsidy and capital needs for institutions. Preparations needed to be started in Thailand for cutbacks that would soon begin. The implication of cutbacks in our institutions carried the same concerns in those days as they do even as I write this, although probably to a lesser extent. Institutional work would receive a close review. Some personnel would be affected. It was not pleasant to deal with.

Other changes were also coming. People were moving to urban centers in great numbers. Economic development was exploding, and Thailand was getting more hints of political unrest. (That was not new. We had been present when a couple of coups had taken place, with curfews in place and gunfire being heard throughout the city.) But the coups rarely affected the foreigners if they behaved. The king usually stepped in and calmed things down at the last minute.

As a mission, we needed to understand the changes and adapt our work and plans to the new reality. As people moved from rural to urban areas and from agricultural work to factory work, they would sometimes be more open to considering new ideas, including a new faith. We needed to capitalize on any new receptivity that appeared.

Along with changes that were taking place on foreign mission fields, the FMB was going through some changes of its own. Mission philosophies and mission strategies were also changing, sometimes to the consternation of field personnel. More decisions were being made in Richmond and less in the field. That was not all bad. Some habits, activities, and work needed to be evaluated and revised, but field personnel—knowing the country, the culture, the language, and having years of in-country experience—also had wisdom that needed to be considered. Sometimes it was, but many times, it wasn't. Morale was affected, and it directly impacted our work in the field.

New Doors Opening

Our Thai work was going well. Response was still minimal when compared with some areas of the world, but we were seeing evidence of increasing interest. There were hints of changes in the air, especially in Southeast Asia. Upheavals in the political and military status, combined with the impact of the refugee movements, led to thoughts of innovative ways to penetrate the region with the gospel.

The refugee crisis had prompted a major outpouring of financial resources to address hunger issues. When the crisis eased, doors began to open slightly in previously closed, or almost closed, areas. With resources available and the possibility of capitalizing on a few of those fuzzy opportunities, the FMB created a new entity to try to enter those doors. The new entity was called Cooperative Services International: CSI. One new element with CSI was that it was free to initiate probes into all areas of the world with a possibility of establishing a presence. Previously, new outreach ministries in each area of the world, divided into nine areas by the FMB, were the responsibility of the area director for that specific area.

It is beyond the scope of this family history to go into details of the organization and its mission. The above paragraph is included only to provide the background for my brief time as director/ coordinator of CSI in Indochina. I continued as the consultant for hunger relief and disaster response for South and Southeast Asia, but there were specific opportunities to explore in Laos, Vietnam, and Cambodia. I was asked to assist in coordinating a committee to explore some of those opportunities. The title was window dressing—to be used according to what was appropriate at any given time in our specific geographical area. The international director of CSI, based in Richmond, was a former missionary in Vietnam prior to the fall of Vietnam in 1975 and knew the area well.

The survey trip to Laos that Bill Wakefield had asked me to make in 1981 was made prior to the organization of Cooperative Services International, but it dovetailed with the mission and scope of CSI. It was a part of the overall intent to touch every possible people group in South and Southeast Asia, even in closed countries, with the gospel.

A Surprising Invitation

A confluence of circumstances came about at that time and revealed again that God was exercising His sovereignty and had His own plans. A series of three typhoons battered the east coast of Vietnam in late 1985 and early 1986. The last one occurred just before rice harvest time, destroying the crop at the worst possible time. To add to the destruction, the storm surge destroyed multiple large storage warehouses containing reserve stocks of rice and other food goods. It reached inland several miles, inundating many square miles of crop land with salty sand and silt that would greatly reduce harvest yields for years. The combination of disasters left the people in distress.

Vietnam requested help, but other Eastern Bloc nations provided no help. Neither did Western Bloc nations, including the United States, because they had no official relations with the Vietnamese government. When Vietnamese officials learned that Southern Baptists had been in South Vietnam prior to 1975, they got in touch with Dr. Keith Parks at the FMB and requested assistance. (In a personal conversation with Dr. Parks in early 2016, neither of us could remember the details of how the connection came about.)

Bill Wakefield (VP for Southeast Asia) asked me to get some rice to Vietnam, using Hunger Relief funds remaining from the refugee crisis. Although records are long gone and I cannot be sure of the exact figure, I recall using almost $600,000 to purchase a shipload of rice and a variety of medications. I had the rice packaged in fifty-kilogram sacks with stenciled lettering saying: "Donated by Baptist Christians in USA," with a cross stenciled at the top of the sack.

Fifty-kilogram sacks of rice for Vietnamese catastrophic flooding

I chartered a Vietnamese ship, monitored the loading, and arranged to meet them in Da Nang, Vietnam, to monitor the off-loading and distribution.

As a part of earlier discussions with Vietnamese embassy officials in Bangkok about the request from Hanoi for me to visit Vietnam, I had made it clear that we (FMB) would require transportation in order to travel and monitor much of the distribution. They also understood that the food was to be distributed to the civilian population only and not to the military. They agreed. The plan was for me to fly into Hanoi for an initial meeting related to the distribution, fly to Da Nang, go where I wanted to go in central Vietnam, see what I wanted to see, and then be driven back to Hanoi for further meetings with officials.

I was anxious to see Hanoi. The Vietnam War had made it a byword, and I wanted to see as much of it as possible, especially the Hanoi Hilton, the infamous prison where many American POWs were confined and tortured and where some died. My visit was scheduled for February 28–March 9, 1986.

The extensive meetings with senior Vietnamese officials, to take place in Hanoi after the food distribution, were giving me much pause. I had no training or experience in handling discussions and negotiations at that level. It was intimidating. My greatest fear was disappointing the Lord.

In the background of discussions in setting up the food distribution was the possibility of us being allowed back into Vietnam for project activity. This could be the door opening for our return to a presence in Vietnam. That was big. For me to say or do something—even unintentionally or unknowingly—and blow the opportunity was scary. A lot of praying was taking place.

I felt the distribution was handled well. I spent two days going haphazardly to villages in the delta region. At every unannounced, unscheduled stop, the rice sacks, with the stenciling and the cross, were in open and obvious view. I could have been deceived, but I felt they were trying to comply with the conditions we had requested.

After the distribution, they wanted to show me the Hue area. Many centuries earlier, it had been a major city and the cultural center of their nation. It was an interesting, ancient city with its own identity and culture. I enjoyed that visit greatly. Then we left for Hanoi. It was to be a three-day drive for the seven hundred-kilometer trip. We would stop in two provincial capitals for meetings and view some of their priority needs before arriving in Hanoi. There was also food distribution taking place in one of the rural areas en route. I was always accompanied by my interpreter and my "minder," a Communist official who monitored everything I said and accompanied me wherever I went.

Provincial capital visits became endurance trials. They followed a common pattern: a huge meal with a choice of "unusual" food, repeated toasts with a variety of hard drinks (they had difficulty understanding that I did not drink liquor), and then conversation. The conversations also followed a pattern. They first tried to determine who I was and who I represented. In their very centrally controlled, authoritarian system of government, there was no place for someone like me. I was a common United States citizen, not connected to the United States government, but I was meeting with high government officials in Hanoi. Political issues were skirted, rarely mentioned, but they were curious.

"Are you a government official?"

"No."

"Are you CIA?"

"No."

"Who are you? What is your organization? Where do you get resources to help with these projects? Why do you do this?"

I was prepared for that. I gave a brief statement explaining who I was as a Christian, the Christian organization I represented, who we worshipped, and that we were following the example of our God in showing love and concern for those who were in great need. There was always a moment of silence after I spoke. They had heard the words, but they had trouble processing what the words meant. With their worldview, they never could really comprehend. After a bit, we went on with the business at hand.

I have wanted to recapture and explain the dynamic of those discussions, but it is almost futile to attempt it. The discussions were courteous, framed in diplomatic language, but there were several returns to the question of who I was and how I had come to be in that situation. They did not know much about Baptists, but they did know about Christians. Behind the diplomatic language was the understanding by both of us that we were desirous of dialogue but wary of entangling agreements. They were hard-core believers in their system, avowed atheists, and adamantly opposed to the Christian worldview., I was a committed Christian, adamantly opposed to the Communist worldview, and unwilling to compromise any of my Christian convictions, yet I was willing to meet with them and provide substantial assistance to their hurting people if they were willing to cooperate. Neither of us tried to convince the other to change our belief systems.

The conversations were never confrontational or adversarial. There were conditions each imposed on the other, but they were related more to operational matters than philosophical ones. I was tense as we began the discussions, but I was more comfortable when they returned to questions concerning who I was and why we were willing to provide assistance without demanding concessions in return. It was a strange meeting in many ways, but both sides wanted some kind of relationship established—and we were willing to take some risks to bring it about.

Each province had overwhelming needs. The coastal central provinces, from Da Nang northward, had suffered most from the typhoons. They desperately needed food and medical supplies. Later, they would need more general agricultural production help and any kind of medical help.

Each province had tea plantations in the mountains, and each felt theirs was the best in the country. As a going-away gift for my offer to help, they gave me a huge sack of tea leaves. By the time we got to Hanoi, the van was packed with tea leaves. Some days later, when I was taken to the airport to return home to Bangkok, my driver was stumped when he suddenly inherited a van load of tea leaves. I would still be drinking tea from that load if I had taken it with me.

The Hanoi meetings appeared to go well. The subjects, concerns, and issues were similar to those we had discussed in the provincial meetings. They wanted—and desperately needed—immediate help and development assistance.

They had conditions for our presence in Vietnam, but we also had conditions. One of their conditions was that I was not to make the assistance known to the world media. They were embarrassed that they could not feed themselves. Though I could not document it, it seemed to me that they felt that accepting assistance from a Christian organization was an insult to their political system. Anything, any comment, that reflected negatively on their Communist system, was anathema. They had total belief in their system. All failures in providing the necessities of life for their people were the result of other circumstances, never of their system of government.

Another condition was that I was prohibited from going to certain places. They did not name them, and would not be specific, but I had not planned to try to see any sensitive areas anyway, so it was no problem. I was free to walk the streets and talk with people. I took advantage of that. I accepted the conditions.

One final condition was that they wanted us to commit at least $50,000 in food and health-care projects before they would commit to cooperation. When I told them we had already provided over $500,000 in food and medical assistance, and named the specific areas, they were surprised. I was surprised that they were surprised. There was an immediate increase in cordiality—and no more mention of conditions.

I also had conditions. One was that I, and all in our organization who followed me, would immediately be granted a visa upon request and have unfettered access to monitor and evaluate every project in which we had a part.

They agreed.

I also stated that we should be free to meet with national Christians and that neither they nor we would be harassed by officials. I told them I would be questioning their compliance.

They agreed.

I had one final condition. If I heard, saw, or found any evidence that any of our resources had not been used as requested, our assistance would end immediately.

Again, they agreed.

I was not naive enough to think I could ensure compliance with everything I had stated, but I could, and did, follow up on some of it. While I was present, I think they did make an effort to comply, but the reality was that our help was not large, in national terms, and could not make much of an impact on the entire nation. They were not about to change their policies for a relatively small amount of help. I did hear later that some leniency had been granted to some of the Christians for a brief period of time, but then the harassment began again.

The big issue had been addressed: We were back in Vietnam. We were not looking at just that one episode. That was just the first open door. It would be another few years before we had resident missionaries there, but one of our doctors followed me in a few weeks and began responding to and initiating additional medical projects. It was a part of our ongoing plan to have permanent personnel back in Vietnam. Our physician had been the medical director of a hospital in Cambodia, was familiar with the region, and also spoke some French. He was a part of our CSI team, along with Joann and me.

Our business was about finished. We had a couple of ceremonial meetings remaining, but we had a working agreement and could build on that. I was free to explore Hanoi. I was glad to be free of my interpreter and my minder. I may have been followed, as I had been in Vientiane, Laos, but it did not concern me.

Hanoi was filled with monuments to Ho Chi Minh. Museums and other major buildings were filled with homage to him. Some of the buildings were impressive, but they were all surrounded by raw poverty and dilapidation. It reminded me of scenes in India: a palatial monument surrounded by abject poverty. There were several street-side shops, but they were poorly stocked. I went to the Hanoi Hilton, but I could only see it from the outside.

Vietnam: The Weird, the Quirky, and the Wonderful

Our purpose had been achieved, and I thanked the Lord many times for that. What I have included here is only a very brief summary of all that occurred. It was a tremendous experience for me—far too much to explain in detail—but the incidental side events and encounters provided fascinating and colorful experiences that made the trip even more memorable. I'll mention only a few of them in no particular order or sequence.

During the rice and medical supply/equipment distribution, I was blessed by several people who risked personal danger when they came close to me and carefully moved a piece of clothing to reveal a cross. They were aware that I was a Christian. They were believers who were maintaining their faith in difficult circumstances and wanted me to know it. We often exchanged looks and shared silent, unobtrusive moments of fellowship as fellow believers.

The drive from Da Nang through Hue brought a surprise. We passed many large cemeteries filled with crosses. The area had a significant Catholic population before the war as evidenced by the huge cemeteries. Another surprise was to learn, from statistics they showed me, there were almost 300,000 evangelicals in the country, many of whom identified as Baptists, but the incoming Communist government had tried, and was still trying, to suppress Christians and limit the number of churches. Life for Christians had become more threatening, and many church buildings had been confiscated by the government to be used as government buildings or storage facilities.

Those realities caused me to struggle with conflicting emotions as our meetings took place. In the provincial meetings and the Hanoi meetings, I was dealing with hard-core believers in their Communist doctrine. They were using words and phrases that I had read, but they were being used to conform to their definition, and their reasoning did not relate to cause and effect. I quickly learned we could not carry on a rational conversation about some subjects. The discussions were not heated (in fact, there was a very cordial atmosphere) and there was no argument. It was just that their worldview was 180 degrees different from mine. With that attitude, and with their conviction that there simply was no God and no spiritual world, I was ambivalent about coming in to offer assistance to such a government.

323

Then the Bible started meddling with me. During our discussions in Hanoi, my daily Bible reading one day was a passage in Luke 2, dealing with the birth of Christ. There came a night in Bethlehem, after many years of subjection to a godless government, when God said it was time to appear. God obviously thought it was worth it to attempt to break the cycle of silence and evil suppression. The thought came to me, unbidden, that perhaps there could come a night in Hanoi when the cycle of silence and oppression might also be broken by an awareness of a newborn Savior.

Then the Bible meddled again, as if to emphasize the message. Immediately after returning to Bangkok, my daily Bible reading was in John 4. Verse 4 states, "Jesus must needs go through Samaria." He, being who He was, could not, would not, detour. He would not perpetuate a problem created by man's rebellion, resentment, and sin. Whatever detours others might choose, we—Christians, TBM—should not turn away and ignore an open door. We too might should go through our Samaria: Vietnam. This is a severely abbreviated summary of my thoughts and feelings during and after the meetings.

Now back to my interesting, bruising, bouncing hop to Hanoi. It was a three day, life-threatening, hair-raising marathon. We left Da Nang in a new, well-equipped Toyota van with a new driver (new, meaning he had just begun driving). After multiple minor and major incidents, we barely made it to Hanoi. Highway 1 was narrow, mostly gravel, and packed with people, bicycles, water buffalo, and carts (not many vehicles at that time), each believing they had the right-of-way. All the bridges had been destroyed by bombing; we forded streams when possible, at high speeds. We crossed larger rivers by pontoon, boat bridge, or ferry. Our newly licensed driver was unaware of safe-driving techniques and could not understand the space required to stop a speeding, fairly heavy vehicle. We knocked several bicycles off the road—with riders knocked into the fields—but the driver never stopped. My "minder" ordered him to keep moving. We failed to make a curve on at least three occasions, flying off an abrupt drop of three feet or more. We had no suspension system when we finally arrived in Hanoi, and the muffler had long since disappeared. The van was suffering a terminal illness.

My hotel in Hanoi was unexpectedly primitive. The toilet was broken and stopped up. All foreigners (mostly Russians) were required to stay in the same hotel at a cost of thirty-five dollars per day, payable only in American dollars. Meals were three dollars each. (Conditions were greatly improved when I returned to Vietnam in 1991.) The hotel restaurant had a facade of modernity, and the menu was in French only. (Most of the officials in Hanoi preferred to speak French, considering it the language of diplomacy. My college French was sorely tested.)

After the meetings, there was one final project they wanted to show me as an example of the kind of assistance they needed. It was located several miles west of Hanoi at the foot of the mountains. There was a broad valley opening to an even larger farming area through which a creek flowed throughout the year. They wanted to build a coffer dam that would be able to hold back enough water to allow them to irrigate a large area and have two crops of rice each year instead of only one. They needed reinforcing steel to build the dam. It was not available within Vietnam and could be purchased only with hard currency, meaning American dollars. The more I looked at the land, water supply, and their survey drawings, the more I felt it was a feasible project. It looked like a good start. (The completed project did work well. I estimated four thousand to five thousand acres of productive land were added.)

A side activity in the valley caught my attention. There was a coal mine back in the mountains with a narrow-gauge railway coming out and running to an electric-generating plant near Hanoi. The train pulling and pushing the coal cars back and forth was a fascinating improvisation. The original Russian train engines had worn out and been discarded, and they could not get replacements.

With a little shade-tree engineering, they took two old Russian diesel trucks with still-working engines, removed the original rubber wheels and axles, and replaced them with wheels and axles from the original train engines. They then attached coupling mechanisms to each end of the trucks and mounted the trucks on the rails, one on each end of the train, facing opposite directions. Reverse gears in the trucks would have been too slow to be practical. With a truck on each end of the train, the truck in use would always be going forward. Neat, but it looked a little peculiar the first time I saw it smoking across the country side.

My last full day in Hanoi was a Sunday, and it turned out to be a wonderful day of worship. Shortly after I got up, I heard bells faintly ringing. I thought it was a radio. I went outside to listen, but I could not find the source. As I walked around, I began hearing other bells ringing and realized they were church bells. All the churches that had bells were ringing them, including at least one Protestant church. Explanations were difficult to obtain. As best as I could piece it together, the churches were defying a regulation that permitted only one church to ring bells on Sunday. For whatever reason, on that particular Sunday (it was just a few weeks before Easter), they decided to ring their bells anyway. It just happened that my morning Bible reading that day had been about the resurrection of Christ. The thought came to me, perhaps nudged by the scripture I had read, that the Christians had spontaneously decided to declare, on His day, to all visitors to Hanoi who could hear and might be Christians, "We are here! We are alive! We worship a living God! We will announce it—come what may!" At least that's what I felt as I listened to the bells and worshipped. It was a good last day in Hanoi.

The tension and emotions of the past ten days left me tired and ready to go home. All I had to do was get on the plane and go. Well, not exactly. In the first place, when I checked in at the airport, I was told that my scheduled flight to Bangkok was a nonexistent flight. My only option was to fly to Vientiane, Laos, and then get a flight to Bangkok. Okay, no problem. I proceeded to customs for clearance. (As part of my initial preparation for the trip, I had asked the Vietnamese embassy in Bangkok for any and all requirements related to Vietnamese customs regulations affecting foreigners, both coming and going. I had learned the hard way that, in some countries, it could be a sticky time. I was prepared; every cent was accounted for, all receipts were in order, I had nothing sensitive, and I had my remaining cash in a container. Everything was ready.) Everything checked, and I was told to proceed.

The agent looked me over for a moment, pointed to my left hand, and asked, "Where you get that ring?"

"It is my wedding ring. I have had it for almost thirty years."

"No, you bought it here. Where is receipt?"

"I did not buy it here. There is no receipt."

"You will pay."

It had never occurred to me (or been mentioned in the more than forty countries I had visited) that I should declare my wedding band when entering the country. Thus began a few minutes of intense fellowship. The line behind me was getting longer and more impatient. He would not let me go, and I would not pay a bribe. I finally told him I was a guest of the Vietnamese government and suggested he ask his boss to call the minister of interior for verification. About that time, a government official who had been in our meetings recognized me as he walked by and ordered the agent to let me go. I was free to leave the country. I was ready. Getting an onward flight out of Vientiane worked out okay, and I headed home. Bangkok looked like the promised land.

But Bangkok was not a rest stop. I returned to two days of executive committee meetings and three days of conferences, and then I went directly to India for a week of hospital board and other meetings.

The threatening hospital financial situation was becoming more real, and restrictions on visas for hospital personnel were becoming critical. Finally, the hospital labor problem was becoming more volatile. BBH was the only nonunion hospital in Bangalore, and union activists would not accept that. The combination of problems compelled us as a board, as well as the FMB, to look immediately at our options.

We had problems, problems, problems, but they had existed since the hospital was established. Rebekah faced them with perseverance throughout her years in India. She is greatly admired. Satan stayed active in his attempts to throttle all missionary presence, but thousands of people had been led to the Lord—and many churches were established. Obviously, God was at work, and we wanted to keep the hospital serving. With fewer missionary personnel and my previous time in the hospital, I was asked to spend several weeks at the hospital when Joann and I went home on furlough. I was torn, but I felt like I had to say no.

Back to Thailand, our schedule was filled until our furlough in August 1986. Joann was going to the Philippines for two weeks of meetings with the women of the mission. She had been recognized for the benefits she brought in addressing women's health issues, especially in the areas of emotional, hormonal, and stress issues. With more than 160 missionaries, the Philippines was a large mission, divided into two areas: Luzon, the northern island area, and Mindanao, the southern area. She would spend a week in each area, speaking and counseling. Upon her return, she would need to return to Bangkla to help cover the hospital again.

Our Indochina work was going well. The refugee crisis had prompted SBC churches to increase their nontraditional giving for disaster and hunger relief. Those resources could now be used to offer assistance in medical and agricultural development in previously closed areas of Asia. Visas for Christian missionaries were an endangered species. Visas for health care and agricultural-development workers were being granted, but the doors that were opened had to be entered and utilized carefully. My work in Thailand and India, combined with my ongoing relief and disaster consulting for South and Southeast Asia, limited my CSI involvement. My head was spinning; it was time for furlough.

We were blessed again when we were provided furlough housing by the First Baptist Church of Irving, Texas, adjacent to Dallas. It was a good central location between Joann's family in West Texas, my family in Arkansas, and both children in the Dallas area.

Furloughs are not vacations. Missionaries are usually given assignments of various kinds, and they are to take advantage of every opportunity to share the mission story with churches. We did that, and we enjoyed it, but we also took some time just to relax and recharge our spiritual batteries.

One of my tasks was to return to M. D. Anderson Hospital in Houston for follow-up cancer testing. They did their thing and said, "Everything looks good. Let us know if you have any problems. See you next time."

One additional furlough blessing was that Lisa gave us our first grandchild. Juli was born in November 1986.

It was back to Thailand again for a busy schedule. Joann was needed at the hospital in Bangkla and was there five or six days a week. Soon after our return to Bangkok, I left for India for a full week of meetings. Surprisingly, and gratefully, and for a variety of reasons, the hospital had moved back from the brink of closure. Our discussions and decisions still took place in a crisis setting, but that was normal for India.

A small FMB reorganization had resulted in an organizational change for CSI. It was now to be directly under the leadership of one director, based in Richmond. No longer would field directors be required. That move relieved me of any further responsibility for Indochina development, and I resigned from the committee. It was a very welcome relief. Joann also resigned. Bill Wakefield and his team were in the formative stages of development work in the three Indochina countries, and they were now requiring more attention. I simply did not have the time to give to it. My work outside my responsibility as mission administrator was taking too much of my time. As a mission, we had our own issues that needed attention, and I needed to stay around for a while.

I did have one more trip I had to take. I would need to be in Seoul, Korea, for several days in April. I was not excited about the meeting, but I was excited about seeing Seoul again, especially the bell pavilion I had helped build thirty-five years earlier.

We flew in shortly after dark to a city extending for miles in all direction with brightly lighted high-rise skyscrapers. I was just absorbing that sight when I realized hundreds of those lights were lighted crosses scattered all over the city. It was thrilling to see. Thirty-five years earlier, it had been a scene of almost total devastation. There had been few intact buildings in the city and not one church that I was aware of. Now the Christian presence was everywhere, and Korea was sending missionaries all over the world. The growth of the Christian faith in what previously was primarily a Buddhist nation was a miraculous demonstration of what God would do when people responded, obeyed, prayed, and went where He led them.

The bell and pavilion were no longer in the heart of the city. Seoul had grown to encompass all land for miles on both sides of the Han River, extending to all nearby valleys. My taxi driver, however, had no trouble understanding where I wanted to go. My first view was a little unsettling; the pavilion seemed so small compared to all the surrounding skyscrapers. When I left in 1952, it stood intact and impressive by itself. All around were potholed streets winding through the former city with bombed-out buildings in all directions. Now the pavilion was almost toylike as it sat amid canyons of buildings and vehicle-clogged streets.

I became excited as I approached the pavilion. It had been well preserved, and the surrounding grounds, with all the carved granite figures, were maintained perfectly. It was still impressive. As I drew closer, however, I was taken aback: the bell was not inside. Questioning a nearby attendant, I learned that a crack had appeared in the bell some years earlier and the decision was made to move the bell. They prepared a special exhibit room in the National Museum and transferred the bell to a climate-controlled space, but the pavilion had not been ignored. They had extended two sides and installed dramatic nighttime lighting that made it even more beautiful and impressive. The whole scene brought back heartwarming memories of a special time and place in my life.

My Thai MA responsibilities were becoming a little more routine. The challenges were always there, but they were somewhat less intimidating than in the beginning. In May 1987, I received another one of those surprising phone calls.

CHAPTER 11

Another Call to FMB Staff

I mentioned earlier that the refugee crisis in Southeast Asia, plus other crises in other parts of the world, had prompted an outpouring of offerings from Southern Baptists. Partly in response to that, the FMB established a new office at the board to capitalize on the opportunities it afforded. The office was to encourage giving as well as conduct hunger relief and health-care projects in previously closed areas of the world. Dr. John Cheyne, a former missionary in Africa, was the director of the new department, called the Human Needs Department. My phone call was from John. He asked me to consider moving to Richmond to become his associate director for community development. My job would be to provide consultation and guidance in evaluating, establishing, and monitoring health-care and agriculture projects on a worldwide basis.

My decision to accept it or reject it was difficult; it was not a matter of a simple change of jobs. I had been offered other Stateside opportunities since returning to Thailand but had declined them. We were in Thailand because we felt the Lord had led us there. Every major work or ministry in which we had been involved since we were married had always been a team effort. I could not unilaterally make a decision to leave.

Joann and I took off a few days, went to a hotel on the coast, and secluded ourselves. We prayed and talked about it for many hours. She, as always, said, "Wherever the Lord leads you, I'll go with you."

What a wife! What a woman! What a partner!

Finally, with very mixed emotions, I accepted it. We trusted the Lord to open a door to ministry by Joann in the Richmond area. The more we prayed and thought about it, the more we felt a sense of "rightness" about it. That sense of rightness was colored by a sense of grief and an element of guilt. We were leaving Thailand again—this time permanently. I will note, appropriately or not, that our return to the States was with less excitement than our original move to Thailand.

Life back in the United States began with familiar activity: travel. Shortly after moving into our house in Richmond in September 1987, I left for the semiannual board meeting of the hospital in India. Preparations and decisions were needed to help determine the future of the hospital. Threatening challenges that could close the hospital were coming from several directions. Options to stay open were being considered.

In the midst of those and many other urgent discussions, a surprising, very serious problem popped up, growing out of the labor agitation and allegations made by nonhospital employees. Rebekah received an official letter stating the hospital was a factory engaging in illegal labor practices.

Rebekah, as the medical director, was charged with criminal conduct as head of the factory. The board was stumped. The Indians on the board had never heard of such a thing. The allegations behind the charge were false and ridiculous, but that was beside the point. Rebekah could be in trouble. That was the beginning of a five-year battle to refute the charge. It was finally resolved in 1993 when the higher courts declared the hospital was not a factory, and all charges were dropped. In the interim, Rebekah, the hospital attorney, and

I spent many hours struggling with the issue. Rebekah and the attorney more so since I retired in 1991.

The criminal charge issue had to be dealt with—and so did the future status of the hospital. I noted earlier that Rebekah took the lead in the India-based discussions reviewing the options. Multiple issues were common in all the options, especially legal questions concerning ultimate liability as interpreted by Indian law. Answers were hard to nail down. There were meetings dealing with endless issues involved in forming the framework for a management contract and the official signing of the documents in it. The framework for the final agreement and contract was formed in a meeting in our home in Richmond in September 1988, and the contracts were officially signed in January 1989.

Stateside: Refugee Work Again

One of my first tasks when I arrived in Richmond was to visit refugee camps in Middle America. That was needed before I actually started work in Richmond. The internal unrest and frequent fighting in Nicaragua had caused thousands of residents to flee to adjacent countries for refuge. A variety of camps sprung up spontaneously in Costa Rica, Guatemala, and Panama, and all had a variety of needs, ranging from minor to very severe.

I spent several days with the local mission leaders reviewing the camps in the different countries. It was similar in some ways to the Southeast Asia refugee situation, except for the lower number of refugees and the less severe living conditions. The mission leaders were not inclined to request additional personnel to deal with the problem, and I agreed with their decision. Based on what I had seen in Southeast Asia, I was able to offer some options that would provide ministry opportunities and assistance to those with the greatest need. That could be done with existing missionary personnel.

I was back in Richmond just in time to see Joann off to do a previously scheduled women's conference in Indonesia. I could now get on with learning the computer systems, familiarizing myself with my new responsibilities, and adapting to a different work situation.

I was deep into my computer class maze when I was called to the phone. When I answered, a strange foreign voice asked, "Where is your wife?"

It took a moment for my brain to adjust. "Who is calling?"

"Singapore Airlines."

"Where are you?"

"San Francisco."

"What happened?"

"She was on our manifest to go from San Francisco to Singapore, but she was not on the flight. Do you know where she is?"

I will omit the details of the following discussion and search. We did find her. She was not lost. Apparently, the travel agent in Richmond had forgotten to consider the international date line in dating her onward flight beyond San Francisco. She arrived in Singapore twenty-four hours later than scheduled. Singapore Airlines discovered the ticket-dating problem, found her, and booked her on to Jakarta, Indonesia. She also arrived there twenty-four hours late, arriving at the conference center (in the mountains, outside of Jakarta) five minutes before she was scheduled to begin the conference. Almost forty hours of travel and airport layovers was not good preparation for the conference, but as usual, she waded into the meeting at full speed and must have done a great job since other conferences were requested in Southeast Asia.

I lost my concentration in studying computers, and I don't think I ever got it back. After those first few rambunctious weeks in Richmond, our lives became more normal. Joann wanted to continue her medical practice, but it was more as a ministry than to make money. FMB personnel policy did not allow both spouses of a family to be employed at the board. They did, however, permit her to serve as a part-time contract physician, and she served in that role for several years, doing initial medical screenings and evaluations of individuals and families who were candidates for appointment as missionaries.

Her second part-time work was as the examining physician for the more than three thousand special education children in Henrico County, of which Richmond was the county seat.

Her third part-time job was to serve as a clinician for the state of Virginia in a juvenile correction center. That was a particularly daunting ministry. It was a different world of patients, with teens and preteens suffering from the devastating effects of abuse, drugs, violence, and sexually transmitted diseases (STDs). Her compassionate, caring attitude sometimes penetrated the resistant, often hard, and tough facade of many of the kids. Although she could not initiate conversations concerning the gospel, she could answer their questions and explain the reason she loved them. She also gave much time to our church (Derbyshire Baptist Church) and many of its ministries.

Worldwide: Hunger and Health Care

Word of the availability of Hunger Relief funds began to spread throughout the missionary world, especially in Asia, Latin America, and Africa. Requests began to come in. The variety of requests, some of which are better left untold, made it apparent that guidelines and criteria for use of the funds needed to be determined and made available to all missionaries. Our department, with Dr. John Cheyne as director, Dr. Van Williams (medical), and me (community development) as associate directors, had that task.

We already had one major guideline: it was to be used for hunger needs only. That had been specified by the donors at the time it was given. That eliminated many requests that were for valid needs but which could not be tied directly to a hunger need. Tents for housing in refugee camps and clothing and bedding for the destitute were examples of general relief needs. Hunger funds could not be used for them. We contacted many donors (churches and individuals) to request permission to use their gifts for whatever the most acute need might be, but the great majority declined to allow any change of use.

I'll make a greatly abbreviated statement concerning just a few of the multitudes of philosophical and strategic challenges we faced in our development work and then move on to review some of the projects.

Our basic motivation (and this was true of most development organizations) was to assist people in learning how to help themselves. There were some obvious situations where that approach was not practical, but it was basic in our actions. It was obvious that we as outsiders could not provide all that was needed on an ongoing basis. We agreed on the philosophy; defining and achieving the goal was the challenge.

Providing the initial resources for projects—finances, equipment, supplies, and know-how—was important, but it was only a small part of the long-term goal of self-sufficiency. It was easy for the initial help to lead to an attitude of dependency. We were always in tension between providing required assistance while avoiding creating dependent relationships. Our efforts to minimize dependency were often in conflict with the need to make a project succeed. When, where, and how we should cut the cord was always a consideration. And it did not take long to realize that dependency could be mutual. Missionaries could unintentionally become dependent on the programs. Avoiding the pitfalls was not simple. Cultural mores often played a part, especially the role of the women. The lack of cultural understanding limited the potential benefit of many good ideas.

Conceptions of accountability and responsibility varied greatly from culture to culture. That was a hard lesson for missionaries to learn and to apply tough love solutions. I saw it in my early projects. We would drill a well and install a pump, and the village would rejoice at having good water. In spite of our constant reiteration that the pump was now their responsibility to maintain, when it broke or wore out, it was never fixed. It took a while for us to learn that it was a cultural thing. We installed it; therefore, it was ours. They should not touch it. They heard our words that it now belonged to them, but that was contrary to their concept of responsibility. Regardless of what we said, they could not understand accountability.

Many other examples could be given, from a variety of projects, but I think this provides a hint of the challenges all of us faced in trying to provide the right kind of help and for how long. For our purpose, as a Christian mission organization, I came to feel that "small but beautiful" programs were usually more effective than huge programs. Our purpose was greater than just providing water, physical health care, or a bigger harvest—as important as they were. We felt strongly that a spiritual component was a necessary part of all our development work. Small projects gave us more opportunities to develop close personal relationships, and those relationships were what often led people to understand and accept the gospel.

Requests from the field varied from being almost ideal to being nonsensical. Many project requests were so vague it was obvious there was no specific plan. "We need $25,000 to help a bunch of people in our area." That was not adequate justification for us to transfer funds. Guidelines and criteria were needed, and workshops were needed to enable field personnel to understand and use funds appropriately. John had already started those when Van and I joined the department. Van and I worked specifically to determine how many medical problems could be traced to malnutrition and other food-related conditions, thereby allowing us to use hunger funds to meet many medical needs. Determining those criteria and making them understandable to field personnel meant John, Van, and I spent a lot of time traveling the world to conduct human needs conferences. I started my part of that assignment shortly after I joined the FMB staff upon our return to the States. I spent a couple of weeks reviewing the refugee situation in Middle America, especially Costa Rica and Guatemala, in October 1987. Those conferences, and the projects that grew out of them, gave a better understanding of how best to use the funds, but they also led to much world travel in the following years.

Many of the projects had so much in common that a full review was not needed. I'll relate only a few that were unusual, significant, or just interesting.

The Mexico mission had requested a conference. In a telephone call with the Mexico mission administrator and Dr. Lee Baggett, a missionary physician at our hospital in Guadalajara, we agreed that a few missionaries and a variety of national Christian attendees would be best combination of attendees. (We had known Lee from our Van Horn days when Joann had asked him to join her when she met with the Mexican minister of health in Mexico City.) We wanted a representative selection—rural and urban, professional and farmer, missionary and national—to be present. We were looking for church leaders in their areas who would be aware of problems and needs in the areas of hunger and human needs. Lee and the mission administrator made a brilliant representative selection of attendees that resulted in a huge leap forward for farmers in the mountains.

About midway through the conference, we had a general question-and-answer meeting with all attendees. I asked the farmers if they had a particular, recurring problem they wanted their brothers to be aware of and to pray about. One of them told of a problem that occurred frequently and caused much hardship in his village and area. He was a part of an indigenous group of people who lived and farmed in the mountains at altitudes between seven thousand and nine thousand feet. At that altitude, the growing season was short. Their corn—their staple food—needed a minimum of 120 days to grow to maturity. The problem was that a late frost in the spring or an early frost in the fall, which happened frequently, shortened the growing season and sharply cut back the corn harvest. That left many farmers with an inadequate food supply for their families. Many of them often went hungry. (Lee told me later of their chronic malnutrition.)

A man in the audience stood up immediately and excitedly said, "We can help!"

In the discussion that followed, we learned that he was a plant science professor on the faculty of an agriculture university and was a leader in one of the Baptist churches near Guadalajara. The university had an experimental farm where they had developed a hybrid corn that matured in about one hundred days or less. The two groups worked together to bring about a solution that brought great benefit to the farmers.

Today's genetics and plant pathology are beyond the scope of this story. To those who do understand, it will also be obvious that I have left out a major problem in the use of hybrid seed: replanting with seed from the same plants.

For the benefit of nonfarmers, the problem with hybrid corn (or any hybrid seed) is that seeds produced by hybrids provide a decreasing harvest with each succeeding season. That meant the farmer had to purchase new hybrid seed every year to ensure a good crop, but the cost was high, the farmers were poor, and the idea was new. They were hesitant to risk it. They had always used regular corn, from which they set aside enough seed to plant next year's crop. It was obviously a low-cost procedure, but it also produced a low and very uncertain harvest. The hope was that the increased, more certain hybrid harvest would produce more than the cost of the seed, resulting in a greater net harvest, perhaps even enough to have some to sell.

The change to the hybrid seed did not happen overnight, but it was gradually adopted by many of the farmers and did prove its worth. The benefit outweighed the risk. It was gratifying to see the benefit provided by the exchange of ideas. It was even more gratifying to see the increased sense of fellowship among the variety of attendees as they came to know each other and realize they were brothers in the Lord.

Another interesting conference and project review trip came up soon after the Mexico trip. It was along the Pacific of South America, including Peru, Ecuador, and Bolivia. I was to go into Colombia also, but terrorist fighting stopped that.

Lima, Peru, was a little surprising. We landed in heavy fog, and it persisted, which was usual for that time of the year. On the coast, not far south of the equator, Lima was adjacent to the cold ocean current coming up from Antarctica, causing fog to be present much of the time. Plant life depends on it for moisture, and rainfall is usually less than two inches per year. Reviewing the Lima area and the Trujillo area in the even more arid northern part of the country, I was not impressed with project prospects.

The flight from Lima to La Paz, Bolivia, must be the most spectacular in South America. Over the Andes Mountains, with peaks over 20,000 feet, then into La Paz where the airport is at 13,300 feet, it is one breathtaking sight after another. We descended in a weaving path between sheer mountain walls, close in on both sides. I was grateful to be arriving in VFR conditions. I was hoping we could depart VFR also. Having seen the twisting flight path that had to be followed precisely, departing IFR in thick clouds over that same path would have been a white-knuckle time. We flew in over Lake Titicaca, the largest lake, by volume, in South America. It is at an altitude of 12,500 feet. The high airport elevation at La Paz got my attention quickly; lugging heavy baggage up and down stairs from the international terminal to the domestic terminal had me puffing.

The flight on to Santa Cruz, in the southeastern part of the country, was anticlimactic. I would be conducting a human needs conference in the city where we had a veterinary missionary who had some good projects underway and where several churches had been established. I needed to arrive early so I could better understand the situation before we started the conference.

My final project review in Bolivia was the most memorable and the most encouraging. It was an agriculture project in a remote jungle area in the extreme southeastern part of the country, not far from Paraguay. It was well into the Amazon River basin. It was another case of where getting there—and back—was a bunch of fun.

There was only a trail into the area, and access was primarily by aircraft. I chartered a Cessna 206 from Missionary Aviation Fellowship. After the first few miles, we were over thick jungle for the more than 230 miles to our project. The pilot was doubly careful in his flight preparation. Everything and everyone was weighed carefully. With travel so expensive and so infrequent, the plane was loaded to maximum capacity. I was glad he asked me to ride as copilot; I was going to be eyeballing in all directions.

I had flown a Cessna 206, and it was familiar except for some of the radio equipment. He noticed my look and told me it was a ham radio. I began to understand. There were no radio navigation aids where we were going; the flight would be dead reckoning, by VFR only. He had a ham radio installed in the plane and a matching unit in his house. On every flight over the jungle and other uncharted territory, his wife would monitor the home radio. Every fifteen minutes, he would call home and identify his position as best he could; identifiable landmarks were scarce. He had flight charts for the area, but they were of no help. He picked up the chart of the area over which we were flying and indicated our approximate position, then pointed to a large printed statement on the chart: "Area Not Surveyed: Chart Unreliable." I believed it; the chart showed mountains at our location, but we could see it was relatively flat jungle.

We were flying at 1,500 feet and could see the ground okay, but visibility in all directions was limited. There was a thick, smoky haze coming off massive fires in the Amazon basin, extending into Paraguay. They were clear-cutting thousands and thousands of acres, burning the poor-quality trees, logging the good timber, and then converting it all to farmland. I was saddened to see it happening. Our short landing strip was a curving runway cut into slightly sloping, cleared area. Our pilot set the plane down perfectly.

Getting to know the young missionary couple, seeing what they had already done, and hearing what they dreamed of doing left me excited and thrilled at what could be accomplished in that primitive setting. Both the man and his wife had grown up on small farms in rural Mississippi. They understood small-scale farming and the struggles to make ends meet. They also understood the people with whom they worked, a previously isolated tribal group only two generations from living by hunting and gathering. They needed to understand basic farming procedures, and they were eager to learn. They were also responsive to the gospel; several had already become believers and were leading others to the Lord. They were open to learning, adapting to, and adopting a new way of life. I was delighted to encourage them and assure them of full project assistance.

I had one other project to review and a conference to conduct in Ecuador before heading home. The project was agriculture development. The location was a village and farmland in a valley at an altitude of about ten thousand feet. They had the same problem as the villagers in Mexico—corn was the staple crop, the source of most of their food—but the growing season was so short they often faced crop failure and then hunger. I talked with the resident missionary about hybrid corn as a possible solution. He followed up with the idea, but that area of Ecuador was lacking in resources (primarily hybrid seed), and he was unable to make a major impact. He did attempt a few test plots to demonstrate the possibility of increasing yield, but the circumstances were not yet geared for success.

He did have success with another project (vocational training) that had impressed and pleased the villagers. They wanted to show their appreciation by preparing an elaborate dinner for the local missionary and me. Such occasions made me uncomfortable. They used scarce food, and sometimes expensive specialty items, to express their thanks. They would deny themselves needed food to show their gratitude to us. On that occasion, they went all out. After a soup appetizer, they brought the piece d'resistance and prized delicacy: a whole guinea pig, roasted, with head, teeth, and tail still intact. It was about the same size as a large rat. They ceremoniously placed it before me and signaled me to begin eating. I was not thrilled about it, but it would have been culturally insulting to refuse it. I picked it up, took a bite, and passed it on to the village headman. He did the same thing. Unknowingly, I had done exactly what I was supposed to do: take a bite and pass it on. That was just one of countless times I have thanked the Lord for taking care of me—even in the minor things.

The next conference was at the seminary in Quito, Ecuador. The seminary was in a valley on the edge of town, surrounded by snowcapped mountains, highlighted by Cotapaxi, a nineteen-thousand-foot, snowcapped volcano just a few miles from the seminary. (As I write this in 2015, the news media is showing Cotapaxi erupting, but not a major eruption.) After we completed the conference, I was ready to go home. After a brief time in Manaus, Brazil—on the Amazon River—and Caracas, Venezuela, I was happy to be home.

My transition from the hectic pace on the mission field to the hectic pace of the home office was becoming more routine. It was different with Joann. Her hectic pace continued for a brief few weeks, fulfilling earlier commitments. Then the pace slowed. She had picked up some part-time work, but that activity did not provide the same sense of accomplishment as her work in the field.

The move from the field back to the United States had more ramifications than either of us realized at first. Others who joined the staff from the field had a similar experience. The move was more difficult for the spouse. From having a significant role in the field, the spouse sometimes became almost a nonentity with the board. For Joann, the loss of the "immediacy" of her work in the field was especially difficult. She had become a physician to serve the Lord in needy areas of the world. That desire had now apparently been short-circuited. She needed a place where she could fulfill her calling to ministry. That was not achieved quickly in Richmond.

But Joann, being Joann, did not throw in the towel and become discouraged. She responded to, created, and kindled ministry wherever she found herself living or serving. In some of her part-time positions, she was prevented from overtly sharing the gospel, but that did not prevent her from sharing love and compassion. And that sharing was fruitful in the lives of her patients and in the lives of several staff people who were blessed by her ministry.

Her pace gradually picked up again as her work expanded, and she became better known. She eventually spent about half of her working time with the board and the other half with the Virginia Department of Corrections. Both of the positions allowed her to fulfill the increasing number of requests she received to speak. Those requests were at the state level as well as the national level, and a few continued to come from South and Southeast Asia. She became very busy again, which was the way she liked it.

There was one activity we both enjoyed: speaking in churches and associations and visiting places in Virginia that had histories going back nearly three hundred years. It was exciting to hear some of the old-timers with their unique Virginia accent relating stories from their early years. It was a striking contrast with our days in Van Horn when we were able to hear the stories from some of the old-timers who were direct descendants of the original settlers who had arrived in covered wagons. What a history and legacy we have as a nation!

Back to Travel and Project Evaluations

My last major trip of 1987 was to the semiannual board meeting of the hospital in Bangalore, India, in October. The multiple issues to be considered in the merger of our hospital with Christian Medical College Hospital in Vellore occupied much of our attention. Although the merger would not be formalized until January 1, 1989, the ramifications needed to be explored in depth with a fine-tooth comb. It was a new and major undertaking, raising questions we had never faced before, but the merger was not the only issue. The never-ending problems caused by the labor agitators, including the charges levied against Rebekah Naylor, were very costly. Added to those two huge issues was the imminent implementation of the subsidy cutback by the FMB. It was a challenging time.

The motivation to struggle through and overcome the obstacles was evident all around us. Many people were coming to know the Lord, and many churches were being established. It seemed the more problems and persecutions the people had, the greater their response to the gospel. That phenomenon has been present for centuries, but to be present and witness the faith of new believers in such trying times was exciting and very encouraging. There was a strong desire to press on, believing God would reward our efforts.

All of 1988 through 1991 brought a bunch of travel in Africa and Latin America. The countries visited included Kenya, Tanzania, Ivory Coast (Cote d'Ivoire), Ghana, Mali, Burkina Faso, Cameroon, Liberia, Senegal, and Nigeria. What an itinerary! I'll just summarize the gist of those travels and project reviews. They are not in chronological order.

- Kenya and Tanzania are mentioned first because of their great variety of notable features and because they were often my point of entry. When our semiannual hospital board meetings were finished in India, I often returned to the States via Africa for project reviews and evaluations. Sometimes the flights were from Bombay (or New Delhi) to Nairobi, Kenya, or Dar es Salaam, Tanzania. They were good starting points for a look at the many projects we had underway or were being proposed in East Africa. From there, it was convenient to fly on to West Africa for reviews and then fly on home.

- On a flight from Dar es Salaam, Tanzania, to Nairobi, Kenya, the pilot descended to give passengers a close-up view of Mount Kilimanjaro. Majestic! That detour in flight would not be permitted today.

- Project review possibilities for water in a small section of the Rift Valley, west of Nairobi. It is a dry, sparse grazing area used by the Maasai people. An area of much historical and anthropological significance.

- Ferry boat ride across Lake Victoria. Wow! But I missed seeing Victoria Falls.

- Reviewing project requests for Kariobangi, a high-density concentration of about two hundred thousand refugees (a various mix of tribal groups when I was there) living in a slum-like camp on the edge of Nairobi. The Kenya mission had a medical clinic that was doing greatly needed work, craft training, and vocational training. Unbelievable needs. No sanitation facilities and only a few flowing faucets.

- Review the Mwanza area (in Tanzania) south of Lake Victoria, deep in the bush, for agriculture development. Needs not as great as other areas. Flight by mission plane over the Serengeti National Park on the way back to Nairobi. Not able to see the wide variety of wildlife, but the park was beautiful.

- Dining at the Carnivore Restaurant in Nairobi. When I ate there in 1990, the choices were giraffe, wildebeest, camel, elephant, zebra, and crocodile (and some unnamed). Conservation laws have now eliminated many of the choices. It was a wonderful experience.

None of the stopover points between East and West Africa were vacation destinations. For me, Cameroon was the most forgettable. Our stop was in Douala, the capital. The airport looked like a twentieth-century ghost town. The recently built terminal and Jetways had been built for the country by the Russians. It was typical Russian architecture of the time: unpainted concrete block construction with no finishing touches. It felt like entering a prison.

None of the Jetways worked; they were just parked haphazardly. Grass was growing around them, and passengers deplaned well out on the tarmac and walked to the terminal carrying their luggage. It was a relief to leave. Lagos, Nigeria, about 550 miles farther on, was not much better.

Accra, the capital of Ghana, and Abidjan, in the Ivory Coast, were actually very nice—and much-appreciated stops. Most of my time in Ghana was spent at the Baptist Hospital in Nalerigu, a small town in the northern part of the country near the border of Burkina Faso. The medical staff, in a very commendable desire to provide the best possible care, had asked for a hospital evaluation.

Dr. Van Williams, my coworker in the Human Needs Department, and I were given the privilege of doing the review. Van had come out of the more advanced medical facility in Bangalore and was of much help in capitalizing on medical practice advances. For me, it was déjà vu, very similar in many ways to our situation in Bangkla. Without having any professional administrative personnel, they had used some good common sense and cultural sensitivity to establish excellent administrative procedures. They were a very effective Christian medical institution reaching out to a wide area that had great needs and little knowledge of the Lord. Churches were being established. There was little I could add to their already effective ministry.

Van and I used a modified version of the Accreditation Manual of the Joint Commission for Accreditation of Health Care Organizations (JCAHO) as a basic reference for standards of quality.

I attended some rural clinics conducted by one of their nurses, which were similar to our Bangkla mobile clinics. The nurses in Nalerigu did more in providing vaccinations and inoculations than we did in Bangkla. Thailand was more advanced than Ghana in preventive medicine. The hospital was an outstanding example of the best possible care being given in the remote African bush. We were blessed to see high-quality medical care being provided in circumstances beyond imagining in high-tech American hospitals.

Van and I were thoroughly enjoying ourselves until the next-to-last day. As we were beginning the day, the missionaries informed us that the harmattan was coming in—and we should leave early. Harmattan? The harmattan is a dry, parching breeze, appearing often on clear days, loaded with almost microscopic dust, the residue of sandstorms coming off the Sahara Desert just north of Nalerigu. It filled the air, made breathing difficult, and wreaked havoc in the hospital. The OR staff showed us surgery packs that had been tightly wrapped and sterilized, yet when opened, they revealed small amounts of residual dust. Maintaining sterile equipment and supplies was a never-ending battle.

But more immediately threatening to Van and me was that aircraft, especially jets, were grounded when the dust was thick because of the damage the dust would do to the engines. We needed to get to the nearest airport, Tamale, which was almost two hundred miles away, before the flights were grounded.

We barely made it on time. The radio navigation aids were not working, so the airport personnel did not know if the plane was coming or not. It did, and we all boarded okay, including the goats. The man seated next to me carried his goat in his arms. He was on his way to Accra to a particular mosque for some celebration calling for a goat to be sacrificed. I was grateful no bathroom facilities were needed en route.

From Accra, Van headed back to the United States. I flew to Abidjan, in the Ivory Coast, for some conference time with the missionaries, and then I met with most of the Liberian missionaries who had evacuated to Abidjan. They were in distress, in mourning, and angry. A civil war was tearing Liberia to pieces. Churches, families, and communities were being split. Many of the missionaries had to evacuate. Some stayed in remote areas of Liberia, and others went to Ivory Coast. When I was there, some of them were planning to return to Liberia, but others said it was premature.

The stress and uncertainty led to emotional discussions. It was not the best time to consider development projects, and I was not in any administrative role. After much discussion and listening, we had an extended time of prayer before I left. In that three-year period, I was speaking to an area-wide group of missionaries in Africa, and I asked how many had been present when a coup occurred or had been required to evacuate their home stations. To my surprise, more than half raised their hands. Missionaries soon learned that the mission field was not a secure place, but there really were no secure places. I was reminded of the Cambodian refugees in the Kamput refugee camp singing, "This world is not my home, I'm just a-passing through."

Burkina Faso and Mali were totally new challenges. We had projects in both countries, but the largest were in Mali. One was a water-development project (Kenieba Circle; well above one million dollars) utilizing large equipment (Caterpillars, earthmovers, well-drilling rigs, low-boy tractor trailers, and others). I chartered a Missionary Aviation Fellowship plane in Bamako (the capital) and flew west a couple of hundred miles to review it. It was impressive—with impressive challenges. I could only shake my head as I saw the logistical difficulties of maintaining and operating such equipment in such a remote place. There were no supply houses anywhere near and very few trained operators. One Caterpillar had been parked for two years because of a lack of parts. On the plus side, several productive water wells had been drilled.

I returned to Bamako to review a vocational training center the mission had established to provide greatly needed skills training. It was an encouraging project.

From Bamako, it was eastward again to Ouagadougou, the capital of Burkina Faso, where the mission had established a few smaller projects, mostly related to water development. That was a natural; the whole area was in the southwestern part of the Sahara Desert, and water was a constant critical issue.

Ouagadougou was fascinating, as was the nearby town of Koudougou, both of which had mission-directed projects of vocational training. The projects were greatly needed, but they faced the perennial problem of insufficient qualified personnel to properly direct the programs. The mission was also facing difficulties in a lack of missionary personnel. Some had illness that required treatment in other countries, some were on furlough, and some were so new they could not yet provide much assistance. French was the official language, limiting those not yet fluent. Most of the missionaries also wanted to learn one of the dominant tribal languages to enable them to communicate with unreached people groups, but that was a slow process.

Ouagadougou, in Burkino Faso, and Bomako, in Mali, were prominent historical cities. They formed the two major bottom points of a triangle, with the top point being remote Timbuktu, in the northern part of Mali. For many centuries, Timbuktu had been a prestigious university center of Islamic studies, serving as the intellectual and spiritual capital for Islam in West Africa. The encroaching of the Sahara Desert in recent centuries has caused Timbuktu to lose prominence. It is now a town of about fifty thousand with very little infrastructure, leading the mission administrators of West Africa to decide not to initiate any projects at that time. I wanted to see the "remotest part of the earth" (although I have seen a few other places that could vie for that honor), but it was simply not worth the effort. It is no longer on my bucket list. I've seen about all the remote places that I care to see. After I finished the reviews in Burkina Faso, I was ready to head west to Senegal, my final stop before the hop across the Atlantic to New York City. Well, not quite.

We took off for some intermediate stop (I can't remember the city or country) that was almost due west. When we got to cruising altitude, I realized we were not flying west—we were flying east. After a bit, I asked a cabin attendant why we were going east. With a casual shrug, she said there had been a coup d'état in the country of our scheduled stop, and the airport was closed. Instead, we would be going to Niamey, the capital of Niger, to make other arrangements.

Surprise! Surprise! Never mind. We finally did make it to Dakar, Senegal.

Taking off from Dakar was a happy time because my landing would be in the United States. I was ready. As we began our descent into New York, we entered thick clouds. That was not unusual, and I was not concerned. After the flaps were lowered, the speed brakes were deployed, and the landing gear was dropped, I knew we were at the point of landing, but the clouds were still too thick to see the wing tips. When the pilot flared for landing, I still could not see the ground. I began to think he was preparing to abort the landing and go around. At that moment, he touched down. It was a totally blind landing. I leaned back in my seat with a huge sigh of relief and thanked the Lord. The flights on to Richmond were anticlimactic.

Concurrently with the travels and Africa project reviews between 1987 and 1991, I was doing similar reviews in Latin America and Asia. I have already commented on some of them. The one remaining project in Latin America that deserves comment is the "Living Water Project" in North Brazil. I reviewed it in March and April 1989. It was the largest development project the FMB had undertaken up to that point (and probably even up to this time), calling for several million dollars. It involved establishing factories, city water systems, demonstration farms, irrigation projects, and smaller projects. It was a joint undertaking of the FMB, various entities of the Baptist General Convention of Texas, and various governmental entities of the state of Paraiba in the northeastern portion of Brazil. It was planned as a five-year project with possible extensions of some individual projects. The area chosen was a densely populated, mostly rural, economically depressed region that extended over hundreds of square miles. It required several days of travel to see all the projects.

The summary statement in the paragraph above will quickly reveal why I will not go into great detail about the project. It was massive and very comprehensive, which, in itself, contained lessons for us in doing community development. We learned from it.

One of the lessons we learned, and tried to pass on to other missions around the world, was that in most instances involving development projects by the FMB, smaller is better. In Brazil, with several entities involved—Texas Baptists and Brazilian city and state governments—leadership change was inevitable. In this case, when political leadership changed, the commitment changed. Cooperation that had been promised did not materialize. The FMB was sometimes left with an incomplete project, but now it was the only participant. The only options were to drop the project and lose the investment or commit more resources we did not have. We needed to be careful about joint commitments with governmental entities.

Another lesson learned was that a project could be so big and so complex that the spiritual component could be left as a lower priority.

1991: Back in Vietnam and Cambodia

In Asia, there were two major projects that merit wider comment. They are just two of many projects that made significant impacts in their area, but one of those made an impact on an entire nation— and even into other countries.

Dr. Van Williams and I flew into Vietnam and later drove into Cambodia in the spring of 1991. Van would be reviewing the medical project possibilities, and I would be looking at the nonmedical possibilities. It was his first visit to Vietnam and my third visit. We reviewed some areas and projects—I had approved the coffer dam project on an earlier visit—and they wanted us to see the completed project. The dam was working as planned, and thousands of acres of rice paddy land were now producing two crops a year. We were pleased. So were the officials. Some project prospects had improved since my last visit, and some had not. Van was struck by the primitive state of health care and the lack of medical and surgical equipment in the hospitals. Every kind of assistance was needed.

Our discussions in Hanoi were benign and cordial—just as they had been on my initial visit. We met with lower-level officials who were apparently satisfied with our joint efforts and were open to an ongoing relationship. So were we. They took us to several possible project sites, including two or three hospitals and two possible dam sites. One of those caught us by surprise. It was in the mountains and involved a steep climb to reach the dam site high in the mountains and some distance from the water source, which was a surprisingly big spring issuing from the side of a mountain near the foot of a major mountain range.

Van and I had not dressed for mountain climbing. We had on leather-soled shoes that had no traction on the grass-covered mountainside. After a long climb, we asked how much farther. They said it was only about three hundred meters. "Okay, we can handle that." They meant three hundred meters higher; it was over a mile in actual climbing distance. Their plans, the geography, the survey drawings, the water source, and the potential addition of thousands of acres of cropland combined to make it a viable project.

The following day, they took us to an agriculture university north of Hanoi, almost to the China border. It was their major project proposal for consideration. I don't know how it had come about, but two or three of the university faculty members, one of whom was what we call a dean, had visited Harold Watson at the Baptist Rural Life Center in the Philippines. They were overwhelmed at what they saw and at how Harold had changed the entire approach to farming and food production. What he had done with a minimum of outside resources and how it had made such outstanding contributions to the life of the poor and rural of the Philippines amazed them. They became excited about the potential for their own similar agriculture development in Vietnam. It was a worthwhile project.

I will digress a moment. When they learned that Harold and the Rural Life Center were part of the same organization as Van and me, already working in Vietnam, they were thrilled. They became even more excited about telling us of their vision for the university and how our assistance could help bring to Vietnam what Harold was doing in the Philippines. We had an excellent visit and conversation that became a major factor in our reentry into Vietnam and a joint effort with the university.

That thrilling story of Southern Baptist's return to Vietnam is not really a part of our history so I won't pursue it, except to note that the missionary who became the first resident missionary back in Vietnam was a friend, a missionary kid whose father was an agriculture missionary in Thailand. The son, also an agriculture missionary, would be the first returning resident missionary to Vietnam. As with most of the stories of our work and travel, this one has been enormously abbreviated. There are countless omitted details that, taken all together, clearly reveal the sovereign hand of the Lord working faithfully in the background. What a privilege to be a part of such an action by our Lord. Our God is a God of history!

Philippine Award to Harold Watson

An additional comment is necessary concerning Harold Watson and the accomplishment of the Rural Life Center. Years of outstanding agricultural development that brought national benefit resulted in a very prestigious award being given to Harold. The presentation was made in 1989, although the award had actually been granted a little earlier. In a widely distributed news release, President Corazon Aquino of the Philippines announced that the Philippine government and President Aquino were presenting the Special President's Award to Harold Watson in a ceremony in Washington DC.

With Harold still in the field in the Philippines and Dr. Keith Parks and Dr. Bill Wakefield unable to attend, I was asked to represent Harold and the Foreign Mission Board in receiving the award. It was a high honor for Harold and highly deserved. It was also an honor for me to represent him. I had visited him at the Rural Life Center and had seen, firsthand, the wide range of accomplishments Harold had brought about. It was a most appropriate award.

Joann and I went to Washington for the ceremony on November 10, 1989. There was a private reception prior to the ceremony at which President Aquino and several of her chief ministers met with the honored attendees. Joann and I were highly impressed with the group. We visited with President Aquino, John "Jay" Rockefeller, senator from West Virginia, his brother David Rockefeller, president and CEO of the Chase Manhattan Bank Corporation in New York (the Rockefeller Foundation was also receiving an award), Senator Nancy Kassebaum of Kansas, Senator Richard Lugar of Indiana, and others

Award for Harold Watson from President Aquino of the Philippines

Two of President Aquino's chief ministers sought me out to inform me that they knew Harold, that they were also Christians, and they were proud of what Harold had accomplished for their country. We visited with the Rockefeller brothers at length, particularly David. He wanted us to understand that he strongly identified as a Baptist and was especially proud of what Harold and the FMB had done. What a night!

When Van and I finished our reviews in Hanoi and other northern areas of Vietnam, we flew to Saigon, now calling itself Ho Chi Minh City. Since the entire country was now considered one country, our reviews in the south were just extensions of our reviews in the north. Our reviews were primarily of farming operations, cashew orchards, and experimental farms for testing a variety of crops. The projects extended well up into the area north of Saigon, including some familiar names from battles fought in the area during the war. Much travel but most of it was rather routine.

It was time to take off for Cambodia by highway, road, trail, and ferry. Driving from Saigon to Phnom Penh was an unusual drive, even for Southeast Asia. Much of the lower portion of Vietnam and Cambodia is low-level wetlands made up of several swamps, canals, and rivers, with the Mekong and its tributaries being dominant. Crossing the Mekong River and delta area was similar to crossing the Brahmaputra River and delta area in Bangladesh. Both rivers are huge, both areas were low-lying, built-up silt—and subject to flooding every year. It did not lend itself to major bridges. Ferries were common. It took a long day's drive to make it.

I had been invited to come to Phnom Penh by government hospital officials because our office had funded some of their equipment. They were anxious to make a good impression and generate a willingness to provide further funding. They were delighted that Van, a physician, was also present. There was really nothing unusual in our reviews and discussions. By that time, I had had similar meetings and discussions in many other countries, so there was rarely a surprise. I had been in Cambodia previously for discussions with officials, but I can't remember all the places I visited. Van and I visited the usual places, the most unusual being a portion of the killing fields and then seeing the Tuol Sleng Genocide Museum: (www.tuolslenggenocide,museum.com/).On

one of my earlier visits I had gone to the museum to see a huge map of Cambodia on a wall, composed entirely of the skulls of people killed by Pol Pot. The place, the torture, the killing, and the whole saga are too horrible to describe.

On this visit, we had an experience that made the visit one of our most wonderful. On the Sunday we were there, we went to church. For the first time in twelve years, the churches (there were six house churches in Phnom Penh) received permission from the government to hold a baptismal service. Van and I joined others in the back of a truck to go out to the house of a believer who lived on the bank of a major branch of the Mekong river, right at flood stage. Seventy-seven adults were baptized, which was the most ever in one service in Cambodia, we were told. It was an all-day affair. There would be preaching, then there would be a Communion service, then a meal would be served, then preaching, and singing, on and on through the day.

It is hard for us as Americans—with all our freedoms—to realize what that service meant to those people that day. Many had suffered for their faith in God. Many had lost loved ones because of their faith. The tears of hundreds of believers joined the waters of the Mekong on that day of remembering and rejoicing. The gates of hell had not prevailed against their faith. Van and I left with great gratitude and the highest possible admiration and respect for believers with such faith.

We went on to Bangkok for a visit (I was back in my second home again—with friends!) and a couple of meetings. I also went to the semiannual board meeting at the hospital in Bangalore before I went home.

One More Tall Travel Tale from That Era

All international travelers have their funny/horrible/weird tales of navigating peculiar customs regulations. I have already mentioned my wedding band episode in Hanoi, but I had another one, in India in 1990, and I have to admit that it involved a rather unusual baggage item.

Dr. Rebekah Naylor was an accomplished musician as well as a physician and surgeon. She also directed the hospital bell choir in Bangalore. While speaking at a Stateside church during furlough in early 1990, the church decided to order her a new set of bells to take back to India. However, it was not really a set of bells—it was a full set of tongs, similar to tuning forks. There were eighty-eight tongs, corresponding to the eighty-eight keys on the piano. The tongs did not arrive at her house before she returned to India. When they did arrive, her dad, knowing I would soon be leaving for India, asked me to take them to her. They arrived in Richmond in a large, specially prepared container, with each tong having its own cradle. I bought the largest suitcase I could find, barely got the container in, and added it to my luggage.

The airport in Madras (now called Chennai) was my port of entry and had the usual two categories of lines through customs: one for duty-free goods and one for duty items, primarily liquor, cigarettes, and electronic goods. As usual, I went through the duty-free line. This time, however, I was picked on a random basis to have my bags checked. When I opened the suitcase and they saw the tong containers, they asked what it was. I told them it was bells for a children's bell choir. They wanted it opened. Inside was a brochure showing children playing the tongs. They were about to pass me on through when the curiosity of one of the agents impelled him to ask what it sounded like. I tried to explain, but he wanted to hear one. I opened the case, picked up a tong, and handed it to him. He examined it a moment and then shook it. *Ding!* Big smile. He reached over, picked up another one, and shook it. *Dong!*

An agent in an adjoining line heard it, came over, picked up a tong, and shook it. *Ding!* Then another. *Dong!*

By that time, all the agents were deserting their battle stations and coming over to do their own ding-donging. All the checkout lines came to a halt. One of the female agents picked up a tong, began ringing it, and then started doing a traditional Indian dance, using the tong as a stage prop. That really got the adrenaline going. Talk about hearing bells ringing! It was total chaos. All the agents were singing, dancing, ringing bells, and having a ball. For them, it was a happy interlude in a day usually filled with shoving, shouting, angry passengers demanding immediate attention. Now they were all being ignored, and pandemonium reigned. I was standing there in total frustration, but all I could do was wait it out.

After a while, the situation began to return to the normal chaotic state.

One of the agents decided the item should not be duty-free; it was too much to allow to pass free. Surely something could be gained from it. "How much did it cost?" the agent asked.

"I don't know. I have not seen the invoice. Maybe $400."

"No! It cost $2,000." (They usually charged half the cost of the item as the import duty fee.)

I said again, "Maybe $400."

"No. It cost at least $1,500. You pay me $200."

I learned later the tongs cost about $1,000.

We had some close fellowship for about ten minutes. We finally settled on a hundred dollars as duty, and I felt fortunate to get by with that. With great relief, I repacked the tongs—they were all there—and left the airport over two hours after I landed.

During our last year in Richmond, James took on an interesting challenge. After returning from the college in Thailand, he decided to establish his own consulting business, including an international component. He was in Moscow investigating an export business opportunity just before the Soviet Union disintegration occurred. It was not the time or place to invest resources. He put his consulting business idea on a back burner and went to work with Perot Systems in Dallas as a computer-systems engineer.

There is one final note concerning a task I had in Richmond. The FMB and the other SBC institutions were dealing with the uncertainties that were prevalent in the SBC at that time. One of the steps taken by the FMB in an attempt to be transparent with the government concerning FMB actions and decisions was to establish a "liaison" position. An FMB staff member with a background in certain states was chosen to establish a relationship with the state Baptist convention leadership. I was asked to fill that role in Arkansas. The role was separate and apart from the role of the two FMB board members elected by the state conventions to serve as members of the FMB trustees.

As the liaison for Arkansas, I was to meet with the state convention executive director and executive committee when possible and also attend the annual Arkansas Baptist State convention. My purpose was to share with Arkansas Baptist leadership current issues the board was dealing with. It was also to hear and respond to questions related to positions taken and decisions made by the board. Dr. Don Moore was the executive director of the Arkansas Baptist State Convention at that time, and a close friendship grew out of our working together.

CHAPTER 12

Joann's Ministry Established: The Dark Side of Travel

While I was tumble-weeding around the world between 1987 and 1991, Joann was reestablishing her life and ministry in a very different world in the United States. I have already mentioned the three part-time jobs she had, but I want to speak in more detail about her sensitive time as a medical consultant with the FMB.

The title was benign, even friendly, but non-revealing. The job description was also nonthreatening—review and make a recommendation concerning the medical condition of missionary candidates and their families prior to appointment—but the consequences of those consultations could be shattering if they revealed a medical condition in the family that threatened, or even prohibited, appointment. It was not unusual for candidate families to have medical problems.

Weighing those problems against the threat posed by living in remote areas or in third world countries with poor-quality health care sometimes posed a difficult dilemma when Joann made a recommendation. On one side, the family (parents) felt called by the Lord to go as missionaries. They had passed all other preliminary qualifications, the board wanted to appoint as many missionaries as possible, and the family was willing to take the risks involved. So why not give the green light and send them on their way?

But there was another side to be considered before a recommendation could be made. Joann had dealt with many family medical problems in the field, and she had seen the consequences of inadequate care. She had also seen latent symptoms become suddenly acute and life-threatening. Her medical experience gave her, more clearly than the family (and more clearly than the FMB trustees who had rarely served in the field) a better perspective of potential difficulties they would face in the field.

Another element to be considered was the very high financial exposure to the FMB of a family in the field needing to travel to another area to obtain adequate, but often expensive, continuing care. In her position, she sometimes reviewed medical invoices. Extrapolation of the growing expenses was a warning flag. With about 3,900 missionaries under appointment (at that time), accompanied by an almost equal number of missionary children, medical costs constituted a major part of the total FMB budget. In those years, the board could absorb the cost.

When the number of missionaries under appointment exceeded five thousand, the cost became a serious matter. The signs were already indicating an upward trend in medical (and other) expenses that the board could not sustain. In fact, that point has now been reached; it has become totally unsustainable. Drastic personnel reductions are being taken to cope with the consequences even as I write this. Those factors, and others, were considered by Joann in making her recommendations. The situation became more tenuous when a few members of the board indicated a personal policy of thinking all candidates should be appointed—even those with severe medical problems. Any future financial concern or personal risk due to the absence of medical care was irrelevant. "If they feel called, send them!" Now, in 2015, there are more missionaries in the field than can be supported. Up to eight hundred of them are being forced to take early retirement or be terminated. The signs have been there, but the warnings went unheeded.

Now back to Joann's establishment of new ministries. As the story of the dramatic work Joann had done in our eighteen years in the field became known, speaking requests began to come in. The Bangkla hospital years, especially her work with leprosy patients, was a fascinating story. The magnitude of her refugee medical work on the border was apparent with just a simple relating of the story. Then the successful saga of the Khond Hills primary health-care training program elicited an excited appreciation of all she had done in just a few years. When it was all summarized, it became obvious that God had been at work through it all. Sometimes He worked openly and miraculously. At other times, it was obvious He had been working in the background for long periods of time, but it was just now coming to light. To all who heard the stories, it was apparent that God's sovereignty was directing the entire drama. It was an exciting story, and she was ready and willing to share it.

The invitations to speak came first from local churches and associations and then more widely on a national level. She had loved being a missionary, and she loved telling how God brought it all about. Her emphasis, over and over, was that God had done it. She was just following where He led. To Him be the glory!

Two of her speaking engagements merit sharing with more detail. One of those was serving as the featured speaker at the annual Mission Day Emphasis at the Southern Baptist Theological Seminary in Louisville, Kentucky, in March 1990. It was an honor to be asked to speak. Southern Seminary was the original Southern Baptist Seminary and had been in the forefront of theological education for many years. Many nationally recognized evangelical authors, pastors, and scholars were products of Southern. Many missionaries were alumni, and it was still producing pastors, preachers, missionaries, and scholars. Joann could match any of them in scholarship, but hers was in medicine, not theology. She was just a tad intimidated, but she did a wonderful job and was highly commended. I was a little proud of her too.

The other occasion was perhaps of even greater significance. In June 1990, she was asked to present the theme interpretation at the national Women's Missionary Union (WMU) annual meeting in New Orleans. She would speak on five occasions to approximately four thousand women at the New Orleans Convention Center. Part of the significance came from the fact that her close friend, Dr. Dellanna O'Brien, was the national executive director of WMU at that time. (She and her husband, Bill O'Brien, executive vice president of the Foreign Mission Board, had been appointed missionaries at the same time as Joann and I. Dellanna and Joann had been in high school together in Odessa, Texas.)

She illustrated the convention's theme of "Hearts of One Accord" with a dramatic multimedia presentation. Sounds of a heartbeat reverberated through the convention center in concert with the animated pulsations of a heart flashing on two very large overhead screens. In her series of presentations, she drew many analogies between the critical role of the heart in the human body and the equally critical role required of believers to have a heartbeat for missions … for sharing His love.

I'll give just one of the many analogies she used. In our physical heart the electrical impulse or signal that triggers the heartbeat is initiated in the top of the heart. In a similar, spiritual way, the impulse that triggers our heartbeat for missions originates at the top—from Christ our Head. His command, the impulse, is just as critical to our spiritual lives as the electrical impulse is to the physical heart. The signal to the physical heart can be short-circuited. It can be diverted, blocked, or weakened not because of a faulty signal but because of a fault in the heart. The point is clear. We can hear a thousand signals from the world that divert, block, or weaken the signal—the command—from the Lord. When that occurs, we will not have a heart that is in accord with the Lord.

The response to those two presentations, and the others she gave, was widespread and heartwarming. It was especially encouraging to Joann because she was still coping with the sense of loss she felt in being out of the mission field. She did not feel public speaking was her gift, but if the Lord could use her speaking to touch hearts and draw people closer to the Lord, then she could accept that as one of her ministries.

As a side note, her speaking continued after retirement. More about that later.

Travel: The Dark Side

I have enjoyed travel since my early years, and I have been privileged to travel in much of the world, but there can be too much of a good thing. To many, it sounds interesting, even glamorous. It wasn't. For me, the reality was different. Travel became less desirable. Long check-in lines, repeated security checks, delayed and canceled flights, countless hours waiting for the next flight, and then countless hours sitting in a cramped seat. The list could go on, and it all wreaked havoc on the body's circadian rhythm. I frequently went into meetings or project reviews after twenty or thirty hours of travel and waiting.

But those were actually the minor inconveniences. In our Richmond years, the greater wear and tear came from the physical and emotional isolation from home, family, and familiar surroundings when I would be gone for weeks at a time, but it had actually begun earlier, in the refugee work in Thailand, when Joann and I were separated most of the time. The separation itself was wearying, but it was exacerbated by dealing constantly with human and spiritual needs beyond describing. It was difficult to find a "place" needed for renewal.

I say that, even while remembering my earlier comment about Psalm 90:1, which affirms that our home, our renewal, comes from a "person," not a "place." But we do not and cannot live happily in isolation. For me, family is a necessity of life. I know the day of ultimate earthly separation is coming, and it will be a time of suffering for those who remain, but until it comes, I want the companionship of loved ones. My travels in later years denied me that, and it finally began to wear me down. The needs were still there, and I knew it, but compassion fatigue finally took its toll on me. I was tired of waking up and having to stop and think, *Where in the world am I?*

Those statements are made as a confession. I became less excited about the work I was called to do. I noticed a certain lassitude of spirit in myself. And therein lay part of my dilemma. The sense of being in the Lord's will was still with me. There was also a sense of accomplishment as I saw lives helped and changed because of our involvement. That sense of achievement helped offset the sense of loss, but I came to feel it was an unequal balance after years of travel and separation.

Those thoughts, feelings, and emotions were not the only factors I considered. There was growing evidence that external circumstances might be changing. The FMB philosophy of "doing" missions and the framework of an administrative structure required to accomplish that change were always subject to review and revision. That turned out to be the case when my position was not filled after I retired.

Those factors, plus others related to family needs, especially of Joann's aging parents, led me to submit my notice of retirement from the board, effective in June 1991. Leaving a work to which God had called me and leaving coworkers who had become dear friends was hard, but as with previous hard decisions, there was a sense of "rightness" about it. It was time.

CHAPTER 13

Retirement Era: Flip-Flop Family, Parents Gone

Our planning for retirement activity had begun years before retirement. We had taken to heart the truism, "Retirement must be *to* something and not just *from* something." It should be for positive reasons, not negative. We had seen friends retire with no plans at all, only to begin to experience declining health. For many, retirement travel was a pleasing prospect; for Joann and me, travel was not a priority, except by our schedule and our choices. The one certain plan we had was to keep busy. I think we succeeded.

We had blueprints ready when we arrived in Arkansas. It was primarily a matter of Joann letting the architect know what she had in mind. She had done thorough research. She had every kitchen cabinet, including several specialty cabinets and drawers, dining room cabinets, and bathroom cabinets and drawers planned in detail long before construction began. No messing around with her! Get with the program!

I had limited construction experience, but after some extensive, selective conversations, I decided to serve as my own general contractor. To take advantage of wholesale prices, I formed my own company: Piney Ridge Construction Company. I hired a respected builder to serve as my foreman. He had four grown sons who had grown up helping him build houses, so he had a built-in, experienced crew, cross-trained in all phases of construction. We were building in a rural area, so abiding by building codes was not necessary, but we complied with applicable codes in every detail.

We were off the highway and secluded in the woods, so we prepared for any utility outage. For electricity, we wired the place for emergency power, provided by a generator operated by our tractor power take-off (PTO) that could handle the entire house. For heat and cooking, we had electricity, LP gas, a wood stove, and a fireplace. For water, we drilled a well with an interconnect capability with city water. Our primary uses for the well were to irrigate our garden and landscaped area and to provide water for the courtyard waterfall. All utility lines were underground.

We gave much thought and discussion to the house design. Part of it was dictated by the terrain: a sixty-foot bluff on the west and a sloping hill on the east. Our back deck, extending the length of the house, overlooked the bluff, Ol Piney, and Culpepper Mountain.

The size of the house was not easily decided; we were torn between two options. One was that there were only the two of us, and we were getting older. "Let's build small." The other option presented three major issues to consider: our growing family of grandchildren, a desire to have a home large enough for ministry to church and other groups, and providing space to care for Joann's aging parents when necessary. The second option prevailed, and we built large.

The fellowship and joy we had in the great number of times we had groups of people in our home remain some of our best times. We had the entire church at least once each year, usually at Christmas. We had summer cookouts on our deck, swimming parties for the church youth, and the medical staff from the hospital. We entertained prospective new physicians for the community and often brought church visitors home for lunch. For a number of years, we had the Goatcher family reunion on alternate years. We sometimes had up to seventy people for sit-down dinners. We kept a guest book to note the occasion and record the names of the people who attended. That book is a source of many happy memories. As we review those twenty-two wonderful years in our retirement home, we are glad we decided to build it large enough to accommodate such occasions.

A Tangent

Joann and I were often conscious of the flip-flop arrangement in our family life. Usually, the parents stayed home, and the kids took off into the world. In our case, the kids stayed close to home, and the parents worked and traveled the world. No one was unhappy with the arrangement; we were just different. Our children have never indicated any resentment at our nomadic lives. In fact, they have expressed gratitude for the privilege of living in another country and culture and being able to see much of the world. Whether that had anything to do with relationships or not, James and Lisa did some things for us on special occasions that have meant much to us through the years. I'll relate only a couple of the many. Both occurred not long after we were settled in our retirement home. I'll relate Lisa's first.

Our children, their spouses, and the grandchildren came to see our home as the epitome of what "home" should be (as Joann and I did). It was in the country, in the woods, with creeks, waterfalls, swimming holes, trails, wildlife, a garden to till and see from whence came their food and plenty of room to roam and explore. It had a mother and grandmother who prepared unending, delicious feasts and created an atmosphere that said *home*. It was a sanctuary of peace and spiritual renewal.

All of them expressed their love, appreciation, and gratitude countless times and in many ways, but Lisa found a way to express it in a little different manner. She wrote a poem, laboriously embroidered it on a portion of thick cloth, and framed it for hanging.

Come with me, let's go
To the house on the hill,
Where the fire is warm,
Though the wind blows chill.
A quiet sanctuary,
With peace your heart will fill,
Oh, come let us go to the house on the hill.
Come with me, let's go
For a walk by the creek,
Where the clear water rushes
Over rocks to pools so deep.
A deer! An armadillo! (Augh!)
Who knows what else we'll meet!
Oh, come let's go for a walk by the creek.

James has a unique ability to choose gifts that became special. He did that numerous times for both of us. Not always expensive (although sometimes we knew it was an almost sacrificial gift), he managed to make the occasion memorable. I'll tell of only one.

We had gone to Dallas to visit him close to my birthday. He surprised and blessed me with tickets for the two of us to attend a Texas Rangers baseball game. I liked baseball and had played it in my younger years, but I had never attended a Major League game. I couldn't have been more pleased. The fact that the Rangers won an exciting game just added to the enjoyment. It remains one of my favorite memories.

A Great Discovery

Joann received a surprising, serendipitous gift just as we began construction. It came about after we had purchased a four-acre tract of land between our house site and Highway 9. We bought it to provide a visual and sound buffer between our house and the highway and also to prevent any unwanted construction or trash accumulation adjacent to our homesite. Several years earlier, a mobile home had been placed on the plot, but a major flood had destroyed the place. It had been abandoned. It was overrun with brambles, thorns, junk trees, and discarded trash—an unattractive sight. After buying it, we decided to set out 2,400 pine trees and two hundred white oak trees to increase the buffer effect and enhance the looks. (Now, twenty-four years later, many of those trees are large enough to harvest.)

On an impulse, I decided to wade through the almost impenetrable undergrowth of brush and take a closer look at the entire tract. That was when I found the surprise. At some point, while the mobile home resident was living on the site, he had built a waterfall. It was not a miniature yard decoration, but an eight-foot structure built of unusually shaped volcanic rocks brought in and sunk several feet into the ground. Water pipes had been installed inside the rock structure as it was built. The rocks had been laid to make it appear that a spring was issuing from near the top of a bluff. It was partially buried in the ground, obviously abandoned for many years. Even in the rough setting, I could see its beautiful potential.

How was I going to tell or show Joann? For years, she had dreamed of having a home with a waterfall. When we bought our retirement place, she could visualize the ideal type and placement of the waterfall in the courtyard. She had thought, planned, and looked at many home-landscaping waterfalls, but none had really been appealing. Neither of us were landscapers or designers. We did not know what to do about a waterfall. When I saw that half-buried monster, I imagined Joann's reaction. When she came home from work, I told her to put on her heaviest grunge clothes and go for a walk with me.

I led the way, parted the brambles and briars, and stood aside as we came to the waterfall. It took a moment for the reality to hit home—and then she laughed and yelled like a little girl. She proceeded to plan the whole layout in the courtyard in just a few moments. It was her dream fulfilled. She is convinced it was a gift from God.

Moving that four- or five-ton waterfall into its precise place at the appropriate time was a touchy project. One of my builders was a large-equipment operator. He rented the biggest front-end loader available, picked up the waterfall (barely), and slowly brought it almost half a mile to the house. I am convinced that loader actually groaned as the operator maneuvered the waterfall into position and gradually lowered it into its prepared location in the courtyard. It was too tall to just place on the ground, but we excavated a couple of feet and then lowered it into place. Plumbing connections were completed, and skilled rock masons built a pool at the foot of the waterfall with an overflow space into a rock-bordered channel down to another pool from which the water was pumped back up to the top of the waterfall to provide a continual flow of water.

There also had to be a garden! We prepared the garden area. Since we were in the woods, much clearing was required. It was a sloping area, fairly close to the house, so erosion had to be prevented. I built three dry-stack rock walls the length of the garden to create three tiers of level ground. The soil was clay and rocks, hardly ideal for a garden, so I added more than a hundred cubic yards of good topsoil to improve the fertility. We ended up with about seven thousand square feet of growing space. In addition to the usual vegetable growing area, we added a place for grapevines, a blueberry patch (we already had a blackberry patch), a strawberry bed, an asparagus bed, a watermelon and cantaloupe patch, and apple and peach trees.

The garden was ready, Joann was ready, the labor was rewarding, and the harvest was delicious. What we did not eat fresh, Joann canned, dried, or preserved. We were not the only ones to enjoy it. Our grandchildren loved to come visit us to plow the ground, pick the ripe produce, and help Grandmother can and preserve what was not eaten. Wildlife, especially deer and raccoons, also enjoyed it. I built an eight-foot fence around it, but that did not stop the birds and squirrels that would take a bite and discard the remainder of the fruit. What a waste! That garden provided a bountiful harvest of delicious food and a wonderful therapeutic benefit for both of us. We miss it.

Another serendipity popped up soon after I registered our place for inclusion as a Stewardship Farm with the Department of Agriculture and the Arkansas Forestry Department. Planned as a way to assist local farmers, including tree farmers, to enhance the environment in forest management, mast production, wildlife benefit, crop selection, and insect infestation, the program also encouraged the development of forest-hiking trails on privately owned land. When the specialists in the Agriculture and Forestry Department looked at our land, they suggested that I apply for assistance in building a trail. They had noticed several attractive features on our place, including waterfalls, overlooks, and bluffs that warranted a trail. I applied for the program, it was approved, and we were on our way.

The trail began at the north end of our back deck, went to the pinnacle overlooking Ol Piney and the confluence of Wolfe and Choctaw Creeks, up Wolfe Creek by a hundred-yard rock wall, which was composed of rocks cleared from the adjacent field in the late 1800s, on up the creek past the beaver hole, the Blue Hole (eight feet deep with an eight-foot bluff on three sides, fed on the upper side by a six-foot waterfall, then another two hundred yards up to another waterfall, up and over the high elevation on the place, and back down to a bluff overlooking Choctaw Creek to the south end of our back deck. It was exactly one mile in length. A professional trail builder did a beautiful job choosing the best locations for viewing the woods, waterfalls, bluffs, and glades for wildlife sightings. That trail was walked and enjoyed countless times by family members, church groups, and others. Through all seasons, Joann and I walked that trail, marveling at the hundreds of dogwoods in bloom, listening to the snow crunching under our feet, and watching startled deer and turkeys leap away at our approach. What memories!

We had a professional landscaper design the area in front of the house, including the stairway leading from the driveway up to the second (main) level and the area immediately surrounding the waterfall. Across the driveway from the courtyard and into the woods, we had short walking trails bordered by rhododendrons, azaleas, hydrangeas, roses, and smaller annuals and perennials, according to the season and Joann's preference. You can perhaps imagine the satisfaction, pleasure, and renewal we experienced as we enjoyed the blessings of that place for so many years.

Sitting together on the front porch at the end of a summer day was one of our most treasured times. As twilight faded into darkness, the chorus of insects, birds, and nightlife would change with the time of day and the season. In the summer, the katydids and cicadas could be so loud it was uncomfortable. At other times, it would be totally quiet. To sit quietly together in the swing after a long day of labor and consciously sense the presence of the Lord in the midst of His creation was to worship.

An element of fun and laughter was added when we brought our little dachshund home with us. She loved to be outside and just run and play. Before the squirrels headed home to their high-rise nests for the night, GiGi loved chasing them from tree to tree. She never caught one, but she thoroughly enjoyed chasing them. When she became tired, she came up on the porch and lay down by Joann. Happiness.

Joann loved birds, and one of our sweetest memories is sitting on the porch and listening to the great variety of birdcalls, including turkeys, and the staccato hammering of the woodpeckers. Sometimes, whippoorwills, doves, and mockingbirds would continue calling on into the night. Nighttime was the favorite time for owls, both screech and hoot, although the sound of the screech owl was not pleasant.

For daytime viewing, Joann hung a variety of birdfeeders just outside the breakfast nook windows and the kitchen. Migrating hummingbirds came to love the buffet selection she set out for them. If she delayed setting out the feeders or brought them in too quickly, the tardy hummingbirds would hover near the windows looking for their handouts. It looked like they remembered the feeders from an earlier migration and knew where to get their food. Could they do that?

Joann also set out a variety of feeders for other birds and kept notes of the variety that came by. She was surprised and thrilled at the great number, many of which were migrating and rarely seen in the area.

There were also many wonderful solo times for me. I loved to go out on the porch and then into the woods, watching a full moon rising through the trees and brightening the entire area. I recalled my times in Van Horn when the moon was full and going out into the desert to enjoy the night. I also did that in Choctaw, Nepal, Colorado, and India. Walking through the woods—or just sitting and listening when a full moon was moving through the trees—was exhilarating.

Retirement had financial implications for us. Both of us were frugal, and we had been able to save some money—even in the tight times. We were fortunate to make some real estate transactions when the market favored our decisions. Also, our time in Van Horn coincided with an inflationary period, bringing us unexpected financial benefit. We were not wise in finances and investing, but we did live conservatively. The Lord blessed us in a surprising way. It all combined to allow us to pay for our retirement home as we built it.

However, transitioning from two incomes to only one retirement income brought an abrupt reduction in income. Joann was not yet eligible for Social Security, and the board had miscalculated my total time with the board. They had determined it to be a little over twenty-five years (required for full benefits) when it was less. That reduced my monthly income. We had to transition quickly back to a very frugal lifestyle.

It required about a year for our house to be finished, and since I was serving as my own general contractor, I could not do any outside work. Joann had been assured of a position with an organization, but it fell through at the last minute. As a physician, she was able to find work, but she preferred part-time positions in our immediate area. Those positions were scarce.

There was another option, but neither of us was excited about her establishing a private, full-time practice. Many people in the community wanted her to do so. Having been there and knowing how demanding that role could be, it was just not wise. Fortunately, and thankfully, opportunities began to open and Joann, being Joann, quickly turned them into ministry opportunities. The Lord had come through again.

Joann had two major practice opportunities in her Choctaw retirement years. The first one was with the Greers Ferry Medical Clinic in Greers Ferry, owned and managed by Baptist Health System in Little Rock. It was a family practice clinic, but with retirement communities nearby, she did a lot of geriatric medicine. It was part-time work, three days a week, with coverage provided by a nurse practitioner when Joann was absent.

She retired from the clinic in 1996 and was immediately recruited by a mental health organization to provide mental health coverage in several clinics in north-central Arkansas, including Clinton. She had dealt with many patients with mental and emotional problems— both adults and children—in her years of family practice, and her success in treating them was recognized in the medical community. It was a difficult and challenging practice, but it was rewarding in many ways. She spent many continuing medical education (CME) hours in psychiatric study and seminars to keep abreast of the most effective treatment protocols for mental and emotional problems. Dealing with all varieties of drug addictions and abuse victims was often a heart-wrenching, emotionally draining time, yet it too had its rewards. She retired from that practice in 2011.

As we were preparing to move into Parkway Village (the retirement village in Little Rock where we now live) she stopped in the administrator's office to see if they needed any medical assistance. As a matter of fact, they did. She immediately began work on a one-day-a-week basis, primarily in the 105-bed nursing home. That continued until the end of 2013. At that point, she had been practicing medicine for fifty-nine years. At eighty-two, she felt it was time to stop practicing since she did not want to place any patient at risk. (It has been interesting to see a large number of village residents continue to seek her advice and counsel relating to medical issues.)

One of our priorities when we moved to Clinton was to find a church home. The Clinton area, like most rural areas in the South, had little country churches all over the place, including my old home church in Formosa. Started when most people walked to church, there are multitudes of small, barely existing churches in close proximity to each other that are still hanging on because Grandpa or Grandma was an early member and don't want the old church to close.

Joann and I visited several of those little churches before we settled on Formosa. Like many others, attendance at Formosa had dropped, with people becoming more mobile and able to go to larger churches with more programs for their children. Joann and I—perhaps Joann more than I—saw it as mission field with possibilities for growth. The church had come alive in recent years. The fact that it was the church where I had been saved and baptized and where many of my ancestors had been charter members were factors in our joining, but there were many other factors.

The pastor retired several months after we joined the church. It was his second retirement, but it was not surprising since he was well up in years. What was really surprising was that the church immediately called me as pastor. I explained my thoughts about my lack of a specific call to preach and that it had been more than thirty years since I had served as pastor, but they would not rescind the call.

I had another task, and I served for more than four years. One of our many blessings was to help establish a Spanish-speaking mission of the church. Many dairies had been established in the area, staffed primarily with Spanish-speaking workers. The mission field next door needed to hear the gospel. Joann and I did some intense review of our Spanish in order to understand and say more than "¿Còmo estas?" We were delighted when several of those who attended the Spanish-speaking congregation were baptized in one of the swimming holes on our place.

A big part of the reason the church did so well was Joann. She was the church pianist and a teacher, but that in no way conveys the full extent of her influence in the church. She was not only my helpmate—she was the helpmate for the entire church in a hundred different ways. She was, and continues to be, greatly loved and respected.

After a little over four years, I felt the church was on fairly solid ground and submitted my resignation/retirement notice. I was a little surprised when the church immediately elected me as treasurer. A little later, the new pastor wanted me ordained as a deacon. I thought one ordination was enough, but he felt a deacon had a different, unique role that called for another ordination. I relented. We remained as members and enjoyed many good years at the church until we moved into our retirement home in Little Rock.

Logging: Another Vocation

When Joann and I bought the land for our retirement home, part of the appeal was the many beautiful, tall pine trees growing all over the place, mixed with a variety of hardwoods. The land had been unused for more than sixty years, and some of the trees on the hills were well over one hundred years old. I decided to clear out the thick undergrowth of trash bushes and selectively cut many of the junk/ dead/skeleton trees to enhance the beauty and productivity of the woods, but I was not aware of the potential value of the pines. That changed after we completed the house and I began to consider the tree concentrations on the place. I also saw the results of tree planting done by Truett while we were overseas.

Joann and I had three small tree farms, giving us a total of 190 acres. While we were overseas, Truett had the creek place and the Formosa place set out in pine tree seedlings—between thirty-five thousand and forty thousand trees. On the undisturbed seventy-five-acre Choctaw portion, there were several hundred natural-growth mature pine trees ready to harvest. The trees on the other two places were not yet mature, but their potential was evident. It was time to consider what to do and how to do it.

I had thought of having a commercial logger do the work, but that idea died quickly. The logger's fee would be well over half the value of the timber. He would do only clear-cutting and no selective cutting. For me, that was totally unacceptable. Clear-cutters used massive equipment that wreaked havoc on the woods and destroyed most of the smaller, good trees. It also destroyed many of the hardwoods that produced mast for wildlife.

Consideration quickly led to the decision to hire a forestry consultant. He was of great help in providing a quick summary of forest management, particularly the criteria for choosing trees for selective thinning. It provided me with much-needed information that was important for when I began doing my own solo logging. I needed to accurately determine diseased, stressed, overcrowded, and commercially acceptable trees to harvest—as well as knowing which healthy seed trees should be left to ensure continued sustainability. One other need was to determine the maximum cuts possible for each tree, within the parameters established by the lumber companies.

After a thorough review of the woods and consideration of other factors, my consultant suggested doing my own logging. He felt that

I would realize enough financial benefit within a few years to pay for most of my equipment.

That took some thought. By that time, I had done enough in the woods with a chainsaw to partially realize what I would be getting into. I decided to do it. Deciding to do it, then doing it, however, was not a simple step.

I'll omit the details of the first few years of my logging. I started small, without the tractor and other major equipment. I did get an eighteen-foot gooseneck, tandem wheel trailer to haul the logs to the mill—that was a necessity. Without the other equipment, it was slow going, but that was okay. It allowed me to learn at my own pace.

One of the first requirements was to complete a forty-hour course on logging procedures. All loggers were required to complete the course and be entered in the computers of the major purchasers before they could sell logs. It was a condition imposed to forestall legislation that would usurp many of the prerogatives of individual landowners who desired to do their own logging. It was actually a good, worthwhile study of legal, tax, safety, environmental, and forestry-management issues. I was glad to do it.

It was time to make the big step. I had done enough in the woods and had talked to several equipment dealers, and I knew what I needed. I bought a thirty-nine-horsepower Kubota four-wheel drive tractor with a PTO, front-end loader, and a box blade. I added a specially fabricated steel log-loader, capable of handling a 2,500-pound, eighteen-foot log, and an 8,000-pound-capacity winch operating off the tractor PTO. It had a 180-foot wire cable, enabling me to pull heavy logs out of ravines or other difficult places. I added two more chainsaws: one large one for the large trees and a trimmer to clean up the tops of the felled trees. (Some of the trees were thirty inches in diameter, requiring special attention.) I later added a brush hog for grass and brush clearing all over the place. Extensive use of the tractor proved it to be the precise one needed; it was large and powerful enough to handle any tree, yet small enough to maneuver in the woods without harming the other trees. With all equipment and permits in place, I could easily cut a trailer load of trees and take them to the mill in Clinton in one day. That began several years of very satisfying logging activity that enhanced the woods on our place, gave me plenty of hard labor to stay in shape, and provided a little eating-out money.

Since our place was hilly and thickly wooded, I hired a Caterpillar operator to cut a logging trail through the woods to allow full access to all the trees. Negotiating a long, heavily loaded trailer in the woods was tricky, so I had all the logging trails cut in circular patterns so the trailer would not need to be backed up.

Next to the tractor, the winch was the wisest buy I made for harvesting timber. It enabled me to fell trees exactly where I wanted and to extract trees from locations that would have been impossible to reach otherwise. Many of the trees were so closely spaced because they had grown very tall to reach the sunlight. In many cases, the first limbs would be fifty or sixty feet above the ground. That was great for lumber production, but it made felling the tree in a particular location a dicey process. Falling a few feet off the intended track could result in the tree getting hung up or tangled with other trees. When that happened, getting it down and out could be tricky—and dangerous. The winch, combined with strategically placed pulleys, enabled me to guide it down in just the right place almost every time. There were enough trees ready for harvest that I was able to cut only the oldest for lumber. The mill in Clinton recognized the quality and paid me accordingly.

There was a little issue stalking around the edges of our awareness throughout all my logging activity: the inherent danger of logging work. It was a little more of a concern to Joann than to me perhaps because she had extensive experience in repairing the damage done by a chainsaw. It was made worse in my case because I usually worked alone. That was not a good practice, but I had no choice. Accidents could happen even to the strongest and most experienced, and I was already a little past seventy when I was at my peak logging activity. In spite of great caution, trees and limbs can exhibit a mind of their own. Logging is not an exact science. Many experienced loggers have been injured, and a few even killed, by a falling limb while cutting a tree. In the walk-around before cutting a tree, a close look had to be taken to try to identify dead, or potentially deadly, limbs that could fall easily. You can't be looking up or around when you are felling a tree.

I did all I could to mitigate the danger. I wore chaps, hard hats, and goggles, and I reviewed instructional videos about safe and unsafe procedures, but the danger was always there. I came close to injury several times, and I often fell while maneuvering to cut up the tops of the trees, which was not at all uncommon and not much of a threat. I feel strongly that the Lord kept me mindful of the danger and helped prod me to exercise extra caution. I have thanked the Lord countless times—Joann has also—for keeping me safe through almost twenty years of logging.

When I reached age eighty-three, I realized I was not as agile or as strong as I needed to be to continue logging. I stopped my logging, but I continued to cut our winter firewood. I had a log-splitter to help with that task. It had its own danger, but I was careful there also—and the degree of danger was lower. I was glad when the buyer of our retirement home expressed an interest in doing some logging and wanted to buy my logging equipment.

Cutting and using firewood was a rewarding part of our retirement life. There is great satisfaction and comfort in being by a warm stove on cold winter days and nights. We had a fireplace in our living room and a stove in our den—both with catalytic combustors that greatly increased their heating efficiencies. Each had long-burning capability; fill them with wood, set the damper, and they kept the place warm for twelve hours. Our den was our favorite place of refuge, especially in the wintertime. GiGi loved it as much as we did. She would curl up on a mat next to the fire and almost refuse to move.

I have been grateful for my logging experience. It did, in fact, almost pay for the equipment, and the equipment was of great help in other work around the place, especially the brush hog. The hard work also kept me in good physical condition, and I think it contributed to my continued ability to stay active. It was just one more of many serendipities the Lord provided in our retirement years.

Early Retirement Years

Logging was enjoyable and gratifying for me, and it was beneficial to the land in many ways, but a bird's-eye view of our retirement years would reveal that it occupied a relatively small amount of my total time. Far too much took place in those twenty-one years to note in detail. It was a wonderful, significant era in our lives, with significant events that I must relate. Some of them were personal and family events, important primarily to the family, but some of them were ministry related and reemphasize the desire and ability of God to continue to use us, His people, to the end of our days.

An unexpected opportunity to continue in ministry came in December 1992: our church called me as pastor. I had never felt a call to the preaching ministry. I have never been gifted with preaching or speaking skills. I felt more at home in a pastoral role, and I accepted the call on that basis. Several people joined our fellowship during those years, and the church grew and became financially stable.

Although I am an ordained minister and was a pastor for six years, I objected to being addressed as "Reverend." I know enough of the etiology of the word to dislike the implied superior status of one so addressed. I did like the term "Pastor." Or, just call me by my name.

It was a small church with several faithful, mature believers who wanted and needed spiritual feeding. Preparing three appropriate messages weekly was a time-consuming process. Seminary training from my early years really came to my rescue. How grateful I was that it had been a prerequisite to missionary service. Rightly or wrongly, preaching was a difficult task for me. I never identified with preachers who were always just itching to preach. To share His Word, to witness at every opportunity, and to serve in every way possible was a welcome undertaking, but preaching and public speaking was not my gift.

One part of my ministry that I particularly enjoyed was that of unofficial community pastor, simply because of my heritage. My family had been in the area for well over a hundred years. Joann and I were often called at crisis times by nonmembers. I was glad to be seen in that role; it opened many doors for ministry.

We had a special time when Joann's medical school class had its fortieth reunion in June 1995. Joann was chosen as one of the keynote speakers because of her "unusual" medical career. As she summarized her forty years of medical practice, much of it as a medical missionary in the undeveloped world, it touched a responsive chord. Perhaps because her life of ministry and service epitomized the aspirations of many of her classmates in their beginning years, but which went largely unfulfilled, her living out that original vision brought wonderful inspiration. Whoever thought a medical school class reunion could be transformed into a time of worship? It was a tremendously moving time to see sixty or seventy culture-hardened doctors, many shedding tears, and many others seemingly realizing that they had missed the point in their lives. Afterward, they waited in line to talk with Joann about her experiences. They wanted to talk to one of their own who had stayed true to her call and commitment.

That class is still highly recognized for the accomplishments of its graduates. One was president of a medical school, three were deans of medical schools, one was president of a huge pharmaceutical company, two were world-famous award winners for research success, one was the author of the standard medical school textbook on internal medicine, and one was well-known for software development in the health-care field. There were others with major accomplishments, but less well-known. Talk about a room full of high achievers! It was hard to keep my husbandly pride subdued as I observed their recognition of Joann.

Travel: Our Choice

That reunion was a high point, but it was not the only one that year. Shortly after returning from the medical school reunion, we joined Norman and Kay Roberts on a tour of Israel. (Norman, Kay, and Joann had been at Baylor together, and Norman and I had had joint hospital administrative responsibilities together in the States and in India. They were serving as volunteer missionaries in Europe at that time.)

We traveled the length and breadth of the country and saw the usual highlights: the Sea of Galilee, the synagogue at Capernaum, the confluence of streams forming the Jordan River, the Dead Sea, the Mount of Olives, the Dome of the Rock, Bethlehem, the Garden of Gethsemane, the Jericho Road, and many others. The reality of being there and reading scriptural accounts of events at the actual places where they occurred made a visual and emotional impact that has to be seen to be understood. It was a time of inspiration, worship, and blessing.

We returned home through Germany, with a boat trip down the Rhine River and a side trip to Mainz to obtain a portion of John's Gospel printed using the original Gutenberg press. That year, 1995, was a good one for us.

Our move back to Arkansas brought a temporary decline in speaking engagements for Joann, but just as she had become recognized quickly after our move to Richmond, she also gained recognition quickly in Arkansas. First, at the local level and then statewide. She spoke and conducted conferences in churches, associations, and at the state WMU convention. She also continued to be invited to speak to overseas missions on a reduced level.

In addition to the subjects noted earlier, there was one additional subject that came to be a major part of her presentation: aerobic exercises. Many missionary women (and other women too) were in situations where extensive physical activity was limited, yet it was an important component of good overall health. She began offering aerobic exercises as a part of the conference, and it soon became one of the favorite times of the conferences. That idea quickly grew to the production of an exercise video that could be reproduced and used by the women at any convenient time. The exercises were set to Christian music to enhance their enjoyment of the time.

Her first video was produced when she was fifty-eight years old. It was widely reproduced and used in many areas. An updated video was produced when she was sixty-eight—while she was conducting a conference in Singapore. It was professionally produced by the Christian Media Center in Singapore and was also widely distributed. She continued to use that video until she was seventy-five. (Yes, she was still high-stepping at that age and outlasting many younger participants!)

She finally had to discontinue doing the full workout because she had injured her hip while running in a 5K race in Little Rock. The heated pool in our retirement village has enabled her to resume a very active water aerobics and water volleyball regimen—in her eighties. I'm trying to get a little sympathy here in my struggles to keep up with "the weaker vessel."

The mid-to-late 1990s brought a heavy schedule. My logging activity reached its peak, yet I was constantly interrupted by other priorities. It was a continual struggle to keep the garden and landscaped portion of our place in top condition. I retired as pastor of the church in early 1997. In January 1998, I was asked to become interim director of missions for the North Central Arkansas Baptist Association. I continued in that role until July 1998. By that time, as noted earlier, I had become treasurer of the church.

Of all our activities in 1997, a trip to Alaska was the most memorable. We were joined by the Roberts and by Frank and Carolyn Shell. Frank had been asked to become director of missions for the North Central Baptist Association, but when we got Frank, we also got Carolyn. No superlative is too high for them—both as individuals and as a team. They made a huge impact for the Lord throughout the state. Joann and Carolyn were like two peas in a pod and the greatest of friends for each other. Joann gave the eulogy at Carolyn's funeral, which was a time of great sorrow.

We flew into Fairbanks for our first night and then marveled the next day at the staggering views as we rode the train slowly southward to Anchorage. We were fortunate to have the clouds part as we neared massive Mount McKinley. Denali is the highest mountain in North America, giving us a grand panoramic view. After a brief time in Anchorage, we flew southeastward to Sitka to begin our small ship ride through the Inland Passage and down to the Lower 48.

Norman had made the arrangements for us to travel by day on a ninety-passenger boat and then dock and stay at a hotel. The boat was small enough to ease up close to huge glaciers (and see them calving to produce small icebergs) and then move out to open water and maneuver quickly when the whales were cavorting all around us. The passengers were ecstatic as the whales, acting like kids in a playful mood, would come close to the boat, breach, and then circle around to do it again. Even the boat captain was shouting with delight.

We made our way over to the Chatham Strait and then up to Haines for a couple of days of sightseeing and then back down to Juneau for a couple of days. While we were in Juneau, we had another wonderful experience. Seeing the bears on Bear Island is a must-see event. The salmon were running, and the bears were making the most of their big chance. We decided to go watch— without asking about the details. We forgot that the devil can be in the details. We boarded a DeHavilland Beaver pontoon aircraft, the workhorse airplane of the Alaska bush country, for a ride out to the island, but we didn't land at Bear Island. As it turned out, we were there in the midst of the spawning season, a time when aircraft were forbidden to land near Bear Island. We had to land at another island where passengers would get out and paddle over to Bear Island in small two-person canoes. That was when the fun began. It was open ocean between the islands, which were almost a mile apart. That was not the ideal canoeing location for novice canoeists. Fortunately, we had no mishaps, but a few couples had struggles.

Bear Island, the salmon runs, the bears catching the salmon, eagles all over the place catching the salmon—it was breathtaking to be so close and see it all unfold. We often just stopped and looked and listened. Several of the bears had cubs, and it was fun watching the little cubs try to catch the salmon. It was a 3-D documentary, up close and personal, but all good things (or at least some good things) must come to an end. Our eyes and our hearts had been filled as we viewed God's beautiful creation. It is easy to understand how people can come to love Alaska so deeply. We headed home.

When Joann retired from the Greers Ferry Medical Clinic, she had been almost immediately asked to join a mental health provider with clinics in several north Arkansas locations. She went from being busy to being very busy in her medical practice.

In 1998, we brought Joann's parents to live with us. Both had come to the point of requiring total care. Her dad, particularly, had severe Parkinson's disease, which totally immobilized him. He had been in a nursing home in Dimmitt, Texas, close to her brother James. Her mother had severe cancer. Joann felt we should bring them to live in the downstairs apartment we had prepared for them. Both of us retired from most of our outside responsibilities in order to take care of them. Joann, torn between competing, urgent needs, continued to work at a few mental health clinics as the only psychiatric professional in the region. There were a great number of severely afflicted patients in the area who constituted a danger to themselves as well as to others. Someone had to do something. After thirteen years with the organization, treating thousands of mentally and emotionally ill patients and many hundreds of hours of CME training at the medical school in Little Rock, she had become a very competent non-board-certified psychiatrist. I'll refrain from listing all the medical specialties at which she became an expert in her fifty-nine years of practice.

Her love and devotion to her church remained a priority. She continued as church pianist and Sunday school teacher. Since one of us always needed to be at home, she went on Sundays while I went on Wednesdays.

In early 1999, Mom Horton passed away in our home. A few months after her death, Dad Horton became lonelier and wanted to go back to the nursing home in Dimmitt. We delayed for a couple of months, trying to get him to change his mind. We knew his return would not be as he remembered. Many of his friends were gone, and he would be a stranger, but he insisted, so we finally returned him to Dimmitt. As we feared, it was not as he remembered, and he never recovered his zest for life. Finally, he developed pneumonia and died on October 8, 1999.

Not long after her Dad's death, Joann received word that she had been given the 1999 McCall Humanitarianism Award by Baylor University. It was given in recognition of her accomplishments as a missionary physician in some of the neediest areas of the world. Particularly significant were her years as a refugee camp medical director in the Southeast Asia refugee crisis and the years of training "barefoot doctors" in the remote hills of India.

I had seen her go the second mile in loving service to those difficult areas and was pleased and proud that others saw it also. It was a well-deserved award. Both of us were saddened that her dad could not be present. Throughout her life, her dad had been a constant encourager and supporter. A man of strong Christian faith and total integrity, he instilled those same qualities in Joann. Now she was being honored, but he was not there to see the results of his significant part in her receiving that award.

Our aversion to extended travel began to dissipate after the first three or four years in our new home. Establishing our landscaped home and developing our garden out of thick woods, while finding new avenues of ministry, was enough to keep us fully occupied around home, but once we became more settled in and had a routine somewhat in place, we were ready to travel again. The years 2000 through 2004 were filled with memorable travels and events. This time, however, we went on our own schedule to places we chose. Our first trip began in Asia. Joann had a conference for the Singapore Baptist women in Singapore (sensing a good thing, a bunch of men showed up too!), a place we loved to visit. That was work for her; the other five of us managed to survive. We traveled with the Shells and the Roberts. We had enjoyed our trip together to Alaska and decided to do more of it.

Joann and I were particularly blessed on that trip because we were able to make a side trip through Thailand and attend the fiftieth anniversary of the beginning of our Southern Baptist mission work in Thailand. Words can't convey the joy and gratitude we felt as we gathered with more than 1,500 Thai national Baptists at our camp on the Gulf of Siam for a two-day worship and celebration time. We remembered the early years when the response was discouragingly slow. It had been a time of sowing seeds, working hard, and praying for a harvest. Now we could see the beginning of the harvest. We rejoiced as we saw and heard those we had worked with as new believers now serving in national leadership roles as wise and mature pastors and people of God. The nationals had done all the work, planned the entire program, made all the arrangements for speakers and music, and invited some Karen Hill Tribe choirs that would grace any program anywhere with their music. Joann and I were in tears much of the time. Those memories are precious to us.

In Singapore, Joann did her usual great job in leading her conference. We flew to Beijing to begin a tour that was similar to the one Joann and I had made almost twenty years previously. One thing that was strikingly different was the extent of the modernization of China. It was apparent everywhere. In many ways, it was a welcome improvement, especially in the food, but the air pollution was unreal. It was terrible for breathing, and the traffic was in close competition with India and Thailand.

Toward the end of the tour, we flew to Chongqing (called Chungking in 1982) to begin our Yangtze River cruise. Joann and I had not been in that area before, and we were delighted when our guide took us to a museum dedicated to the United States Army Air Force. The Chinese vividly remembered the encroachment of the Japanese army, including many aircraft units, that were coming near the city in the early 1940s. The United States Army Air Force began flying in supplies and ammunition that enabled the Chinese army to repulse the Japanese. It saved thousands of lives and prevented much destruction. All the freight to support the fighting had been flown in over the "hump," the high Himalayan mountain range separating Chongqing from Kunming. It had been brought to Kunming from Burma and India, much of it over the historic Burma Road.

What really caught my attention was that my cousin, J. C. Evans, had been in the air force in World War II in the early 1940s and had flown the "hump" many times. He would not talk about it until the 1990s when Truett and I were visiting him in Mississippi not long before he died. For the first time, he began talking about it, describing what some of the flights were like. It had been so dangerous and traumatic that he could not verbalize it until that time. They were flying transport aircraft, primarily DC-3s, that were slow and unarmed; they were sitting ducks for Japanese fighter aircraft. It was considered one of the most dangerous flight routes of World War II. The casualty rate was extremely high.

There were many photographs in the museum of flight crews who had flown in from Kunming. The pictures were too fuzzy to identify individuals definitely, but I could easily imagine J. C. being in one of the photographs. The museum had been established (and continues to be), supplied, and maintained by the people of Chongqing in appreciation for what the United States military had done to protect the city. I had not seen the museum the last time I talked with J. C. I have often wished I could have told him about it.

On Board and Down the River

The Yangtze River is a storied river, much like the Nile, the Amazon, the Ganges, the Mississippi, the Congo, and others. Flowing through some of the most ancient portions of early Chinese civilization, it is especially significant for China. It has been the primary transportation route through the mountains for centuries. It was already a large river by the time it reached Chongqing (population over ten million), but that city had become the preferred starting point for many of the cruises. The portion we cruised was primarily in the mountains—rugged mountains—and they kept the river contained. The river was rarely very wide (compared to the Ganges), but it was deep, often between five hundred and six hundred feet deep. The ship captain said he sometimes dropped a microphone near the bottom to hear large rocks being rolled along by the current.

There were approximately 250 passengers on board, plus a very full crew. All the staterooms had large picture windows for viewing the constantly changing scenery. We stopped several times to view facilities, temples, scenes, or historic places that would disappear when the water rose upon completion of Three Gorges Dam. Over thirty centuries of Chinese history and culture would be buried underwater, perhaps never to be seen again. More than one million people would be displaced.

The scenery was spectacular, especially a side trip we took up the Daning River. It was just one of many tributaries that came tumbling out of the mountains to join the Yangtze. It was about half the size of the Colorado River, rolling down a steep decline for miles before its confluence with the Yangtze, an almost continuous stretch of twisting, turning whitewater confined between towering canyon walls. Exploration sounded exciting, and we went for it.

There were ten or twelve passengers in a partially glass-enclosed boat, accompanied by many other similar boats, that made the run up and down the river. After a few miles of struggling to make headway up a continually turbulent stream—while avoiding huge boulders and other boats—we came to a relatively smooth stretch of the river. Another boat driver, impatient at our slow, underpowered progress, decided to pass us. Not a good decision. He was unable to pass in the space available.

Our driver did not want to be outdone and kept trying to maintain his lead. We crashed. Shattered glass fell all around us. Our boat was momentarily out of control. No one had on a life vest.

Joann immediately tried to find the life vests, and Carolyn remained calmly seated. We later asked her about it. She said, "Frank can take care of me. If he doesn't, the Lord will. Not to worry."

The hard-sell advertisers of the boat excursion had been right. It was exciting—almost too exciting. Frank goaded me into writing a note about it:

> We were cruising the turbulent Daning,
> Awed by spectacular scenes,
> When quick as a flash,
> Our boat broke in a crash,
> And a nightmare emerged from the dream.

The ride through the Three Gorges portion of the river down to the Three Gorges Dam was all it was claimed to be. After exiting the gorges, the river had become less deep but far wider. It was massive. A bypass channel, with a lock, had been excavated adjacent to the river to enable the heavy river traffic to continue during construction. While transiting through that lock, we had our best view of the construction of the dam not long after it was begun. Several sky-cranes, hundreds of feet high, had already been assembled across the river to place the tens of millions of cubic feet of cement required to complete the dam. It is beyond the scope of this story to repeat the statistics of the overall project. They are hard to imagine.

Millions of people downstream have expressed concern about the danger of a break in the dam. The extreme pressure resulting from the massive amount of water impounded by the dam has created a potentially catastrophic disaster. Many engineers are concerned because they believe the reliability of the dam, with some known foundational weaknesses, cannot be projected with certainty. It is too big, with too many uncertainties, to guarantee total safety. What is known is that a break in the dam could cost hundreds of thousands of lives and untold damage.

After touring Guilin and cruising the Li River again, we boarded a large, ultra-modern catamaran in Canton (Guangdong) for a beautiful ride down the Pearl River, through the estuary, out to and around Macao to Hong Kong, and then back home. What a trip!

A Mountain-Sized Challenge

The year 2000 was another good retirement year for us. The fiftieth anniversary reunion in Thailand had been a soul-satisfying experience that continued to bless us. The China trip, especially the cruise down the Yangtze, which allowed us to see much of ancient China, provided a last-in-a-lifetime opportunity to view portions of that ancient land. Joann and I have a deep affection for the Chinese people and are blessed to know of the emergence of many new believers from difficult circumstances.

James added a new dimension, and challenge, for Joann and me. He decided to climb the highest mountain in several western states. He had already climbed Guadalupe Peak in Texas, near our former home, several times, and then he climbed Mount Wheeler in New Mexico (13,161 feet). His next goal was Mount Elbert, the highest mountain in Colorado at 14,439 feet. The catch was he wanted me to do it with him. Well, okay. I began preparations with training hikes in the mountains near our home.

In late July, James and I headed out. We camped the first night near Salida, Colorado. It was after dark when we arrived, and I had to applaud him as he set up the tent in a very short time in a light rain. We left early the next morning, arriving at the trailhead (about ten thousand feet) outside of Leadville in good time. The climb went well until we reached thirteen thousand feet, and James began to have symptoms of altitude sickness. We stopped for a while, and then we decided to go back down, spend the night at the motel in Leadville, and try again the next day.

When we got up the next morning, I decided I was not up for another climb just yet. I left him at the trailhead and spent the day exploring the area around the town where a variety of mining activity had been going on for years. I went back to the trailhead at about the time he was due down from the mountain. After a short wait, he came swaggering down the trail with both thumbs pointed up. He had done it. He didn't have a T-shirt, but he had a picture.

Not long after we returned home, and James returned to Dallas, Joann began to get itchy feet. She quizzed me repeatedly about the climb. How steep? How dangerous? How long? "Could I do it?" We decided to give it a try.

First, we had to do some intense preparation. We bought backpacks, loaded them with about thirty pounds of "stuff," and took off for the Buffalo River in north Arkansas to train for the climb. We started at a trailhead near the top of a mountain and climbed down a very steep trail (Hemmed-in-Hollow Trail) to the base of the trail at the Buffalo River. It is also the location of the Hemmed-in-Hollow Waterfall. At 220 feet, it is the highest waterfall between the Appalachian Mountains and the Rocky Mountains. Then we climbed back out—a total distance of five miles on a trail that proved almost as difficult as the trail up Mount Elbert. Over the next few weeks, we walked that trail several times, knowing it would be more difficult when we were climbing at a much higher elevation.

Joann's camping came to a halt after our Canadian Rockies romp. We stayed in a motel in Leadville. From our motel, and even better, from the airport, we could see the full length of the massive mountain. Even though it is the highest mountain in the state, it is not topped off with rocky, craggy peaks. It has a rounded top. We hit the trailhead early on a beautiful, clear morning. The total distance up and back was more than eight miles, most of which was not extremely difficult, and there were sections that required care to prevent falling. The elevation change from the trailhead to the top was about 4,500 feet.

We reached the timberline at about 12,300 feet, and the woods disappeared. As we continued to climb, we found ourselves standing in a place of unsurpassed beauty. We were on a shoulder of the mountain that allowed us to see clearly almost two hundred degrees around us. Extending in all directions were mountains just above fourteen thousand feet, many with large remnants of snow. We saw lakes, towns, and Mount Massive nearby, only twelve feet lower than Mt Elbert.

After climbing another thousand feet, we entered more snow. We stopped frequently just to view the panorama and try to absorb the immensity with which we were surrounded. One of those sights, easily missed in the great distances around us, was looking down on eagles soaring far below. They were poetry in motion as they caught the rising thermals and rose almost to our level, then began their descent, looking for any unsuspecting snack or lunch while gliding near the mountain at great speed.

Our enjoyment pulled our attention away from the rapid buildup of a thunderstorm quickly coming our way. It was a common occurrence in the high mountains in the summer.

Joann and I were torn momentarily about which way to go. We were at a little over fourteen thousand feet, just short of the peak, which was barely over a ridge immediately in front of us. It was so close, but danger was close also. We were the tallest things on the mountain, and lightning was beginning to strike rock outcroppings around us. I had been near lightning strikes many times, but the thunder on that mountain was so loud and reverberating that it was painful. We could not afford to linger. It was time to move—and we did. We almost ran down the mountain until we reached the woods.

It was disappointing that we did not actually reach the peak, but the fact that we could certainly have achieved it had the storm not come made it a most rewarding experience.

One of the fascinating things about being on the mountain was that we saw hundreds of small rivulets of snowmelt runoff, forming into little creeks that became larger on down the mountain where they came together to form the headwaters of the Arkansas River. We are not mountaineers, but that adventure, and responding to that challenge, is still a high point for us.

Back to a Busy Retirement

We needed to get back home and stay for a while. Much was going on. Joann's practice was increasing (a pattern wherever she worked). She continued as church pianist, Sunday school teacher, ESL instructor, and board member of Williams Baptist College. The college also asked her to give the endowed lectureship on the relationship of science and faith.

I had the Wednesday evening services at church through the year while also serving as church treasurer. The tempo of my logging increased. Extended heat and drought of the previous three years stressed many of the pine trees, leading me to give as much time as possible to harvesting those trees before they died.

Every two years, the Thailand Baptist Mission has a reunion somewhere in the States. It is a greatly loved time when former and retired missionaries and their children get together and renew the close ties that have bound us together as a family through the years. In October 2001, Lisa, Chris, and their family joined us in Mississippi for a good time of renewal.

Making it an even better time, Juli and Rebecca, our two oldest grandchildren, joined Joann and me after the meeting for an extended driving trip through New England, southeastern Canada, Nova Scotia, and Prince Edward Island. Crossing the ten-mile-long

Confederation Bridge over the Northumberland Strait onto Prince Edward Island was a gorgeous drive.

Juli and Rebecca had fallen in love with *Anne of Green Gables* and just had to explore the house and area on which the book was based. It turned out to be an idyllic place, just as in the book. The entire island had retained the Christian influence of previous years, making it especially heartwarming.

Adding to our pleasure was the Scottish and Irish culture that still permeated the island. We spent a night in Charlottetown, the largest town on the island, and attended a ceilidh (pronounced "Kayla") presented by a local Scottish music and dancing group. The band was composed of fiddles, flutes, pipes, whistles, and bagpipes and played a variety of folk music and dances enthusiastically and beautifully. Step dancing, sometimes called clogging, was our favorite. The dancers vigorously beat their heels, toes, and feet on the floor in hard-soled shoes, in as many ways as possible, keeping time with the rhythms of the music. Juli and Rebecca, excited and expectant, sat on the front row, very close to the dancers, and could hardly restrain themselves.

To top off the evening, the final part of the program was a brief statement by the leader of the group. He summarized the desire of the group to retain much of their cultural heritage and keep their Christian history and faith alive and flourishing. The program was closed by all of us singing "Amazing Grace." It was a beautiful, delightful time of fun and worship that we still remember with joy.

One of our side trips in New Hampshire became more memorable a couple of years after we completed it. All of us wanted to see the unique mountainside granite formation that came to be called the "Old Man of the Mountain." The profile of the formation has long been the state emblem. Nathaniel Hawthorne used the feature for *The Great Stone Face* in 1850. We spent just a brief time admiring the profile, easily seeing the hints of traits Hawthorne saw: strength of character, compassion, reliability, fearlessness, and others. We were shocked and a little saddened a couple of years later when reports and pictures showed the collapse of the formation. We were grateful we had had the privilege of seeing it before it fell.

We returned through southern Canada to Montreal, Buffalo, and Niagara Falls. Our hotel room overlooked the falls, capturing the sight and sound that is beyond description. The kids, like their parents, are adventurous and insisted on boarding the boat that took passengers up to and into the falls. They just squealed with delight.

The fall colors in Vermont and New Hampshire lived up to their reputation. In fact, they exceeded it. A ten-inch snowfall covered the mountains and the woods while we were there, then the clouds cleared out, leaving the brilliantly colored trees, the mountains, and the snow to display their splendor in full, contrasting color. The memory of that experience is still a much talked-about event. The younger grandkids fuss at us for not providing a similar experience for them.

Not long after we returned to Arkansas, James joined us for a trip to Florida for a front-row seat to watch a space shuttle launch. It didn't happen. The weather turned sour, and the launch was canceled. So, we went with plan B. We drove to Key West and then back through the Everglades to Callaway Gardens, Georgia, and then home.

In November 2001, Joann received an early, surprising, and wonderful Christmas gift. The Baylor University Alumni Association called and informed her she had been chosen as a Distinguished Alumnus for 2002. It would be presented to her at a special awards ceremony in January. The name of the award conveys something of its significance. She had devoted years of distinguished service to people in desperate need, often in difficult, even dangerous places. She had taken "the road less traveled" to go into the byways and backsides of the world to suffering people to model and talk about the living, loving Savior she served. Joann will always be the first to recognize that she could never have accomplished what she did without the help of others, especially the Lord.

In her response to the presentation, she expressed her deep gratitude to many who had been her enablers along the way. Among those she especially desired to thank was Baylor itself. She was grateful that her school, which had prepared her in such a wonderful way, had provided an atmosphere that encouraged her in her calling to ministry and continued to be true to its original purpose. She was thankful the university still considered the missionary calling a vocation worthy of recognition. It was a high honor and a high hour for her. My pride in her and admiration of her could hardly be contained.

Boards, Hospitals, and Associations

While Joann continued on the board of Williams College, I was asked to join the board of Ozark Medical Center in Clinton in April 2002. It is a 157-bed, 300-employee combination hospital and nursing home. It was just beginning a $30 million construction program for a completely new facility. It came to be a long, challenging, but rewarding twelve years for me as I returned to active involvement in hospital administration.

The British Isles was one of our favorite places we had never visited. Much of our Christian heritage and history had begun in those four small countries, and we had longed to see the whole area. The ancestors of both our families came from Scotland or England. It was time to go. We visited the usual sites, and the places we visited hold a special place in our hearts because of their direct influence on us. Our Christian heritage and hard-won freedoms came alive as we worshiped where John Knox was a pastor in Edinburgh, Scotland; saw the site in England where the Magna Carta was signed and then saw a copy of it; stood where the Pilgrims had boarded their little ship to sail to the New World; and heard many of the old, classical, great hymns as sung by Welsh choirs.

No trip to Great Britain is complete without a visit to Waterford, Ireland, to observe the world's greatest display of crystal and watch master craftsmen fashion such works of art. "Yield not to temptation" is wise biblical advice, but we yielded a time or two to get a couple of small pieces.

There was something in Scotland and England—and to a lesser extent in Ireland and Wales—that strongly attracted Joann and me. It was almost like sensing a kindred DNA. The evidence of our Christian history, the expressions of our faith, and sometimes even the expressions of our secular freedoms resonated deeply with us. We felt such an affinity with the area and the people that it seemed almost like home. We loved seeing the region.

After our British trip, I served a few months as unofficial interim pastor of my brother's church in Little Rock.

After a dozen or so years of retirement, we began to think our schedule should level off—or maybe even drop off somewhat—but it did not happen. In retrospect, I think it was a blessing in disguise. For our continued health, we stayed active mentally, physically, and spiritually. We think that busy schedule delayed the aging process.

That busy schedule became unexpectedly busier when I was asked to become interim CEO of the hospital in Clinton. The former administrator resigned less than a year after I went on the board, and I was asked to take the position until we had a permanent replacement. I faced a steep learning curve. It had been more than twenty years since I served as a hospital administrator, and much had changed in the health-care field. I had been active on hospital boards through most of that time, but much of it was overseas. Daunting new government rules, regulations, and reimbursement procedures were in place, but my background and experience as a hospital administrator helped in my transition back to everyday administration. The 130-bed nursing home was a new and strange animal—or perhaps *can of worms* is a better term. Nursing home care has its own dynamic, but even in the nursing home, there were enough similarities that I began to catch on. Challenges or issues with personnel, finances, equipment, and regulations often have similarities across a broad spectrum of commercial activity.

As I was struggling to get up to speed again as an administrator, Joann and I often laughed and talked about our work histories. For Joann, becoming a general practice physician provided the requisite background to becoming a pediatrician, mental health specialist, leprosy specialist, tropical medicine expert, and geriatrician. She had unusual knowledge in many other medical areas. She was able to provide leadership in a wide variety of medical situations because she had acquired the necessary first step of being a medical doctor. That was what enabled her to transition to so many other responsibilities.

In a similar but far less dramatic way, I had enough basic training and experience in hospital administration and other administrative responsibilities to move back into administration and other roles without causing a total foul-up, but I was glad to have my replacement in place after several months and was relieved to revert to being chairman of the board. (I was later interim CEO on two other occasions.)

The premier family event of 2003 was the marriage of James to Zarella Rendon. That is a simple statement about a common event, but the story leading up to their marriage adds a new twist to it.

James had had one or two semiserious girlfriends, but none had resulted in marriage. I accused him of being married to computers. He was approaching forty years of age and kept hoping the Lord would drop his future wife in his lap. I gently reminded him that the Lord sometimes needed a little help. He finally agreed in a different way. He went online to a very reputable Christian dating site, provided the requested information, and waited with skepticism. It just so happened that a fine Christian woman had made a similar decision at about the same time. Their individual histories had enough similarities in beliefs, hopes, and preferences that James called and set up a luncheon meeting.

The rest, as the old saying goes, is history. I had the privilege of conducting their wedding ceremony in the Armstrong Browning

Library on the Baylor campus on September 20, 2003. One of many pleasant memories from that wedding was the background classical music provided by Juli and Rebecca, our two oldest granddaughters, on the violin and piano. All of us have been blessed with the addition of Zarella—a very sweet, very sharp (coauthor of a computer science textbook), very wonderful woman—to our family. We are grateful and proud. Over a year later, they gave us another blessing, a grandson, Ryan James, giving us a total of eight grandchildren. At the last count, we have six granddaughters, two grandsons, and five great-grandchildren.

Long before the phrase *bucket list* came en vogue, Joann and I had some places in mind we wanted to see. We had seen several of those places (primarily national parks in the West) with the children, but a few remained. We completed another one in 2003 with a tour of the California national parks. Yosemite was the highlight. It is just one of countless places that have to be seen up close (meaning doing some hiking) to begin to comprehend the immensity and grandeur of God's creation.

A couple of years later, we toured the upper Midwest, which was the first time Joann had seen that part of our nation. The Black Hills, Badlands, buffalo herds, Mount Rushmore, unending miles of corn, wheat, and other crops, the Great Lakes, the Mackinac Bridge, and the whole area had a strangely quiet and serene atmosphere that was most appealing. The area was not as dramatic as the Rocky Mountains, but it had its own special attraction.

There was one remaining place on our list that we were finally able to see. It was a cruise through the Caribbean—with a side trip to Costa Rica. We went in January and February 2008 as our slightly delayed fiftieth wedding anniversary celebration, which was on December 21, 2007.

Costa Rica was chosen partly as a tiny makeup attempt to Joann. In all of our years in Asia (and even back in Van Horn), we had been a team. Whatever we did, in work or travel, we did together. We liked being a team. That changed in 1987 when we came back to the States for me to be on staff at the FMB. I began working and traveling alone. When I came home and tried to tell her where I had gone and what I had done, I could never convey the full story. We had become almost addicted to sharing work, sights, events, and experiences. That sharing had become tremendously important to us. I wanted her to see at least a little of what I had seen. Costa Rica was the only place where we could arrange it. In Costa Rica, I had been asked to review the refugee situation in Central America. Now was my chance—Joann and I would see it together as a shared experience.

The Caribbean cruise destinations need no further comment—with one exception. Inside one of the island bays, we anchored near a shallow area that was teeming with stingrays that were two or three feet in diameter. They had become tame and friendly with people and swam between and among us, totally unafraid. Joann and I locked our hands together while a large stingray came up and just settled on our arms. While we were holding it, other stingrays were swimming around and between our legs, maneuvering like little kittens. It was a wow moment. That cruise was all that a cruise was supposed to be. I'll move on to Costa Rica.

After a brief look around San Jose, we joined a small group for a winding ride through brilliant green volcanic mountains (with two over twelve thousand feet) toward the Caribbean coast of Costa Rica. Before reaching the foot of the mountains, we stopped to enjoy a wild, speedy zip-line ride down to a white-water river at the base of the mountains. At that time, zip-lines were relatively new, and we had never ridden one. We did not really know what to expect, but our first view gave a second-thought hint.

A small platform was attached high in a tree near the top of a mountain, forty or fifty feet above the ground. Six of us climbed up to the platform: four younger people, Joann, and me. From the platform, two steel cables, suspended one above the other, extended from the tree down to another tree, anywhere between three hundred and eight hundred yards down the mountain to another tree platform. There were about seven segments in the total descent, the final segment ending at the river.

When it was time to strap in and go, Joann and I deferred to the younger ones, thinking they would jostle to be first. Surprise! They all backed up, reluctant to start. Finally, Joann looked at me and said, "Let's go!" She stepped up, was strapped in, and zoomed off. I followed, still shaking my head in wonderment at my wife. She had ridden a camel in Israel, elephants in Thailand and India, ridden with crazy taxi drivers in many cities, gone white-water rafting in Nepal, and now jumped off on a wild zip-line escapade in Costa Rica. And she would not join me on a looping, rotating roller coaster in Branson, Missouri? Who can predict a woman?

Each rider was strapped into a one-person harness and given two thick leather gloves. The gloves were worn to grip one of the cables, which served as the braking system. Gravity propelled the riders. The cables sagged between the platforms, with the low sag point being lower than the destination platform to allow enough speed to build up during the downward sloping first portion of the ride to coast beyond the sag point and arrive at the next platform just as forward motion stopped. Speed could build quickly on the first part of the ride, making it tempting to grip the cable and slow down. If you did that, you could slow down too much. Your momentum would be inadequate to take you up to the landing point. Then you had to pull yourself, hand over hand, up to the platform, which was not easy. After a couple of segments, we got the hang of it and began to enjoy the experience.

It was an exhilarating ride! At times, we were at least a hundred feet above the canopy of the forest, giving us an unmatched view of the surrounding mountains, volcanoes, and waterfalls. We could not see the wildlife on the forest floor, but we could get glimpses of monkeys in the trees and birds of all kinds. It was one breathtaking scene after another.

The last segment was the longest—about 2,500 feet—crossing a white-water river just a few feet above the water before terminating at the platform near the bank of the river. We unbuckled, still trying to absorb what we had just experienced, and then immediately climbed into rubber rafts for another wild float ride down the river. It was not as turbulent as the river in Nepal, but it had its own special appeal. This time, the wildlife was more easily seen in the trees, in the water, and along the banks. Flowers, especially orchids, were growing all over the place.

We headed back to the Pacific side of the country, crossing through the mountains in the Arenal region where I had reviewed the refugee camps. All evidence of any refugee presence was gone.

We were taken to a port city west of San Jose where we boarded our cruise ship, the *Crystal Symphony*, for a ride down the Pacific side of Costa Rica, then an eye-popping squeeze through the Panama Canal into the Caribbean. The immensity of the Panama Canal, with its massive widening project in full view as we passed through, reminded us of the Three Gorges Dam construction project in China. One of the little surprises as we navigated the locks was that the clearance of the ship was only about one foot on each side when we were in the locks. The ship did not propel itself through the locks; it was pulled by mechanical "mules" alongside the lock walls.

My cup of flying interest and enthusiasm was filled to overflowing in 2004 when Bob Rollins, my commercial pilot brother-in-law, invited me to go with him to Oshkosh, Wisconsin, for the biggest annual air show in the nation. Attended by more than seven hundred thousand people, flying in with thousands of planes, it was a continuous, one-week spectacle of sights and sounds. The variety of aircraft on display is beyond describing; just listing categories is lengthy:

- restored aircraft from the beginning of flight by the Wright brothers
- military aircraft from World War I and World War II to the newest experimental models, including all types of fighters, bombers, and transports

- home-built airplanes of every conceivable design
- commercial jets of all kinds, including jumbos
- helicopters, gyrocopters, powered gliders, and individual jet-pack fliers
- personal airplanes, flown by the owners, parked in every available space

Many airplanes had tents pitched under the wings—and families camped out for the week. With the static displays, flight demonstrations, military dogfights, and aerobatic contests, something was going on constantly through all the days and much of the nights. My legs were tired, my neck was sore, and my brain was overloaded before the week was out, but there could not have been a better finale to my personal flying experiences than those days in Oshkosh.

Five years after what I thought was the grand finale of my flying experiences, Joann gave me a totally unexpected birthday present: a flight in a North American T-6 Texan, the advanced flight trainer of World War II. Fully aerobatic, it could handle any flying situation a pilot could handle. Her gift enabled me to fulfill a lifelong desire to go up and do all the acrobatic maneuvers I had read about. Accompanied by an instructor, I did all that I had dreamed of doing: barrel rolls, aileron rolls, hammerhead stalls, Immelmann turn, loops (but not an inverted loop), and spins. That was just one of many magical birthday gifts she sprung on me.

Our Home: A Museum of Memories

Like most families, we had many special occasions, events, and celebrations that remain vivid in our memories. They all became important milestones in our family journey, but they are too numerous to relate in total. I'll provide just a few brief summaries.

Our retirement home in Choctaw (and now in Little Rock) has always reflected much of our world travels. It is similar to a museum in many ways. As we traveled, we obtained more than a hundred special or unique items from many of those countries. Several of them are delicate ivory carvings (obtained while it was still legal). Others are crystal, jade, silver, gold, ebony, and other distinctive materials. Many are original oil paintings depicting familiar scenes from around the world. Because Joann loves birds, I brought her carved birds from at least twenty countries, made from a great variety of materials. We have intricately carved teakwood and rosewood furniture and other items that are irreplaceable. Few, if any, of these many mementos have any great monetary value, but their sentimental value to us is beyond measure. In any room, at any time, a glance at one of those items will trigger a significant memory, often related to a spiritual event that brings back the joy of that time. All of those mementos help make our home a haven, a special sanctuary of peace.

All of it together—the mementos, the places we visited, the unusual sights, the experiences, the establishment of churches, the growth of the Lord's kingdom, the friendship of fellow believers all around the world—reveals a lifetime of transcendental moments and events that bring forth continual thanksgiving to God.

Christmas

The following are cherished Christmas memories while living in our retirement home at Choctaw.

- Decorations in the courtyard, a spotlight on the waterfall, roof-line lights, stairway and column lights, door and window decorations and lights, a large lighted star on the peak of the house, and reading the biblical story of the birth of Jesus on Christmas morning with the children and grandchildren.

- Christmas reception for the entire church each year. Part of the preparation for the reception included a display of gold, frankincense, and myrrh, reminders of the gifts brought to Jesus at His birth by the wise men. We bought a small gold chain while we were in Thailand; we purchased the frankincense and myrrh in Israel. It was a fascinating display, but no samples were offered.

- Taking the entire family (Lisa, Chris, their seven kids, and James) to Branson, Missouri, for Christmas. While there, Rebecca and I were the only ones willing to take a wild roll-over, looping roller coaster in Silver Dollar City. When we returned, Rebecca (our Granddaughter) insisted on another time around. A few years later, I gave her a training flight in an airplane. She loved it too.

- Joann taking the time to teach the grandchildren how to decorate for special occasions, especially Christmas and the Christmas tree. Most of the tree decorations came from all over the world—many with a story and history of their own. She had a knack/touch/skill for making the house a home of refuge and restoration and peace. They admired and envied her for her many gifts.

Additional Memories of Choctaw

We never tired of watching the changing seasons. From our many windows, it was a delight to watch the bright white service (Sarvice) berries appear as the first blossoms of spring, followed shortly by a small grove of brilliant, fuchsia red buds in full color just across the creek from our house. A little later, hundreds of dogwoods would burst forth in all their brilliance all through our woods. The man who cleared our logging road opened a trail through a thick grove of huge, mature dogwoods. They overlapped to form a spectacular tunnel drive that, when in bloom, seemed to illuminate the area with the brightness of the blossoms.

A wonderful surprise came to us during our first spring in the house. On the steep slope, just below our back deck, a large group of bushes suddenly erupted in bloom, producing a fragrant, colorful display. They were wild azaleas, sometimes called mountain laurel. We had never seen the plants before. They extended from our house up Wolf Creek to the Blue Hole, covering the hillside in some areas. Springtime in our little woodland retreat cottage was just one visual feast after another. The fall colors were also spectacular, especially the maples we had set out in the yard. All of the beauty was in addition to the colorful courtyard that Joann kept in bloom with a variety of flowers, shrubs, annuals, and perennials.

Additional Memorable Events

- Our fiftieth wedding anniversary in 2007. James put it together in Austin, Texas, with all the family.
- Missionary reunion in Glorieta, New Mexico, for all retired FMB missionaries. There is a tie, a bond, and a fellowship among missionaries unlike any other. Experiences, struggles, and stresses of being in the mission field can be fully understood only by other missionaries.
- Vacations back to Big Bend National Park in far West Texas. I loved them, and Joann tolerated them.
- Baptizing two of our grandchildren. Performing the wedding of James and Zarella.
- Jane Doe (the name I gave her): a tame deer from some unknown owner that came out of the woods and lived with us for several months. She was absolutely delightful—even when she ate Joann's favorite hostas in the courtyard.
- I had a bleeding episode in 2009, but seven days in ICU and six units of blood brought me back to normal. William

Wordsworth's "Intimations of Mortality" became more than just a poem. The theme became much stronger as a certain reality after that episode.

- Occasions when I loaded about a dozen bales of hay on my logging trailer, hooked it to my tractor, and took a bunch of kids, including our grandkids, for Halloween rides through the woods.

- Goatcher family reunions were great times for getting reacquainted with relatives not seen in many years. We had three, in alternate years, with up to seventy in attendance. Joann laid out a bountiful buffet that was greatly admired and enjoyed. It was a wonderful time for the children to meet cousins they had not seen before and for the younger generation to gain a sense of family, identity, and belonging. Our guestbook, recording those times with names and special notes, is a special memento of those occasions.

Other Responsibilities After Retirement

Joann served on the Williams Baptist College board of directors for fourteen years. She has had many key committee roles. The quality of the college graduates makes it a major player in the higher education system in Arkansas. Education majors, recognized throughout the state as the best qualified teachers, are always immediately hired. Preprofessional students rarely have any difficulty gaining admittance to law and medical schools. Perhaps most important of all, the college prepares hundreds of students for vocational Christian ministry. Joann has a great love for her alma mater, Baylor, but she has also developed a great love and loyalty to Williams College for its outstanding quality and wonderful success in preparing thousands of young people to go out into the world as well-educated, committed, and faithful Christians.

Joann spent many pleasant hours in the kitchen with our granddaughters, teaching them how to cook the delicious dishes for which she was famous, but it was not only in the kitchen. She also taught them the many fine points of gardening: when to plant what seed, how deep, and what plants to set out and when. They learned well. All six of them love gardening and are excellent cooks. She also demonstrated fruit and vegetable preserving, canning, and drying.

I enjoyed teaching many of our grandchildren how to drive the truck, operate the tractor, handle the power mowers, use the log-splitter, and maneuver the garden tiller. I assisted Chris in his early use of the chainsaws, and then I let him decide how much he wanted his children to be trained to use them. It can be a dangerous activity.

I was on the board of directors of Ozark Health Medical Center for twelve years, president/chairman for four years, and interim CEO three times. I was a board member of the Arkansas Hospital Association for two years, receiving the Chairman's Award in 2012. I served on the board of directors of the Arkansas Association of Hospital Trustees for four years, the last year as president.

Joann consistently ran the 5K Susan Komen Race for the Cure (for breast cancer) in Little Rock for more than ten years.

At eighty-three, I decided to stop logging. My strength and agility had decreased. Using the chainsaws alone in the woods became too dangerous.

At eighty-two, Joann decided to retire from the practice of medicine. After fifty-nine years of obedient, rewarding, God-honoring, compassionate care, she felt she should bow out of practice before any harm could be done to a patient inadvertently. It was not an easy decision; she loves serving and taking care of people.

After twenty-one unbelievably wonderful, golden years in our dream retirement home, we felt it was time to sell our place and move into a retirement community in Little Rock. We made the move in November 2012. As acutely as we felt the loss in leaving our dream place, our children, and especially our grandchildren, felt it even more. It had also been their dream place, impossible to replace, but the source of a thousand heartwarming memories will remain with them for as long as they live.

Our retirement village covers eighty-eight acres along Chenal Parkway in west Little Rock and is convenient for all our needs. It is part of a continuing-care community. Joann and I live in a cottage in the independent living section. There is also an assisted-living facility, an Alzheimer's unit, and a ninety-five-bed nursing home. Because Parkway Village is a part of the Baptist Hospital System, we also have immediate access to the nearby Arkansas Baptist Hospital when acute care is needed. Every day, Joann and I thank the Lord that we are able and privileged to live in such a place. One of the many fun things about Parkway Village is the golf cart we use to move about. The area is too large to walk everywhere, yet it is too small to require a car. The golf cart is the perfect answer—and it is fun to drive. It also happens to be a drawing card for the grandkids; they love it even more than we do.

In 2013, I received the first of a series of correspondence from the Department of Justice of the United States government. It was a follow-up of my involvement in the atomic weapons testing program in Nevada. There had been an unusual incidence of medical problems among some of the military participants in the program, primarily related to cancer. That occurrence finally led to litigation, then research, and finally to congressional legislative action authorizing the Department of Justice to partially reimburse those who had been treated for cancer that could possibly be related to the testing program. Somehow, in the arcane, mysterious meanderings of government bureaucracy, my name appeared. After more than a year of correspondence, including multiple forms, questionnaires, and requests for military, medical, and marital records—with no indication of an end to the process—I decided to answer only one more letter and then drop it. The next letter I received indicated that I qualified for some reimbursement. In July 2014, I received a check. It was not large, but it was a welcome surprise and greatly appreciated. The saga had ended after sixty-four years.

Our move to Parkway Village, even with our advanced years, has not brought much of a decrease in activity. Our church home, Immanuel Baptist Church, is an unbelievable beehive of activity, seven days a week. With more than two hundred touch points of ministry outreach, every member is constantly encouraged to be involved.

Joann is active in the choir (a world-class, hundred-voice choir with a full orchestra), the WMU, Twice Blessed (a ministry to homebound members) and the Worship Prayer Team. She does water aerobics three days a week, plays water volleyball three days a week (Parkway Village has a fully equipped workout room and heated swimming pool and spa), is in the Parkway Village choir, and is active in the WMU. In her spare time, she visits patients in the nursing home, residents of the assisted-living facility, and shut-ins in Parkway Village. Just writing about it tires me out.

I can opt out of the women's programs, but being a deacon in Immanuel Baptist Church is almost like having a part-time job. The church takes the deacon's ministry seriously, as it should. We have regular assignments in visitation, service, and ministry. I also maintain a regular exercise program. It's a tough life. We thank the Lord every day for it. We continue to redeem the time in every way possible, realizing that every day brings us nearer to our final transition day.

EPILOGUE

One Final Word

Our lives are always in transition—until the Lord calls us home. That is the last and greatest transition. We will not always be here. Death is certain, but it isn't the end. All of our time here on earth is supposed to be preparation time for eternity with our heavenly Father. He has prepared a place for us. Are we prepared for that place? We see our time here in the village in our declining years as a continuing time of preparation for that final transition. If these comments seem morbid, then I have not conveyed what I intended. Our death will be a graduation time, a time of celebration, celebrating both our earthly life and journey being led by the Lord, and our future heavenly life in the presence of the King. That final transition will be our home going, a joyous time of reunion with those who have gone before us and fulfillment of the Lord's promise that we will eternally dwell in His presence.

Our spiritual preparation should be our highest priority, but practical preparation is important also. The death of a loved one often wreaks emotional distress on those loved ones who remain, yet it is at that very time that many critical decisions must be made. Joann and I have tried to make those preparations in an attempt to alleviate as much distress as possible for our children.

Words are inadequate to fully express our gratitude to God for the journey on which He has led us and for His presence with us every step of the way. May all that is recorded in this chronicle bring glory to God.

Printed in the United States
By Bookmasters